Money & Banking

5th Edition

David H. Friedman

AMERICAN
BANKERS
ASSOCIATION ®

The American Bankers Association is committed to providing innovative, high-quality products and services that are responsive to its members' critical needs.

To comment about this product, or to learn more about the American Bankers Association and the many products and services it offers, please call **1-800-BANKERS** or visit our Web site: www.aba.com.

This textbook has been approved by the American Institute of Banking for use in courses for which AIB certificates or diplomas are granted. The American Institute of Banking is the 102-year-old professional development and training affiliate of the American Bankers Association. Instructional materials endorsed by AIB have been developed by bankers, for bankers.

American
Institute of
Banking

AMERICAN
BANKERS
ASSOCIATION ®

CONTENTS

EXHIBITS

ABOUT THE AUTHOR

David H. Friedman is an economist, author, banking instructor, and former vice president at the Federal Reserve Bank of New York.

Mr. Friedman designed the Essentials of Banking seminar and the General Banking Curriculum for the Professional Development Program of the American Bankers Association. He is the author of the ABA textbook *Deposit Operations,* "A Preface to Banking" and "The Bank Book," four booklets on economics and banking subjects, and several segments of *The Money Encyclopedia.*

Since 1974 Mr. Friedman has been on the faculty of New York's Center for Financial Training. He is an associate professor of economics at Brooklyn College and the lead faculty member of the Global Institute of Finance–Mercy College Masters Degree program in banking. Mr. Friedman has conducted seminars and training programs on banking operations, the U.S. payments system, and a broad range of economic and management subjects for the ABA Business of Banking School.

Mr. Friedman has a Bachelor of Arts and a Master of Arts in economics from Brooklyn College and has completed course work and examinations for a doctorate in economics at New School University. He lives in East Brunswick, New Jersey.

ACKNOWLEDGMENTS

The American Bankers Association and the author acknowledge Linda McElroy, instructional designer, for her professional attention to the refinement of the textbook's presentation and instructional components. We also acknowledge Theresa Londquist, instructional designer for the American Bankers Association, for her innovations and revisions to the Instructor's Manual, which is a teaching guide for the Money and Banking course. Ms. Londquist also provided much-appreciated assistance with the final production phases of the textbook.

The American Bankers Association, the author and the instructional designers, thank the task force members who reviewed and commented on the textbook outline and manuscript. They provided valuable guidance on both substance and depth of content. Special appreciation is extended to

Ray Albo
Vice President
Continental National Bank
Miami, Florida

James Chessen
Chief Economist,
Director Economic Policy and Research
American Bankers Association
Washington, D.C.

J. Michael Cutshaw, Esq.
Mc Glinchey Stafford P.L.L.C.
Baton Rouge, Louisiana

Nessa Eileen Feddis
Senior Counsel
Government Relations
American Bankers Association
Washington, D.C.

Richard Ferguson
Vice President
Commercial Lending
Adirondack Trust Company
Saratoga Springs, New York

David Gire
Vice President
Transaction Processing
Bank of Hawaii
Honolulu, Hawaii

Charley Hoffman
Group Director
Electronic Delivery
American Bankers Association
Washington, D.C.

Doug Johnson
Senior Policy Analyst
Economic Policy and Research
American Bankers Association
Washington, D.C.

Keith Leggett
Senior Economist
Economic Policy and Research
American Bankers Association
Washington, D.C.

Rolando M. Ochoa
Vice President
Bank Atlantic
Aventura, Florida

John J. O'Leary
Assistant Vice President
Ridgefield Bank
Ridgefield, Connecticut

Janita L. Ponze
Project Manager
Professional Development Group
American Bankers Association

David Rios, CLBB
Owner and Consultant
Corporate Financial Group
Corpus Christi, Texas

Richard Schubert
Community Banking & Facility Manager
UMB Bank of Kansas City
Kansas City, Missouri

James Halstead Smith, CCM
First Vice President
Treasury Management
SunTrust Bank, Nashville
Nashville, Tennessee

Paul Smith
Senior Counsel
Government Relations
American Bankers Association
Washington, D.C.

Donna Stake
Vice President and Banking
   Center Manager
Bank of America
Fernandina Beach, Florida

Robert W. Strand, Ph.D.
Senior Economist
Economic Policy and Research
American Bankers Association
Washington, D.C.

Steven L. Wrangler
Vice President
Commercial Lending
Bank Center First
Bismarck, North Dakota

PREFACE

The fifth edition of *Money & Banking* is a revision of the text that was published in 1998. The revision incorporates new and updated material on the changes that have occurred in banking and the economy during the past five years. The updates cover

- the increase in foreign use of U.S. currency and the inroads the dollar coin, stored-valued cards, e-cash and e-checks have made on domestic payments patterns, in chapter 1
- the declining reliability of the money supply measures as guides for policy control, in chapter 1
- the business cycle decline (recession) that occurred in 2000, in chapter 2
- financial holding companies and their new powers, in chapter 4
- the growth of defined-contribution pension plans, such as 401(k) plans, and the credit union membership issue, in chapter 4
- new sources of noninterest income and noninterest expenses that are shaping banks' income statements, in chapter 5
- Internet banking and electronic bill presentment and payment (EBPP), in chapter 6
- the Federal Reserve's response to the terrorist attacks of September 11, 2001, in chapter 7
- the Gramm-Leach-Bliley Act of 1999, which repealed the Glass–Steagall Act, and the issue of deposit insurance reform, in chapter 8
- the impact of the wealth effect on spending and savings behavior in the late 1990s, in chapter 9
- America's productivity growth surge since the mid-1990s, in chapter 10
- the shift in monetary policy targeting from money supply growth to real interest rates and other financial and economic measures, in chapter 11
- the government's management of the federal budget, the federal debt, and America's international balance of payments, in chapter 12
- the increase in foreign ownership of the national debt, in chapter 12
- the euro, in chapter 13
- the changing profile of foreign banks' activities in the United States, in chapter 13

A fundamental restructuring of the text was undertaken in this fifth edition. Most notably, the chapters were reorganized, condensed, and repositioned. The primary sources for the data cited in the text were the Federal Reserve Board's monthly *Bulletin* and the monthly publications of the Federal Reserve banks, most notably the Federal Reserve Bank of St. Louis' *Monetary Trends* and *International Economic Trends*.

This edition of *Money & Banking* also has been redesigned to make it easier to use for both teaching and learning purposes. Among the text's practical features are

- objectives at the beginning of each chapter, which tell students what they can expect to learn from the material presented
- introductions to each chapter, which tell students and instructors where the chapter is heading and why specific topics are important for exposition
- boxed informational inserts that contain topical information related to the concepts in the chapters or provide real-world applications of the concepts
- tables, graphs, and other exhibits that update information and data to the early-2000s and help students understand key interrelationships and principles
- extended study presentations following selected chapters, which provide for in-depth exposition of selected topics, either to establish historical context for material discussed in the chapter or to provide a review of more advanced technical information
- a summary at the end of each chapter, which reviews the chapter's main points
- a list of key terms at the beginning of each chapter, which highlights concepts that will be discussed in the chapter
- end-of-chapter questions, which help students learn the subject matter by applying concepts explained in the chapter
- exercises at the end of selected chapters, which help students add to their subject knowledge by applying concepts learned in the chapter
- lists of additional resources, including both print resources and suggested web sites that contain information about material related to the chapter content
- a separate section at the back of the book that contains the answers to all chapter discussion questions, exercises, and balance sheet review problems
- a comprehensive glossary that provides definitions for terms used in the text
- an index that can be used by students to quickly locate concepts

Money and Banking is intended to serve both as an introductory text for new bankers and as a refresher text for experienced bankers who are preparing for advanced coursework. The specific needs of bankers also have been kept in mind in establishing the learning objectives of the text. These objectives are to

- explain the basic functions of money, the types of money and payment devices used in the United States, and the concepts and measurement of the U.S. money supply
- describe the important role of savings and lending in the U.S. economy, and the various measures that are used to assess the performance of the U.S. economy
- summarize how banks create money when they make business loans and the multiple expansion of bank deposits that follows lending
- describe the principal financial institutions in the United States today and how increased competition has changed the way they do business
- explain how banks work and the features of a bank's balance sheet and income statement
- explain how banks, through the check collection and electronic funds transfer processes, facilitate payments and settlement transactions in the United States
- describe the structure and functions of the Federal Reserve and the impact that this institution has on banks and the economy
- summarize the responsibilities of the major banking regulators and the banking laws that have affected the current competitive and regulatory environment
- explain the theories that underlie the role of money and interest rates in the economy

- summarize the basic goals of economic policy—full employment, price stability, and economic growth—and actions that have been tried to achieve these goals
- describe the monetary policy tools, the effects of monetary policy among various borrowers in the credit market, and the role of banks in implementing monetary policy
- summarize the federal budget process and the various actions the government can take to manage the federal debt and the U.S. balance of payments
- explain the role banks play in international trade and payments and the workings of the foreign exchange market

Chapters 1 through 4 provide a broad overview of money and the U.S. economy. The evolution and basic functions of money are examined, followed by the principal payment devices and money supply measures used today. The discussion continues with the role of savings and lending in the economy and reviews various measures of U.S. economic activity. The creation of money through the lending process is thoroughly explained. Lastly the role of banks is compared with that of other financial intermediaries, and the many types of deposit accounts in existence today are examined.

Chapters 5 and 6 present an overview of the business of banking. The text considers banks as business firms, examining the important sources of bank earnings, types of bank loans, banks' funds management, and other profit-generating strategies. Bank operations and the crucial role of banks in the nation's payments system are then discussed.

Chapters 7 and 8 focus on the Federal Reserve, other banking regulators, and how legislation and regulation affects the business of banking. The unique quasi-governmental structure of the Federal Reserve is examined, as are its multifaceted roles as the nation's central bank. This examination is followed by a review of the responsibilities of the other banking regulators. Banking legislation and regulation is then introduced, with a look at major laws and regulations that have shaped the current regulatory and competitive environment.

Chapters 9 through 12 provide insights to the theoretical underpinnings that guide policymakers' approaches to economic activity. The tenets of Keynesian and monetarist theory are examined first, followed by a review of the nation's policy goals of full employment, price stability and economic growth. Factors that have spurred U.S. productivity in recent years also are examined. The tools of monetary policy—the discount rate, reserve requirements and open-market operations—and the Federal Reserve's strategies for implementing monetary policy are discussed. Chapter 12 ends with an examination of the tools of fiscal policy, government spending and taxation, and the debt and balance of payments management policies the government can use to guide the economy.

Chapter 13 shifts the focus to the world of international banking, with an emphasis on the role banks play in facilitating world trade and payments through foreign exchange markets. The special role of the U.S. dollar in the international financial system is examined, followed by a review of foreign exchange rates and the foreign exchange market. The role of, and our regulatory treatment of, foreign banks operating in the United States also is discussed.

I hope you will agree that this new edition provides a flexible teaching tool for instructors, as well as an effective learning vehicle for students.

—David H. Friedman

1

MONEY

LEARNING OBJECTIVES

After studying this chapter, you should be able to

- list the basic functions of money
- trace the three-stage evolution of money
- summarize how the valuation of money has evolved from the past to the present
- explain the importance of the different types of U.S. money
- describe the payment devices used in the United States today
- explain the basic differences between the M1, M2, and M3 measures of money supply
- define the key terms listed in this chapter

KEY TERMS

barter economy
commodity money
electronic funds transfers
fiat money
gold standard
legal tender
medium of exchange

money
money supply
near monies
purchasing power
representative money
store of value
unit of account

INTRODUCTION

In ancient Egypt, money was sacred: only mystical items issued by pharaohs and blessed by the gods served as money. Modern money is commercial rather than sacred, and mystical only in the article of faith that has always supported money's value—our willingness to accept money in exchange for goods and services.

Money is an accepted means of making and receiving payments, a common frame of reference for determining value or comparing worth, and an efficient method of storing purchasing power and accumulating wealth.

In this chapter, we explore the concept of money and its functions, the evolution of money, ways the value of modern money is determined, and what constitutes money in the United States today. We also examine how the nation's supply of money is measured and controlled.

THE FUNCTIONS OF MONEY

Economists commonly define **money** in terms of its three basic functions: to serve as a medium of exchange, to serve as a unit of account, and to serve as a store of value. Its importance lies in what it does, not in its physical characteristics.

A MEDIUM OF EXCHANGE

Throughout the ages, people have used countless items as mediums to facilitate the exchange of goods. The ancient Greeks and Romans, for example, used longhorn cattle as a **medium of exchange.** Similarly, brass rings were used by the pharaohs of ancient Egypt, and shark's tooth money was still used by the people of Micronesia early in the twentieth century. If people are willing to accept an item in exchange for goods, services, or settlement of debt, that item serves as money. In the simplest sense, then,

money is nothing more than a nation's generally accepted medium of exchange.

For an item to work well as a medium of exchange, it must be uniform, easily portable, readily divisible, and relatively scarce. Historically, not every item selected as a medium of exchange served this function well. In the seventeenth century, for example, settlers in Virginia used tobacco leaves as money. But tobacco leaves varied greatly in size, texture, and shape, so they were ill-suited as a standard of value. No uniform price could be established for like goods and services because the medium of exchange was not uniform and making exact change was a physical impossibility. Ultimately, tobacco leaves were abandoned as a medium of exchange because they failed to accommodate all three functions of money.

A UNIT OF ACCOUNT

Any item accepted as a nation's medium of exchange also serves as that nation's **unit of account.** In this capacity, money serves as a standard of measurement for the relative value, or worth, of goods and services.

In the United States, the dollar represents a standard of value: it acts as a unit of account. As a consumer, you know that a $500 television set is twice as expensive as a $250 suit. If your after-tax income is $2,000 per month, you know that buying the television set will cost the equivalent of one week of labor.

Money is used similarly to represent the value of items in a company's balance sheet. When a bank loan officer examines the inventories, fixed assets, and raw materials listed in the balance sheet of a company that has applied for a loan, the officer is actually assessing the value of those items using dollars as the unit of account.

A Store of Value

A **store of value** is a means to hold and accumulate purchasing power for future, general use. In its function as a store of value, money allows us to buy goods and services without having to exchange other goods and services. This characteristic distinguishes a money economy from a **barter economy,** an economy in which goods and services are directly traded. For example, in a village community a farmer may exchange a cow for a piece of machinery, or a barber may exchange a haircut for a basket of corn or a small chicken. In a barter exchange, the value in the exchange is determined by the traders.

One drawback to a barter economy is the lack of assurance that any given item in your immediate possession will be accepted in trade for a different item you might want from someone else. Another drawback is the need to preserve the quality and physical condition of goods held in storage for future exchange. A cow, for example, may sicken and die, leaving its owner with nothing to barter. In contrast, dollars can be efficiently stored and accumulated for future use.

THE EVOLUTION OF MONEY

Since ancient times, many diverse items have served as money for the peoples of the world. Some money items, such as cattle, furs, bark, cloth, and tea have been useful commodities in themselves. Others, such as the paper money used in fifteenth-century Europe, have been exchanged as representations of value. In addition, the currency issued periodically in seventh-century China and the paper money that constitutes modern national currencies, have had the backing of state powers. These various types of money are called *commodity money, representative money,* and *fiat money*, and their use traces the evolution of money from earliest times to the present.

COMMODITY MONEY

The world's earliest monies were mediums of exchange that were also useful commodities. The inherent value of the commodity supported its use as an exchange medium for goods and services. In ancient Rome, for example, salt served as a **commodity money** because of its great desirability as a food additive. In fact, salt has held universal appeal as a valued medium of exchange.

While ancient Romans were exchanging bricks of salt, their contemporaries in China were already purchasing goods and services with the world's longest-reigning commodity money—gold. The scarcity and luster of gold and the mystical properties attributed to it made this commodity money universally accepted throughout the ancient world.

Commodity monies are acceptable to people who share little else but an awareness of the intrinsic worth of the commodity. Unfortunately, most commodity monies lack the physical characteristics necessary to ensure their performance as uniform standards of account and good stores of value. Even gold lacks the easy divisibility and portability necessary for a truly efficient and practical exchange medium.

Salt-bricks, wrapped in leather, were used as money by the people of Ethiopia from the fourteenth century to the 1920s. *Photo courtesy of the Smithsonian Institution, NNC, Douglas Mudd.*

Although gold coins still circulate as a medium of exchange in a few countries, the role of gold as a monetary metal today is primarily that of a store of value. Commodity monies still play an important role, however, in countries where recurring economic and political upheaval, war, and invasion have eroded confidence in government-issued paper money and bank deposits.

REPRESENTATIVE MONEY

The impracticality of using commodity money for widespread commercial transactions first became apparent in Europe during the fifteenth century. As trade and economic activity began to expand, the need for a more efficient medium of exchange became pressing.

European tradesmen and merchants began to deposit their precious-metal money with goldsmiths, the earliest bankers. Having gold inventories of their own, the goldsmiths had the vault space and security necessary to safeguard the money. The goldsmiths gave receipts for these precious-metal deposits. Soon, tradesmen and merchants began exchanging their goldsmiths' receipts, a more practical, rapid, and safe method of payment than exchanging precious-metal money. These receipts, the precursors of our modern currency, were **representative money.** They represented claims on items of value held at a central depository. Because the holder of representative money could redeem the receipt at the depository for commodity money or bullion, people were willing to accept the receipt as money. Therefore, this representative money functioned as an effective medium of exchange.

FIAT MONEY

Fiat money represents the third major stage in the evolution of money. It began to take hold in sixteenth- and seventeenth-century Europe with the emergence of strong nation-states and central governments. **Fiat money** is a medium of exchange mandated by a government and backed by the law and power of the state. Virtually all coin and currency used today is fiat money issued by the governments and central banks of the nations of the world. Modern paper currency can no longer be exchanged or redeemed for commodity money or precious-metal bullion. Both coin and currency function as money by government decree. The ease of making change, the portability, and the familiarity of modern-day coin and currency enable them to function effectively for the myriad small personal and commercial transactions that take place daily in marketplaces worldwide.

Fiat money works as a store of value because people are willing to accept fiat money in exchange for goods, services, or settlement of debt. It would be wrong to conclude, however, that this willingness is rooted in law or in the power of the state. No body of law or power of state can guarantee or force acceptance of a medium of exchange, in any form, unless it ensures that the exchange medium will be a good standard and store of value. The money problems of modern economies no longer involve the search for items to serve as effective mediums of exchange, but rather the ability of governments to remain stable and to maintain the purchasing power of the world's monies.

THE VALUE OF MONEY

The value of modern money is based on what it can buy in the marketplace—that is, its **purchasing power.** The value of one U.S. dollar is the same whether that dollar takes the form of a metal coin, a currency note, or a bookkeeping entry in a bank account. This was not always the case. In America's early history, the intrinsic worth of money was an important measure of its value.

Today the purchasing power of money relates directly to the prices of the goods and services on which that money is spent. As prices rise, the purchasing power of a given amount of money declines. As prices fall, the purchasing power increases. For example, from 2000 to 2001, the prices for U.S. goods and services increased by 2 percent, resulting in a small reduction in the dollar's purchasing power.

Government efforts to regulate money in a modern economy are an attempt to maintain and enhance the purchasing power of money. This involves controlling the quantity of money in the economy to stabilize prices. When there is too much money in an economy, the prices of goods and services generally rise. This is because consumers, businesses, and governments with excess money all compete for available goods and services. Competition drives up prices and, in turn, reduces money's purchasing power, generating the phenomenon known as inflation.

The value of money is inversely related to its availability. The greater the quantity of money in circulation, the smaller the purchasing power of each unit of money. The smaller the quantity of money in circulation, the greater the purchasing power of each monetary unit. Today, with checkbook money used as the predominant money in most countries, governments attempt to control the quantity of money (and thus its value) through the monetary policy powers of their central banks.

THE GOLD STANDARD AND THE BIMETALLIC STANDARD

During the nineteenth century, many industrial nations, including the United States, attempted to regulate the value of their national money by operating first under a gold standard and later under a bimetallic (gold and silver) standard.

Under the **gold standard,** these nations defined the value of their money not in terms of its purchasing power but in terms of a fixed weight of gold. The United States, for example, allowed its paper money to be converted into gold at a predetermined rate of exchange. The gold standard worked well as long as gold supplies kept pace with national production and income. In the late 1800s, however, with the end of the California and Australia gold rushes, gold production slowed and prices of goods and services fell throughout the world.

In many countries, declining prices and wages caused by the gold shortages led to economic unrest. Strikes, rising unemployment, and political instability soon followed. In the United States, falling prices prompted farmers and unions to pressure the government to use silver as well as gold as a monetary standard. As a result, the government adopted a bimetallic standard.

Under the bimetallic standard, the U.S. Treasury agreed to exchange U.S. currency for either gold or silver at a predetermined weight ratio. For example, currency could be exchanged either for 16 ounces of silver or 1 ounce of gold. However, this dual standard worked even more poorly than the gold standard in maintaining the value of U.S. money because other countries did not agree to maintain the same ratio of exchange. As a result, different value systems existed throughout the world for the same commodity monies.

Changes in the relative demand and supply for either gold or silver in any part of the world led to a rapid disappearance from circulation of the more expensive money. For example, as changes in supply and demand drove up the price of gold, the cheaper silver was circulated whereas the more expensive gold was hoarded, melted down, or sold abroad, causing it to disappear from circulation. The principle that "cheap money" tends to drive "dear money" from circulation is known as Gresham's Law. It is named for Britain's sixteenth-century Master of the Mint, Sir Thomas Gresham, who first identified this economic phenomenon.

Exhibit 1.1
Personal, Commercial, and Financial Payment Transactions

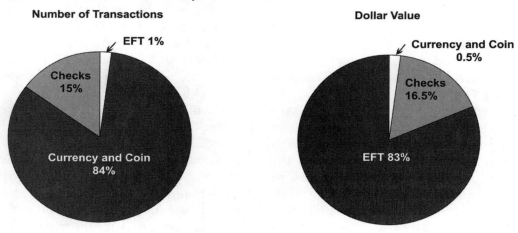

Source: Federal Reserve Bank of Kansas City, *Economic Review,* Fourth Quarter, 1999.

U.S. MONEY TODAY

In the United States today, coin, paper currency, and checkable deposits (deposits from which payments can be made by check or electronic funds transfers) are the accepted mediums of exchange. Credit cards, a commonly used payment device, do not qualify as a medium of exchange. By extending credit to the bearer, credit cards simply delay payment. Exhibit 1.1 compares the use of these various payment devices. It shows that while about four out of five payment transactions involve coin and currency, they constitute only about 1 percent of the total dollar volume of all payment transactions.

COIN

Coin is indispensable to countless daily purchasing transactions, yet it represents a very small percentage of the total dollar volume of transactions. Coin is minted by the U.S. Treasury and distributed by the nation's 12 Federal Reserve banks. It is carried as a liability on the Treasury's books and as an asset on the books of all other institutions that hold coin.

CURRENCY

Like coin, currency is widely used by individuals for relatively small transactions. About 90 percent of all currency transactions involve amounts of less than $20. Today's currency consists almost entirely of Federal Reserve notes printed by the Treasury and issued by the nation's 12 Federal Reserve banks. Unlike coin, U.S. currency is not a direct responsibility of the Treasury but of the Federal Reserve, the central bank of the United States. When issued, currency is carried as a liability on the Federal Reserve's books and as an asset on the books of all other institutions that hold currency, including the Treasury.

From 1914 to 1968, Federal Reserve notes were partially backed, or collateralized, by gold. Gold backing was seen as a means of tying U.S. currency into the gold standard. It ensured that Federal Reserve banks would not issue too much paper money, and thereby generated public acceptance of the currency.

The gold and eligible-paper backing requirements initially were designed to regulate the issuance of currency to match the pace of economic growth. Economists believed that the backing requirements would automatically ensure that currency

THE DOLLAR COIN

In 2000 the U.S. Mint issued a new gold-color dollar coin. The coin bears the image of Sacagawea, the Native American woman who guided the Lewis and Clark Expedition, and was the eighth attempt by the U.S. to put a dollar coin into widespread circulation. The prior dollar coin issue had been the Susan B. Anthony dollar in 1979.

Proponents of dollar coins contend that if the coins were widely used, the government would save a substantial amount of money. Coins cost about 12 cents each to produce and last, on average, about 30 years. Dollar bills cost about 3 to 4 cents to produce, but last, on average, 18 months. The government's continuous need to replace dollar bills so frequently makes them much more expensive than dollar coins over the long run.

The American public, however, prefers dollar bills to coins for day-to-day transactions. Dollar coins have generally been rejected as being too bulky, too hard to distinguish from lower denomination coinage, and too heavy to carry in a pocketbook or wallet.

Some evidence supports the idea that dollar coins would be accepted and widely used by the public if the government removed the dollar bill from circulation. Several countries have successfully put a high denomination coin in circulation, but only by discontinuing the issuance of the corresponding denomination notes.

In 2000 the U.S. mint produced more than one billion Sacagawea coins. Through 2002, however, almost half of these coins remained stored in Federal Reserve Bank and U.S. Mint vaults. Although millions of coins were put into circulation, most are rarely used in day-to-day transactions, and they do not show up in cash registers or vending machines. The most widely accepted explanation for what happened to the circulating Sacagawea coins is that the public is holding them as collector's items. This explanation is supported by the massive public demand for the commemorative state quarters that the U.S. Mint began issuing in the late 1990s.

would not be over issued because only short-term bank loans, such as those made to expand manufacturing or farm production, were designated as eligible collateral by the Federal Reserve. Thus, only increased business activity, as evidenced by increased bank lending, could generate the collateral necessary for issuing additional currency.

Since 1968, Federal Reserve notes have been backed only by the assets of the Federal Reserve banks. Today about 85 percent of these assets consist of government securities owned by the Federal Reserve, valued at more than $540 billion in 2002.

FOREIGN USE OF U.S. CURRENCY

U.S. currency is a widely used medium of exchange, unit of account, and store of value in other countries. Its popularity is so great that in 2002 about two-thirds of America's $590 billion supply of currency circulated exclusively overseas. As seen in exhibit 1.2 on the following page, some 65 percent of America's currency consists of $100 bills, with the share of $100s held abroad increasing steadily since 1980 to more than 70 percent.

In many nations, economic and political instability make U.S. currency a more appealing store of value and medium of exchange than the domestic currency. For example, in Argentina, which experienced severe inflation from the 1960s to the early 1990s, U.S. currency is the only acceptable way to settle large value transactions, such as land and car purchases. An estimated $80 billion in U.S. currency circulates in Argentina and neighboring South American countries. In the nations of the former Soviet Union, high inflation in the 1990s, domestic

Exhibit 1.2
U.S. Currency in Circulation, $100s in Circulation, and $100s Held Overseas (in billions)

Year	Total	$100s	Share of $100s in Total	$100s Held Abroad	Share of $100s Held Abroad
1980	$124.8	$49.3	39.5%	$23.8	48.4%
1985	182.0	81.2	44.6	45.8	56.4
1990	268.2	140.2	52.3	85.7	61.1
1995	401.5	241.5	60.2	169.2	70.1
1996	427.1	261.4	61.2	186.6	71.4
1997	458.0	291.6	63.7	211.4	72.5
1998	492.2	320.1	65.0	228.0	71.2

Source: *Report to Congress: The Use and Counterfeiting of U.S. Currency Abroad*, U.S. Treasury Department, January 2000.

currency recalls, and a weak banking system have encouraged people to hold U.S. dollars as a store of value and to use dollars instead of rubles as a domestic medium of exchange. An estimated $130 billion in U.S. currency may be held in Russia alone.

Practical business considerations in other nations have added to overall foreign demand for U.S. currency in recent decades. In the Caribbean, for example, using dollars as a medium of exchange that circulates together with domestic currency helps attract tourists from the United States. In the oil-producing countries of the Middle East, U.S. currency is routinely used to pay foreign workers, many of whom send those dollars to their families in Europe and Asia. In countries that host U.S. military bases, U.S. currency circulates with domestic currency to accommodate the spending of the troops stationed there. In Liberia and Panama, two countries with long-standing economic ties to the United States, the U.S. dollar is the official currency.

Foreigners' preferences for U.S. currency relate to the compactness, anonymity, and portability of large-denomination U.S. bills. Even in large quantities, U.S. currency is easily transportable. Furthermore, U.S. currency has never been subject to government recall and has always been exchangeable at face value, regardless of when the specific bill was issued.

CHECKABLE DEPOSITS

Most of us rely on checking accounts to buy goods and services and pay bills. United States consumers, businesses, and government entities use checks to make more than 90 percent of all commercial and personal payments, as measured by dollar volume.

Checkable deposits are the total amount of account balances on the books of banks and other financial institutions against which checks are drawn. Checkable deposits constituted about $600 billion in 2002, a large portion of the nation's money.

Individuals draw about half of all checks written in the United States, and more than half of those checks are for amounts less than $50. Payroll checks from businesses are the source of most of the money against which Americans write their personal checks, and about two-thirds of the checks written by businesses are payroll checks. Exhibit 1.3 shows that the predominant use of checks by individuals, businesses, and government entities is to pay bills.

In 2002 Americans wrote about 50 billion to 65 billion checks. From the early 1950s to the early 1990s, the total number of checks written by American consumers, businesses, and government entities grew by about 5 percent annually. During the late 1990s, however, check volume growth began to slow to about 1 percent annually. Economists

Exhibit 1.3
U.S. Check Payments Profile, 2001

Motive	Percentage of Total Checks Written
To pay bills	38
To pay wages or remit income	18
To pay for over-the-counter retail purchases	19
To make personal payments such as gifts and charitable contributions	11
Motive not known	14

Source: Study of the Retail Payment System, Financial Services Policy Committee, Federal Reserve Bank of Boston, November 2001.

believe this slowdown may reflect consumers' increasing use of debit cards and other electronic forms of payment.

Demand deposits, or checking accounts, make up the core component of the nation's money supply. Demand deposits in the U.S. banking system pay no interest but allow the holder or holders to withdraw funds on demand and to transfer funds by check. Because demand deposits are created in the commercial lending process, mainly by the nation's banks, the Federal Reserve's attempts to control the money supply focus on regulating the ability of banks to create demand deposits.

Only since the late 1970s have commercial banks and thrift institutions, such as savings banks, savings and loan associations, and credit unions, been allowed to offer checkable deposits that pay interest. In 2002 Americans held nearly $2,000 billion in money market deposit accounts at banks and savings institutions. Although these accounts pay interest and allow limited check-writing privileges, they are legally classified as savings deposits rather than as checkable deposits.

LEGAL TENDER AND CHECKBOOK MONEY

Checks carry no status as legal tender. Only U.S.-minted coin and Federal Reserve-issued paper currency are designated as legal tender. The term **legal tender** refers to money items designated by the government and the courts as acceptable payment for goods and services or settlement of debt. In effect, the designation of certain items as legal tender leaves sellers of goods and services and creditors with no legal recourse to demand any other form of payment.

Americans prefer using checkbook money to make payments despite its lack of legal tender status. Checks are convenient,

ADVANTAGES OF CHECKBOOK MONEY

A check offers consumers numerous advantages, such as

- the ability to spend small or large amounts with the same instrument
- deterrence to theft or counterfeiting because of the signature requirement
- the ability to stop payment after a transaction has been made
- written proof of payment in the form of a canceled check
- a clear audit trail through the check collection process, which allows for identification of errors or improper transactions
- consumer float, which is extra use of account funds because of the time required for check collection by recipients and their banks, although advances in technology have been steadily reducing the time required

and for many transactions checks serve as a more efficient medium of exchange than coin or currency.

In today's economy, the reliance on legal tender has been supplanted by public confidence in the strength, safety, and soundness of the American banking system. This confidence has been bolstered by ongoing government supervision and inspection of banks and by the insurance of deposits by the Federal Deposit Insurance Corporation (FDIC). The Federal Reserve also has helped make checkbook money highly acceptable by promptly crediting banks with payments for checks drawn on other banks and by speeding up the check collection process nationwide.

ELECTRONIC FUNDS TRANSFERS

About 1 percent of payments in the United States are made by means other than coin, currency, or check. These financial payments are routinely made electronically by computer or terminal between banks, between banks and the Federal Reserve, or between banks and large corporations. As exhibit 1.1 shows, although the percentage of payments is small, the dollar value of these **electronic funds transfers** (EFTs, also called wire transfers) represents more than 80 percent of the total dollar volume of personal, commercial, and financial payment transactions in the United States today.

EFTs also are gaining in popularity among consumers, businesses, and the government for payment transactions. Today nearly half of American workers receive their pay by electronic transfers of funds to their bank accounts. And approximately three-fourths of America's 45 million senior citizens receive Social Security benefits electronically. The federal government has been the leading force behind the development of EFTs in an attempt to cut the cost of using paper checks and to use the increased efficiency that EFTs allow.

CREDIT CARDS

Credit cards, used by 80 percent of all American families, are extremely popular payment devices. About 15 percent of all consumer spending in the United States is done with credit cards. Credit cards are not a medium of exchange, but a deferred-payment device that allows consumers to acquire goods and services immediately while making payment by check or electronic funds transfer at a later date. In effect, using a credit card is akin to accepting a prearranged loan.

In 2002 Americans held more than 500 million credit cards. Many of these cards reflect two-party arrangements made directly with consumers by department stores and gasoline companies. These arrangements simply allow the credit card user to buy goods and services on credit from the institution, merchant, or chain that issues the card. The most popular form of credit card, however, reflects a three-party, or multilateral, arrangement entered into by consumers, the banks that issue the cards, and groups of participating merchants. VISA and MasterCard are examples of this type of credit arrangement, which allows consumers to buy goods and services on credit from thousands of participating merchants. Most multilateral credit cards also allow the user to draw cash on credit from participating banks.

Credit card use has increased dramatically over the last two decades, primarily among those two-thirds of credit card users who opt to use the revolving credit feature of the cards to pay off charges in monthly installments. In the 1990s, a surge in e-commerce propelled this increase, reflected by household purchases of goods and services over the Internet. Most Internet purchases are made with a credit card.

The popularity of bank credit cards during the 1990s and early 2000s has been matched by their profitability for banks. On average, banks earn a higher return on credit cards than on most other bank loans. One reason is that credit cards represent loans that are not backed, or secured, by collateral. As such, credit cards carry a higher risk to a bank than do other kinds of loans. Banks seek to cover this risk by charging high interest rates and by assessing annual fees. Another reason is the large difference between the interest banks charge on credit cards and the interest banks pay on deposits. During the 1990s, banks lowered the interest paid on deposits, which reduced the banks' costs of obtaining funds. At the same time, banks continued to receive high interest from credit card users who were paying off charges monthly on transactions made, in some instances, years earlier. The result has been a wider profit spread for banks between costs and income.

NEW PAYMENT DEVICES

Several new payment devices came into limited use in the United States during the 1990s. Those devices that offer the greatest promise for changing America's payment practices in the future are stored value cards, e-cash, and e-checks.

STORED VALUE CARDS

A stored value card, or electronic purse, is a prepaid, wallet-size card that contains a microchip. The microchip stores data representing a predetermined amount of money usable for purchases or other transactions until the dollars are used up. When necessary, the cardholder can add new dollar value to the card by recharging the card's microchip. Virtually all stored value cards in the United States today are single-purpose cards that limit the cardholder to one type of transaction, such as paying for telephone calls or paying subway or bus fare.

Since the 1980s, public transit authorities in New York, San Francisco, and Washington, D.C., have been issuing stored value cards to riders. During the 1990s, America's major regional telephone companies began to issue stored value cards for customers' use in making local and long-distance calls. Many colleges also issue stored value cards for students' use in paying for on-campus meals.

A growing number of Americans find using stored value cards more convenient than using coin or currency for many small-ticket transactions. Card users can avoid having to hold or carry loose change, and the cards speed transactions because card users do not need exact change.

Many bankers are enthusiastic about the public's growing acceptance of stored value cards and believe that, in time, people will begin using them for a broad range of retail transactions. With a universal or multi-purpose card, banks could routinely recharge cards for customers, transferring dollars from customers' bank accounts to the cards. Banks would save millions of dollars they now incur in handling cash and debit card transaction processing, and could generate fee income from the initial issuance of the cards. The way Americans hold and use money also would profoundly change. If, for example, stored value cards displaced all coin and all currency denominations of $10 and under, America could reduce its need for cash by more than half, as shown in exhibit 1.4 on the following page.

E-CASH AND E-CHECKS

E-cash consists of a predetermined amount of dollars that are digitally deposited by the bank into an account-holder's personal computer. The user can draw on the e-cash to make purchases over the Internet. E-cash payments are sent to participating merchants as strings of electronic digits. Like currency, e-cash does not have to be cleared or settled by the user's bank. Recipients of e-cash can reuse it or deposit it into participating banks for account credit.

E-checks are electronic checks that are prepared on a personal computer and sent in payment over the Internet. Upon receipt of an e-check, the recipient forwards it electronically to a participating bank, which clears and settles the check payment.

Exhibit 1.4
Composition of U.S. Currency, 2000

	Number of Units (in billions)	Value (in billions)	Share of Total Value
Coin	—	$ 25.4	4.9%
$1	7.0	7.0	1.4
$2	0.7	1.5	0.3
$5	1.6	8.0	1.5
$10	1.4	14.3	2.8
$20	4.5	90.9	17.6
$50	1.0	50.5	9.7
$100	3.2	320.1	61.8
Total	19.4	$517.7	100.0%

Source: Federal Reserve, U.S. Treasury, First Quarter, 2000.

Unlike stored value cards, e-cash and e-checks have had a smaller impact than many bankers and Internet companies had initially projected. Most merchants and personal computer users have been reluctant to invest in the software that is necessary to allow e-monies to be sent and received. Merchants see such investments as costly and unwarranted until many of their customers indicate a willingness to pay in e-money. Personal computer users, in turn, have little interest in acquiring e-money software until numerous merchants begin offering e-payment capabilities. Uncertainty over Internet security and information privacy, the lack of software standards for assuring compatible exchanges of e-money among personal computer users, and the lack of a single, common e-money system also have slowed merchant and household acceptance of e-money.

THE MONEY SUPPLY

A nation's **money supply** is the sum of all the funds that individuals and businesses have immediately available for spending in the domestic economy. In the United States, the Federal Reserve applies its monetary policy to regulate the nation's money supply.

The growth of the nation's money supply has long been monitored because of the effects that money supply growth is believed to have on economic activity. Too-rapid growth is inflationary; too slow, recessionary. From 1971 to 2000, the Federal Reserve established specific numerical targets for money supply growth and sought to hit those targets. During the 1980s and 1990s, the relationship between money supply growth and economic activity weakened, however, causing the Federal Reserve to de-emphasize its targeting of money supply growth as the primary means of guiding monetary policy.

DEFINING THE MONEY SUPPLY

The concept of money supply is based on the theory that people and businesses hold and spend money in predictable ways. Individuals, for example, hold and spend money primarily to satisfy their wants and needs in accordance with their incomes. Businesses hold and spend money to enhance profits or prospects for profit. If we know how much money is immediately available for spending by individuals and businesses and if we know what their preferences are for holding, saving, and spending money, we can predict the course and pace of economic activity. More importantly, in theory the economy can be controlled to some extent by increasing or decreasing the money supply. The Federal Reserve's success in controlling the nation's money supply over long periods ultimately affects economic production, employment, income, and price levels.

The money supply is not synonymous with the amount of coin, currency, and checkable deposits in the economy because spending decisions are not based solely on how much of these money items we hold. Actually, most of the public's financial wealth is not held in money, but rather in near monies. **Near monies** are noncash items that are good standards of value and can be rapidly converted into cash, which means they can substitute for money in some respects. Near monies include U.S. government and corporate bonds, life insurance policies, pension funds, money market shares, and various types of interest-earning time deposits in financial institutions. Near monies generally are highly *liquid,* which means they can be quickly converted into money.

In 2002 individuals and businesses held more than $20 trillion in total financial assets. Of this amount, about $1.2 trillion, a little more than one-twentieth of the total, took the form of currency and checkable deposits. By contrast, $4.2 trillion, or about one-fifth of the total, was held by individuals and businesses in time and savings deposits in the nation's banks and thrift institutions.

As consumers, we take at least some of these near-money financial assets into consideration when facing major spending decisions. We may look to our savings and time accounts to draw on savings, or look to our credit cards as a source for borrowing funds, or convert a near-money asset, such as funds in a money market account, into spendable money. What is not apparent to economists, however, is just which assets consumers prefer for long-term savings and which near-money assets typically enter into spending decisions. This uncertainty makes it very hard to predict spending behavior.

The same assessment problem applies to business spending because businesses generally evaluate their spending decisions against the broad range of their financial assets rather than solely against their holdings of cash and demand deposits. Businesses frequently use certificates of deposit, U.S. Treasury bills, and other financial instruments to store purchasing power while assessing their spending options.

PROBLEMS OF CLASSIFICATION

The problem of what near-money assets to count as part of the money supply is complicated by two factors. First, banking innovations and changes in banking law in the 1980s allowed banks and thrifts to offer new types of deposit accounts that pay interest yet are checkable; that is, they are subject both to claim and to transfer by check. Second, these accounts have blurred the distinction between funds held for spending transactions and funds held for long-term savings.

The classification of savings and spendable funds also has been complicated by the rapid transfer of vast amounts of funds by consumers in search of greater interest earnings or greater safety. During the 1980s, high interest rates on deposits induced consumers and businesses to transfer non-interest-earning demand deposit money into a broad range of interest-earning near monies and new, interest-bearing checkable deposits. Then, during the 1990s, low interest rates on deposits induced consumers and businesses to transfer low-paying time and savings deposit money into higher-earning near monies, such as stocks and bonds. In the early 2000s, a sharp decline in stock prices induced consumers and businesses to transfer stock and mutual fund near monies, which were subject to risk of further losses in value, into low-earning, but safe, time and savings deposits. These kinds of movements of funds greatly complicate the tasks of classifying spending money and savings money and interpreting money growth.

MEASURING THE MONEY SUPPLY

The Federal Reserve uses a variety of money-supply measures to predict and control the pace and direction of U.S. economic activity in order to ensure the purchasing power of money and maintain a growing economy. The most important of these measures are M1, M2, and M3. The Federal Reserve also factors in a measure of debt. Exhibit 1.5 shows the relative size of these various measures in 2002 and the components of

each. Exhibit 1.6 then shows the relative growth rates of these measures in 2001.

M1 MEASURE

M1 refers to the most commonly used and narrowest measure of the money immediately available to the public for domestic spending. This measure counts all mediums of exchange, including interest-earning checkable deposits held by individuals at both banks and thrift institutions. M1 consists of

- currency and coin outside the Treasury, Federal Reserve banks, and commercial banks

---

Exhibit 1.5
Components of the Money Supply and Debt Measures (as of January 2002)

			Amount (in billions)
M1:	Currency and coin		$587
	Demand deposits		327
	Other checkable deposits		261
	Traveler's checks		8
		Total	1,183
M2:	M1		1,183
	Savings deposits and money market deposit accounts		2,345
	Small-denomination time deposits		954
	Deposits in retail money market funds		984
		Total	5,466
M3:	M2		5,466
	Large-denomination time deposits (more than $100,000)		819
	Repurchase agreements (RPs)		374
	Eurodollars		212
	Deposits in institution-only money market funds		1,167
		Total	8,038
Debt:	Federal debt		3,384
	Nonfederal debt*		15,944
		Total	$19,328

* Includes state and local government debt and private debt.
Source: Federal Reserve Board, *Statistical Release H.6 (508).*

- demand deposits at all commercial banks, except those deposits due to domestic banks, foreign commercial banks, and certain foreign official institutions or the U.S. government, less cash items in the process of collection and Federal Reserve float
- Negotiable Order of Withdrawal (NOW) accounts
- interest-earning checking accounts provided by credit unions
- savings deposits subject to automatic transfers
- demand deposits at thrift institutions
- traveler's checks

M2 MEASURE

M2 is a broader measure of the money the public has immediately available for domestic spending. In addition to the mediums of exchange included in M1, M2 counts near monies that are close substitutes for money, quickly mature into cash, or are readily sold for cash. M2 consists of

- M1
- savings deposits and money market deposit accounts at banks and savings institutions
- time deposits with minimum denominations of less than $100,000, except individual retirement accounts
- balances held in retail money market mutual funds (funds with minimum investments of less than $50,000)

M3 MEASURE

M3 is a still broader measure of money supply. It includes not only the categories of money and near money counted in M1 and M2, but certain highly liquid assets used mainly by big business firms. M3 consists of

- M2
- time deposits with minimum denominations of $100,000
- repurchase agreements issued by commercial banks
- balances held in institution-only money market mutual funds (funds with minimum investments of $50,000 or more)
- Eurodollar deposits held by U.S. residents at foreign branches of U.S. banks and all banks in the United Kingdom and Canada

A repurchase agreement involves the purchase of a security with an agreement that the seller will buy back the security within a specified time and at an agreed-upon price. Most repurchase agreements involve three-month Treasury bills with the buy-back scheduled within a day or two. *Eurodollars* are broadly defined as any dollar-denominated deposits on the books of banking offices outside the United States, including non-European banks.

Exhibit 1.6
Money Supply and Debt Growth, 2001
(percent change at seasonally adjusted annual rates)

	M1	M2	M3	Debt
Three months, from October 2001 to January 2002	6.9	6.9	7.9	6.8
Six months, from July 2001 to January 2002	7.6	9.2	9.9	6.6
Twelve months, from January 2001 to January 2002	7.8	9.6	11.3	6.1

Source: Federal Reserve Statistical Release H.6 (508), Table 10, February 28, 2002.

DEBT MEASURE

In its efforts to predict and control the pace and direction of U.S. economic activity the Federal Reserve also considers the growth of debt in the economy. The debt measure used by the Federal Reserve includes

- outstanding debt instruments issued by the U.S. government and the nation's state and local governments
- private debt in outstanding corporate bonds; commercial and residential mortgages; consumer, business, and other loans made by banks; and commercial paper
- other debt instruments

CLASSIFYING THE MONEY SUPPLY MEASURES

Each of the money supply measures shares common characteristics. Each successive measure is broader than and includes the measure that preceded it. Thus, M2 includes all of M1 plus near monies, and M3 includes all of M2 plus additional near monies. Also, none of these measurements counts the monies or near monies held by banks or the government.

Banks hold money primarily to meet the Federal Reserve's reserve requirements and bank's liquidity needs. The government manages the money it holds through two sets of accounts: Treasury Tax and Loan (TT&L) accounts at thousands of banks and thrifts into which tax receipts and loan proceeds (receipts from the sales of newly issued securities) are deposited, and accounts at the Federal Reserve banks from which disbursements are made. To include monies held by banks and the government in the money supply measures would distort the predictive link between money supply growth and economic activity because those funds are not held for immediate spending on goods and services.

Checking accounts kept in U.S. banks by foreign commercial banks and official institutions also are not included in any money supply measure because these deposits are not generally used in domestic commercial transactions.

Finally, cash items (checks) in the process of collection in the banking system and Federal Reserve float, the credit banks receive for checks deposited with Reserve banks before the checks are collected, are subtracted from the total of demand deposits. This is done to avoid double counting and thus overstating the size of the money supply measures.

MONEY SUPPLY AS A POLICY GUIDE

Since the 1930s, M1 and M2 growth has had mixed success in predicting the course of the economy. Beginning in 1933, the government imposed ceilings on the interest rates that banks could pay on time and savings deposits. These ceilings and the prohibition on the payment of interest on demand deposits tended to distort M1 and M2 trends. During periods when rate ceilings were well above interest rates on U.S. Treasury bills and other money market instruments, funds tended to flow into time and savings deposits at banks, speeding the growth of M2 and slowing the growth of M1. When market interest rates exceeded the rate ceilings, growth of M2 slowed as time deposits were transferred into higher-earning Treasury bills and money market instruments.

During the 1960s, the growth of the narrow M1 measure of the money supply seemed to offer better predictions of the course of the U.S. economy than the growth of the broader money supply measures. In the 1970s, the M2 measure came closer to the mark.

In the 1980s, the Federal Reserve began to broaden its monetary policy focus from M1 to the M2 and M3 money supply measures, contending that the growth of the M1 measure was being particularly distorted by changes in bank deposit products and the way the public was holding spending and savings monies. By 1987 the Federal Reserve concluded that M1 had lost its predictive link to the economy and stopped using it as a target for guiding monetary policy. Instead, the Federal Reserve began to rely solely on M2 and M3.

The Federal Reserve became increasingly suspicious of the predictive qualities of the M2 measure during the 1990s. Accordingly, it decided to abandon M2 as a policy target and rely instead on the predictive qualities of other financial and economic measures, such as real and nominal interest rates, commodity prices, and the growth of the nation's production. In 2000 the Full Employment and Balanced Growth Act of 1978, known as the Humphrey-Hawkins Act, expired. This legislation had required the Federal Reserve to set target ranges for money supply growth. On its expiration, the Federal Reserve announced that it would no longer set such targets because money supply growth was not providing a useful benchmark for conducting monetary policy. The Federal Reserve did say, however, that money supply growth would still be taken into account in evaluating economic and financial conditions and formulating a monetary policy response.

SUMMARY

Money is best understood as a medium of exchange that serves both as a standard unit of account and as a store of value. As a medium of exchange, money allows goods and services to be sold at different times and in different places. As a unit of account, money enables comparable values to be placed on diverse goods and services. As a store of value, money enables purchasing power to be stored for future use.

Money has evolved over the years from commodity money to representative money to fiat money. An example of commodity money is salt, which has inherent value; an example of representative money is goldsmith's receipts, which are redeemable

for something of value; and an example of fiat money is U.S. currency, which is money by government decree.

Only coin and currency are designated as legal tender in the United States today. Nonetheless the vast majority of payments by dollar volume are made by checks and electronic funds transfers drawn against checkable deposits in banks.

In the modern era, the acceptability and value of money are rooted not in money's intrinsic worth but in its purchasing power. Governments attempt to maintain the purchasing power of money by controlling the quantity of money in circulation. During the eighteenth and nineteenth centuries, governments relied on the gold and bimetallic standards to ensure appropriate control. Since the twentieth century, government control over money has been maintained through the monetary policy powers of nations' central banks.

In the United States, the Federal Reserve has long monitored, and at times targeted, the nation's money supply growth because of the effects such growth is believed to have on economic activity.

REVIEW QUESTIONS

1. Briefly describe the three functions of money. Explain which function, if any, holds the greatest importance.
2. What is the difference between barter and the use of commodity money?
3. "Gold as a commodity money would be a poor medium of exchange in today's American economy." Do you agree or disagree? Explain your answer.
4. Must fiat money be designated as legal tender by a government for it to be generally accepted as a nation's money? Does legal tender status ensure the general acceptability of money? Does government insurance for deposit money affect its acceptability as money? Explain your answers.

5. What are the basic differences between the M1, M2, and M3 measures of money supply?

ADDITIONAL RESOURCES

Federal Reserve Economic Data (FRED®) and FRED II. Databases maintained by the Federal Reserve Bank of St. Louis providing current and historical trend data on money supply and other financial measures. Information about FRED® is accessible at *http://research.stlouisfed.org/fred/;* information about FRED II can be found at *http://research.stlouisfed.org/fred2.* FRED II allows data downloads in Microsoft Excel and text formats.

Fundamental Facts About U.S. Money, Federal Reserve Bank of Atlanta, 1993, 16 pp. Provides historical information about U.S. money and describes the features of today's currency and coinage.

History of Money from Ancient Times to the Present Day, 2d ed., by Glyn Davies. A history of money from ancient times to the present day. A description of the book is available at *http://www.ex.ac.uk/~RDavies/arian/llyfr.html.*

Monetary Trends, Federal Reserve Bank of St. Louis, 2002. Provides current monthly data and charts on money supply, interest rates, and related measures of U.S. financial performance.

Money Matters, Federal Reserve Bank of Chicago, 1994, 18 pp. Examines the role of money and gold in U.S. history.

Understanding the Ms in Monetary Policy, Federal Reserve Bank of New York, 1994, 8 pp. Defines the key money supply measures and discusses how these measures are used in the formulation of monetary policy.

2

MONEY AND ECONOMIC ACTIVITY

LEARNING OBJECTIVES

After studying this chapter, you should be able to

- describe gross domestic product and other customary measures of U.S. economic activity
- state ways in which saving and lending are important to our economy
- compare the role of banks, other financial intermediaries, and brokers and dealers in our economy
- explain how the Federal Reserve uses its monetary policy to achieve economic balance
- give reasons why the impact of monetary policy differs among various borrowers in the credit markets
- define the key terms listed in this chapter

KEY TERMS

brokers
dealers
disposable personal income
financial intermediaries
gross domestic product
inflation
monetary policy
money creation

national income
net domestic product
nominal GDP
price index number
prime rate
real GDP
recession
usury laws

INTRODUCTION

Economic activity as we know it would not exist without money. The administration of our country's material resources would not be possible without an acceptable medium of exchange and a standard and store of value. A money economy expedites the production, distribution, and consumption of goods and services.

Consider the American economy and your place in it. The capital formation process was made possible by a money economy. Industrialization, mass production, and economic growth would not have taken root in the eighteenth century without money. Because of money, specialized jobs and geographic mobility are common today. Spending, saving, and lending relationships are now an acceptable fact of modern life.

This chapter explores the way money relates to economic activities such as production, income, spending, saving, and lending. It begins by examining the various measures of economic activity and then explores the important roles that banks and other financial intermediaries play in the economic process. Lastly it analyzes how the Federal Reserve's monetary policy affects the nation's economic balance.

For a detailed exposition of the economy's sporadic imbalances, known as business cycles, you are encouraged to examine Extended Study 1.

THE CIRCULAR FLOW OF ECONOMIC ACTIVITY

The most basic measure of an economy's size and performance is its **gross domestic product** (GDP), a measure of the total value of all new goods and services produced within a country in a given period, typically one year. In 2001 the United States generated a GDP of more than $10.2 trillion, mainly in the form of services.

The nation's GDP reflects the interaction of the consumer, business, and government spending sectors in our economy (see exhibit 2.1). These economic sectors supply each other with factors of production in the form of land, labor, capital, and entrepreneurial talent. In return, the various sectors receive money income in the form of wages, rent, interest, profits, and, in the case of government, taxes. They then spend this income to buy the goods and services they have helped produce. Consumers, businesses, and governments need income to generate demand for goods and services.

MOTIVATIONS FOR SPENDING

Economists divide the economy into consumer, business, and government sectors because motives to spend, save, and borrow differ for each group. Consumer spending is motivated by people's wants and needs. The U.S. economy is a consumer-oriented economy, with consumption spending on food, housing, medical care, and transportation accounting for about 60 percent to 65 percent of the GDP.

Business spending is motivated by profit. Business decisions to invest in new factories and equipment, hire new workers, replace old machines, or build inventories of raw materials are based essentially on the desire for financial gain. Although business spending or investment represents only about 10 percent to 15 percent of the GDP, this spending is profoundly important to the economy's well-being because it typically creates new jobs.

Government spending is motivated by the desire to achieve various social and public objectives. A very important factor in the spending plans of the nearly 80,000 state and local governments in the United States is their ability to collect taxes. For the federal government, tax collection is less of a constraint in spending. Since the 1930s, the federal government has used spending and taxation as major tools for achieving economic objectives. Government spending is approximately 20 percent to 25 percent of the GDP.

Exhibit 2.1
The Circular Flow of Economic Activity

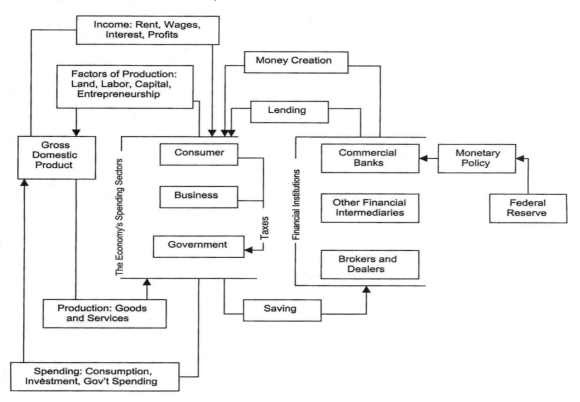

THE ROLE OF SAVINGS AND LENDING

Consumers, businesses, and government entities do not spend all of their income; some of it is saved. Economists define savings as income not used to buy goods and services. Using this definition, consumers typically save about 4 percent of their disposable (after-tax) personal incomes; most businesses retain a portion of their earnings as savings; and some state and local governments end their fiscal years with budget surpluses. In effect, savings represent a leakage from the economy's circular flow of income and spending (see exhibit 2.1). Money that is saved might otherwise have been used to buy goods and services and to generate income.

If savings were literally kept out of circulation by being hoarded in mattresses or cookie jars, the economic consequences could be devastating. Goods and services might remain unsold without an offsetting infusion of new money. Given this situation, producers faced with declining sales might cut back production and lay off workers. In turn, unemployed consumers would spend less, worsening the economic slump and generating even bigger layoffs. Eventually, the entire economic system would spiral down as production fell and unemployment rose.

If a pattern of falling GDP and rising unemployment lasts for two or more consecutive quarters, economists say the economy is in a **recession.** Only when those consumers, businesses, and governments that had hoarded their savings began to use that money to sustain themselves would the downward spiral begin to reverse.

In another scenario, producers faced with declining sales caused by a shortage of money might cut prices. Lower prices and a smaller supply of money could absorb all available goods and services and maintain the economic balance. The problem here is that wages, rents, and interest are prices, too; yet even in a deflationary period of falling prices, workers, landlords, and creditors are normally reluctant to accept cuts in their incomes. It is uncertain whether a deflationary contraction would be any less devastating to the economy than a recession.

In reality most of the money saved by consumers, businesses, and governments is not hoarded, but instead is deposited in a vast assortment of financial institutions and invested in various financial instruments. Commercial banks and other financial intermediaries then pump the money back into the economy's spending stream by lending it to consumers, businesses, and governments that want to spend more than they currently have (see exhibit 2.1). Savings, and the resultant lending, are needed for businesses to undertake large projects that require long-term financing. The economy maintains its balance as long as the volume of money that flows out of the spending stream as savings is offset by money pumped back in through lending by commercial banks and other financial institutions.

CREDIT AVAILABILITY AND ECONOMIC GROWTH

Money saved by consumers, businesses, and governments, combined with the money created by commercial banks, provides the U.S. economy with a vast pool of loanable funds. Loans enable the various economic sectors to spend more than their current incomes would allow. The growth of our economy and other modern industrial economies depends on the ability to obtain credit. Fewer consumers would be able to buy cars, houses, and vacation trips if they had to finance such purchases solely with savings or current income. Businesses might be unable to replace obsolete machinery or buy the raw materials required for continued high levels of production. Governments would have to reduce the scale of their public works and social programs, including payments to Social Security recipients, the unemployed, and those on welfare. The ability of the economic sectors to obtain substantial amounts of credit has been a key factor in the growth of the U.S. economy.

During the course of any given year, U.S. consumers, businesses, and governments typically borrow funds and repay loans. Each year, however, the nation's financial institutions extend more new credit than is repaid. As a result, the total amount of credit outstanding in the United States has increased annually. During the 1990s, total credit increased by about $500 billion to $700 billion a year. In 2002 the total of all outstanding consumer, business, and government debt stood at more than $19 trillion.

MEASURES OF ECONOMIC ACTIVITY

The U.S. Department of Commerce uses statistical records called national income and product accounts to track the economy's performance. These accounts include measures such as real GDP, net domestic product, national income, personal income, and disposable personal income. Exhibit 2.2 illustrates the relationships between these accounts and shows how money links production and consumption in a complex, circular flow of economic activity.

REAL GDP

The gross domestic product represents a country's total output of goods and services measured at market prices over a one-year period. Because the GDP measure reflects both the price and quantity of goods and services, an increase in prices can generate a measure of apparent growth that does not reflect an actual increase in production or national living standards. For this reason, the **nominal GDP,** which measures total production using current prices, is adjusted for **inflation,** as evidenced by rising prices.

Exhibit 2.2
National Income and Product Accounts

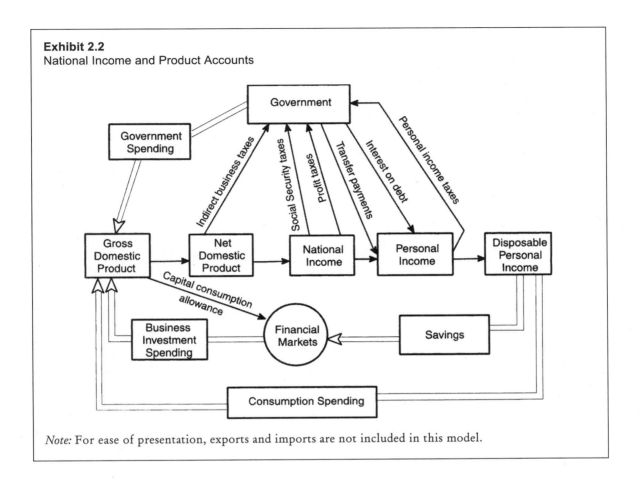

Note: For ease of presentation, exports and imports are not included in this model.

The resulting figure is called **real GDP.** The real GDP calculation is made by selecting a base year against which prices for the current year can be compared. Then a **price index number** is developed that reflects the percentage change in prices between the two years. Real GDP is calculated by using the following formula:

$$\frac{\text{Nominal GDP}}{\text{price index number}} \times 100 = \text{real GDP}.$$

The current base year is 1996. In 2001 the price index number was 109, meaning that 2001 prices were 9 percent higher than 1996 prices. The nation's GDP in 2001 totaled $10.2 trillion. This nominal GDP translates into a real GDP in 2001 of $9.4 trillion, calculated as follows:

$$\frac{\$10.2 \text{ trillion}}{109} \times 100 = \$9.4 \text{ trillion}.$$

NET DOMESTIC PRODUCT

Each year, while producing new goods and services, an economy consumes some portion of its existing capital goods (buildings, machinery, and equipment) through wear and tear and obsolescence. This economic cost of production is subtracted from the GDP to obtain the **net domestic product,** which reflects more accurately the dollar value of all goods and services produced during the year. In 2001 U.S. producers consumed more than $900 billion worth of capital goods in generating the year's production. This consumption of capital, called depreciation, equaled about 9 percent of the year's total nominal GDP. For 2001 the nation's net domestic product totaled about $9.3 trillion.

NATIONAL INCOME

Manufacturers incur additional production costs from sales, excise, real estate, and other indirect business taxes. Typically the prices of manufactured goods reflect these added costs. By subtracting indirect business taxes from the net domestic product measure, we obtain a measure of the cost of resources used in production and the income received by the sellers of these resources. This measure is called national income.

National income is the sum of all wages, rents, interest, and profits received by entrepreneurs and the suppliers of land, labor, and capital. In short, it is the total income of the U.S. economy. In 2001 U.S. national income amounted to about $8.4 trillion.

PERSONAL INCOME

Not all income received by business owners is available for personal use or disposition. A portion of the income goes to the federal government to pay employees' Social Security taxes and taxes on corporate profits. These two outflows of money are subtracted from the national income measure when calculating personal income.

Consumers and businesses also receive income from government sources that must be added to the national income measure when calculating personal income. The two sources of government payments that must be considered are transfer payments and interest paid by the government on its outstanding debt. Transfer payments are monies that the government pays directly to people, such as Social Security payments, veterans' payments, and unemployment insurance payments. Personal income, the net result of these two subtractions and two additions to national income, totaled about $8.7 trillion in 2001.

DISPOSABLE PERSONAL INCOME

Disposable personal income is a measure of the amount of income people have available for spending and saving after they pay taxes. About 96 percent of this after-tax income is spent on goods and services (consumption). The remainder is saved, with the monies going into a broad range of time and savings deposits at commercial banks and other financial intermediaries and into financial instruments that have different degrees of liquidity, risk, and return. In 2001 disposable personal income totaled about $7.4 trillion.

GDP AS A MEASURE OF SPENDING

The gross domestic product is a measure of production, income, and spending, where

- production equals the total dollar value of all newly produced goods and services
- income equals the total income received by consumers, businesses, and governments
- spending equals the sum of all the monies spent by consumers, businesses, and federal, state, and local governments

In the GDP formula, consumer spending is generally called *consumption* and represented by the letter *C.* Consumer spending generally relates to purchases of goods or services. Business spending is considered *investment* spending and is represented by the letter *I.* Business spending typically goes to rebuild inventories, expand factories, and replace deteriorated equipment. Government spending typically is represented by the letter *G.*

An additional component of GDP as a measure of spending is the net flow of money reflecting imports and exports. Total expenditures on domestic goods are reduced when Americans spend part of their incomes on imports and are increased when foreigners spend part of their incomes on American exports. The net effect of these international transactions on GDP spending is the difference between the value of our imports and exports. If exports exceed imports, the GDP will be slightly greater than the sum of $C + I + G$; if imports exceed exports, as they did in 2001 by about $350 billion, the GDP will be lower.

DEBTORS AND CREDITORS IN OUR ECONOMY

In recent decades, consumers, businesses, and governments have borrowed funds equal to about one-sixth of the GDP each year from the nation's banks, other financial intermediaries, and credit markets. The consumer sector, through its savings, provides about two-thirds of the funds supplied to all borrowers. The business sector provides most of the remaining funds.

As previously noted, the total of all outstanding consumer, business, and government debt in the United States in 2001 exceeded $19 trillion. The composition of this debt is shown in exhibit 2.3.

CONSUMERS

Through savings, consumers supply most of the funds available for lending and investment in the United States. About 80 percent of consumer savings is placed with banks and other financial intermediaries. The other 20 percent of consumer savings is invested directly in credit market instruments. Consumers also borrow. In 2001 consumers were responsible for $7.2 trillion in outstanding debt (see exhibit 2.3).

More than two-thirds of consumer debt is mortgage debt assumed in the purchase of residential housing. Less than one-third of consumer debt represents funds borrowed for installment buying and other short-term personal purposes.

The consumer sector has total financial assets of about $19.8 trillion, including holdings of money; highly liquid near-money instruments, such as savings and time deposits at banks and savings institutions; and stocks and bonds, about half of which are held indirectly in pension plans. But the consumer sector's actual wealth, or net

---

Exhibit 2.3
Outstanding Debt of the U.S. Government, Consumer, and Business Sectors, 2001

Sector		Amount (in billions)	
Federal government		$5,800	
Federal debt held by federal agencies and trusts		2,400	
Net federal debt			$3,400
State and local government debt			2,800
Consumers	Mortgages	5,000	
	Other loans	2,200	7,200
Business	Mortgages	500	
	Bonds	2,800	
	Loans	1,600	
	Market instruments	300	5,200
		Total	$18,600

Source: Federal Reserve Bank of St. Louis, *National Economic Trends*, February 2002, and *Federal Reserve Bulletin*, February 2002.

Changing from Gross National Product to Gross Domestic Product

The U.S. Commerce Department's Bureau of Economic Analysis collects and publishes America's national income and product accounts data. In 1991 the Bureau changed the key measure it uses to determine the economy's production and spending levels from gross national product (GNP) to gross domestic product (GDP).

For more than 50 years, the U.S. government and American economists had used GNP as a measure of the total value of all newly produced goods and services and the sum of all consumer, business, and government spending. Most other countries did not use GNP, however, because it was seen as an inaccurate measure of a nation's production and spending.

GNP counts goods and services produced and money spent by resident workers and business firms without distinguishing whether the production and expenditures take place in the country whose economy is being measured. For example, the U.S. GNP counts goods and services produced by American companies operating in other countries but excludes all goods and services produced in the United States by foreign workers and foreign companies.

By contrast, GDP focuses on where goods, services, income, and spending are produced. Thus the U.S. GDP measures only production, income, and spending that occurs in the U.S. GDP includes all goods and services produced in the United States, whether they are produced by American or foreign-owned companies. GDP excludes goods and services that are produced abroad even if they are produced by American companies.

The Commerce Department switched to using GDP because it gives economists and government officials a more accurate picture of the links between these economic activities and other important economic performance measures, such as employment, productivity, and investment in factories and equipment. Using the GDP also enables the U.S. to more readily compare its overall economic performance with that of other countries.

Surprisingly, in the United States, total GNP and total GDP differ very little; about one percentage point or less difference separates the two. In other countries, however, the differences can be substantial. For example, because so many American companies manufacture goods in Canada, its GNP is almost 4 percent smaller than its GDP. By contrast, Kuwait has made enormous investments in other countries, which generate interest, rents, and profits. Because of this pattern of investment, Kuwait's GNP is one-third larger than its GDP.

worth, far exceeds the difference between its financial assets and its financial liabilities (outstanding debt). This is because consumer net worth includes not only financial assets but nonfinancial assets such as real estate and household goods. Economists estimate that in the United States, the consumer sector's net worth is about $40 trillion.

BUSINESSES

The business sector is the second largest net debtor in the U.S. economy, with total outstanding debt of $5.2 trillion in 2001 (see exhibit 2.3). The cash flow from retained earnings of business firms provides only part of the funds the business sector needs for annual capital spending. The remaining funds must be borrowed from banks and other financial intermediaries through loans, borrowed from the financial market by issuing market instruments, or raised by selling stock to raise new equity capital. Most business debt represents funds borrowed to finance inventories and to replace and modernize production plants and equipment.

GOVERNMENTS

Government debt accounts for about one-third of the nation's outstanding debt. As shown in exhibit 2.3, the federal government owes $5.8 trillion. About two-fifths of this total is held by federal agencies and trusts, however, which reduces the net federal debt to $3.4 trillion. State and local government debt totals $2.8 trillion.

BORROWING AND LENDING RELATIONSHIPS

To a borrower, a loan represents a debt; to a lender, it represents an asset. When a commercial bank or other financial intermediary makes a loan, it obtains a financial asset. A promissory note or loan agreement from the borrower stipulates the terms and conditions of repayment.

When a bank or other financial intermediary buys a corporate or government note or bond, it also obtains a financial asset. In effect the note or bond represents the making of a loan to the corporation or government unit. The note or bond is itself a promise to repay the note holder or bond holder under terms and conditions usually stipulated on the instrument. Thus the $19 trillion in outstanding debt owed by U.S. consumers, businesses, and governments in 2001 represents $19 trillion in assets or financial wealth to the holders of the loan agreements, notes, bonds, and other financial instruments that constitute the total debt.

SOURCES OF CREDIT

About 75 percent of all funds borrowed in the nation's credit markets are loans made by financial intermediaries, including banks, to consumers and businesses. The remaining funds are obtained by businesses and governments directly from the nation's credit market; that is, from people and institutions that buy debt instruments.

Consumers rely almost exclusively on loans from banks and other financial intermediaries as a source of credit. Commercial banks, savings banks, finance companies, and credit unions are primary sources of short-term, intermediate-term and mortgage credit for personal spending and home purchasing needs.

Most business debt is owed to commercial banks and other financial institutions. Businesses rely on two major sources of credit: loans from commercial banks and funds obtained directly from the credit market through the sale of short-term and long-term debt instruments ranging from commercial paper to bonds. Businesses often sell new bond issues to raise money for long-term building and capital investment programs.

The equity market provides a third important source of funds for most businesses, but this source does not involve borrowing or lending. When a corporation raises capital by issuing new shares in the corporation, it is in effect selling small portions of equity ownership of the corporation itself. Purchasers of newly issued corporate stock are not lending the company money, but rather buying an asset that may increase or diminish in value depending on whether the corporation prospers. Stockholders typically share proportionally in the company's earnings through dividends and a higher market price for their stock. If the corporation does poorly, stockholders may see the value of their stock decline. Because stockholders are not creditors but owners, they rank low in terms of the legal priority of their claims against the assets of a corporation unable to repay its debts.

While many small local governments rely on bank loans, the federal and state governments rely almost exclusively on selling their own debt instruments in the credit market. These debt instruments include notes and tax warrants issued by states and localities, as well as Treasury bills, notes, certificates, and bonds issued by the federal government. Most of these government securities are purchased by commercial banks and other financial intermediaries and become part of their investment portfolios.

FINANCIAL INTERMEDIARIES

Financial intermediaries take in funds from consumers who choose to save and then lend these funds, principally to consumers who choose to borrow. These loans, together with the business and consumer loans of commercial banks, provide the economy with most of its investment funds. Financial intermediaries include commercial banks and savings institutions, such as savings banks and credit unions, along with insurance companies, pension plans, and money market funds. The investment activities of these institutions provide loan funds to the issuers of the notes and bonds they purchase.

The nation's commercial banks are the largest suppliers of loan funds to consumers and businesses. As shown in exhibit 2.4, however, America's mutual funds, through their investments in stock, bonds, and other debt instruments, are the major providers of funds for America's corporations. Commercial banks had long held this position, but new competition from nonbank companies and new forms of corporate borrowing in the 1980s and 1990s ended banks' dominance.

During the 1980s, major nonbank companies, such as Sears, American Express, General Electric, and Westinghouse began to expand their businesses to include financial services and loans to consumers and other companies. At the same time, mutual funds began to offer shareholders checking account services that paid higher interest on deposits than did banks. In 1980 mutual funds had total assets of $135 billion—equivalent to less than 10 percent of the $1,537 billion in assets held by commercial banks. By 2002 mutual funds' assets had grown more than 50-fold and exceeded banks' assets by $400 million.

During the 1990s, the nation's large corporations also began to increase their use of direct financing to obtain funds. Instead of borrowing from banks, these companies borrowed funds by selling their own commercial paper (short-term, uncollateralized promissory notes) directly to the public. During the decade, the amount of commercial paper outstanding increased by more than 85 percent. The growth of the commercial paper market also enabled finance companies, which issue commercial paper to fund their lending, to expand their activities at the expense of commercial banks.

Exhibit 2.4
Assets of Selected Financial Intermediaries, 1980–2002 (in billions)

	Commercial Banks	Savings Institutions*	Credit Unions	Life Insurance Companies	Mutual Funds**
1980	$ 1,537	$ 803	$ 72	$ 479	$ 135
1985	2,329	1,291	137	880	495
1996	3,669	910	277	1,630	2,300
2002	6,500	1,100	375	2,500	6,900

* Includes savings banks and savings and loan associations.
** Includes both open-end and closed-end mutual funds and money market mutual funds.
Source: Federal Reserve Bulletin, February 2002, U.S. League of Savings Associations.

BANKS AND MONEY CREATION

Traditionally, banks differed from other financial intermediaries in that only banks could "create" money by making loans that generate new demand deposits. Demand deposits, or checking accounts, represent the core medium of exchange in the U.S. economy, and commercial banks still create most of the demand deposit dollars that circulate in the U.S. economy. Because of this, the Federal Reserve primarily uses the nation's banks to implement its monetary policy. The Federal Reserve's **monetary policy** is designed to influence the nation's money supply, helping to ensure the availability of credit in quantities and at interest rates consistent with specific economic objectives (see exhibit 2.1).

A bank that makes a loan monetizes a private debt by accepting as an asset the debt obligation of the borrower; that is, the borrower's promise to repay. The bank simultaneously creates a liability on its books in the form of a demand deposit balance in the amount of the loan.

To create money, a bank must have reserves, either funds on deposit at a Federal Reserve bank, or in vault cash, or in a correspondent bank pass-through account. The bank's reserves must be at least equal to the amount of money to be created. The more reserves a bank has, the greater its potential for expanding earnings because it can continue to make new loans and investments. The fewer reserves a bank has, the closer its reserves are to its own liquidity margin or to the reserve requirements of the Federal Reserve and the smaller it's potential for expanding earnings.

Commercial bank lending creates more demand deposits throughout the economy. This **money creation** by the banking system is constantly being modified by the flow of money between banks and other financial intermediaries, the movement of funds from checking to savings accounts, and the cashing of checks. But changes in the level of reserves available to banks are the chief factor determining how much money can be created by banks through the commercial lending process.

BROKERS AND DEALERS

The interaction between borrowers and lenders in the U.S. economy is made more efficient through the work of a relatively small group of securities dealer firms and several thousand brokerage firms. **Brokers** and **dealers** serve as important intermediaries between borrowers and lenders seeking to make a match in the credit markets. These firms maintain markets for trading both new and outstanding issues of notes, bonds, and other debt instruments.

Brokerage firms, which are typically associated with the stock market, sell their services for a fee. Dealer firms, which are typically associated with the bond markets, assume risk on their own behalf. Dealer firms often buy outright the new debt issues of a corporation or government agency. They then seek to make a profit by reselling the debt instruments at a higher price to banks, savings banks, insurance companies, pension plans, and other financial intermediaries as well as to individuals.

Brokers and dealers help facilitate a rapid and efficient flow of credit from lenders to borrowers in the U.S. economy. On a daily basis, the nation's major government securities dealer firms serve as a primary market for the Federal Reserve's open-market operations, buying and selling outstanding U.S. government securities.

MONETARY POLICY, CREDIT MARKETS, AND INTEREST RATES

Monetary policy affects the cost and availability of credit to consumers, businesses, governments, and the nation's depository institutions. When monetary policy is expansive, credit usually is available at relatively low interest rates. However, when monetary policy becomes restrictive and interest rates begin to rise, competition in the marketplace determines how demand for credit will be matched with a limited supply of loanable funds.

THE FEDERAL RESERVE AND MONETARY POLICY

The Federal Reserve controls money creation by banks so that the economy does not get either too much money, which can lead to inflation, or too little money, which can lead to recession.

If the economy is experiencing inflation, the Federal Reserve will try to slow the growth of the money supply by restraining bank lending. The Federal Reserve will pursue a tight or restrictive monetary policy that is typically characterized by higher interest rates. If the economy is in a recession, the Federal Reserve will try to encourage growth in the money supply by stimulating lending. The Federal Reserve will pursue an easy or expansive monetary policy that is typically characterized by lower interest rates. The objective is to keep income, spending, savings, lending, and bank-created money in balance. Keeping the economy's money flows in balance promotes relatively stable yearly increase in real GDP and helps avoid the sporadic imbalances associated with business cycles (see Extended Study 1, Business Cycles).

CREDIT MARKETS AND INTEREST RATES

When they find they cannot satisfy all of the credit demands of potential borrowers, banks typically post higher interest loan rates. As a result, some corporations may borrow less and thus spend less in periods of tight credit. However, smaller and newer businesses may find they cannot afford the higher interest rates on loans. Large corporations tend to be less concerned about rising interest rates for bank loans. Corporations often bypass the banking system entirely, either by raising funds directly in the credit market through selling commercial paper or bonds or by financing capital spending through retained earnings.

Higher market interest rates generally compel mortgage lending institutions to increase the rates they pay on deposits, but

---

THE PRIME RATE

Traditionally, banks charge a preferential interest rate on loans to their most creditworthy corporate customers. This lower rate is called the bank's **prime rate**. The availability of prime rate loans is generally based on the length and scope of a bank's relationship with a corporate borrower, the level of compensating deposit balances maintained by the borrower at the bank, and the corporation's loan and repayment history.

The prime rate of large money center and regional banks is frequently reported in the business media as the interest rate that all banks charge for business loans. In fact, many banks base prime rate loan charges on a cost-of-money rate plus a spread to cover operating costs. Other banks use a cost index to develop a multiple-rate structure for business loans. Most banks have changed the name from prime rate to base rate.

The base rate is the bank's starting point to begin negotiations of a specific rate for a specific customer. The lending bank looks at the anticipated cost of money for the length of time desired by the borrower and then adds a margin on top of that cost.

Banks often are criticized for implicitly discriminating against small and new businesses during periods of tight money and rising interest rates by channeling scarce credit primarily to prime-rate borrowers. Although many banks specifically allocate a portion of their lending to small and new businesses, this controversy tends to resurface whenever bank credit becomes scarce.

also to charge more for mortgages. As a result, economists estimate that a one percentage point rise in mortgage rates results in 200,000 fewer new housing starts.

In some states, consumers find that, as interest rates rise, installment credit becomes harder to find. This phenomenon occurs because maximum consumer loan rates, set by state usury laws, crowd these loans out of the market. **Usury laws** stipulate the maximum rates of interest to be charged on various types of loans. If market interest rates and business loan rates, which are not covered by usury laws, are higher than the usury ceilings, banks channel funds from potential consumer borrowers to higher-paying business borrowers or to higher-return investments. As a result, sales of big-ticket consumer items tend to decline. Economists have estimated that a one-percentage point rise in interest rates can result in 500,000 fewer automobile sales.

Governments tend to finance spending by borrowing directly from the credit markets, not from banks. Most states and localities have maximum limits for the interest rates they would pay to obtain credit. Thus, when interest rates rise, they often get a smaller share of the money available in the credit markets. The federal government is not bound by statute or policy to a maximum interest rate that the Treasury may pay to sell its new bills, notes, or bonds. Nonetheless, the federal government is not immune to rising interest costs. About one-third of the federal government's debt has to be refinanced each year at prevailing interest rates.

INTEREST RATES AND BANK LOAN CHARGES

Bankers assess a broad range of factors in determining loan charges. The interest rate a bank charges for its loans generally reflects the bank's assessment of its credit risk, its cost of funds, administrative costs and profit margin, and the possible effects of inflation.

A primary concern in determining loan charges is the bank's perception of the loan's credit risk, the risk that the borrower will not repay the loan when it is due. Accurately assessing and charging for the credit risk associated with a loan is one of the most difficult tasks that banks face.

In determining loan charges, banks also must consider what they have to pay to depositors or to other sources in the money market to obtain funds. This general cost of funds may differ, even for banks of like asset size in the same region of the country, because different banks rely on different sources and types of funds. For example, Bank A may borrow from Bank B, while Bank C may take in large deposits.

Bank loan charges also reflect an assessment of the rate of inflation over the term of a loan. The bank considers the probable decline in the purchasing power of money during the time that the loan is outstanding. This assessment is important because banks want to be repaid in dollars equal in value to those loaned.

Bank loan charges also reflect the administrative costs incurred in maintaining and servicing loans, as well as the bank's desired margin of profit. Banks often express their profit margin as a percentage spread over the costs they incur in obtaining reserves to support loans, plus an allowance for administrative costs and their assumption of risk.

SUMMARY

Consumer, business, and government spending generates demand for the production of goods and services. The income received by consumers, businesses, and governments for producing these goods and services is used to exercise that demand and to generate saving, investment, and further spending. Money links these processes in a complex circular flow of economic activity. Important measures of the nation's economic performance include real

GDP, net domestic product, national income, personal income, and disposable personal income.

Financial intermediaries take in funds from consumers, businesses, and governments that choose to save some of their income. The financial institutions then lend those funds to consumers, businesses, and governments that choose to borrow. These loans provide the economy with most of its investment funds and are an important factor in its long-term growth.

When commercial banks make loans, they create new money in the form of demand deposit balances. If the amount of bank-created money adds too much to the existing money supply, inflation can result; if it adds too little, recession can result. The Federal Reserve's monetary policy attempts to control the money supply by influencing commercial bank lending to prevent or counter such economic imbalances. It does this by changing the cost of money through interest rates, or the availability of money through the growth of the money supply.

REVIEW QUESTIONS

1. How does the economy benefit when consumers place their savings in banks and other financial intermediaries instead of holding their savings as cash?
2. What functions do financial intermediaries, brokers, and dealers perform that lenders and borrowers could not perform for themselves?
3. What would be the economic and financial consequences if consumers and businesses could not obtain credit from financial intermediaries?
4. Why does the Federal Reserve focus primarily on controlling commercial bank lending as opposed to other financial intermediary lending?
5. How and why do rising interest rates differently affect consumer, business, and government borrowers?

ADDITIONAL RESOURCES

Economic Indicators for Consumers, Federal Reserve Bank of Richmond, 1994, pamphlet. Explains key statistical indicators used to assess the economy's direction.

Economic Report of the President, U.S. Government Printing Office, 2002. Provides data on nominal and real GDP growth and other economic performance measures.

Economics: Fundamentals for Financial Services Providers, Jon A. Hooks, Ph.D., American Bankers Association, 1998. Explains basic economic theory, statistics, and indicators for forecasting the economy's direction.

Free Enterprise, the Economy and Monetary Policy, Federal Reserve Bank of Dallas, 1994, 15 pp. Examines the workings of the household, business, and government sectors of the U.S. economy.

Macroeconomic Data: A User's Guide, Federal Reserve Bank of Richmond 1994, 70 pp. Explains key macroeconomic statistics and provides information on price indices and the GDP accounts.

National Economic Trends, Federal Reserve Bank of St. Louis, 2002. Provides current monthly data and charts on components of the U.S. national income accounts, prices, employment, and other measures of the U.S. economic performance.

EXTENDED STUDY 1: BUSINESS CYCLES

The U.S. economy is highly susceptible to imbalances in economic activity. These imbalances, called business cycles, are recurrent, periodic fluctuations in business activity in which stable business conditions decline and then improve again. Although economists do not understand precisely why business cycles occur, in the United States they can trace economic disruptions as far back as the 1790s.

Business cycles disrupt almost all sectors of the U.S. economy, but never quite in the same way or to the same degree. During the twentieth century, the U.S. economy had an average growth rate of about 3 percent to 5 percent of real GDP each year. That growth was very uneven, however, surging well above the average in some years and declining into recession and even depression in others.

CHARACTERISTICS OF BUSINESS CYCLES

Business cycles are characterized by phases of recession, recovery, and expansion that occur at irregular intervals and last for indeterminate periods of time. A recession can be defined as the downward phase of a business cycle. To qualify as a full-fledged recession, a decline in real GDP generally must last for two consecutive quarters, or six months. A depression is a severe and extended recession during which the decline in real GDP is precipitous. During the Great Depression (1929 to 1933), for example, real GDP fell 50 percent. In contrast, during the 1990 recession, real GDP fell only about 2 percent; and, based on current estimates, during the 2001 recession, real GDP fell only six-tenths of one percent, making it one of the mildest recessions on record.

During the recovery phase of the business cycle, the economy regains the level of production that preceded the recession phase. In the expansion phase of the cycle, the GDP surpasses the pre-recession level of production. Since the end of World War II, the U.S. economy has experienced ten recessions and subsequent recoveries and expansions, as shown in the next two tables.

Business cycles can trigger sporadic imbalances in the economy's money flows. Some current economic analysts attribute these fluctuations to

- changes in money supply growth
- changes in consumer spending
- changes in business investment spending

If the amount of bank-created money adds too much to the supply of money flowing from income and other borrowing sources, prices inflation can result. However, if too little newly created money is added to the existing supply, the economy can begin to contract and move toward recession.

Shifts in consumer expectations about the course and direction of the economy or changes in disposable personal income levels can lead to spending changes that catch producers off guard and can help precipitate a business cycle.

The economy responds unevenly to sudden speedups or slowdowns in business firms' accumulation of inventories,

Duration and Severity of Post World War II Recessions			
Recession	Duration (in months)	Peak Unemployment (percent of labor force)	
November 1948 to October 1949	11	7.9	October 1949
July 1953 to May 1954	11	6.1	September 1954
August 1957 to April 1958	9	7.5	July 1958
April 1960 to February 1961	11	7.1	May 1961
December 1969 to November 1970	11	6.1	August 1971
November 1973 to March 1975	17	9.0	May 1975
January 1980 to July 1980	7	7.8	July 1980
July 1981 to November 1982	17	10.8	December 1982
July 1990 to March 1991	10	7.8	June 1992
March 2001 to November 2001	8*	6.0	April 2002

* Estimated.
Sources: Bureau of Labor Statistics, National Bureau of Economic Research.

Economic Expansions Since World War II		
Begin	End	Duration (in months)
October 1945	November 1948	37
October 1949	July 1953	45
May 1954	August 1957	39
April 1958	April 1960	24
February 1961	December 1969	106
November 1970	November 1973	36
March 1975	January 1980	58
July 1980	July 1981	12
November 1982	July 1990	92
March 1991	March 2001	120
	Average expansion	56.9

Source: National Bureau of Economic Research

replacement of depreciating equipment, or purchases of new capital goods and technology. Such changes in business investment spending also may disrupt the economy.

Businesses usually try to keep their inventories of unsold merchandise at the lowest level consistent with continued efficient operations. Inventory levels cannot be precisely controlled, however, because in most cases they reflect businesses' expectations of future sales. If the nation's retailers find they have underestimated consumer demand, they rush to stock up on merchandise to avoid losing sales. This sudden upsurge of orders generates unexpected business for wholesalers and manufacturers and propels the economy ahead. If, on the other hand, retailers overestimate demand and find themselves with several months' supply of unsold inventories, they stop or sharply cut back their purchases from wholesalers and manufacturers. This sudden decline in orders blunts the economy's expansion and slows economic activity.

During a recession, changes in money supply growth, consumer spending, and business inventories all may contribute to the slowing of the economy.

In recent decades, the economy's recessions, recoveries, and expansions have become more readily recognizable and predictable. Recessions have become milder and shorter, averaging about 12 months, and periods of expansion have become longer. Earlier in the twentieth century, recessions averaged close to two years, and a full business cycle averaged about four years.

In the 100 years that preceded World War II, the U.S. economy was in recession much of the time: for every 48 months of declining production, there were only 52 months of expansion. Since World War II, however, the economy has registered 80 months of expansion for every 20 months of production decline. The economic expansions of the 1990s (120 months), the 1980s (90 months), and the 1960s (105 months) are the three longest periods of expansion on record.

EFFECTS OF BUSINESS CYCLES

Economists recognize that different sectors of the economy experience recession, recovery, and expansion in disproportionate ways.

The nation's heavy manufacturing industries, which produce steel, oil, machine tools, and automobiles, experience sharp reductions in demand for their products during recessions and sharp increases during recoveries. These changes usually precipitate rapid layoffs of production workers during recessions and almost equally rapid work recalls during recoveries. A deep and long recession also may lead to delays in planned price increases or to selective price cutting in an effort to maintain sales.

The nation's light industries usually experience smaller fluctuations in product demand than do the heavy industries. When profits and wages begin to decline, business purchases of capital goods and consumer purchases of big-ticket items, such as new cars and furniture, tend to be postponed; however, purchases of less-costly consumer goods tend to continue.

Service industries, which include banking, finance, insurance, and medical care, usually are only mildly affected during a recession. As a result, employment in the service industries tends to be more stable during a recession than employment in other sectors of the economy. Analysts of business cycles contend that the evolution of the U.S. economy from a goods economy to a service economy has made modern recessions weaker because the service economy offers greater stability of employment.

The housing, government, and agricultural sectors of the economy are affected indirectly by recessions. Activity in the housing industry and employment in the construction trades are determined primarily by mortgage interest rates and the availability of funds for mortgages. Therefore, the housing sector is vulnerable to the effects of business cycles.

Because federal government spending and employment are largely determined by public policy, they are generally immune from the effects of business cycles. At the state and local levels, however, shortfalls of tax receipts during a recession can lead to reduced spending and employment. Tax revenues typically decline during a recession because businesses earn less profit and workers earn less income, resulting in less tax revenue.

In recent decades, agricultural production, long considered invulnerable to cyclical swings in economic activity, has become more responsive to changes in investment spending and business cycles. This trend reflects the replacement of small farms by large farming corporations that rely on mass production and extensive investments in capital and technology.

RECESSIONS AND EXPANSIONS IN THE 1990s AND EARLY 2000s

Most economists who have analyzed the nation's business cycles agree that no two recessions and subsequent expansions are alike. The data suggest that business cycles vary sharply from the average in their duration and severity. Nonetheless, economists use averages as a yardstick for comparisons.

From 1948 to 1982, the average duration of eight recessions was about 12 months. During those recessions, real GDP fell, on average, by about 2.5 percent. More recently, the 1990 recession and the 2001 recession (as estimated at time of printing) were both milder than average in terms of length (10 months and 8 months respectively) and severity (a real GDP decline of 2 percent and 0.6 percent respectively).

Expansions can be similarly categorized. During the 18 month periods immediately following recessions from 1948 to 1982, real GDP grew at an average annual rate of about 5 percent. However, during the 18 months that followed the end of the 1990 recession, the economy's real GDP grew by less than 2 percent. Projections of economic growth through May 2003 (18 months from the estimated November 2001 end of the 2001 recession) are that real GDP will have grown by only 2.5 percent to 3 percent.

A slower-than-average rate of growth during a business cycle expansion typically keeps unemployment high. Unemployment, which generally declines in an expansion, increased in 1991 and 1992 above the level registered during the 1990 recession and most economists are projecting that unemployment will increase during the 2002 expansion.

Economists are unsure why the economy's expansion after the last two recessions has been slower than average. Some economists believe the slow pace of GDP growth may be part of a long-term trend related to structural changes that businesses began making in their operations during the 1980s. Other economists believe that the high level of consumer and corporate debt accumulated in the 1990s has acted as a drag on economic expansion. They contend that consumers and businesses have been reluctant to step up spending by borrowing additional funds, even at very low interest rates, because of difficulties in repaying outstanding loans. Still other economists point to the meager growth in disposable personal income in the 1990s as the reason for the slower pace.

3

Banks and Money Creation

LEARNING OBJECTIVES

After studying this chapter, you should be able to

- explain how the banking system creates money through multiple deposit creation
- contrast the lending process of a commercial bank with other financial intermediaries
- describe how banks gain and lose reserves, and how these reserve changes affect bank lending and economic activity
- evaluate the role of banks in implementing monetary policy
- define the key terms listed in this chapter

KEY TERMS

bank notes
cash assets
coefficient of demand deposit expansion
excess reserves
fractional reserves

loan assets
multiple deposit creation
reserve requirements
reserves
T-accounts

INTRODUCTION

For many years, commercial banks in the United States could issue their own paper currency. In 1863 the National Banking Act ended this practice among state-chartered banks, but nationally chartered banks continued to issue currency until 1913. In that year, the newly established Federal Reserve banks were given the exclusive franchise to issue U.S. currency. Commercial banks no longer issue currency, but they still create money on their balance sheets through the lending process.

This chapter examines how commercial bank lending traditionally differs from other financial institutions whose lending does not create new money on their balance sheets. It also examines the Federal Reserve's use of banks and bank reserves to implement monetary policy and the impact of this practice on the lending process and on U.S. economic activity.

OVERVIEW OF BANK LENDING AND MONEY CREATION

Financial intermediaries are institutions that transfer funds from savers to borrowers. They do this by taking excess funds from consumers, businesses, and governments and lending these funds to other consumers, businesses, and governments that need additional funds for spending and investing. In so doing, financial intermediaries help maintain a balanced economy and stimulate growth in production, employment, and income.

A financial intermediary may lend funds directly, or it may make loans indirectly by buying an interest-earning asset, such as a government security or a corporate bond. When a financial intermediary invests in an earning asset, it is in effect lending funds to the government or corporation that issues the security.

Until 1980 commercial banks were unique among financial intermediaries in having the power to create demand deposit

money through the lending process. This explains why the federal government's monetary policy traditionally has been directed primarily at commercial banks.

The pace at which a bank can make loans, and thus create demand deposits, depends on the amount of **reserves** it holds as cash in its vaults and deposits at its district Federal Reserve bank or in a pass-through account at a correspondent bank. An underlying principle, called **fractional reserves,** holds that only part of a bank's assets must be held as liquid assets. Liquid assets, such as vault cash or near-money assets, can be converted to cash with minimal cost or risk of loss to meet the claims of other banks presenting depositors' checks for collection or of depositors withdrawing cash.

This principle of fractional reserves is the basis for the modern practice of central banks establishing reserve requirements as a tool of monetary policy. The Federal Reserve sets **reserve requirements:** stated percentages of liquid assets that depositories must hold by law against outstanding transaction account liabilities, including demand deposits. Congress granted money-creating power to other types of depository institutions in 1980. Accordingly, since 1980 the Federal Reserve's reserve requirements have been extended to cover all depository institutions, not just commercial banks. Even without established reserve requirements, however, a bank or thrift would need to hold some fraction of its assets in liquid form, either as cash or as deposit balances with other banks, to maintain its day-to-day viability as a depository institution.

A bank's reserves are the raw material it uses for making new loans and investments. Through its regulation of bank reserves, the Federal Reserve maintains tight control over lending and investing because, in the aggregate, the nation's banks can create amounts of money several times larger than the original reserves. This phenomenon, called multiple deposit creation, profoundly affects the economy. The regulation of bank reserves controls the growth of the money supply and influences the cost of funds in the banking system along with the profit potential of bank lending and investing.

THE LENDING PROCESS OF A SAVINGS INSTITUTION

When a thrift institution, such as a savings bank or a savings and loan association, takes in funds and then lends them out, it simply exchanges a cash asset for a loan asset. We can trace the typical lending process of a thrift making a loan by using **T-accounts,** which are abstracts of an institution's balance sheet that show only those changes in assets and liabilities being examined.

Assume, for example, that the First Intermediary Savings and Loan Association receives a total of $100,000 in cash deposits from a number of different depositors for credit to their savings and time deposit accounts. Further, assume that First Intermediary's management believes it should hold **cash assets,** which are liquid assets or reserves, equal to 10 percent of its deposits at all times to meet customers' demands for cash and to pay other banks for check collection.

If First Intermediary decides to hold $10,000 in cash assets against its new $100,000 in deposits, it then has $90,000 in funds available for lending. Suppose that First Intermediary chooses to redistribute its assets by using these funds to make a $90,000 mortgage on some real estate.

In granting the mortgage, the borrower receives a $90,000 check drawn on First Intermediary or on its account at a correspondent bank. In exchange for providing $90,000 of its cash assets to the borrower, the savings and loan obtains a new earning asset (the mortgage). This redistribution of First Intermediary's assets increases its earnings and profit prospects because purely liquid cash assets do not earn a return, whereas earning assets do. The loan has not increased the amount of money in the economy, however. Before the loan was granted, various depositors deposited $100,000 in cash in First Intermediary. After the loan, the borrower holds $90,000 of those funds, and First Intermediary holds the remaining $10,000 as necessary liquidity against the claims of its depositors.

The following T-accounts show how First Intermediary's balance sheet is affected first by the cash deposits and then by the loan. Notice that the T-accounts show only the asset and liability accounts affected by the transaction, with a plus or minus sign to indicate an increase or decrease for each account. Because a T-account is a microcosm of a full balance sheet, it must balance—that is, the change in assets and liabilities must match (equal pluses and minuses on each side or offsetting plus-minus entries on one side).

Although in recent years thrifts have been given the power traditionally reserved to banks to create money through the

First Intermediary Savings and Loan
(before the loan)

Assets		Liabilities	
Cash assets	+ $100,000	Savings deposits	+ $100,000

First Intermediary Savings and Loan
(after the loan/redistribution of assets)

Assets		Liabilities	
Cash assets	+ $10,000	Savings deposits	+ $100,000
New mortgage	+ $90,000		

business loan process, most thrift lending still takes the form that has just been described. It is also worth noting that although banks and thrifts are not required to hold reserves against personal time and savings deposits, their need for liquid assets serves as a form of reserve requirement.

THE LENDING PROCESS OF A COMMERCIAL BANK

During the 1850s, commercial banks in the United States literally created money by issuing their own **bank notes,** or paper currency. The federal government ended this practice among state-chartered banks when it passed the National Banking Act in 1863. Nationally chartered banks stopped issuing notes in 1913 when the newly established Federal Reserve banks were given the exclusive franchise to issue U.S. currency. Since 1913 commercial banks no longer issue currency, but they still create money on their balance sheets through the lending process.

Commercial banks are institutions that accept demand deposits and make business loans. The lending process of a commercial bank is similar to that of a savings institution in that the receipt of cash from depositors increases both its assets and its deposit liabilities, which enables it to make additional loans and investments. But cash received by commercial banks is rarely loaned out in the same form. It is normally deposited in the bank's account at its district Federal Reserve Bank as additional reserves. These reserves in turn enable the bank to create new money through the lending process.

For example, assume that First Commercial Bank takes in $100,000 in cash deposits from businesses and individuals for credit to their checking accounts. For the sake of simplicity, further assume that the Federal Reserve requires the bank to meet a 10 percent reserve requirement, which in this case means that the bank must hold $10,000 in reserves against these new deposits. (Actual reserve requirements vary

National bank notes of the 1860s decorate a song sheet.
Photo courtesy of the Library of Congress, Prints and Photographs Division [LC-USZ6219191].

depending on the amount of total transaction deposits a bank holds.)

Given these assumptions, First Commercial Bank now has $100,000 in cash assets (held either as vault cash or as a deposit balance at its district Federal Reserve bank), giving it $90,000 in excess reserves against which it can create $90,000 in new demand deposits by making a commercial loan. A bank's total reserves are those cash assets it holds or owns that are eligible for meeting the reserve requirement. Remember, only vault cash and deposit balances held at the Reserve bank or in a pass-through account at a correspondent bank are eligible. **Excess reserves** are those reserve assets held above and beyond the amount required by the Federal Reserve. An easy way to remember these terms and relationships is through the following equations:

$$\text{Total reserves} = \text{required reserves} + \text{excess reserves.}$$

$$\text{Excess reserves} = \text{total reserves} - \text{required reserves.}$$

When a commercial bank makes a business loan, it accepts as an asset the borrower's debt obligation (the promise to repay), and creates a liability on its books in the form of a demand deposit balance in the amount of the loan. The deposits that banks create when they make business loans are generally backed by financial or physical assets, which collateralize the promissory note or loan agreement. Assume that First Commercial agrees to lend $90,000 to a local merchant. Again, the loan transaction can be shown using T-accounts.

The First Commercial Bank loan created a sum of money ($90,000) that did not exist before by generating a demand deposit balance for the merchant who received the loan. This money creation increased the bank's assets and liabilities by $90,000 each. The loan did not simply bring about a redistribution of assets as occurred when First Intermediary Savings and Loan made its loan.

In the case of First Commercial Bank, the new $90,000 in demand deposit money does not disappear when the merchant uses the loan proceeds to buy inventory. The supplier of the merchandise deposits the $90,000 check in its own bank. This bank forwards the check for collection to First Commercial, which pays the check by transferring $90,000 of its cash assets to the supplier's bank. Having paid the check, First Commercial also strikes from its books the

First Commercial Bank
(before the loan)

Assets		Liabilities	
Cash assets	+ $100,000*	Demand deposits	+ $100,000

* Required reserves	$10,000
Excess reserves	$90,000

First Commercial Bank
(after the loan)

Assets		Liabilities	
Cash assets	+ $100,000*	Demand deposits	+ $100,000
New business loan	+ $ 90,000	Demand deposit created for business borrower	+ $ 90,000

* Required reserves	$10,000
Excess reserves	$90,000

$90,000 deposit liability previously carried for the merchant borrower. The next T-account shows First Commercial's balance sheet after check collection.

The $90,000 that First Commercial created as a demand deposit balance still exists, but now it is entered on the books of another bank (in the account of the supplier that sold the merchandise to the merchant borrower).

RESERVE REQUIREMENTS AND LIQUIDITY CONSTRAINTS

A bank's ability to create additional money depends on its excess reserves. When a bank has no excess reserves, it cannot create any more demand deposits. To do so would result in a reserve requirement deficiency as soon as the newly created funds were

First Commercial Bank
(after check collection)

Assets		Liabilities	
Cash assets	+ $10,000*	Demand deposits	+ $100,000
New business loan	+ $90,000		

* Required reserves	$10,000
Excess reserves	$ 0

spent. Furthermore, a financial penalty would be imposed by the Federal Reserve for failing to adhere to banking law.

At this point in our example, First Commercial bank no longer has any excess reserves. If First Commercial tries to increase its earning assets by making a $5,000 loan, the effects will be as shown in the T-account below.

The T-account at the top of the followng page indicates that after the check collection process was completed, First Commercial's books would show a reserve deficiency.

First Commercial Bank would now have only $5,000 in cash assets (vault cash and/or a deposit balance at the Federal Reserve).

However, the law requires the bank to hold an amount equal to 10 percent of its $100,000 in demand deposits, or $10,000. In essence, the $5,000 loan would have generated a reserve deficiency of $5,000. In payment for the new business borrower's check, First Commercial would have had to transfer $5,000 of its reserves to another bank. As a result, even though its balance sheet continues to balance (assets equal liabilities), First Commercial has a reserve deficiency.

Even in the absence of legal reserve requirements, the senior management of First Commercial might determine that $5,000 in cash assets would represent too little liquidity; that is, $5,000 would be insufficient

First Commercial Bank
(after the second loan)

Assets		Liabilities	
Cash assets	+ $10,000*	Demand deposits	+ $100,000
Initial business loan	+ $90,000	Demand deposit created for new business borrower	+ $ 5,000
New business loan	+ $ 5,000		

* Required reserves	$10,000
Excess reserves	$ 0

First Commercial Bank
(after check collection)

Assets		Liabilities	
Cash assets	+ $ 5,000*	Demand deposits + $100,000	
Initial business loan	+ $90,000		
New business loan	+ $ 5,000		

* Required reserves (deficiency) $5,000

to protect the bank against the likely demands of its depositors to withdraw funds in cash form.

The First Commercial example illustrates an important principle of the deposit expansion process: a bank cannot create an amount of money greater than its excess reserves. This is because the bank loses a dollar in reserves, or cash assets, for every dollar it creates. The loss occurs when the proceeds of the bank's new loans are disbursed and the loan funds are transferred through the check-collection process. Significantly, this limitation applies to individual banks, but not to the banking system as a whole.

MULTIPLE DEPOSIT CREATION

Multiple deposit creation describes the ability of the banking system to create an amount of deposits many times greater than the bank's initial amount of reserves. Again, we can illustrate this concept by using T-accounts to trace a commercial bank loan. This time, however, the effect of the loan on other banks will be followed as newly created deposits move from bank to bank. To keep the example simple, we will assume

that all bank-created deposits stay in the banking system, that all newly created funds are held as demand deposits, and that each bank creates loans equal to every available (excess) reserve dollar. Although these assumptions are unrealistic, they do not distort the fundamental process by which banks collectively create multiple deposits.

Assume that Bank One receives a cash deposit of $100,000 from a corporate customer for credit to the customer's checking account. Also assume that the Federal Reserve's reserve requirement for such transaction accounts is 10 percent. Bank One must hold $10,000 in required reserves against its new $100,000 deposit, which leaves $90,000 in excess reserves. Bank One can thus create $90,000 in additional funds through lending.

When Bank One makes the initial loan, both its assets and its liabilities temporarily increase to $190,000, reflecting the addition of the loan to its earning assets portfolio and the addition of the newly created demand deposit to its total liabilities. As soon as the borrower uses the newly created funds, however, Bank One's assets and liabilities decline to their pre-loan level.

Bank One
(after the initial loan)

Assets		Liabilities	
Cash assets	+ $100,000*	Demand deposits	+ $100,000
New business loan	+ $ 90,000	Demand deposit created for borrower	+ $ 90,000

* Required reserves	$10,000
Excess reserves	$90,000

Suppose that the borrower, a small business firm, uses the loan proceeds to buy new computer equipment and pays with a check drawn on Bank One. The computer manufacturing company deposits the check in its account at Bank Two. When the borrower's $90,000 check clears, Bank One strikes from its balance sheet the $90,000 demand deposit liability carried for the borrower. After the check clears, Bank One again has $100,000 in assets and $100,000 in liabilities. Note, however, that the composition of its assets has changed. Before the loan, Bank One held $100,000 in cash assets. Now it holds $10,000 in cash assets and $90,000 in **loan assets,** which are contracts in which borrowers agree to pay interest for the use of the bank's funds. The $10,000 in cash assets meets the bank's 10 percent reserve requirement. Bank One's T-account now looks like the following.

The $90,000 in deposit dollars created by Bank One now appears as a deposit by the computer manufacturing company on the balance sheet of Bank Two, increasing that bank's liabilities. Bank Two's cash assets also increase by $90,000 when it receives payment for the check from Bank One. Bank Two is subject to the same 10 percent reserve requirement on transaction accounts, so it must keep $9,000 in reserves against that new deposit. However, Bank Two can loan an amount equal to its remaining $81,000 in excess reserves.

When Bank Two makes a loan, its assets and liabilities increase temporarily, but return to their pre-loan level when the amount of the borrower's check is collected by yet another bank. Assume that Bank Two makes an $81,000 loan to a borrower who uses the loan proceeds to pay for data processing services. When the service corporation deposits the check in its account at Bank Three, Bank Two's newly created $81,000 in demand deposits will then move to Bank Three, together with $81,000 in cash assets transferred by Bank Two in payment for the borrower's check.

Bank Three (following page) is now in a position to create demand deposits equal to $72,900, or 90 percent of its new reserve assets. When it does so, Bank Three will

Bank One
(after check collection)

Assets		Liabilities	
Cash assets	+ $10,000*	Demand deposits	+ $100,000
Loan assets	+ $90,000		

Bank Two
(after check collection)

Assets		Liabilities	
Cash assets	+ $90,000*	Demand deposits	+ $90,000

* Required reserves	$ 9,000
Excess reserves	$81,000

Bank Two
(after loan and check collection)

Assets		Liabilities	
Cash assets	+ $ 9,000*	Demand deposits	+ $90,000
Loan assets	+ $81,000		

* Required reserves	$9,000
Excess reserves	$ 0

Bank Three
(after check collection)

Assets		Liabilities	
Cash assets	+ $81,000*	Demand deposits	+ $81,000

* Required reserves	$ 8,100
Excess reserves	$72,900

give still another bank the ability to create new deposits.

In theory this process could continue through many banks. Taken together the banks could generate deposits up to 10 times greater than the $100,000 in cash deposits that initially started the process (see exhibit 3.1 on the following page).

The multiplier, or **coefficient of demand deposit expansion,** is the reciprocal of the reserve requirement ratio. For example, if the reserve requirement is 10 percent, or $\frac{1}{10}$, the multiplier, or reciprocal of $\frac{1}{10}$, is 10. Theoretically, the banking system could generate $1 million in total deposits using a $100,000 initial cash deposit as a base. Of this $1 million, $900,000 would be newly created money. If the reserve requirement were 20 percent, or $\frac{1}{5}$, the expansion coefficient would be the reciprocal of $\frac{1}{5}$, or 5—and a $100,000 initial cash deposit could increase to only $500,000.

The lower the reserve requirement, the greater the money expansion potential of the banking system. The higher the reserve requirement, the smaller the money expansion potential of the banking system.

LOAN REPAYMENT AND DEPOSIT CONTRACTION

Just as the lending process affects a bank's balance sheet, so do loan repayments. The lending process creates money through the multiple expansion of bank deposits, whereas the net repayment of loans reduces the banking system's assets and liabilities and effectively contracts the multiple expansion of deposits. Individual banks find it difficult to perceive these effects because their receipts of loan repayments and new loans are typically combined in an ongoing process. The effects of a loan repayment, however, can be examined by using T-accounts.

Assume that First Commercial Bank is fully loaned and is subject to a 10 percent reserve requirement on demand deposits. Its books look like the next T-account.

Now assume that Borrower repays Loan B to First Commercial with a $50,000 check drawn against an account at another bank. Once First Commercial collects the check, its books look like the T-account on the following page.

First Commercial Bank
(fully loaned)

Assets		Liabilities	
Cash assets	+ $10,000*	Total demand deposits	+ $100,000
Loan A	+ $25,000		
Loan B	+ $50,000		
Loan C	+ $15,000		

* Required reserves	$10,000
Excess reserves	$ 0

Exhibit 3.1
Multiple Expansion of Bank Deposits

Position of Bank	New Deposits	New Loans and Investments	Required Reserves
Bank one	$ 100,000	$ 90,000	$ 10,000
Bank two	90,000	81,000	9,000
Bank three	81,000	72,900	8,100
Bank four	72,900	65,610	7,290
Bank five	65,610	59,050	6,560
Bank six	59,050	53,140	5,910
Bank seven	53,140	47,830	5,310
Bank eight	47,830	43,050	4,780
Bank nine	43,050	38,740	4,310
Bank ten	38,740	34,870	3,870
Sum of first ten banks' deposit expansion	651,320	586,190	65,130
Sum of remaining banks' deposit expansion	348,680	313,810	34,870
Total for banking system	$1,000,000 (multiple expansion)	$900,000 (net creation)	$100,000 (original deposit)

Note: Reserve requirement = 10 percent.
Multiple expansion equation:

$$\frac{1}{\text{reserve requirement}} \times \text{initial deposit} = \text{total deposits.}$$

Multiple expansion in above example:

$$\frac{1}{0.10} \times \$100,000 = 10 \times \$100,000 = \$1,000,000.$$

Note that the loan repayment did not increase First Commercial's total assets or total liabilities, but did change the composition of its assets. First Commercial now has $60,000 in cash assets, of which $50,000 is in excess reserves. First Commercial now could make another $50,000 loan, creating $50,000 in new demand deposits.

The repayment of Loan B has added to First Commercial's reserves and expanded

First Commercial Bank
(after external loan repayment)

Assets		Liabilities	
Cash assets	+ $60,000*	Total demand deposits	+ $100,000
Loan A	+ $25,000		
Loan C	+ $15,000		

* Required reserves $10,000
Excess reserves $50,000

its lending capacity. The reserves it acquired came from another bank, however, and that bank's reserves and lending capacity were reduced. In order for a loan repayment at one bank to lead to further multiple expansions of deposits or loans in the banking system, a net addition to the reserves of all banks must occur.

What happens if Borrower B repays its loan to First Commercial with a check drawn against funds in an account at First Commercial? After First Commercial posts the check internally, its balance sheet will reflect a reduction in assets and liabilities of $50,000.

First Commercial has not gained or lost any reserve assets. Its cash assets remain

First Commercial Bank
(after internal loan repayment)

Assets		Liabilities	
Cash assets	+ $10,000*	Total demand deposits	+ $50,000
Loan A	+ $25,000		
Loan C	+ $15,000		

* Required reserves $5,000
Excess reserves $5,000

unchanged at $10,000. However, the bank's lending capacity has increased. Because its deposit base has contracted, or been reduced, First Commercial can now meet its 10 percent reserve requirement with only $5,000 in reserve assets. This puts the bank in a position of having $5,000 in excess reserves.

If we assume that First Commercial will fully use this $5,000 gain in excess reserves to expand its loans, the banking system would be capable of generating $50,000 in additional deposits. First Commercial would then have the same $100,000 total deposit base it had before Loan B was repaid.

INFLUENCES ON MULTIPLE DEPOSIT CREATION

The multiple expansion illustrated in exhibit 3.1 is based on a simplified set of assumptions that only partially reflect the world of banking. In reality, some deposits created by banks flow out of the banking system into non-depository financial institutions such as mutual funds insurance companies, and into money market instruments such as U.S. Treasury bills. In addition, consumers and businesses typically convert some of

their newly acquired demand deposits into cash and time deposits. Notably, time deposits cannot be withdrawn before a specified date or without advance notice.

Under the law, the Federal Reserve may vary reserve requirements depending on the amount of deposits a bank holds. For example, as of 2003 banks and other depositories were subject to reserve requirements of 3 percent on transaction deposits of $6 million to $42.1 million and 10 percent on any transaction deposits above that level. The reserve requirement on the first $6 million of transaction deposits was $0. This variability adds to the complexity of multiple deposit expansion. Moreover, reserve requirements change every year.

The fact that banks usually do not create money equal to every available excess reserve dollar further complicates the calculation. This is because each day's check collections are subject to next-day corrections or adjustments that can increase or decrease the previous day's deposit balance and reserve totals. Furthermore, given the rapid pace and large volume of deposits flowing in and out of a bank on any given day, it is only at the end of a day, or perhaps a day or two later, that the bank can determine precisely how much in excess reserves it has available to support new loans. To ensure that they remain in compliance with the required minimums, banks tend to retain some excess reserves even when loan demand is very strong.

Cash held by banks is an asset that can be counted to meet reserve requirements. Therefore, depositors' cash needs also affect the mathematical progression of new money creation. Every request for cash from consumers and businesses requires the bank, in essence, to dip into its reserves. As depositors cash checks against their own deposits, a bank loses reserves in an amount equal to the sum of the cash withdrawals. With a smaller amount of excess reserves, or with no excess reserves, a bank's ability to lend, and thus create money, is blunted.

The public holds cash as well as checkable deposits. It is reasonable to assume that for every new deposit of checks, the public will request some of the deposit back in cash. Conversely, every time cash is deposited for credit to a checking or savings account, banks' reserves increase on a dollar-for-dollar basis. During the course of any given week, the cash position of most banks fluctuates on a fairly predictable basis. Most banks take in more cash than they pay out on Mondays and Tuesdays, largely reflecting the accumulated weekend cash receipts deposited by merchants. On Thursdays and Fridays, most banks pay out more cash than they take in, reflecting business and consumer demands for increased weekend liquidity and pocket money.

The movement of funds from checkable deposits into time and savings deposits also affects the money expansion process by changing the amount of required and excess reserves held by banks. Banks are required to maintain reserves against transaction accounts but not against time and savings deposits. Whenever consumers transfer funds from their checking accounts into savings or time accounts, banks' required reserves decline and excess reserves increase.

Take the case of an individual with $10,000 in a checking account. If the reserve requirement is 10 percent on transaction accounts, the bank holding this account would be required to hold $1,000 in reserves in vault cash or in a deposit balance at its district Federal Reserve Bank. If that individual transfers the $10,000 into a certificate of deposit at the same bank, the bank's required reserves would decrease by $1,000 because banks are not required to keep reserves against certificates of deposit. As a result, the bank would now have $1,000 in excess reserves and, thus, $1,000 in new lending or investing capacity.

Reserve requirements represent a cost to banks because reserves are assets that must be set-aside in non-interest-earning form. Banks take reserve requirement costs into consideration when they determine loan charges and the interest rates they pay on deposits. Because a bank can increase its earnings by investing funds that do not need to be held as reserves, banks typically pay one-eighth to one-quarter of a percent higher interest on certificates of deposit than would be the case if they had to hold reserves against certificates of deposit.

More Realistic Multiple Deposit Creation

If we examine the money-creation process using more realistic assumptions, we can see a more accurate picture of the multiple expansion process in the banking system. Assume now that there is a 10 percent reserve requirement against checkable deposits. Now assume that for every new demand deposit dollar held by depositors, they choose to hold $0.50 in cash and $1.00 in time deposits. Finally, assume that Bank One has $100,000 in excess reserves, which enables it to create $100,000 in new demand deposit money by making a loan.

The borrower of Bank One's $100,000 uses the loan proceeds to pay, by check, various outstanding bills. The recipients of these checks deposit them in Bank Two, but prefer to hold $0.50 in cash and $1.00 in time deposits for every dollar of demand deposits they hold. The recipients of the $100,000 in checks wind up with $20,000 in cash, $40,000 in time deposit accounts, and $40,000 in demand deposits, as shown here:

Bank Two must now hold an additional $4,000 in required reserves, or 10 percent against its new $40,000 in demand deposits. Bank Two's total reserve gain is $80,000, reflecting the $100,000 reserve account credit

Bank One

Assets		Liabilities	
Loan	+ $100,000	Demand deposit created for borrower	+ $100,000

Bank Two

Assets		Liabilities	
Reserve account	+ $100,000*	Demand deposits	+ $40,000
Cash	– $ 20,000	Time deposits	+ $40,000

* Required reserves	$ 4,000
Excess reserves	$76,000

it received in the check collection process, partially offset by the $20,000 paid out in cash. By subtracting the $4,000 in required reserves from the bank's $80,000 in total reserves, we see that the bank's excess reserve position is now $76,000. Bank Two now has the capacity to create $76,000 in new demand deposits by making loans. Assume that it does so, and that the borrowers deposit the loan proceeds at Bank Three.

Suppose that the recipients of these loan proceeds also prefer to hold a portion of their newly acquired funds in cash and savings accounts. Using the same ratio that was used for Bank One's depositors, the $76,000 in loan receipts takes the following form: $15,200 is held as cash, $30,400 is held in time deposit accounts, and $30,400 is held as demand deposits. This is reflected on Bank Three's books as follows:

Bank Three

Assets		Liabilities	
Reserve account	+ $76,000*	Demand deposits	+ $30,400
Cash	$ 15,200	Time deposits	+ $30,400

* Required reserves	$ 3,040
Excess reserves	$57,760

Bank Three must hold $3,040 in required reserves, or 10 percent against its $30,400 in demand deposits. Because the bank's total reserve position is $60,800, its excess reserves equal $57,760. This sum represents Bank Three's maximum potential contribution to the money creation process of the banking system—assuming it too will make loans in the amount of its excess reserves.

We can compare these three banks' more realistic experience with the simplified example summarized in exhibit 3.1. Under the more realistic assumptions, each of the three banks has less in excess reserves because some reserves are used in paying out cash. This condition holds even though the three banks have no reserve requirements for the amounts held in time deposits. Under the more realistic scenario, the banking system might generate new demand deposits equal to only about 1.5 times the initial amount of excess reserves, rather than the 10-fold increase shown in exhibit 3.1. The T-account balance sheet for the banking system after full multiple expansion in our realistic example is as follows:

Banking System

Assets		Liabilities	
Cash paid out	− $ 84,000	Demand deposits	+ $166,000
Loans	+ $416,000	Time deposits	+ $166,000
Total	+ $332,000	Total	+ $332,000

Banks would be able to create $416,000 in new money, corresponding to the amount of all loans, while generating $166,000 each in demand deposits and time deposits and paying out $84,000 in cash.

In reality it is difficult to calculate a precise multiplier or coefficient of expansion. For one reason, reserve requirements differ for different amounts of deposits. In addition, bank customers move funds from cash to demand and time deposits and back. A single multiplier is valid only in theory. The underlying concept of the multiple expansion of bank deposits, however, is valid in both theory and in practice.

CONTROLLING THE MONEY-CREATION PROCESS

The Federal Reserve strives to ensure that the amount of deposits created by the nation's banking system is neither too much nor too little for the needs of the economy. The Federal Reserve does this by controlling the amount and cost of reserves available in the banking system. However, the Federal Reserve does not involve itself with the daily management decisions of individual banks. To obtain reserves, banks are free to compete against each other, against other financial intermediaries, and in other markets for customers' deposit and loan business. The Federal Reserve focuses on the total amount of reserves available in the banking system, not on the amount available to any individual bank.

During periods of declining production, the Federal Reserve typically seeks to stimulate bank lending to spark needed business and consumer spending. The Federal Reserve tends to provide the banking system with reserves that banks can use to expand loan activity. Low demand for loans is a characteristic of recession, and banks often find interest rates declining as new reserves expand the base of available reserves. Banks tend to see this stimulative Federal Reserve policy as consistent with their own goals because an expansion of excess reserves increases banks' earnings potential. Declining interest rates themselves increase the value of the securities held in banks' portfolios, a major component of most banks' earning assets.

During periods of rising prices, on the other hand, the Federal Reserve's policy goals may directly conflict with the lending goals of banks. To counter inflation, the Federal Reserve seeks to restrain bank lending in order to hold down credit-induced buying. To do this, the Federal Reserve typically attempts to reduce or hold back excess reserves. In this environment, as demand for bank loans increases, interest rates often rise. Banks tend to see anti-inflationary monetary policy as reducing their earnings prospects. It cuts them off from the reserves they need to meet their customers' loan demands and raises their cost of doing business. Rising interest rates therefore generate paper losses on the securities held in bank portfolios that were purchased when rates were lower.

EFFECTS OF CONTROL

An increase in the quantity of reserves available to banks typically spurs bank lending. When a bank accepts a new deposit, it must keep required reserves against the new deposit. However, the bank has a margin of excess reserves against which new loans can be made. The bank will seek to turn its excess reserves into income-generating assets by making loans or investments. As the recipients of these bank loans or investments spend their money in the economy, these funds are deposited in other banks. As total deposits in the banking system increase, there is more money creation for the economy, and therefore, increased earning assets for banks. As we have seen, the multiple creation of bank deposits expands the nation's money supply by an amount many times greater than the initial expansion generated by the first loan.

In a similar fashion, reserve losses may depress bank lending. When a bank pays out previously deposited funds, it loses reserves. If the bank has no excess reserves, it faces a reserve deficiency. It must then seek to obtain the reserves it needs to meet reserve requirements by selling its secondary reserve assets (government securities held in the bank's investment portfolio), borrowing from other banks, borrowing from the Federal Reserve, or quickly attracting new deposits.

An individual bank can meet a reserve deficiency by borrowing from another bank or selling securities to a private dealer firm. However, the banking system as a whole can meet a reserve deficiency only with an infusion of reserves from outside the system. Banks cannot simply adjust assets and liabilities to create new reserves. At best a given bank can transfer its reserve deficiency to another bank, or a group of smaller banks can redistribute their reserve deficiencies to one or two larger money market banks. However, the banking system itself will still hold the same amount of reserves.

The Federal Reserve could, as a matter of policy, generate a reserve deficiency in the banking system as a means of reducing the money supply. It could do this by raising reserve requirements or by selling government securities in the open market. Within days, the money supply would decline as bank loans were repaid and, with no excess reserves, no new loans are made. When the total deposit base of the banking system has declined sufficiently, the amount of available reserves meets the reserve requirements.

BANK RESPONSE TO CONTROL

When the Federal Reserve wants to restrain bank lending and money supply growth, it generally implements restraint in a gradual and subtle way by reducing the growth rate at which it supplies reserves to the banking system. As the expansion of reserves begins to slow, the continued strong demand for reserves by banks wanting to make loans and increase their earning assets leads the cost of reserves to rise. Almost immediately, the increased cost of reserves is reflected in an increased cost of federal funds, the reserves that banks sell to one another.

Federal funds transactions are the primary reserve adjustment device used by the nation's biggest banks. The cost of federal funds, known as the federal funds rate, increases as banks compete for reserves to expand individual loan and investment portfolios. The trading of reserves among banks is known as the federal funds market because banks, in effect, buy or sell their Federal Reserve account balances to one another. When the cost of reserves increases, banks must charge more on loans and command more on investments to make any expansion in earning assets profitable. Some banks will be induced to cut back on loans as their management responds to rising costs or to a decline in loan demand from customers unwilling to pay higher loan rates for borrowed funds. Banks that respond in this way typically allow loans to be repaid without extending new ones; this reduces their deposit base and as a result, their need to maintain a high level of reserves. These adjustments invariably reduce the amount of demand deposits in the nation's banking system and the amount of required reserves needed to support these deposits.

SUMMARY

Commercial banks create money in the form of new demand deposits when they make commercial loans. In contrast, other financial intermediaries primarily lend out existing funds taken in from depositors, a process that does not create money. The ability of banks to create new demand deposits depends on their level of reserves, which comprise the amount of vault cash held and the amount of funds on deposit at the district Federal Reserve bank or the amount of funds on deposit in a pass-through account at a correspondent bank.

When new reserves enter the banking system, banks can expand demand deposits by a multiple of those reserves. When reserves are withdrawn from the banking system, deposits must contract by a multiple of the lost reserves. The deposit multiplier shows how much demand deposits can change when reserves change. Using simplified assumptions, the multiplier is the reciprocal of the reserve requirement ratio. The mathematics of new money creation, however, are affected by several complex factors, such as the public's ongoing shifts of funds between cash and time deposits and the varying reserve requirement percentages applied to banks of different deposit size.

In implementing monetary policy, the Federal Reserve does not involve itself with the specific management decisions of individual banks. Rather, the Federal Reserve focuses on the total amount of reserves available in the banking system to support all loans. Its attempts to restrain or spur bank lending and money supply growth influence the federal funds rate, which is the cost of reserves that banks buy and sell to one another.

REVIEW QUESTIONS

1. Explain the use of T-accounts in analyzing the lending process of banks.
2. Evaluate this statement: "As my bank's commercial loan officer, I do not create money; I simply loan the money that depositors have placed in the bank."
3. If there were no reserve requirements, could banks create an infinite amount of demand deposits? Why or why not?
4. How can a bank that finds itself with a reserve deficiency obtain new reserves? Would these options work if the entire banking system needed additional reserves? Explain your answers.
5. How do banks use federal funds transactions to adjust their reserves?

ADDITIONAL RESOURCES

Bankrate.com, at *www.bankrate.com*. Provides data on banks current interest rates offered on deposits and charged on loans.

Federal Reserve Bulletin, Board of Governors of the Federal Reserve, monthly publication. Provides statistical tables with up-to-date data on banking activity and the performance of various sectors of the economy and articles on selected banking, business, and economic topics.

Modern Money Mechanics, at *www.geocities.com/tthor.geo/mmm3.html*. Provides access to the Federal Reserve Bank of Chicago's workbook on deposit expansion and to information on the money supply measures.

Modern Money Mechanics: A Workbook on Bank Reserves and Deposit Expansion, Federal Reserve Bank of Chicago, 1992, 8 pp. Uses T-accounts to describe money creation and the factors affecting bank reserves.

Principles of Banking, 7th ed., by G. Jay Francis and Susan M. Siegel, American Bankers Association, 2001. Explains deposit expansion as well as other principles of the business of banking.

EXERCISE 1: MULTIPLE EXPANSION OF BANK DEPOSITS

This exercise deals with the multiple expansion of bank deposits under the following simplified assumptions:

- All bank-created deposits stay in the banking system.

- All newly created funds are held as demand deposits.
- All banks create loans equal to every available (excess) reserve dollar.
- Reserve requirement for all deposits is 8 percent.

1. What is the multiple expansion equation?
2. What is the multiplier, or expansion coefficient?
3. Complete the chart based on the assumptions given above.

Multiple Expansion of Bank Deposits

Bank Position	New Deposits	New Loans and Investments	Required Reserves
Bank One	$100,000	$ _____	$ _____
Bank Two	$ _____	$ _____	$ _____
Bank Three	$ _____	$ _____	$ _____
Sum of first three banks' deposit expansion	$ _____	$ _____	$ _____
Sum of remaining banks' deposit expansion	$ _____	$ _____	$ _____
Total for banking system	$ _____	$ _____	$ _____

4

FINANCIAL MARKETS AND FINANCIAL INTERMEDIARIES

LEARNING OBJECTIVES

After studying this chapter, you should be able to

- describe the principal financial intermediaries in the United States today
- summarize how increased competition has changed the business orientation of banks and other intermediaries
- distinguish between demand deposit accounts, savings and time deposit accounts, negotiable order of withdrawal accounts, and money market deposit accounts
- cite the major deposit liabilities of banks
- define the key terms listed in this chapter

KEY TERMS

bank holding company
commercial banks
credit unions
defined-benefit plans
defined-contribution plans
demand deposits
finance companies

financial holding company
money market deposit accounts
money market funds
proprietary funds
savings institutions
time and savings accounts
transaction accounts

INTRODUCTION

Financial intermediaries link savers with borrowers. They accept money from individuals or businesses that want to save it and lend it to consumers, businesses, and governments that choose to borrow funds. These institutions are essential in our modern economy. As we engage in the many financial transactions of day-to-day living, financial intermediaries enable us to manage our money with great efficiency, safety, and convenience.

This chapter takes a broad look at the important financial intermediaries, including depository institutions such as commercial banks and savings institutions, and at nondepository institutions, such as mutual funds and finance companies. It also looks at the major types of deposit instruments, including both transaction accounts and various types of time and savings accounts. It examines the competitive relationships that form the basis of our nation's financial system and discusses how changes in the financial markets affect these relationships.

For additional study of related topics, you are encouraged to examine the extended studies. Extended Study 2, The Failure of Savings and Loan Associations During the 1980s, traces the main causes of the collapse of many savings and loan associations during that decade and the measures taken to address the problem. Extended Study 3,

Bank Holding Company Activities, reviews the activities bank holding companies can engage in and the criteria used for determining their approval.

THE CHANGING COMPETITIVE ENVIRONMENT

Commercial banks are the most important depository institutions among the nation's major financial intermediaries. They are essential to the economy's savings and lending process (see exhibit 4.1). In 2001 the nation's commercial banks held $6.5 trillion in assets, more than four times the nearly $1.5 trillion in assets held by all of the nation's other major depository institutions.

In recent decades, however, the importance of other nondepository intermediaries in the savings and lending process has grown. These institutions also have become more competitive with both commercial banks and savings institutions, which include savings and loan associations (S&Ls), savings banks, and credit unions. Commercial banks and savings institutions have had to contend with the rapid asset growth of such nondepository intermediaries as money

Nineteenth-century bank note issued by the U.S. Treasury.
Photo courtesy of the Library of Congress, Prints and Photographs Division [USC-6240571].

Exhibit 4.1
Financial Intermediaries

Type of Financial Intermediary	Number of Institutions	2002 Asset Size (in billions)
Commercial banks	8,375	$6,500
Savings institutions		
Savings and loan associations	775	200
Savings banks	1,300	900
Credit unions	10,600	375
Nondepository financial institutions		
Insurance companies	5,000	2,500
Mutual fund companies*	440	6,900
Finance companies	1,000	1,200
Private pension plans	7,800	5,000
State and local government pension plans	**	3,000

* These companies offer 8,200 different stock, bond, and money market funds. The stock and bond funds hold $4.7 trillion; the money market funds hold $2.2 trillion.

** Indeterminate. The top 10 government pension plans hold 30 percent ($900 billion) of the industry's total assets.

Sources: Federal Deposit Insurance Corporation and *Federal Reserve Bulletin,* First Quarter 2002.

market funds, pension funds, and finance companies. They also have faced emerging competition from such nonfinancial intermediaries as brokerage firms and retailers.

During the 1980s, these nonfinancial intermediaries began offering banking-type services, including deposits. These changes significantly affected the nation's financial structure and the competitive relationships among intermediaries.

During the 1990s, commercial banks regained some of the business they had lost to savings institutions in the previous two decades. The nation's S&Ls were hit hard with serious liquidity and earnings problems. Many became increasingly unprofitable as interest rate ceilings were gradually raised after 1980 and then eliminated in 1986. A spate of insolvencies and mergers during the 1980s and 1990s considerably reduced the number of savings institutions in the industry. Over the two decades, nearly two-thirds of the nation's S&Ls and savings banks (some 3,700 in all) were merged, acquired by other institutions, or closed.

MAJOR DEPOSITORY FINANCIAL INTERMEDIARIES

Before the 1980 Monetary Control Act, commercial banks and savings institutions each had characteristic products, services, and customer markets, largely determined by government regulation. These distinguishing characteristics have largely disappeared.

COMMERCIAL BANKS

A **commercial bank** is a private corporation, chartered either by a state or the federal government, which accepts demand deposits, makes commercial loans, and provides other financial services. Most commercial banks are small, state-chartered institutions. About one-third of all banks hold deposits of $50 million or less (see exhibit 4.2 on the following page). One-quarter of the nation's banks hold deposits between $50 million and $100 million. The remaining banks, numbering fewer than 3,500, hold deposits of more than $100 million.

Exhibit 4.2
Commercial Bank Size, 2002

Bank Asset Size	Number of Banks	Percentage of Banks	Percentage of Total Bank Assets
Less than $25 million	1,110	13.3	0.3
$25 to 50 million	1,718	20.5	1.1
$50 to 100 million	2,094	25.0	2.5
$100 to 500 million	2,757	32.9	9.2
$500 million to 1 billion	313	3.7	3.5
$1 to 10 billion	301	3.6	14.3
More than $10 billion	82	1.0	69.1
Total	8,375	100.0	100.0

Source: Federal Deposit Insurance Corporation web site.

Few of the nation's commercial banks are global corporations with hundreds of branches and thousands of employees, yet they hold the majority share of the banking system's total deposits. These banks are concentrated in the nation's money centers: New York, Chicago, and San Francisco.

Accepting demand deposits (non-interest-bearing checking accounts) and making loans to businesses were traditionally the only activities associated with commercial banking. Since the 1960s, however, most commercial banks have become full-service financial department stores serving both consumer and business markets. Banks today derive their earnings not only from loans, but also from financial investments and the sale of financial services.

Making loans remains the primary role of commercial banks. Making loans creates the demand deposit dollars that serve as the nation's principal form of money. In the early 2000s, about 25 percent to 30 percent of commercial bank loans, by dollar volume, consisted of loans made to business firms; about 20 percent consisted of loans made to consumers; and another 40 percent to 45 percent consisted of mortgages on residential and commercial properties.

Most of the nation's commercial banks also offer time and savings deposit accounts, rent out safe deposit boxes, exchange foreign currency, maintain automated teller machines (ATMs), issue credit and debit cards, and sell traveler's checks.

Until the 1960s, demand deposits dominated the deposit structures of commercial banks. Today the predominant types of commercial bank deposits are money market deposit accounts (MMDAs) and time deposits, which are interest-earning accounts that technically cannot be withdrawn on demand. In 2002 commercial banks held nearly $1.8 trillion in MMDAs and passbook savings, and about $700 billion in large-denomination time deposits maintained principally by businesses (see exhibit 4.3). Banks held only $460 billion or so in demand and other checkable deposits, including negotiable order of withdrawal (NOW) and automatic transfer service (ATS) accounts. Account ownership of demand deposits at commercial banks is weighted heavily toward the business sector. More than 65 percent, by dollar volume, are owned by businesses.

BANK HOLDING COMPANIES

A **bank holding company** is a corporation that owns or controls one or more banks. Bank holding companies may own and control any number of commercial banks

Exhibit 4.3
Business and Consumer Deposits, 2002 (in billions)

Type of Deposit	Commercial Banks	Savings Institutions	Total
Money market deposit accounts and passbook savings	$1,796	$590	$2,386
Small-denomination time deposits	622	324	946
Large-denomination time deposits	706	113	819
Demand and other checkable deposits	462	111	573
IRA and Keogh deposits	162	96	258

Source: Federal Reserve Board, *Statistical Release H.6 (508),* February 2002.

within a state. About 6,100 bank holding companies in the United States own or control 7,400 banks, and these banks hold about 90 percent of commercial bank deposits. The significance of this corporate structure is that bank holding companies may engage in financial activities and offer services through their nonbank subsidiaries that banks themselves are not allowed to do. Activities range from providing securities brokerage services to underwriting stocks and bonds.

The holding company arrangement has allowed banks to expand their geographic markets. Until the 1980s, state banking regulations severely restricted intrastate branching, and from 1927 until 1997, the McFadden Act largely prohibited branching between states. The law that, before 1997, prohibited banks from branching into other states—the McFadden Act—did not apply to the activities of bank holding companies.

Bank holding companies enabled large banks to operate outside their immediate local and regional markets. Some 55 multistate bank holding companies had bank subsidiaries in 36 states by 1997. For more information about approved activities of bank holding companies and the criteria used for determining approval, you are encouraged to examine Extended Study 3.

FINANCIAL HOLDING COMPANIES

A **financial holding company** is a corporation that owns one or more commercial banks as well as one or more companies that underwrite stocks and bonds, sell insurance, or provide other specialized financial services, such as portfolio management. Financial holding companies have been permitted only since 2000. They allow banks, insurance companies, brokerage firms, and securities dealer firms to affiliate under common ownership and offer customers a complete range of financial services.

Before 2000 banks that wanted to underwrite stocks and bonds, sell insurance, or provide other specialized financial services had three options. Such a bank could

- operate in a state that allowed the activity
- take advantage of federal law that permitted nationally chartered banks to sell insurance across the country from offices in towns with populations less than 5,000
- have its parent bank holding company establish a subsidiary, although the subsidiary's activities would be subject to regulatory limitations

At the same time, securities dealer firms and insurance companies could position themselves to provide banking services in two ways. They could

- use a legal loophole, discovered in the 1980s and subsequently closed in 1987, that enabled them to own consumer banks, which were essentially commercial banks that did everything but make business loans
- acquire a single savings institution, known as a unitary thrift, and provide banking services through this institution

Financial holding companies provide a more straightforward way for banks and nonbank financial institutions to integrate.

Through 2002 about 500 bank holding companies have established financial holding companies, as have several insurance companies and brokerage firms. In 2002 the ten largest financial holding companies held more than 40 percent of the banking system's assets (see exhibit 4.4).

SAVINGS INSTITUTIONS

In 2002 U.S. savings institutions included about 1,300 savings banks, 775 savings and loan associations, and 10,600 credit unions. **Savings institutions** are depository institutions that primarily accept savings and checkable deposits from the public and use these funds for mortgage loans.

Exhibit 4.4
The 10 Largest Financial Holding Companies in the United States

| Company Name | Assets in 2002 (in billions) | |
	Holding Company	Bank
Citigroup New York, NY	$944.3	$462.3
J.P. Morgan Chase & Co. New York, NY	713.3	660.8
Bank of America Corp. Charlotte, NC	609.8	579.9
Wells Fargo & Co. San Francisco, CA	279.7	287.1
MetLife, Inc. New York, NY	254.1	0.2
First Union Corp. Charlotte, NC	252.9	240.2
Tannus Corp. (U.S. Subsidiary of Deutsche Bank) New York, NY	214.8	42.9
FleetBoston Financial Corp. Boston, MA	211.7	206.4
U.S. Bancorp Minneapolis, MN	160.3	155.1
HSBC North America, Inc. Buffalo, NY	105.9	82.5

Note: In 2002 there were 525 Financial Holding Companies (FHCs) in the United States. These FHCs held $4.2 trillion in bank assets, about two-thirds of total U.S. bank assets.
Source: Federal Reserve Bank of Kansas City, *Financial Industry Perspectives 2001*, Second Quarter, 2002.

The role of savings banks and savings and loan associations traditionally has been to lend people's savings to individuals who want to buy homes. The role of credit unions has been to lend savings for major purchases. However, new payment- and deposit-related powers granted to savings institutions in the 1980s effectively eliminated most of the differences in the deposits taken and loans made by banks and savings institutions. Moreover, during the 1980s, many of these institutions found that expanded powers did not guarantee increased business or profits.

SAVINGS AND LOAN ASSOCIATIONS

Savings and loan associations (S&Ls) specialize in residential mortgage lending. Most S&Ls are small. Some S&Ls are owned by the savers and borrowers who are their members, but most S&Ls are corporations owned by stockholders. Savings and loan associations are chartered by either a state government or the federal government.

During the 1980s, Congress gave S&Ls new powers to make them more strongly competitive with commercial banks. These new powers included

- the ability to make residential mortgages in broader geographic areas and in larger amounts
- broader investment powers
- authorization to issue credit cards, make business loans, and offer interest-earning checking accounts

Using these new powers introduced a degree of instability to S&L operations, however: S&Ls saw their traditional source of funds shift from stable, low-cost, long-term passbook deposits to volatile, short-term accounts that were sensitive to market interest rates. And interest rates were rising at that time. S&Ls' income, which derived mainly from fixed-rate mortgages, failed to keep pace with the rising cost of funds. The result was a substantial squeeze on profits.

To expand earnings, many S&Ls drew on their recently granted powers and switched from making low-yielding residential mortgages to making high-yielding, but riskier, consumer, commercial real estate, and business loans. A large number of S&Ls overextended themselves and suffered substantial losses when economic conditions soured and commercial real estate and business borrowers could not repay. Although interest rates declined sharply in the mid-1980s, many S&Ls continued to lose money because of bad loans, excessive operating costs that included very high interest rates paid on deposits, and fraud.

At the beginning of the 1980s, S&Ls were the second largest financial industry in the United States, with 5,500 institutions holding more than $2.5 trillion in assets. Today, S&Ls are one of the smallest. The collapse of the savings and loan industry in the 1980s wiped out the gains of 30 years of S&L deposit and loan growth. It also eliminated S&Ls as major depository institution competitors of commercial banks.

For a detailed review of the factors that led to the collapse of the S&L industry, you may wish to examine Extended Study 2.

SAVINGS BANKS

America's 1,300 savings banks held some $900 billion in assets in 2002 (see exhibit 4.1). Savings banks are located primarily in the New England and Mid-Atlantic states. They were first organized in the early 1800s, before commercial banks started accepting individual savings deposits, to encourage thrift and to provide a safe repository for public savings.

Until the 1980s, most savings banks were state-chartered, state-supervised, non-stockholder institutions operated by boards of trustees for the benefit of depositors. The depositors owned these mutual institutions and received profits from interest on deposits. In the 1980s, Congress gave mutual savings banks new powers to offer interest-bearing checking accounts, make local business loans, and offer demand deposit accounts to business loan customers as well as to consumers. Congress also broadened savings banks' overall lending and investment powers and gave mutuals the option of converting to federal charter and becoming stockholder institutions. By issuing stock, savings banks could more readily obtain capital to expand and compete more effectively. Most mutuals converted to stock ownership.

Savings banks traditionally have obtained most of their funds from small individual deposits. Passbook deposits typically supply about 90 percent of savings banks' funds. By presenting a passbook, the depositor can have his or her savings converted to cash, although savings banks can require the depositor to provide written notice at least seven days before withdrawal.

CREDIT UNIONS

Credit unions are cooperative associations of people with a common interest or affiliation who pool their savings and can then borrow funds from that pool. Members purchase shares with their savings, which, in turn, allows members to borrow from the pool of all credit union shares. More than one-third of the nation's adult population (70 million) are credit union members. Based on income from the credit union's loans and other investments, members are paid dividends (interest) on their shares.

Although they constitute the largest category of savings institutions in terms of numbers, credit unions hold a relatively small amount of assets. In 2002 there were about 10,600 credit unions in the United States, which held about $375 billion in assets. However, some credit unions have assets that exceed those of many S&Ls and savings banks.

Many credit unions are small, with few, if any, full-time paid employees. They operate on the corporate premises where employees work, with members working at the credit union on a voluntary part-time basis. Rent-free space by the sponsoring employer and no labor costs keep overhead low and often give small credit unions a competitive edge in lending rates over other thrifts.

Members' savings, called share accounts, represent about 90 percent of the total liabilities of credit unions. Loans to members account for more than 60 percent of total assets. Traditionally, credit union loans have been short-term installment loans. However, changes in banking law and regulation during the 1980s drastically altered the scope of credit union activities.

Credit unions now make mortgage loans of up to 30 years, offer checking account services through share draft accounts, and offer certificates of deposit through variable-rate share certificates. Credit unions are also permitted to make overdraft loans on share draft accounts and to make real estate cooperative loans.

In the early 1980s, new services both spurred the growth of credit unions and increased their operating costs. Federal regulations governing credit unions may have spurred their growth even more, and in the view of many banks gave credit unions some competitive advantages over commercial banks.

For example, until the 1980s federally chartered and some state-chartered credit unions were subject to a 12 percent ceiling on loan rates. This rate ceiling made their loans highly appealing to borrowers. At the same time, interest rates on credit union savings accounts were not subject to the low rate ceilings then applicable to savings deposits at banks and other thrifts.

As cooperatives, credit unions are still considered nonprofit entities and are therefore not subject to income taxes. Credit unions also are subject to fewer restrictive and costly-to-administer regulations than are banks. These advantages have raised issues about the fairness of competition between credit unions and other depository institutions.

CREDIT UNION MEMBERSHIP

Until the 1980s, a credit union's membership was essentially limited to people who had a common interest or affiliation, such as working for the same employer, belonging to the same labor union, or being a member of the same fraternal organization. Largely for this reason, membership in most credit unions was small and locally based.

In 1982 the National Credit Union Administration (NCUA), the government agency that charters and regulates federally chartered credit unions, ended this membership limitation by broadening the common affiliation rule to encompass a wide range of indirect activities and relationships, such as working in a given geographic area, sharing a common religion, or having served in the military. This rule change had a profound impact on credit union membership. Between 1980 and 2002, membership increased by 60 percent, from 44 million people to more than 70 million people. Credit union asset growth was even sharper, increasing from $69 billion in 1980 to more than $375 billion in 2002.

Banks had long argued that credit unions' tax-exempt status gave them an unfair competitive advantage by enabling credit unions to pay more on deposits and charge less on most loans. Market surveys show that credit unions, on average, charge 10 percent to 25 percent less than commercial banks for auto loans, credit cards, and unsecured personal loans, and pay one-half to one percentage point more on deposits. The NCUA's membership rule change in the 1980s added to banks' contention that credit unions were being granted unfair market advantages, a contention that banks repeatedly made to Congress and to the courts in the 1980s and 1990s.

In 1996 a federal court of appeals ruled in favor of banks and ordered the NCUA and credit unions to adhere to the narrow pre-1982 common affiliation rule. In 1998 the U.S. Supreme Court upheld the federal court's ruling. However, Congress moved quickly in 1998 to prevent the potential disenrollment of millions of credit union members. It redefined credit unions as "alternative retail banks" that are empowered to serve "local, well-defined communities" and it instructed the NCUA to specifically define those communities. The NCUA responded by establishing a very broad definition of community, which was consistent with the post-1982 broadened common affiliation rule.

Most of the nation's credit unions are small and about 10,000 are federally chartered. However, a growing number have become large. About 1,000 credit unions have assets of $75 million or more, and banks contend that these institutions have unfairly taken business away from small community-based banks by being allowed to open their membership ranks to people outside their local markets.

Credit unions contend that their tax-exempt status is justified by the public-service role they have played over the decades in offering low-cost banking services and credit to low- and moderate-income consumers that, until recent decades, were largely ignored by commercial banks. The broadening of credit union membership is an attempt to strengthen this role. Banks counter by arguing that the social purpose that might have justified special treatment for credit unions decades ago is no longer valid today. Since the 1980s, banks argue, credit unions have come to possess the same product and service powers as banks and today they compete broadly with banks. Thus, market fairness dictates that tax rules and other regulations governing credit unions and banks should be the same.

MAJOR NONDEPOSITORY FINANCIAL INTERMEDIARIES

During the last decade, nondepository financial intermediaries emerged as significant competitors of banks. Nondepository financial intermediaries include money market funds, insurance companies, pension funds, and finance companies.

MONEY MARKET FUNDS

A **money market fund** is a specific type of mutual fund. Technically, mutual funds are investment companies that sell shares in pools of financial assets they purchase and manage for individual or institutional investors. A money market fund specializes in investments in short-term instruments, typically with a three-month average maturity. Examples of such short-term instruments are certificates of deposit, commercial paper, bankers' acceptances, and U.S. Treasury bills. Most mutual funds invest in corporate stocks and bonds and in government bonds. In 2002 mutual funds offered 8,200 stock, bond, and money market funds. Of these about 1,800 were money market funds with assets of more than $2.2 trillion (see exhibit 4.1).

Money market funds are not to be confused with money market deposit accounts (MMDAs). In 1982 commercial banks and savings institutions were authorized to offer MMDAs as a way of competing with money market funds.

Money market funds typically offer a checking account option that enables shareholders to write checks, usually of $500 or more, against their shares. Shares also can be redeemed by electronic transfers (wire transfers) sent by the fund to an investor's bank account. Most money market funds require a minimum initial investment, which can be as low as $500. Some funds require no minimum.

Money market funds attract and retain deposits because they generally offer higher interest rates than banks offer on money market deposit accounts or savings certificates. This interest rate edge reflects the broader latitude that money market funds have to invest and trade in riskier, and thus higher-paying, financial instruments. In addition, because accounts held at money market funds and the money market deposit accounts held at banks have slightly different characteristics, they appeal to different types of investors.

To meet growing competition from money market funds during the 1990s, banks began to offer money market fund services to customers by either selling shares in their own proprietary funds or selling the shares of nonbank funds. A **proprietary fund** is advised and managed by the bank, but the bank itself does not own the fund's assets or actually issue shares to customers. A separate company, not affiliated with the bank, brokers these funds.

Banks that sell the shares of nonbank funds simply act as brokers for customers and split commissions on shares bought and sold. Banks that have proprietary funds earn both management fees and full commissions on shares bought or sold for customers.

Today more than 100 bank-related money market funds hold about $500 billion, or nearly 25 percent of total money market fund assets. The popularity of bank-related funds has raised increasing concerns in Congress that bank customers may not fully understand that shares in bank-related money market funds are not deposits, and thus are not insured by the Federal Deposit Insurance Corporation. To address these concerns, the bank regulatory agencies have issued information disclosure guidelines to banks. When selling money market funds, bankers are required to inform customers that money market fund shares are not insured by the Federal Deposit Insurance Corporation (FDIC) and of the risk that shares can decline in value.

INSURANCE COMPANIES

Insurance companies make up another type of nondepository financial intermediary that competes with banks for individuals' checking and savings funds. By selling risk protection, primarily to individuals, insurance companies receive contractual premium payments paid by policyholders. Policyholders typically do not use their policies as savings accounts, but the accumulated cash value of a life insurance policy can be drawn on to provide the policyholder with liquidity. Insurance companies are thus considered financial intermediaries because they accumulate the funds they receive from premiums and place them in relatively risk-free, long-term investments, such as corporate bonds and multifamily and commercial mortgages.

PENSION FUNDS

Pension funds, another important non-depository financial intermediary, administer savings set aside by employers and employees for retirement income. In 2002 the nation's private pension funds held $5.0 trillion of retirement savings; state and local government pension plans, often called public pension funds, held $3.0 trillion. About two-thirds of private pension assets are managed by private trustees, including bank trust departments; the other third are held in plans administered by insurance companies.

The two most widely used types of pension plans in the United States are defined-benefit plans and defined-contribution plans. In a **defined-benefit plan,** the pension fund makes specific monthly payments to retired employees based on a formula that usually factors in the employee's length of service and earnings. In a **defined-contribution plan,** the pension fund takes in employees' contributions, which may or may not be matched by employer contributions, and invests the funds into one or more investment alternatives determined by the employee. The 401(k) plans are the most popular of the defined-contribution plans, accounting for more than $1 trillion of pension plan assets. The assets held by private and public defined-benefit plans are very similar and are heavily weighted toward investments in stock. The overwhelming investment choice of employees covered by defined-contribution plans also has been stock.

FINANCE COMPANIES

The nation's 3,000 finance companies also are classified as non-depository financial intermediaries. **Finance companies** provide two types of credit: wholesale and retail. Merchants are provided wholesale credit so their inventories can be carried until purchased by consumers. Retail credit is provided to consumers so big-ticket items, automobiles in particular, can be bought on installment. To obtain funds, finance companies borrow from commercial banks and insurance companies and sell their own secured or unsecured promissory notes directly in the credit market.

Merchants that receive wholesale credit do so by signing a promissory note. These notes are ordinarily secured by warehouse or trust receipts covering the merchandise to be financed. Retail credit to consumers involves direct lending secured by a personal promissory note. A lien is placed on the article purchased so that the article can be recovered if the borrower defaults on the loan. For automobiles, insurance policies covering fire, theft, and accident are required.

During the 1990s, finance companies greatly increased their share of the auto loan and general consumer installment loan market in relation to that of banks and other providers of consumer credit. These gains are reflected in the $1.3 trillion in total assets held by finance companies in 2002.

Finance companies have dominated the auto loan market since the 1980s by using below-market financing rates, from 2.9 percent down to 0 percent, in lieu of price-tag reductions to boost car sales. The ability of finance companies to use below-market rates has made it difficult for commercial banks to compete for auto loans.

MAJOR NONFINANCIAL INTERMEDIARIES

Nonfinancial intermediaries are nondepository businesses whose primary activity is not providing financial products and services. In the 1980s, brokerage firms, mutual funds, retail stores, and other nonbank companies that were seeking to enter the banking business found a loophole in the law governing bank holding companies. The law limited the purchase of banks to bank holding companies and restricted such companies from owning any other businesses unless they were closely related to banking. However, the law narrowly defined a commercial bank as an institution that offers demand deposits and makes business loans. Nonbank firms discovered that they could own a bank by purchasing one and then divesting it of either its demand deposits or its business loans. A bank that retained one of the defining characteristics but lacked the other became, in effect, a nonbank bank, also called a consumer bank.

During the 1980s, nearly 200 major companies acquired consumer banks. These companies included nondepository financial intermediaries, such as brokerage firms, mutual funds, and insurance companies, and nonfinancial intermediaries, such as retail stores and manufacturers. Using their acquired banks, these companies began to actively compete for commercial bank and savings institution customers. Of these companies, the top 10, comprising mainly brokerage firms, American Express, and Sears, earned more than $2 billion annually

from sales of financial services. Exhibit 4.5 lists some of the major nonbank corporations that owned consumer banks during the 1980s.

The consumer bank movement of the 1980s presented a formidable competitive challenge to commercial banks and savings institutions. It also posed a real threat to the way the government had chosen to regulate banks at the time.

The consumer bank loophole meant that such companies as Sears and J.C. Penney could provide banking services through a consumer bank subsidiary without having to divest themselves of activities not permitted to bank holding companies. The loophole also meant that bank holding companies owning consumer banks could provide banking services outside their home states without having to obtain the permission of those states, as was required by federal law.

In 1987 Congress closed the loophole by redefining a commercial bank as any institution insured by the FDIC, effectively precluding nonbank companies from establishing any new consumer bank subsidiaries. However, Congress included a grandfather clause in its legislation that exempted consumer banks that had been established before 1987.

During the 1990s, Congress sought to address competitive and regulatory issues raised by the existence of consumer banks. The issues included

- bank ownership
- banks being regulated as a separate line of commerce
- whether bank holding companies should be allowed to underwrite stocks and bonds without restrictions
- whether bank holding companies should be allowed to provide brokerage and insurance services

These issues were addressed by legislation in 1999. The Gramm-Leach-Bliley Act broadened bank ownership rules and allowed

Exhibit 4.5
Major Nonbank Corporations that Acquired Consumer Banks in the 1980s

Holding Company	Primary Business	Subsidiary Consumer Bank
Advest Group, Inc. Hartford, CT	Brokerage/ mutual funds	Advest Bank, Hartford, CT
Aetna Life and Casualty Hartford, CT	Insurance	Liberty Bank & Trust Gibbsboro, NJ
American Express Co. New York, NY	Travel and entertainment card	Boston Safe Deposit and Trust Co.; Advisory Bank and Trust, Minneapolis, MN; American Express Centurion Bank, Newark, DE
Bear Stearns Co. New York, NY	Brokerage	Custodial Trust Co., Trenton, NJ
Chrysler Corp. Highland Park, MI	Manufacturing/ finance co.	Automotive Financial Services, Inc., Highland Park, MI
Dreyfus Corp. New York, NY	Brokerage/ mutual funds	Dreyfus Consumer Bank, East Orange, NJ
General Electric Co. Stamford, CT	Manufacturing/ finance co.	Monogram Bank, Blue Ash, OH
Home Group Inc. New York, NY	Insurance	Premium Bank, Oceanside, CA
J.C. Penney Co., Inc. New York, NY	Retail chain	J.C. Penney National Bank, Harrington, DE
John Hancock Subsidiaries, Inc. Boston, MA	Insurance	First Signature Bank & Trust Co., Boston, MA
Merrill Lynch & Co. New York, NY	Brokerage	Merrill Lynch Bank & Trust Co., Plainsboro, NJ
Montgomery Ward & Co. Chicago, IL	Retail chain	Clayton Bank & Trust Co., DE
Sears, Roebuck and Co. Chicago IL	Retail chain	Greenwood Trust Co., New Castle, DE; Hurley State Bank, Hurley, SD
Travelers Corp. Hartford, CT	Insurance	Massachusetts Co., Boston, MA

banks, through financial holding companies, to underwrite stocks and bonds and provide brokerage, insurance, and other financial services.

MAJOR TYPES OF DEPOSITS

Today's bank liabilities reflect innovations in banking and changes in banking law and regulation that created new types of deposits, altered the definitions and characteristics of existing deposits, and shifted the deposit-taking focus of the banking industry.

Deposits are held either as transaction accounts or time and savings accounts.

TRANSACTION ACCOUNTS

Transaction accounts are deposits from which payments can be made using checks, drafts, payment orders of withdrawal, or telephone transfers drawn against funds on deposit. Demand deposit accounts and negotiable order of withdrawal (NOW) accounts are the two principal types of transaction accounts. Automatic transfer

THE SECONDARY MORTGAGE MARKET

Financial intermediaries routinely assemble pools, or packages, of their mortgage loan assets and, with the assistance from the government and its agencies, sell securities in the market backed by these loan pools. This process, called securitization, has given rise to a large secondary mortgage market in which investors buy and sell mortgage-backed securities collateralized by residential mortgage loans.

Securitization allows initial mortgage lenders, such as banks, savings institutions, or insurance companies, to convert their mortgage assets into cash assets, reduce the risk of default they assume when they hold mortgages, and provide a source of fee income if the initial lender continues to service the mortgages it pools. The government or its agencies guarantee mortgage-backed securities. This feature has enhanced the value of these securitized instruments to investors and has added to their popularity among financial intermediaries.

The government has provided support for the mortgage market since the 1930s. Over the decades federal agencies were established to

- provide liquidity for savings institutions by lending them funds through Federal Home Loan Banks
- promote fixed-rate, monthly payment, fully-amortized residential mortgages and provide insurance to mortgage lenders against default through the Federal Housing Administration (FHA)
- create a secondary market for the buying and selling of mortgages through the Federal National Mortgage Association (Fannie Mae) and Government National Mortgage Association (Ginnie Mae)
- purchase mortgage loans from banks, pool these mortgages, and issue government-guaranteed securities, called mortgage pass-through securities, using these pools as collateral
- guarantee securities issued by banks and other lenders who pool mortgages and issue mortgage-backed securities through the Government National Mortgage Association (Ginnie Mae)

To date, more than one-third of all residential mortgages in the United States have been securitized, including about one-quarter of all conventional mortgages and about 85 percent of all mortgages insured by the FHA or the U.S. Department of Veterans Affairs.

Mortgage pass-through securities are widely purchased by institutional investors and by Fannie Mae and Freddie Mac. (Technically, Fannie Mae, Ginnie Mae, and Freddie Mac are government-sponsored corporations rather than government agencies.) The market for mortgage pass-through securities issued or backed by government-sponsored agencies now exceeds $3 trillion and is the second largest securities market in the United States. The largest securities market is the U.S. Treasury securities market. The development of this market has generated increased mortgage lending from a greater number of financial intermediaries, and has assured a ready supply of funds for residential mortgages.

By selling mortgage loans in the secondary market, banks and other mortgage lenders are able to replenish loan funds for the next loan request. In addition, banks use Fannie Mae underwriting guidelines to make their loans easier to sell in the secondary market. Securitization has also kept mortgage rates in line with market rates and less dependent on the flow of deposits to mortgage lenders.

service (ATS) accounts and credit union share drafts are also checkable deposits. Commercial banks held about $320 billion in non-interest-earning demand deposits and about $140 billion in interest-earning transaction accounts in 2002. Savings institutions held about $111 billion in checkable deposits (see exhibit 4.3).

Depository institutions must maintain reserves against transaction accounts, which are deposits, including interest-earning deposits, on which checks may be drawn. Reserves need not be maintained against other types of accounts.

DEMAND DEPOSIT ACCOUNTS

Demand deposit accounts are checking accounts that allow the holder to withdraw cash on demand and to make payments by writing checks. Since 1933 the federal government has prohibited interest payments on demand deposits. A demand deposit is specifically defined as a deposit payable on demand; that is, a customer may withdraw funds from the account with no advance notice by writing checks or using an automated teller machine.

Most demand deposit balances held in banks are for commercial accounts. Personal checking account balances represent only about 25 percent of total demand deposit balances. However, personal accounts constitute 90 percent of the total number of demand deposit accounts at most banks.

In recent years, with increased competition from interest-bearing transaction accounts, there has been a steady decline in demand deposit balances. Bankers expect little, if any, growth in the number of demand deposit accounts. Nonetheless, although the traditional checking account appears to have little potential for growth, banks continue to be innovative in their demand deposit offerings as a means to entice new customers and sell other bank products.

NOW ACCOUNTS

Negotiable order of withdrawal (NOW) accounts make up the other major category of transaction accounts. NOW accounts are, in essence, transaction accounts that behave like interest-bearing checking accounts. They are interest-earning accounts on which check-like instruments may be drawn. Withdrawals from NOW accounts are made using savings account withdrawal tickets as negotiable instruments that closely resemble checks. Because NOW accounts have the characteristics of savings accounts, the bank can require seven days notice before a withdrawal can be made. However, banks rarely impose this requirement.

NOW accounts may be offered by commercial banks, mutual savings banks, and savings and loan associations, and they may be owned only by individuals, certain nonprofit organizations, and governmental units. For-profit businesses may not own NOW accounts.

TIME AND SAVINGS ACCOUNTS

Besides transaction accounts, the other broad category of deposit accounts consists of various types of time and savings accounts. **Time and savings accounts** are interest-earning deposits that technically cannot be withdrawn on demand. In the past, depositors held their savings funds mainly in passbook savings accounts. Today, in their efforts to compete for depositors' savings, banks and savings institutions offer a broader range of time and savings accounts.

TIME DEPOSITS

A time deposit is defined as any deposit in a bank account that cannot be withdrawn before a specified date or technically without advance notice. Time deposits have a minimum term of seven days. If a time deposit is withdrawn before seven days or before the maturity of the time deposit contract, an interest penalty is charged. The major categories of time deposits are savings accounts, money market deposit accounts, savings certificates, certificates of deposit, and various types of retirement accounts.

SAVINGS ACCOUNTS

Savings deposits can generally be withdrawn without notice and pay interest to the depositor. However, some types of savings accounts limit depositors to no more than six transfers per month, of which no more than three can be by check.

Savings accounts were traditionally the staple deposit of savings institutions. Today, however, funds in these accounts represent only one-third of consumer-oriented time deposits in commercial banks and less than 15 percent of the total deposits of all banks and savings institutions.

Savings accounts were long characterized by the passport-size passbooks that were provided to customers and in which account information was recorded. Most banks and savings institutions have converted their passbook accounts into statement savings accounts. In these accounts, customers receive monthly statements of account activity.

Most passbook savings consumers continue to hold on to their passbooks despite the low rates paid on these accounts. Many consumers like the passbook itself; they like to hold their money and watch it grow. They also like to be able to deposit or withdraw small amounts at will, with no maturity or penalty constraints. Long-standing public familiarity with passbook accounts also may be a factor in their continued popularity.

MONEY MARKET DEPOSIT ACCOUNTS

Money market deposit accounts (MMDAs) are savings deposits on which a limited number of checks can be written each month. In 1982 Congress allowed depository institutions to offer MMDAs so that they could provide an account competitive with money market funds. The new account was not subject to any interest rate ceilings, and holders were restricted to limited check-writing privileges. Unlike money market funds, however, MMDAs were, and are, insured through the FDIC.

An MMDA carries no minimum maturity, but banks may require seven days notice of a withdrawal. Depositors may make up to six transfers per month from the account, three by check and three by preauthorized transfer. Since 1986 money market deposit accounts have not been subject by law to minimum balance requirements. Nevertheless, most banks continue to require a minimum account balance as a matter of management discretion. Minimums range between $500 and $2,500, depending on the market.

Although MMDAs offer limited check-writing privileges, for reserve requirement purposes Congress classified them as savings accounts rather than transaction accounts. Because time and savings deposits are not subject to costly reserve requirements, this classification makes MMDAs more competitive with money market funds, which also have no reserve requirements.

The MMDA became a major deposit category at banks and savings institutions very quickly after it was authorized in 1982. Today it is the largest single deposit category. Contrary to what many bankers had originally expected, however, most MMDA funds were not shifted from the money market funds. Instead, they were redeposited from more traditional and lower-paying demand, time, and savings accounts.

SAVINGS CERTIFICATES

Savings certificates, or certificates of deposit (CDs), are time deposits with fixed maturities and interest rates that are offered in any denominations, primarily to individuals. These certificates are usually nonnegotiable; that is, they cannot be transferred to a third party as payment and they can be redeemed only by the original depositor.

Although savings certificates can be issued in any denomination, most banks require a minimum deposit of $500 to $2,500 for certificates, depending on maturity. Once issued, no funds may be added to or withdrawn from the certificate until it matures. In 2002, banks held more than $620 billion in certificates; savings institutions held about half as much.

Large-denomination CDs

Large-denomination CDs, valued at $100,000 or more, are offered by banks primarily to corporations. Large-denomination CDs have fixed interest rates and are payable at maturity, which can be any date seven days or longer after deposit of the funds. Large-denomination CDs can be issued in non-negotiable bearer form, which makes the CD payable only to the deposit-holder by the issuing bank. However, the most popular CDs among big corporations are negotiable, making them saleable in the secondary market (see exhibit 4.3).

Most of the nation's large banks offer CDs through nationwide brokerage firms as well as through local or regional offices. By using a brokerage firm with an extensive network of nationwide offices, a bank can reach a broader market for its CDs than it could reach on its own. Banks generally have to pay a higher interest rate on their brokered CDs than on those issued locally. But these higher interest rates tend to be less than the rates banks otherwise would have to pay to borrow funds in the nation's money or capital markets. In 2002 banks and savings institutions held more than $800 billion in large-denomination CDs.

Retirement Accounts

Individual retirement accounts (IRAs) are interest-earning accounts that provide individuals with a means to reduce or defer taxes. For self-employed individuals, comparable retirement accounts are Keogh accounts or simplified employee pension (SEP) accounts.

Most banks offer IRA accounts as trust or custodial time accounts. IRAs may carry a fixed or a variable interest rate over the life of the account, with withdrawals not allowed without a 10 percent Internal Revenue Service tax penalty until the depositor reaches age 59½. Individuals not covered by a pension plan can deposit up to $3,000 a year in a tax-deferred IRA account. That is, funds deposited can be subtracted from total income on which taxes are paid. Individuals covered by a pension plan also can open IRA accounts on which interest is not subject to taxation until withdrawal; however the IRA contribution amount cannot be subtracted from their current year's taxes. Beginning in 2002, individuals will be able to deposit increasingly larger annual amounts in IRA accounts, up to a maximum of $5,000 by 2008.

Before 1981 only workers not covered by an employer's pension plan could open IRAs. In 1981 IRAs were made available to all employees as part of broader tax reform measures enacted by Congress. With the liberalization of eligibility rules, IRA deposit growth soared. In 1981 banks, thrifts, brokerage firms, and other financial institutions held about $26 billion in IRA deposits. By 1986, when Congress rescinded the liberalization, more than $350 billion in IRA deposits were being held for 20 million account holders. Commercial banks held about one-quarter of this total.

Since 1987 only workers whose incomes fall below a specified amount have been permitted to deduct IRA deposits from current taxes. Among the factors that influenced Congress in changing IRA rules was a sense that upper-income individuals were using the tax deduction as a shelter and that the Treasury would lose considerable income tax revenue if the deduction were continued.

IRA deposit growth decreased during the 1990s in response to the lack of broad tax deductibility for IRAs, the relatively low interest paid by banks on deposits in the 1990s, and the growing popularity of money market and other mutual funds as preferred retirement assets. In 2002 banks and savings institutions held about $260 billion in IRA and Keogh deposits, the same amount they held in 1996.

SUMMARY

Commercial banks and savings institutions are among the nation's key financial intermediaries. Changes in banking law and regulation have eliminated most of the differences between these institutions and today their business activities and products overlap significantly. At the same time, nondepository financial intermediaries and nonfinancial intermediaries have emerged as sources of competition.

The composition and cost of deposits at bank and savings institutions also have changed significantly. Increasingly, funds have moved from non-interest-bearing demand deposit accounts and low-earning passbook savings accounts into interest-bearing transaction accounts. Competitive relationships among financial intermediaries also have changed as funds have moved from banks to nonbank intermediaries.

The traditional differences between demand deposits and time deposits were modified by changes in banking law and practice during the 1980s. The emergence of interest-earning checkable deposits, such as NOW accounts and MMDAs, and the popularization of IRAs significantly altered the public's savings practices and caused demand deposits to lose much of their appeal.

REVIEW QUESTIONS

1. What are the major differences between commercial banks and savings banks, credit unions, and money market funds?

2. What competitive advantages, if any, do nondepository intermediaries such as Merrill Lynch and General Electric have over commercial banks?
3. What are the major types of time deposits offered by commercial banks?
4. Explain how a money market deposit account operates.
5. Cite three changes in the deposit structure or operations of financial intermediaries that occurred during the 1980s.

ADDITIONAL RESOURCES

American Bankers Association, at *www.aba.com*. Web site of the American Bankers Association; provides current information on bank regulatory compliance issues.

Bankrate.com, at *www.bankrate.com*. Provides data on banks current interest rates offered on deposits and being charged on loans.

"The Changing U.S. Financial System: Some Implications for the Monetary Transmission Mechanism." *The Economic Review,* Federal Reserve Bank of Kansas City, First Quarter 2002. Discusses key developments in the U.S. financial system that have altered the response of interest rates to monetary policy.

The Declining Role of Banking, Federal Reserve Bank of Chicago, 1992, 52 pp. A series of papers on bank structure and competition drawn from the Chicago Federal Reserve Bank's 1992 conference on banking.

Federal Reserve Bulletin, Board of Governors of the Federal Reserve, monthly publication. Provides statistical tables with up-to-date data on banking activity and the performance of various sectors of the economy and articles on selected banking, business, and economic topics.

Instruments of the Money Market, Federal Reserve Bank of Richmond, 1993, 274 pp. Describes the major money market instruments and the institutional arrangements of the markets in which these instruments are traded.

Office of Thrift Supervision (OTS), at *www.ots.treas.gov/*. Web site of the Office of Thrift Supervision; provides current data on savings institutions.

Principles of Banking, 7th ed., by G. Jay Francis and Susan M. Siegel, American Bankers Association, 2001. Provides a basic understanding of banking principles and current issues.

Reference Guide to Regulatory Compliance, by Kathlyn L. Farrell, American Bankers Association, 2002. Provides a detailed outline of the various regulations important to banking by bank functions, including consumer lending, deposit operations, safety and soundness, information reporting, and social responsibility; includes coverage on Regulation D, Reserve Requirements of Depository Institutions, which outlines the legal requirements for demand deposits, transaction accounts, NOW accounts, and time and savings accounts.

EXTENDED STUDY 2: THE FAILURE OF SAVINGS AND LOAN ASSOCIATIONS DURING THE 1980s

The collapse of the savings and loan (S&L) industry had its origins in the deregulation of interest rates that Congress set in motion during the 1980s. Three other contributing factors were

- the increase in deposit insurance coverage from $40,000 to $100,000 per account in 1980
- the low capital requirements and liberal accounting rules accorded S&Ls during the 1980s
- the inability of the Federal Home Loan Bank Board (FHLBB—the agency that regulated S&Ls during the 1980s) to attract and retain enough examiners to monitor and prevent risky and unsound S&L practices

INCREASE IN FDIC INSURANCE COVERAGE

The 1980 increase in FDIC insurance coverage brought large-denomination CDs under deposit insurance for the first time. Owners of these large CDs, typically in amounts of $100,000 or more, could place them in any bank or savings institution, no matter how weak its earnings or how poorly it was managed, without fear of loss.

During the 1980s, many S&Ls relied extensively on brokered CDs to obtain funds when they were nearly insolvent. Working through nationwide brokerage firms, S&Ls offered large CDs to people and business firms in areas of the country that they could not reach on their own.

In some instances, brokerage firms placed the CDs of the S&Ls with groups of individuals, each of whom owned a part of a $100,000 deposit. For such individuals, the joint ownership provided a higher interest return than the return available on smaller savings certificates while providing the same degree of deposit insurance protection. The S&Ls paid high interest rates on these CDs and used the funds to expand unsound lending and investments.

CAPITAL REQUIREMENTS AND ACCOUNTING RULES

A capital requirement specifies how much bank owners' money, as a percentage of the bank's assets, a bank must set aside as a cushion for possible losses the bank may take on loans not repaid or on poor investments. In theory, bank owners who are required to put up a substantial sum of their own funds are more likely to restrain the managers of their banks from making risky or speculative loans and investments. In the case of S&Ls during the 1980s, capital requirements were set at 3 percent, half the requirement for commercial banks at the time.

During the early 1980s, the FHLBB also liberalized accounting rules for S&Ls. The new rules enabled insolvent S&Ls to record the value of their assets, liabilities, and capital in such a way that they appeared to be solvent: the value of assets equaled the value of liabilities plus capital. For example, S&Ls were allowed to mark up capital funds by adding substantial amounts for goodwill, meaning estimates of how much money a potential buyer might pay for the S&L if it were sold.

In 1986 the U.S. General Accounting Office reported to Congress that more than 450 S&Ls were insolvent on the basis of generally accepted accounting principles (GAAP). The S&Ls in question held assets of $113 billion, at the time 11 percent of the total assets of the S&L industry. In 1987 Congress ordered the FHLBB to reinstitute GAAP in evaluating the financial condition of S&Ls. However, the requirement was to be phased in through 1993 in an effort to allow financially troubled S&Ls to meet the stricter solvency requirements. Therefore, reinstituting GAAP had no practical impact on the balance sheets of S&Ls during the 1980s.

S&L EXAMINERS

The FHLBB had too few examiners in the early 1980s to monitor and prevent risky and unsound S&L practices. Indeed, the number of field examiners employed by the FHLBB declined in every year from 1981 to 1984. The FHLBB lost examiners because its pay scale, unlike those of other examining agencies, was subject to federal civil service limitations. In 1985 these limitations were removed and the salaries of S&L examiners were raised to levels comparable to those of bank examiners. The number of S&L examiners grew sharply after 1984, from about 1,300 to 3,400 by 1989. However, by the late 1980s the problems of S&Ls could no longer be contained through the examinations process.

CLOSING FAILING S&Ls

In 1989 Congress enacted legislation that provided a way to systematically close hundreds of insolvent S&Ls while protecting the government's deposit insurance program. The Financial Institutions Reform, Recovery and Enforcement Act (FIRREA) also imposed new stringent capital requirements on S&Ls and restricted some of their activities.

FIRREA established the Resolution Trust Corporation (RTC) to manage the assets of insolvent S&Ls. Its initial holdings of failed S&L assets exceeded $100 billion, but by the early 1990s this total swelled to about $400 billion. Between 1989 and 1995, when the RTC was disbanded, Congress gave the RTC nearly $100 billion to make up the difference between revenue received from liquidating S&L assets and funds paid out to insured depositors.

RESTRICTING RISKY S&L ACTIVITIES

FIRREA limited the activities and investments permissible for S&Ls. They were required to hold a higher percentage of their assets in qualified thrift investments, typically housing-related loans and securities. The list of loans and securities considered to be qualified also was narrowed substantially. Undercapitalized S&Ls were prohibited from soliciting brokered deposits and all savings institutions were prohibited from investing in real estate or in junk bonds (bonds that carry credit ratings below those commonly required for bonds that are purchased for investment). S&Ls also were made subject to legal limits on the amount of loans they could make to any one borrower.

NEW CAPITAL REQUIREMENTS

To bolster the capacity of S&Ls to suffer losses without becoming insolvent, a situation that would create a potential drain on federal deposit insurance fund reserves, S&Ls were made subject to

- a minimum capital requirement of 3 percent
- a requirement that the S&L maintain tangible capital in an amount equal to no less than 1.5 percent of assets
- a minimum risk-based capital requirement

Under the new minimum capital requirement, an S&L was required to maintain capital, or owners' equity, equal to no less than 3 percent of its total assets. Thrifts were prohibited from including most types of goodwill in their measure of capital. (Goodwill is the difference between the worth of a company's assets and the market value of the company itself. In essence, goodwill reflects the value of a company's name, reputation, and customer base.)

Tangible capital excludes the value of supervisory goodwill. Supervisory goodwill is the estimated value above an S&L's net worth that a potential buyer might be willing to pay for, presumably to obtain the S&L's deposit insurance coverage. The tangible capital requirement effectively put a minimum on the amount of real owners' equity that an S&L would have to hold.

Under the minimum risk-based capital requirement, numerical weights (multiples) were applied to S&L assets according to the riskiness of the assets. The sum of these weighted assets determined the risk-adjusted asset base against which a minimum amount of capital was required to be held.

These capital requirements helped shrink the S&L industry during the 1990s. The exclusion of goodwill from capital and the risk-based capital requirements caused some solvent S&Ls to close because they could not raise additional capital. Many other S&Ls were able to raise necessary capital only by selling off assets or by sharply curtailing their growth.

EXTENDED STUDY 3: BANK HOLDING COMPANY ACTIVITIES

Bank holding companies were brought under federal regulation in 1956 when Congress applied federal antitrust laws to the activities of multibank holding companies and gave the Federal Reserve the power to approve or deny applications from multibank holding companies wanting to acquire additional banks or engage in new business activities. The Bank Holding Company Act of 1956 also limited the nonbanking activities of multibank holding companies to those "closely and properly related to banking." In 1970 Congress amended the Bank Holding Company Act to cover one-bank holding companies as well.

If the Federal Reserve deems that a proposed activity is closely related to banking it must then determine whether the proposed activity is properly related to banking by evaluating the public benefits and costs likely to be associated with the activity. If the Federal Reserve concludes that the holding company's activity would lead to substantial market concentration, decreased or unfair competition, conflicts of interest, or unsound banking practices, it denies the request.

To approve an activity, the Federal Reserve must be convinced that the activity meets a public need or provides a social benefit. In effect the holding company must show how its provision of the new service would generate benefits to the public, such as greater convenience, greater service selection, lower price, or greater efficiency.

ACTIVITIES OF BANK HOLDING COMPANIES

Since 1956 the Federal Reserve has approved a broad range of activities for bank holding companies (BHCs), allowing them to

- issue credit cards
- provide trust services

- sell general and portfolio investment advice, general economic information, and bookkeeping and data processing services
- provide courier services
- provide management consulting services
- issue traveler's checks and money orders
- deal in bankers' acceptances and broker gold bullion
- provide services associated with mortgage banking, finance companies, factoring companies, trust companies, collection agencies, and credit bureaus
- service loans
- act as insurance agents or brokers for credit extensions and underwriting credit-related life, accident, and health insurance
- lease personal and real property and providing land escrow services
- sponsor, organize, or control a closed-end investment company
- act as a general insurance agent in towns with populations less than 5,000
- provide investment services that promote the welfare of the community
- provide securities brokerage services
- sell property insurance of $10,000 or less through finance company subsidiaries
- provide advisory services for those seeking to buy commodities or foreign exchange
- act as futures commission merchants
- sell financial counseling, tax planning, and tax preparation services to consumers
- underwrite and deal in revenue bonds, commercial paper, mortgage-backed securities, and consumer-related receivables
- underwrite and deal in corporate bonds and corporate stock, provided the revenue from these activities does not exceed 25 percent of the subsidiary's total revenue
- provide financial advisory services to institutions and high-net-worth individuals
- offer combined investment advisory and securities brokerage services

5

THE BANK AS A BUSINESS FIRM

LEARNING OBJECTIVES

After studying this chapter, you should be able to

- name the principal earning assets and key liabilities on the bank balance sheet
- explain the key characteristics that differentiate the major types of loans banks make
- differentiate among U.S. government securities, federal agency securities, and municipal obligations
- describe the most important sources of bank income and expense
- explain how various funds management strategies, such as asset allocation, liability management, and spread management, are used
- define the key terms listed in this chapter

KEY TERMS

balance sheet
borrowed funds
capital account
capital adequacy standards
compensating balances
derivatives
earning assets
federal funds
income statement

liquidity
loan commitment fee
loan loss reserve account
loan participation
return on assets
return on equity
sweep accounts
term federal funds

INTRODUCTION

At the beginning of the twentieth century, commercial banks primarily focused on meeting the credit needs of businesses. They made short-term loans to businesses to finance traded goods, to manufacturers to buy raw materials, and to merchants to carry inventories.

Today the business of most banks includes originating short- and long-term business and consumer loans; residential and commercial mortgages; and investing in federal, state, and local government securities. Many banks sell a variety of financial services to customers, ranging from overnight investment of account balances for corporations to sales of mutual funds to consumers.

One important way of learning about a business is to examine its balance sheet. A balance sheet is a statement of what the company owns and what it owes. As such, it provides a snapshot of the company's financial condition at a specific time. This chapter examines the balance sheet of the banking system, particularly its earning assets: loans, investments, and other interest- or dividend-bearing assets. It also analyzes the banking system's income statement to learn more about various income and expense items.

The chapter also explores the principles and practices of asset/liability management. Typically, banks are corporations owned by stockholders interested in earning dividends. As such, profitability is clearly a major concern of bank management. Bank earnings are determined by economic forces and management proficiency in continually adjusting the bank's sources and uses of funds. However, banks have adopted strategies to supplement their management of sources and uses of funds, including the securitization of assets and the use of derivatives, specialized financial investments that hedge against risk. Banks also employ these strategies to generate additional revenues.

BALANCE SHEET ANALYSIS

A **balance sheet** is a statement of assets, liabilities, and owner's equity showing a company's financial condition at a specific time. It lists the company's assets on one side and its liabilities and net worth, or capital, on the other. As its name suggests, both sides must balance. The balance sheet is known also as a statement of condition. Exhibit 5.1 shows a balance sheet for the U.S. commercial banking system in 2001. The data in the balance sheet is based on the total amounts of assets, liabilities, and capital of 8,400 commercial banks. However, rather than showing total dollar amounts, each asset account is shown as a percentage of total assets and each liability account is shown as a percentage of total liabilities plus net worth. In this way, the balance sheet provides an industry norm against which individual bank comparisons can be made. This system-wide balance sheet also suggests the relative importance of various types of bank assets and liabilities.

Bank assets are listed on a balance sheet in descending order from the most liquid assets, such as cash, to the least liquid assets, such as the bank's building and equipment. Bank liabilities also are listed on a balance sheet in descending order of liquidity. By examining the various items found on the balance sheet of a typical bank, we gain insight into the basic business of banking. We'll first look at bank assets and then at bank liabilities.

CASH ASSETS

A bank's cash assets provide it with primary liquidity. **Liquidity** encompasses immediate available funds on which banks can draw, such as funds to honor depositors' demands for coin, currency, or to honor requests for payment by other banks in the check collection process. A bank's cash assets consist of cash held in its vault and at tellers' stations, its reserve balance at the district

Exhibit 5.1
Balance Sheet for U.S. Commercial Banks, 2001 (in aggregate percentages)

Assets			Liabilities and Capital	
Cash assets (includes interest bearing balances)		7%	Transaction deposits (demand deposits and interest bearing checking accounts)	11%
Federal funds sold and securities purchased under repurchase agreements		4%	Savings deposits (includes MMDAs)	21%
Securities (to be held to maturity)		20%		
U.S. Treasuries	10%		Large-denomination time deposits (CDs)	17%
Municipals	10%		Small-denomination time deposits (savings certificates)	13%
Mortgage-backed (issued by federal agencies)	65%			
Other securities	15%			
Securities (available for immediate sale or for trading purposes)		3%	Eurodollar borrowings	10%
Loans		60%	Federal funds purchased and securities sold under repurchase agreements	8%
Business	30%			
Consumer	15%			
Real Estate	40%			
Other	15%		Other liabilities	11%
Other assets		6%		
			Capital account	9%
Total		100%	Total	100%

Note: Percentages are based on average total assets/total liabilities and capital of $6,200 billion in 2001.
Source: Federal Reserve Bulletin, February 2002.

Federal Reserve Bank, deposits with correspondent banks, and cash items in the process of collection. These assets generally do not earn an interest or investment return for the bank, but they may entitle it to some services. For example, many small banks pay for the check clearing services provided by their correspondent banks by maintaining an agreed-upon daily compensating deposit balance with their correspondents. On average, banks hold about 7 percent of their assets as cash assets.

FEDERAL FUNDS SOLD

Banks frequently buy and sell excess reserve balances, called **federal funds,** for one-day

use by other banks. Money market banks routinely use federal funds as a mechanism for adjusting their daily reserve positions. The banks operate in this fashion so they neither hold excess reserves, which represent a lost opportunity to earn a return, nor incur costly reserve deficiencies. Small community-based banks that may have excess reserves but no market for overnight loans typically sell their reserves to larger money market or regional banks. Banks throughout the country use Fedwire, the Federal Reserve's funds transfer network, to make instantaneous transfers of federal funds.

Many banks also sell excess reserves by engaging in repurchase agreements. Under these agreements, they purchase securities from other banks with an agreement to sell the securities back in a day or two. The purchase results in a transfer or loan of reserve balances to the buying bank; the subsequent repurchase results in a payback of the borrowed funds. In effect, securities purchased or sold by banks under repurchase agreements are akin to collateralized loans of reserve balances and are thus grouped with federal funds transactions on the balance sheet.

SECURITIES

The second major category of assets on a bank's balance sheet, making up about 20 percent of the banking system's total assets, is the bank's securities investment portfolio. A bank's securities portfolio consists primarily of debt obligations of the U.S. Treasury, state and local governments (called municipals), and agencies of the federal government. These assets constitute a secondary source of liquidity for banks after cash assets. Securities are considered secondary reserves because they are not as liquid as primary reserves like cash, but they are more readily salable than loans.

Banks can carry the value of securities being held to maturity at cost rather than at market value. Securities available for sale and securities held for trading or speculative purposes must be carried at market value. Differences between cost and market value are caused by changes in interest rates. If interest rates rise, securities prices fall and banks face capital losses if they sell securities. If interest rates fall, securities prices rise and banks generate capital gains when they sell securities. By requiring banks to record the current market value of securities available for sale, the balance sheet provides a more accurate reading of a bank's secondary liquidity and the earnings potential of the bank's portfolio. Banks that carry a portion of their securities portfolio at market value can elect to sell this portion at any time they want or need to do so.

Securities investments allow banks to diversify the risks they take in lending funds.

Banks also can meet pledging requirements against trust operations, and they serve as collateral for government deposits. In addition, securities allow banks to promote stronger account and deposit relationships by purchasing local governments' newly issued securities. For all of these reasons, many banks traditionally viewed their investment portfolios as earning assets not subject to complete management control. Today, however, banks increasingly manage investments as a profit-making activity, just as they do lending activities.

U.S. TREASURY SECURITIES

U.S. Treasury securities are direct obligations of the federal government used to meet government expenditures not covered by tax revenue. These debt instruments consist of Treasury bills, notes, and bonds. Treasury bills, or T-bills, are the shortest-term debt obligation of the U.S. government, with original maturities of less than one year. Treasury notes and bonds are longer-term debt obligations, with original maturities of 1 year to 10 years for notes and greater than 10 years for bonds.

U.S. Treasury securities offer banks an investment free of credit risk (the risk of default); a large, accessible secondary market; and income exempt from state and local taxes. For this reason, banks use Treasury securities, primarily T-bills, for major short-term investments and as their backup source of liquidity for meeting seasonal demands for funds and unexpected drains of primary liquidity.

Treasury securities are held in book-entry form at Federal Reserve banks. In this form, they can be transferred instantaneously over Fedwire to buyers throughout the country. The Federal Reserve also buys and sells Treasury securities, primarily T-bills, in implementing monetary policy through open-market operations. The government securities market has so many potential buyers and sellers that most banks can easily buy or sell Treasury bills easily and quickly.

MUNICIPAL OBLIGATIONS

Municipal obligations are securities issued by state and local governments. They consist of short-term tax anticipation notes and tax warrants and long-term bonds issued by states, cities, and counties. Short-term municipal obligations generally come due in one year or less; longer-term obligations, in one year or more.

Many of the nation's 80,000 state and local governments finance short-term revenue needs by selling tax anticipation notes that mature within one year. The notes may be issued not only by the governments themselves, but also by various state and local agencies, including local housing authorities, school districts, and drainage and sewer authorities. As their name suggests, the notes are issued in anticipation of taxes, other revenues, or the proceeds from the sale of long-term bonds pledged to retire the notes.

Most banks purchase the tax warrants and notes of their local municipality directly from the municipality on a negotiated basis. Large regional and money center banks often buy state and local obligations through competitive bidding. Bond issuance requires competitive bidding. Because income earned on all state and local obligations is exempt from federal income tax, municipal bonds pay lower interest returns than do other investment instruments. Commercial banks are able to reduce their effective tax rates by investing in municipal securities. Today these investments account for 10 percent of the banking system's securities portfolio (see exhibit 5.1).

FEDERAL AGENCY SECURITIES

U.S. government-owned or government-sponsored corporations and agencies issue federal agency securities. Agencies that issue these debt instruments include the

- Federal Home Loan Mortgage Corporation (FHLMC)
- Federal National Mortgage Association (FNMA, or Fannie Mae)
- Federal Housing Administration (FHA)
- Tennessee Valley Authority (TVA)
- Government National Mortgage Association (GNMA, or Ginnie Mae)

Banks hold certificates that represent participation in a portfolio of loans held by the agencies; however, these certificates are classified as investments rather than as loans.

Most federal agencies provide support to the housing industry by purchasing existing mortgages from banks and thrifts to replenish the supply of credit available to potential homebuyers. The obligations issued by these agencies are backed by the mortgages that they have acquired. These obligations are commonly known as mortgage-backed securities.

LOANS

Economists see bank lending as a means of creating money that profoundly affects the nation's economic well-being. Bankers see lending as the basic business of banking. Banks held about $3.8 trillion in loan assets in 2001, more than 60 percent of their total assets. Bank loans vary widely in type of borrower, loan size, length of maturity, use of borrowed funds, repayment schedule, and degree of risk. Most banks maintain a diversified loan portfolio that encompasses business and consumer loans and mortgages.

In making loans, banks do not operate on a first-come, first-served basis. They also do not wait for new deposits in order to make a single loan equal to their excess reserves. Rather, banks lend funds in accordance with predetermined loan policies designed to maximize their return on loan assets while minimizing their exposure to risk.

An examination of the major types of bank loans, including business, real estate, consumer, and other loans, illustrates both the diversity of bank lending and some of the factors that affect this basic business of banking.

BUSINESS LOANS

Loans to businesses have traditionally been the single largest loan category on the books of most commercial banks. Today, however, they constitute about 30 percent of all loans of a commercial bank. This small proportion largely reflects changing business borrowing practices.

A business loan is any loan made to an individual, partnership, or corporation other than a financial institution or a farmer for business or professional purposes. These loans can be single-payment or installment loans and either secured by collateral or unsecured. Most business loans made by banks are short-term loans, typically with a maturity of one month to one year.

Business loans usually carry low processing costs in relation to the generally large size of these loans and their relatively low risk. The loss incidence of business loans is low compared with losses incurred in other loan categories. In most states, business loans are not subject to usury limits (maximum interest rates that lenders can charge borrowers), and bank management has considerable flexibility in pricing these loans. Because of strong competition for corporate customers, business loans are some of the lowest-yielding bank loans. To increase the profitability of these loans, many banks charge loan commitment fees or require compensating balances.

LOAN COMMITMENT FEES

A bank will levy a **loan commitment fee** on a corporate borrower in exchange for preauthorizing a loan, usually at a stated interest rate. The loan itself may be made weeks or even months in the future. During the 1980s and 1990s, banks increasingly relied on loan commitment fees to increase

income on business loans. These fees eventually became a significant component of many banks' noninterest earnings.

Loan commitments, however, reduce a bank's flexibility in managing its loan portfolio. A bank can increase or decrease the dollar amount of the loans it makes by changing the interest rates it charges on loans and the noninterest terms it imposes on credit lines. Loan commitments may lock the bank into future loan expansion. When making loan commitments to corporate customers, banks may not know exactly how much the corporation will be borrowing or exactly when the funds will be borrowed. Moreover, repayments of short-term business loans often are tied to the corporation's cash flow, which may vary seasonally. Most banks carefully monitor the dollar amounts of their loan commitments. However, a bank that relies heavily on loan commitment fees can never be sure that on any given day it will have sufficient reserves to honor all the commitments that could be exercised on that day. If banks have to borrow reserves to honor their prepaid commitments, they may find themselves paying more for funds than they are charging for the prearranged loan.

COMPENSATING BALANCES

A bank can increase the profitability of its business loans by requiring **compensating balances.** Under this arrangement, borrowers are required by the loan agreement to maintain deposit balances equal to a fixed percentage of the loan value. Banks require either a minimum daily balance or an average daily balance during the term of the loan.

The additional income a bank generates by investing compensating balances increases the bank's return on the loan. Compensating balances also add protection because the bank has priority over all other creditors with the balances on deposit. If the borrower defaults on the loan, the bank can use any existing deposit balance to offset the outstanding loan balance.

Today most banks no longer follow the practice of requiring compensating balances. Since the 1990s, banks and corporate borrowers have increasingly opted for explicit fee charges to cover loan costs rather than rely on compensating balances. Corporations often find it difficult to maintain compensating balances because they must meet daily cash flow requirements.

CONSUMER LOANS

A consumer loan is a loan made to an individual for a personal expenditure other than the purchase of real estate or securities. Today consumer loans constitute about 15 percent of commercial banks' loan assets. Most consumer loans are short- to medium-term, three- to five-year installment loans that require partial repayments at predetermined time intervals—for example, monthly payments. Because repayment of principal and interest is typically made on a scheduled basis, most consumer loans generate a predictable cash flow return to the lending bank.

A considerable portion of bank consumer lending involves credit extended on bank credit cards. Processing costs for credit card loans tend to be high in relation to their small size. Consumer loans, particularly credit card loans, also carry relatively greater credit risk than do other loans; they are subject to a higher incidence of loan default and fraud losses than are other loans.

REAL ESTATE LOANS

Loans secured by a mortgage, a deed of trust, or some other recorded lien on real estate, in which the bank can take title to the property if the terms of the loan are not met, are classified as real estate loans. Like consumer loans, real estate loans generate a predictable cash flow to lending banks, but earnings yields on real estate loans are typically lower than yields on most other loans. In the past, real estate loans were the lowest-risk loans a bank could make because

they were fully collateralized by property that appreciated while the principal was repaid, thus reducing the bank's credit risk exposure. During the 1980s, however, banks' experience with commercial real estate loans cast doubts on the validity of this longstanding banking premise. Many banks took losses on commercial real estate loans when borrowers defaulted and banks found that the market values of properties collateralizing the loans were less than the amount of the outstanding loans. Nonetheless, most banks fared well during the 1980s and 1990s, on residential mortgages.

OTHER LOANS

Depending on a bank's location and its size, other types of loans may play a significant part in a bank's business. These loans include

- agricultural loans
- loans to securities brokers and dealers
- loans to individuals for purchasing stocks and bonds
- loan participations

For many rural banks in the Midwest and the South, agricultural loans provide a significant source of income. Any loan made to a farmer or rancher for any purpose associated with operating a farm or ranch is considered an agricultural loan.

For large banks in the nation's major cities, loans to securities brokers and dealers and to other financial institutions are common. These loans are generally made to enable brokers and dealers to buy securities for their own accounts or for their customers. High-grade securities typically secure these very short-term loans, which bear relatively low interest rates.

Some banks make loans to enable individuals to purchase stocks and bonds. Banks that make loans of this type must obtain a statement from borrowers about the purpose of the loan proceeds, to determine whether the loan is subject to the Federal Reserve's Regulation U. This regulation limits the amount of credit a bank can extend to an individual to purchase corporate stock when the stock serves as collateral for the loan.

A **loan participation** is the sharing of a loan by two or more banks. Banks often participate in loans too large for them to assume legally on their own. By spreading the loan among several banks, each bank commits less of its reserves and reduces its own risk. Correspondent banks participate in large business loans as part of their respondent relationships and to diversify their own portfolios.

OTHER ASSETS

The last category of assets on the banking system's balance sheet is other assets. These assets include

- small holdings of non-government-related debt obligations, primarily corporate bonds and stock
- Federal Reserve bank stock for bank members of the Federal Reserve
- fixed assets, such as banks' buildings and equipment
- accrued income receivable, which may include interest earned but not yet collected on loans and investments
- assets repossessed, including collateral taken from borrowers who have defaulted on loans

Banks are not permitted to own corporate stock and most corporate bonds for their own accounts. However, banks are permitted by law to hold some corporate obligations. Banks also may legally own stocks and bonds for a limited period of time when the stocks and bonds are acquired as a result of a defaulted loan secured by stocks and bonds. Some banks also have minor investments in foreign securities.

Federal Reserve member banks must purchase stock in their district Federal Reserve bank in an amount equal to 3 percent of their own capital and surplus,

with an additional 3 percent subject to call by the Federal Reserve. Banks that hold Federal Reserve bank stock receive a statutory 6 percent annual dividend on these securities.

LIABILITIES AND CAPITAL

The other side of the banking system's balance sheet is the liabilities and capital side (see exhibit 5.1). We see that deposits make up about 60 percent of banks' liabilities. These liabilities include transaction deposits, time and savings deposits, borrowed funds, and other liabilities, including the capital account.

TRANSACTION DEPOSITS

The first category of deposits on the banking system's balance sheet is transaction deposits. This category includes demand deposits, the traditional non-interest earning transaction deposits of banks, and interest-earning checkable deposits such as NOW accounts. Together these deposits account for about 11 percent of banks' liabilities.

Demand deposits long have been the most stable and least expensive source of bank funds. They are stable because checking account holders typically do not switch accounts from one bank to another. They are inexpensive because, since the 1933 Glass-Steagall Act, banks have not been allowed to pay interest on demand deposit accounts. For these reasons, bankers refer to checking account deposits as relationship deposits. Funds flow to a bank because a customer wants a checking account to make payments and chooses to maintain a relationship with that bank, often because the bank is conveniently located.

During the 1980s, demand deposit totals at banks declined as consumers began to switch funds from non-interest-earning demand accounts into interest-earning checkable accounts. The 1990s saw demand deposits decline further when banks began offering **sweep accounts** to corporate customers. These accounts sweep funds out of transaction accounts into general ledger accounts.

Banks must hold reserves against funds in a transaction account, but need not hold reserves against funds in a general ledger account. Sweeping funds into general ledger accounts reduces the amount of required reserves a bank needs, freeing funds for loans or investments in interest-earning assets and thereby increasing bank profits.

TIME AND SAVINGS DEPOSITS

A bank's balance sheet usually groups major types of time and savings deposits. These deposits constitute half of the banking system's total liabilities and include

- statement savings or passbook savings accounts
- money market deposit accounts (MMDAs)
- savings certificates
- large-denomination certificates of deposit
- retirement accounts, including individual retirement accounts (IRAs)

Like demand deposits, consumer time and savings deposits at commercial banks have traditionally been viewed as relationship deposits; that is, they were seen as a relatively stable source of bank funds. That stability, however, has come into question in recent years.

During the 1980s, most banks were forced to compete aggressively with mutual funds for consumers' savings. Consumers responded to the competition with remarkable sensitivity to interest rate differences and changing rates of return. They demonstrated a willingness to transfer savings funds out of banks into higher-paying Treasury bills and money market funds. When market conditions changed, as they did in the early 2000s, consumers also demonstrated a willingness to transfer monies from mutual funds back into deposit accounts at banks.

BORROWED FUNDS

Another category of liabilities is **borrowed funds,** which include Eurodollar borrowings, federal funds purchased, and securities sold under repurchase agreements. Borrowed funds are major sources of nondeposit liabilities and they constituted about 18 percent of the banking system's total liabilities in 2001 (see exhibit 5.1).

Large banks with overseas offices typically borrow dollar-denominated funds from these offices for a day or two at a time to add to their reserves. These very short-term borrowings are called Eurodollar borrowings. Additionally, most super-regional and many other regional banks throughout the country will operate a branch in the Cayman Islands or the Bahamas. The bank pays a fee to the foreign government to operate the branch although the bank does not set up a brick-and-mortar, physical branch. The branch accepts overnight euro time deposits or term euro time deposits from domestic U.S. customers as well as some foreign customers or providers of funds. The branch then sends these deposits back to the U.S. bank's main banking office.

Most banks buy federal funds from one another to meet reserve requirements, honor loan commitments, or offset unexpected reserve drains from large cash or deposit withdrawals. Immediately available funds obtained for more than one day are referred to as **term federal funds**. Repurchase agreements allow banks to sell securities, thereby obtaining funds, and then repurchase them a day or two later, thus paying back the funds.

OTHER LIABILITIES

Bank liabilities other than deposits and borrowed funds include various payables and contingency reserves. Payables are funds set aside to pay taxes, interest on deposits, and other expenses, such as salaries and dividends. Banks also carry as liabilities unearned loan income; that is, any prepaid interest received on loans. Because unearned income also is routinely recorded on a bank's balance sheet in each loan category, the separate unearned income posting must be subtracted from the bank's total loans to obtain a net measure of the institution's loan portfolio.

CAPITAL ACCOUNT

The last item on a bank's balance sheet is its capital account (see exhibit 5.1). The **capital account** specifically represents a bank's liabilities to its owners. It is the net worth, or owner's equity amount, consisting of stock issued by the bank, surplus (or capital funds not allocated), and undistributed profits. Capital provides a protective cushion against bad loans and bad investments. Thus, a bank with adequate capital is capable of handling riskier transactions than a bank with inadequate capital. The more capital a bank has, the greater the protection the bank provides its stockholders and creditors.

Like any other business, a bank must earn an adequate return on its capital in order to encourage future stockholder investment. Banks, however, typically have less capital in relation to assets than most other businesses. In 2001 the capital of all U.S. banks totaled about 9 percent of the banking system's total assets. However, the amount of capital held by banks varies by size, with smaller banks typically holding more capital as a percentage of assets than larger banks.

To obtain additional capital, many banks issue subordinated capital notes and debentures. A debenture is a type of debt instrument that is considered capital. By relying on debt capital, the issuing bank avoids diluting its earnings or management's current control over the bank. Banks also can deduct interest paid on capital notes and debentures from pre-tax earnings, which provides a considerable tax advantage. In contrast, dividends on preferred and common stock are paid from after-tax earnings.

INCOME STATEMENT ANALYSIS

Unlike a balance sheet, which tallies a bank's assets and liabilities at a particular point in time, an **income statement** shows a bank's income, expenses, and profit or loss over a period of time, usually a quarter or a year. An analysis of a bank's income statement

---

LOAN LOSS RESERVES

Banks are required to take funds from retained earnings and set them aside to cover expected but undetermined losses from borrowers likely to default on their loans. These funds are put into a separate **loan loss reserve account** and are counted as part of a bank's capital. If a borrower actually defaults and the bank has to write the loan off its balance sheet, the bank reduces the value of its loan assets by the amount of the loan and reduces the value of its loan loss reserves by an equivalent amount. Thus, loan losses erode a bank's capital. Unexpected loan losses can dramatically reduce capital. To reduce the risk of this happening, the bank regulatory agencies require banks to set aside funds for possible loan losses, and state and federal bank examiners routinely review each bank's loss reserves for each outstanding loan. If examiners consider a loan uncollectible, the examiners can require the bank to write off the loan, charging it off to the loan loss reserve.

Banks routinely evaluate their loans and loan loss reserves, setting aside a portion of operating profits each month in anticipation of actual charge-offs. Some banks write off bad debts before actual default because it is easier to take losses when earnings are strong than waiting until default, when earnings may be weak.

can provide insight into how well a bank is performing as a business firm. Exhibit 5.2 on the following page is an income statement for the banking system, showing the various sources of bank earnings and expenses.

NET INTEREST INCOME

Net interest income is a bank's interest income minus its interest expense. For the banking system as a whole, net interest income in 2001 was $218 billion ($408 billion in gross interest income minus $190 billion in interest expense (see exhibit 5.2).

Interest income is largely attributable to a bank's **earning assets**; that is, its loans and investments, whereas interest expense is primarily attributable to its interest-bearing liabilities, essentially money market deposit accounts and certificates of deposit. A bank's net interest income reflects both the size of

Exhibit 5.2
Income Statement for U.S. Banks, 2001 (in billions)

Item		Amount
Interest income		
Interest on loans		$314.8
Interest on securities		63.7
Interest on deposits with other banks and federal funds sold		29.8
	Total	408.3
Interest expense		
Interest on deposits		133.3
Interest on federal funds purchased and on other borrowings		19.7
Interest on subordinated debt		37.2
	Total	190.2
Net interest income		218.1
Noninterest income		
Service charges on deposits		27.1
Income from trust activities		22.0
Income from trading securities and foreign exchange		12.6
Other operating income		98.9
Noninterest expenses		
Salaries and benefits		94.7
Occupancy expenses		28.1
Other operating expenses		104.2
Capital gains (losses) on securities portfolio		4.6
Loan loss provisions		43.3
Taxes		37.7
Net income		75.3

Source: Federal Reserve *Bulletin,* June 2002.

the bank's earning assets and the bank's interest rate spread. A bank's interest rate spread, or net interest margin, can be calculated by taking the bank's net interest income as a percentage of its earning assets.

NONINTEREST INCOME

A bank's noninterest income is typically smaller than its interest income. For the nation's largest banks, however, about half of their income now comes from noninterest sources. Traditional sources of noninterest income are service charges on demand deposit accounts, charges for cash management services for customers, income from trust activities, and profits from trading securities and foreign exchange. In recent years, other operating income has been a major source (see exhibit 5.2). Other operating income consists largely of fees, including

- fees for loan commitments and standby letters of credit

- merchant credit card fees
- annual credit card fees paid by cardholders
- fees from servicing and refinancing mortgages
- fees from the sale and servicing of mutual funds
- automated teller machine (ATM) charges
- income from providing lock box (check collection) services to utility companies

NONINTEREST EXPENSES

Banks categorize noninterest expenses separately from interest expenses. Noninterest expenses include salaries, employee benefits, and other personnel expenses; occupancy and equipment expenses; and other operating expenses.

During the 1990s and early 2000s, banks succeeded in holding down the growth of their personnel and occupancy expenses but were less successful in reining in the growth of other operation expenses. Many banks reduced employee fringe benefits and changed their health insurance programs to require employees to pay a larger share of the costs of medical insurance coverage. The nation's larger banks also reduced their employment of back office personnel, consolidating operating departments and, in many instances, outsourcing operational activities. Banks were able to hold down occupancy costs, despite an increase in branch offices in the 1990s, by closing high-cost branches and opening less costly ones, particularly in supermarkets.

Other operating expenses consist largely of fees that banks pay, including

- fees paid to other companies for performing outsourced services
- fees paid to management consultants and to information technology consultants
- merger-related restructuring charges

These expenses reflect banks' changing business strategies and have grown more rapidly than other noninterest expenses.

NET INCOME

Net income is the bottom line of any income statement. Essentially it shows a bank's profit. Exhibit 5.2 shows that after adding capital gains for securities sold, but subtracting loan loss provisions and taxes paid, America's banks made more than $75 billion in profit in 2001.

PROFITABILITY AND OTHER KEY PERFORMANCE MEASURES

Bank profitability is generally measured by a bank's return on assets and return on equity. **Return on assets** (ROA) is a measure of net income as a percentage of total average assets. It gauges how profitably management is using the bank's assets. Expressed as an equation, it is

$$\text{ROA} = \frac{\text{net income}}{\text{total average assets}}.$$

Return on equity (ROE) is a measure of net income as a percent of average equity. It indicates to bank analysts and bank stockholders how much the bank is earning on the book value of stockholders' investments in the bank. In other words, ROE shows the efficiency of capital investment. Expressed as an equation, it is

$$\text{ROE} = \frac{\text{net income}}{\text{equity capital}}.$$

Bank analysts consider a 1 percent ROA and a 15 percent ROE to be the standards for good bank profitability performance. Profitability for banks during the 1990s was good (see exhibit 5.3 on the next page). In assessing a bank's performance, analysts and bankers generally rely on peer group comparison of ROA and ROE as well as other key performance measures. Some of these other measures are

- interest rate spread, also called net interest margin
- rate of return on securities and loans
- capital account as a percent of total assets
- time and savings deposits as a percent of total deposits
- loan delinquencies and loan charge-offs
- earnings per share

In making a peer group comparison, performance measures for a bank are compared with the averages for banks of like asset size to assess relative performance. This analysis yields more meaningful information than does a comparison of one bank with the banking system as a whole. Business markets and competitive forces differ too significantly for banks of widely disparate size to make relevant comparisons. For example, comparing the performance of a community-based bank with less than $25 million in assets against the performance of a money center bank with $1 billion in assets and several foreign branches would not be meaningful.

Income statement analysis is a useful tool for assessing bank performance. But banking is a management-intensive industry. The strength of management determines long-term bank performance, not operating ratios. Analysts usually supplement statistical comparisons with qualitative assessments of bank management before making judgments concerning a bank's asset/liability management strategy or financial condition. These assessments often are made by reviewing a bank's annual report to gain insights to bank management's plans, objectives, and business expectations.

ASSET/LIABILITY MANAGEMENT

Management's proficiency in continually adjusting the bank's assets and liabilities, its sources and uses of funds, determines bank earnings.

Until the 1960s, funds management was largely passive. Bankers focused primarily on managing the banks' earning assets. They did this by taking in additional deposits, maintaining substantial primary and secondary reserve assets, and using any excess funds available for business loans.

During the 1970s, managing bank funds was revolutionized when bankers began focusing on liabilities, meeting demands for new loans by buying or borrowing needed funds. This approach, called liability management, changed again in the 1980s. Reserve requirements were restructured and simplified early in the decade, and interest rate ceilings on time and savings deposits were eliminated by 1986. At the same time, interest-bearing transaction accounts significantly altered the public's deposit

Exhibit 5.3 Selected Performance Measures for U.S. Banks						
Profitability	1990	1992	1994	1996	1998	2000
ROE	7.64	13.24	14.90	14.43	13.95	14.27
ROA	0.49	0.95	1.17	1.20	1.20	1.21
Other measures						
Net interest margin	3.99	4.42	4.37	4.26	4.07	4.00
Capital/assets	6.45	7.51	7.78	8.20	8.49	8.59

Source: Federal Reserve, *Financial Data and Ratios for Insured Commercial Banks*, September 2000.

practices. As a result, banks could no longer rely on stable demand deposits and consumer time and savings deposits as guaranteed sources of funds.

Since the 1980s, banks have drawn on funds management strategies that

- match assets and liabilities by maturity
- match assets and liabilities by duration
- use variable rate pricing on loans and deposits
- maintain balanced or favorable repricing gaps in the timing of maturing assets and liabilities

ASSET ALLOCATION STRATEGY

With an asset allocation strategy, a bank seeks to expand earnings by reallocating funds between loan and investment assets.

The first allocation of funds is to primary reserves, such as vault cash and account balances with the district Federal Reserve bank and correspondent banks. Primary reserves are used to meet reserve requirements and the bank's day-to-day liquidity needs.

The next allocation, called secondary reserves, is based on the bank's forecasted loan and deposit growth over the coming year. Funds are invested in secondary reserve assets of differing maturities—primarily Treasury securities—based on this forecast. After allocations are made to primary and secondary reserves, any remaining funds are used to meet loan demand. If there are residual funds after all loan demand has been met, they are invested in Treasury, federal agency, and state and local securities. Under an asset allocation strategy, banks buy securities when loan demand is soft and interest rates are low. When loan demand builds, banks sell securities to raise funds to meet loan demand. But rising interest rates usually accompany strong loan demand. When interest rates rise, banks take capital losses as they sell securities. Taking capital

losses makes sense as long as the bank can more than offset its losses with interest earnings on loans made using the funds obtained through selling securities. Taking capital losses also may make sense if the losses can be used as a tax offset to shelter other income.

LIABILITY MANAGEMENT STRATEGY

Another widely used funds management strategy is based not on a bank's assets but on its liabilities. Liability management strategy involves funding loan and investment growth by borrowing or buying money. To accommodate desired increases in earning assets, banks try to manage increases in their liabilities by drawing on financial instruments and using market practices they can control. Liability management typically entails borrowing federal funds, issuing negotiable certificates of deposit, borrowing Eurodollars, using the proceeds of commercial paper sold by the bank's parent holding company, and engaging in repurchase agreements.

FEDERAL FUNDS

Federal funds are funds that banks buy from and sell to each other for one business day and are immediately available from reserve accounts at Federal Reserve banks. Most banks that have $1 billion or more in total assets prepare early-morning estimates of the bank's expected reserve positions each day. On the basis of those daily estimates, the banks adjust their reserves using purchases or sales of federal funds. The money market banks in New York City, typically at the vortex of the federal funds market, buy reserves from regional and small community-based banks and channel those funds to their own broker, dealer, or multinational customers.

NEGOTIABLE CERTIFICATES OF DEPOSIT

Another part of the liability management strategy of most large banks is issuing negotiable certificates of deposit (CDs). These are usually large-denomination CDs of at least $100,000 made payable to the holder of the instrument at maturity. With a negotiable CD, the initial depositor can sell the certificate in the secondary market.

When loan demand begins to build at large regional and money center U.S. banks, they send out bids for CD depositors. Bidding continues as long as banks can earn more on loans than they have to pay to attract CD deposits. When loan demand begins to slow, banks allow existing CDs to mature and be withdrawn, and they reduce their marketing efforts among corporations. Banks typically lower their CD rates as loan demand and loan charges (interest rates) begin to fall.

EURODOLLAR BORROWINGS

Borrowing Eurodollars is part of the liability management strategy of many large banks that have branch offices overseas, as well as banks that have offshore branches in name only. Eurodollars are dollar-denominated deposits on the books of banking offices outside the United States. Those offices can be in any country, not just in Europe, even though the deposits are referred to as Eurodollars. When the head office of a U.S. bank wants to borrow funds from its overseas branch, it typically instructs the branch to bid for Eurodollar deposits. Because overseas deposits are not subject to reserve requirements and FDIC insurance premiums, an overseas branch office usually can afford to pay a slightly higher rate to attract funds. Generally Eurodollar depositors are corporations with accounts at U.S. banks.

When the overseas or offshore branch accepts a Eurodollar bid, it instructs the depositor to have its U.S. bank pay the dollars directly to the branch's head office in the United States. When the head office receives the transferred funds, the funds are recorded on its balance sheet on a net basis. The assets due from the bank's own foreign branch are netted against liabilities due to the foreign branch. The head office records the corresponding liabilities as liabilities due to its own foreign branch and not as deposits.

Competition for Eurodollars is generally not as strong as for domestic sources of funds. Nevertheless, large money center

---

THE ORIGIN OF THE NEGOTIABLE CD

In 1961 First National City Bank of New York invented the negotiable CD as a way for corporations to obtain an interest return on their demand deposits. At that time, banking regulations both prohibited banks from paying interest on demand deposits and specified that interest-earning time deposits had to have minimum maturities of 30 days. The negotiable CD offered banks a way to convert high-reserve-requirement demand deposits into lower reserve-requirement time deposits while providing an interest return to holders.

First National City Bank, which is now Citibank, developed a secondary market for CDs by gaining the support of a major government securities dealer firm. The securities dealer firm agreed to buy or sell existing CDs to enable corporations to get their money back without having to wait 30 days. A corporation that had to meet a multimillion-dollar payroll on the 15th of the month, for example, could buy a CD on the 1st of the month and then sell it in the secondary market on the 14th in time to cover its payroll checks. The corporation would receive the equivalent of 14 days' worth of interest on its money, reflected in the sale price of the CD. The purchaser, perhaps another corporation seeking a return on two-week money, would receive 16 days' worth of interest when the CD matured on day 30.

banks that have ready access to the Eurodollar market frequently use Eurodollar borrowings for overnight and weekend funding arrangements. Unlike the CD market, the Eurodollar market is essentially an overnight market, with interest rates subject to larger and more frequent changes.

COMMERCIAL PAPER SALES OF BANK AFFILIATES

Another liability management strategy involves using the proceeds of commercial paper issued by a bank's holding company parent or affiliates. Commercial paper consists of short-term unsecured promissory notes issued by creditworthy corporations that seek to borrow funds for a limited period of time.

Banks are not permitted to issue commercial paper, but holding companies can, and many banks are owned by holding companies. A parent holding company issuing commercial paper can benefit the bank in one of two ways. The holding company can deposit the proceeds from its commercial paper sales in the bank, thereby increasing the bank's funds. Because these funds are classified as borrowed funds rather than as deposits, they are not insured and are not subject to FDIC insurance premiums or reserve requirements. Thus, every dollar received by the bank from its parent holding company's sales of commercial paper can be used to support an additional dollar of new loans. The holding company also can use the proceeds from the commercial paper offering to purchase loans or an investment from the bank, thereby improving the bank's overall earning asset position.

Because the bank subsidiary is usually a bank holding company's major investment or asset, commercial paper issued by a bank holding company is generally considered by investors to be of high quality and is perceived to be implicitly secured by the assets of the bank itself. Technically, however, commercial paper is unsecured and is subject to greater credit risk, so the interest rates offered on commercial paper generally exceed the interest rates banks themselves pay on time deposits of equivalent maturity. Some bank holding companies can combine a strong bank implicitly backing the paper with a competitive interest rate to make their commercial paper easily salable. Although they are not an available source of funds for all banks, commercial paper sale proceeds have become an important source of short-term money for many banks.

REPURCHASE AGREEMENTS

Repurchase agreements are another liability management strategy. Under a repurchase agreement, also known as an RP, or repo, a bank sells government securities from its own portfolio with a promise to buy the securities back at a specified price after a short period of time, usually a few days.

Repos are not subject to reserve requirements. Therefore, banks pay an attractive interest return on them and still profit because they can convert all newly freed reserves into earning assets. Repos also have become essential to the cash management programs that many banks market to corporations, state and local governments, and some individual accounts. Under these programs, corporations, municipalities, and individuals that typically have daily idle funds enter into sweep agreement contracts with their banks. Given the ease with which cash management bank customers may access them, repos are one of the most popular overnight investment vehicles offered by banks.

OTHER SOURCES OF FUNDS

When banks need funds they also can borrow from the Federal Reserve. Most banks do not use this source of funds routinely. Over the decades, the Federal Reserve has come to see its lending as a safety valve, a way of easing pressure on banks least able to cope with short-term asset or liability adjustments during tight money periods. The Federal Reserve discourages banks from using the discount window as an ongoing source of low-cost funds to expand their earning assets.

SPREAD MANAGEMENT STRATEGY

Many banks focus on interest rate spread in their approach to funds management. Because banks typically take in deposits and make loans at different times, increases or decreases in interest rates can place a bank in a position of paying higher interest on deposits than the interest it is earning on loans and investments.

Spread management strategy requires banks to hedge against fluctuations in interest rates. That is, banks strive to maintain a close balance between what they pay for funds and what they charge for funds. With a close balance, the bank's spread will be stable. As market interest rates rise, both the bank's cost of funds and its return on invested and loaned funds will increase proportionally. As market rates decline, both costs and returns will fall in tandem.

If the timing and amount of a bank's deposits and loan repayments perfectly matched its withdrawals and new loans, then the bank would not have to worry about changes in interest rates. It could simply raise or lower the rates it charged to reflect the rates it paid.

But perfect matching of funds flows, is not feasible. Borrowers' scheduled repayments do not match the withdrawal patterns of depositors. If banks tried to force borrowers to tailor their loan requests to the payment patterns of depositors, banks would lose business. Nonetheless, tactics to implement spread management have emerged in which bankers seek to more effectively match or balance their bank's assets and liabilities. These tactics include maturity matching, duration matching, and variable rate pricing of loans and deposits.

MATURITY MATCHING

Some bankers try to match the maturities of specific loan and investment assets with the maturities of specific deposit liabilities. For example, if a bank makes $1 million in new mortgage loans, it might seek to take in $1 million in IRA deposits because mortgage assets and IRA account liabilities are likely to remain on the bank's books for a long time. On the other hand, if the bank takes in $500,000 of funds from 30-day corporate CDs, it might seek to match these funds with a 30-day corporate loan. If interest rates have increased by the time the CDs mature and the bank has to pay more to retain the funds, it can reinvest or lend at a higher rate the funds that are available from the maturing corporate loan. In addition, if the corporation withdraws its CD funds, the maturing corporate loan assures that the bank has ready funds available to meet this withdrawal.

A matching strategy is difficult to implement because demand for loans within specific maturity categories and the availability of high-return money market investments may not always match the maturities of new deposits coming into the bank. In addition, economic conditions may justify holding back on making new loans or investments at the very time that growing deposit inflows to the bank would require a matching of these new funds with new loans or investments.

DURATION MATCHING

Some bankers try to match assets and liabilities on the basis of duration; that is, on the average length of time that assets and liabilities are expected to remain on the bank's balance sheet.

The average duration of a 30-year mortgage is known to be about 5 to 6 years. This is because many mortgage holders sell their homes after a few years, others prepay mortgages, and a few others may default on mortgage loans. Thus, 30-year mortgages carried in a bank's loan portfolio need only be matched against 5- to 6-year deposits.

An effective duration matching strategy requires continual monitoring of a bank's duration positions and constant realignments of bank assets and liabilities. Modern computer technology and specialized software have enabled bank managers to readily implement duration matching strategies.

VARIABLE RATE PRICING ON LOANS AND DEPOSITS

Many banks try to maintain their interest rate spreads by making new loans and new deposits subject to variable interest rates. Variable rates change every month, or every year in the case of mortgages, to reflect changes in the bank's cost of and return on funds. In a rising interest rate environment in which banks must pay increasingly higher rates to attract and retain deposits, variable pricing allows banks to offset these deposit rate increases with higher loan charges to borrowers. The risk banks face is that borrowers will refinance at other institutions to lock in fixed rates rather than face continuing interest rate increases. In a declining rate environment, banks run the risk of losing deposits to institutions that offer fixed interest rate returns.

GAP MANAGEMENT

Gap management involves selectively mismatching assets and liabilities to capitalize on expected interest rate changes. This strategy involves grouping bank assets and liabilities into specific time periods, such as three months, six months, or one year, according to when these assets and liabilities will have to be repriced. The gap is the percentage difference between the amount of assets and the amount of liabilities that will have to be repriced in any given period.

For example, if a bank has more assets than liabilities subject to repricing in the next 90 days, the bank is considered asset sensitive. Asset sensitivity suggests a vulnerability to falling interest rates. If interest rates fall, the bank receives a lower return on assets being repriced; however, the bank is still locked into paying higher interest on liabilities that have not yet matured.

If the bank has more liabilities than assets maturing in a given time period, it is considered liability sensitive for that period and vulnerable to rising interest rates. If interest rates rise, the bank will have to pay a higher rate on liabilities being repriced; however, the bank is still locked into the lower rates it is receiving on assets that have not yet matured.

Some banks try to capitalize on an expected interest rate change by selectively mismatching assets and liabilities. A bank that believes interest rates will fall over the next six months, for example, may try to make its balance sheet liability sensitive for that time period. If rates fall, the bank will benefit because it reprices its liabilities at lower rates while it still receives higher rates on assets that have not yet matured.

A fixed-rate, long-term loan locks a bank into an interest return that cannot be changed if short-term conditions increase bank costs. For this reason, interest rates on long-term loans tend to be higher than those imposed on short-term loans. However, a loan portfolio weighted toward fixed-rate, long-term maturities can generate substantial earnings if interest rates decline for a protracted period after the loans are made.

SUPPLEMENTAL STRATEGIES

Most bankers realize that no ideal funds management strategy exists. Because each strategy is subject to risks, many banks have adopted strategies to supplement their management of assets and liabilities. These supplementary strategies may include securitization, derivatives, or interest rate swaps.

SECURITIZATION

Securitization involves packaging a bank's loans into a pool of loans and selling the pool or parts of the pool to institutional investors. This strategy enables banks to obtain a new source of funds and to keep some revenue, in the form of servicing fees, from the packaged loans. Securitization also can reduce banks' credit risk if the packaged loans are sold without recourse (a legal claim on the selling banks in the event of default).

DERIVATIVES

A **derivative** is a financial instrument that takes, or derives, its value from another underlying or related financial asset that is either underlying the instrument or related to it. Banks use derivatives to try to minimize the effects of changing interest rates on their net interest margins. They do this by adding derivatives to their mix of interest-sensitive assets and interest-sensitive liabilities to achieve a desired gap position over a fixed period of time. In 2000 about 400 banks used derivatives as part of their funds management strategy; most relied on interest rate swaps.

INTEREST RATE SWAPS

An interest rate swap is an agreement, backed by financial instruments, in which one financial institution agrees to make fixed payments to another financial institution and the second institution agrees to make variable payments based on a variable interest rate, such as the federal funds rate. Banks that engage in interest rate swaps exchange payments according to a predetermined schedule for the life of the swap, which may be several years.

A bank might use an interest rate swap under the following circumstances: Assume that a bank performs an analysis of the interest rate sensitivity of its assets and liabilities. The bank finds that for the next 12 months its rate-sensitive liabilities will exceed its rate-sensitive assets by $100 million. If the bank does nothing, an increase in interest rates would shrink its net interest margin over the next 12 months because more liabilities would be repriced at higher rates than assets.

If the bank is concerned with this exposure to changing interest rates, it could reduce its interest rate risk by entering into a one-year interest rate swap for $100 million. Under the swap, the bank would pay amounts based on a fixed rate of interest and receive amounts in return based on a variable rate of interest. Thus, if interest rates increase, the bank gets a larger amount back from the swap than the amount paid, offsetting the bank's interest margin erosion.

OPTIONS

An option contract gives the holder the right to exercise a future transaction, such as purchasing or selling a stock or bond at a currently determined price, for which the option holder pays a fee or a premium.

A bank might use an option under the following circumstances: Assume that a bank experiences a large increase in demand for home mortgages as a result of a drop in interest rates. However, the bank is concerned that if mortgage rates unexpectedly increase, it could be faced with having to honor earlier commitments at the lower rate. Moreover, even if it sells these below-market-rate mortgages in the secondary market, they will sell at a discount; that is, the principal amount will be less than the amount of the mortgage. Under either circumstance, the bank's profits will be hurt.

To hedge against this risk of funding below-market-rate mortgage commitments, the bank can purchase an option on a bond whose market value increases or decreases with the value of home mortgages as interest rates change. The option, called a put option, would give the bank the right to sell the bond at a predetermined price. Thus, if interest rates rise, the bank would profit by executing the option because the bond's market value would be below the option's predetermined price. This profit also would help offset any losses from selling the below-market-rate mortgages.

HEDGING IN THE FUTURES MARKET

A hedge is an attempt to reduce the exposure of securities investments to rising interest rates by selling some securities for future delivery. A futures contract for securities is a commitment to buy or sell securities at a future date at an agreed-on price.

If a bank that engages in hedging expects interest rates to increase, it sells securities in the futures market, locking in a current price for the securities it will deliver at a future date. When interest rates rise, securities prices fall. However, the hedged bank does not sustain a capital loss on the securities it delivers under the futures contract because it locked in the current, higher price before interest rates rose.

A bank that expects interest rates to fall and securities prices to increase can hedge by buying in the futures market. Thus, when rates fall, the hedged bank receives its securities at the lower price agreed to before interest rates fell.

SUMMARY

The business of banking is not limited to making commercial loans. Increasingly, banks make consumer loans and residential and commercial mortgages, invest in government securities, and sell a variety of financial services to businesses and consumers.

A bank's financial statements provide important information about its financial condition. Similarly, the balance sheet and income statement of the commercial banking system provide valuable insights into the business of banks in general. The balance sheet shows the relative importance of various categories of assets and liabilities. Loans still rank first among assets, and

money market deposit accounts and time deposits make up the largest share of liabilities. A review of the banking system's income statement facilitates a comparison of banks' interest income, primarily from loans and investments, and interest expenses, primarily interest paid on time and savings deposits. The income statement also highlights the relative importance of fee income and controlling operating expenses to maintain bank profitability.

Faced with intensified competition in recent years, banks increasingly have turned to aggressive funds management techniques to beef up profits. Banks have found ways to increase their liabilities and expand their earning assets at their own discretion, rather than passively waiting for deposits. Funds management strategies can be broadly categorized as asset allocation, liability management, spread management, and gap management.

REVIEW QUESTIONS

1. What major expense items appear on the bank income statement?
2. Cite the three largest loan categories on commercial banks' books and two characteristics that differentiate each of those loan categories.
3. Why would a business firm pay a loan commitment fee? Why would a bank impose a compensating balance on a loan? Why would a bank participate in a loan with another bank?
4. Why do banks buy securities? Explain the difference between U.S. Treasury securities, federal agency securities, and municipal obligations.
5. What are the objectives of an asset allocation strategy?
6. What is liability management? If you were in charge of liability management at your bank, what sources of managed liabilities would you rely on and why?
7. What tactics can be used to implement a spread management strategy?

ADDITIONAL RESOURCES

The ABCs of Figuring Interest, Federal Reserve Bank of Chicago, 2002, 14 pp., available at *http://www.chicagofed.org/publications/abcsinterest/index.cfm.* Describes some of the more common methods used in banking for calculating interest.

Bureau of Public Debt, at *www.publicdebt.treas.gov.* Provides current data on outstanding issues on Treasury bills, notes, and bonds.

Equity Aanalytics, Ltd., at *www.e-analytics.com/fp24.htm.* Provides information on federal funds.

Federal Deposit Insurance Corporation, at *www.fdic.gov.* Provides access to the FDIC quarterly banking profile, which contains current data on U.S. banks' financial and operating performance.

Federal Home Loan Mortgage Corporation (FHLMC, or Freddie Mac), at *http://www.freddiemac.com/.* This site and the following agency web sites provide information about their missions and include links to useful information about the securities they issue.

Federal Housing Administration (FHA) at *http://www.hud.gov/offices/hsg/.*

Federal National Mortgage Association (FNMA, or Fannie Mae), at *http://www.fanniemae.com/.*

Government National Mortgage Association (GNMA, or Ginnie Mae), at *http://www.ginniemae.gov/.*

In The Money provides access to booklets that explain how derivatives and options work, a glossary, and links to other web sites about derivatives. At www.in-the-money.com/.

Monetary Trends, Federal Reserve Bank of St. Louis, monthly publication. Features charts and tables on money and reserve measures, selected interest rates, and commercial bank loans, with a brief analysis of a current issue.

Principles of Banking, 7th ed., by G. Jay Francis and Susan M. Siegel, American Bankers Association, 2001. Provides a basic understanding of banking principles and current issues.

Reference Guide to Regulatory Compliance, by Kathlyn L. Farrell, American Bankers Association, 2002. Provides a detailed outline of the various regulations important to banking by bank functions, including consumer lending, deposit operations, safety and soundness, information reporting, and social responsibility; includes coverage on Regulation U, which governs extension of credit by banks for purchasing and carrying margin securities.

Tennessee Valley Authority (TVA), at *http://www.tva.gov/.*

EXERCISE 2: BALANCE SHEET PROBLEMS

Problem 1
(Assume that the required reserves against transaction deposits = 10 percent.)

First Commercial Bank
(in millions)

Assets		Liabilities and Capital	
Cash	$ 500	Transaction deposits	$40,000
Reserve account	7,500	Savings deposits	10,000
Correspondent deposits	2,000	Time deposits (CDs)	30,000
Securities	30,000	Borrowing from Federal Reserve bank	1,000
Loan	40,000	Total liabilities	81,000
Building	10,000	Capital	9,000
Total assets	$90,000	Total liabilities and capital	$90,000

Based on this balance sheet, First Commercial Bank's

1. primary reserves are $ 7,500
2. secondary reserves are $ 30,000
3. total reserves are $ 48,000
4. required reserves are $ 4,000
5. earning assets are $ 70,000
6. First Commercial could create 9,000 of new money.

Problem 2
(Assume that the required reserves against transaction deposits = 10 percent.)

National Community Bank
(in millions)

Assets		Liabilities and Capital	
Vault cash	$ 5,000	Transaction deposits:	
Cash items in process of collection	$ 20,000	(private)	$140,000
Federal Reserve balances	$ 29,000	(bank)	$ 10,000
Balance at bank	$ 10,000	(U.S. government)	$ 2,600
Federal agency securities	$100,000	Time deposits	$280,000
Loans	$270,000	Borrowings	$ 1,400
Total assets	$434,000	Total liabilities	$434,000

Based on this balance sheet, National Community's

1. excess reserves are $ _____ 13740_____
2. secondary reserves are $ _____100,000_____
3. required reserves are $ _____15,260_____
4. total reserves are $ _____164,000_____
5. earning assets are $ _____270,000_____

EXERCISE 3: PERFORMANCE RATIO PROBLEM

Balance Sheet of Second Community Bank

Assets

Cash and due from banks	$105,216,000
Federal funds sold/securities purchased	
under agreements to resell	157,998,000
Securities	247,254,000
Loans	340,104,000
Property and other assets	39,798,000
Total assets	890,370,000

Liabilities and Capital

Transaction deposits	$257,403,000
Time and savings deposits	441,810,000
Federal funds purchased/securities sold	
under agreement to repurchase	103,201,000
Other liabilities	24,698,000
Total liabilities	827,112,000
Capital	63,258,000
Total liabilities and capital	$890,370,000

Income Statement of Second Community Bank

Interest Income	
Interest on loans	$48,204,195
Interest on securities	18,522,125
Noninterest Income	21,708,078
Total operating income	$88,434,398
Interest Expense	
Interest on deposits	$56,867,695
Noninterest Expense	
Salaries and benefits	9,382,920
Loan loss provisions	810,204
Other operating expenses	2,044,837
Total operating expenses	$69,105,656
Income before Taxes	$14,328,742
Less taxes	5,292,229
Net Income	$ 9,036,513

Based on the balance sheet and the income statement, Second Community Bank's

1. return on assets (net income/assets) is *1.03* percent
2. return on equity (net income/equity) is *14.29* percent
3. ratio of capital to assets (equity/assets) is *7.10* percent   *699 213 000*
4. ratio of loans to deposits (loans/deposits) is *48.64* percent
5. Interest expenses represent ____ percent of Second Community Bank's total operating expenses. *82.29*
6. Salaries and benefits represent ____ percent of Second Community Bank's total operating expenses. *13.57*
7. What other information is needed to assess Second Community Bank's performance?

   Nothing with these 2 ~~balance~~ or financial statements
   Here is all the information needed for most anybody to
   make an educated statement about SCB's performance

6

BANK OPERATIONS AND THE PAYMENTS SYSTEM

LEARNING OBJECTIVES

After studying this chapter, you should be able to

- cite the major characteristics of the U.S. payments system
- identify three ways interbank checks are collected in the U.S. banking system
- interpret magnetic ink character recognition instructions and other informational check data
- explain how banks process and manage check data
- distinguish between Federal Reserve float and bank float
- list and describe major wholesale and retail electronic funds transfer systems and services
- define the key terms listed in this chapter

KEY TERMS

CHIPS
clearing house
delayed availability standards
Fedwire
magnetic ink character recognition

netting
on-us items
payments system
primary reserves
electronic check presentment

INTRODUCTION

Banks' role in lending money often overshadows their equally important role in the nation's payments system. By meeting the public's need for cash, clearing and collecting checks, and transferring funds electronically, banks provide the power that drives our nation's economy.

Operations are the primary activity of most bank employees. Most bank jobs involve check collection and electronic funds transfers, either directly or in providing the numerous administrative, accounting, computer, marketing, and security-related support services necessary to carry out banks' payment activities.

This chapter examines bank operations within the context of the U.S. payments system, focusing on the key internal processes and activities of banks that relate to payment devices and practices. It looks at the basic features of the U.S. payments system, the check collection process and creation of float, and the major electronic funds transfer systems in use today.

THE U.S. PAYMENTS SYSTEM

The term **payments system** denotes the instruments and procedures used to transfer money, make payments, and settle debts among individuals, businesses, governments, and financial institutions. The U.S. payments system primarily uses checks and electronic funds transfers, and to a lesser extent, cash. It depends on the relationships among commercial banks, other financial institutions, and the Federal Reserve in transferring, processing, and settling money balances.

The U.S. payments system differs in some important ways from those in most other industrial countries. The three features that most distinguish the U.S. payments system are the

- extensive role of the central bank

- number of depository institutions involved
- number and dollar volume of transactions

The 12 Federal Reserve banks and their 25 branches provide a range of payments services, from collecting checks and the electronic transfer of funds to safekeeping securities and providing coin and currency. They also are the nation's centers for the distribution of currency and coin in the banking system.

About one-third of all checks written in the United States are cleared through Federal Reserve banks, branches, and regional check processing centers (RCPCs). The Federal Reserve also operates a funds transfer (wire transfer) system over which money and government securities are transferred instantaneously. Known as **Fedwire,** the system is the primary system through which the nation's major banks do most of their interbank business.

The U.S. payments system is composed of about 20,000 separate depository institutions that receive deposits and make payments for themselves and their depositors primarily through bookkeeping transfers—that is, by check.

The nation's depositories are fragmented into many small, self-contained units. The vast number and dollar volume of money and payment-related transactions that occur between financial institutions also distinguishes the U.S. payments system. For example, in the collection process two or three banks will typically handle a check deposited in the U.S. banking system.

CASH

Meeting the public's demand for coin and currency is a primary responsibility of banks. A bank's cash activities include cashing personal or payroll checks, which converts deposits into currency, and serving as a depository for the public's excess cash, which is credited to depositors' demand and time accounts. The Federal Reserve serves as the source of the nation's coin and currency, providing cash to depositories as they respond to the cash demands of the public.

Monetary policy does not determine the nation's supply of currency. The public freely decides in what form and in what proportions it wishes to hold its money balances. Although cash put into circulation has increased at a rate of almost 10 percent per year for the past two decades, studies of the public's spending habits indicate no such surge in the use of cash to make payments. Two-thirds of America's cash circulates exclusively outside the United States; it is estimated the American public was only using about $200 billion in cash for transaction purposes in 2002.

THE FEDERAL RESERVE AND CURRENCY ISSUANCE

Exhibit 6.1 illustrates the U.S. cash distribution system. The U.S. Treasury mints new coins and prints currency, which is then distributed by the Federal Reserve to the nation's banks. Federal Reserve banks sort and count the millions of Federal Reserve notes they receive each day from depositing

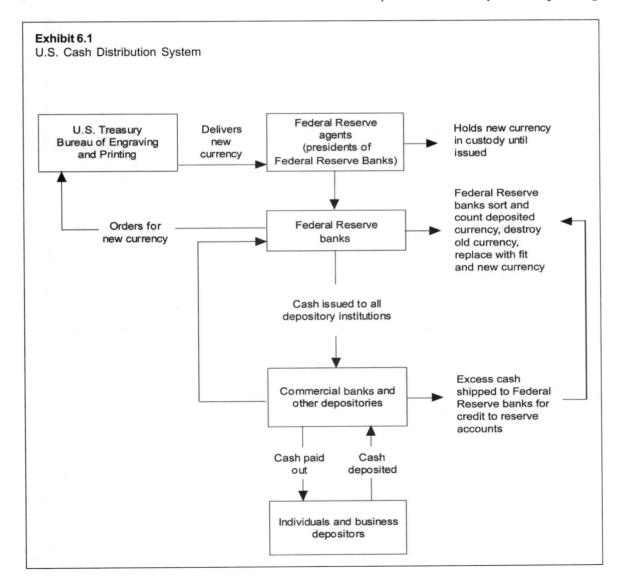

Exhibit 6.1
U.S. Cash Distribution System

banks, withdrawing from circulation worn or mutilated notes (which they destroy and replace with newly issued currency). During the 1990s, the U.S. Treasury's Bureau of Engraving and Printing produced about 8 billion new Federal Reserve notes each year to replace destroyed notes and meet the demand from banks for additional currency.

Banks that want more currency pay for it from the reserve account balances they hold at Federal Reserve banks. When a Reserve bank fills a bank's order for additional cash, it charges the amount ordered against the bank's reserve account. Similarly, banks may ship excess cash to a Federal Reserve bank, which credits it to their reserve accounts. In either case, the result is simply a redistribution of assets on the bank's books.

CASH ASSETS

A bank's cash assets, or **primary reserves,** constitute all of its liquid assets. Cash assets include

- cash held in the bank's vault or at tellers' stations
- deposit balances at correspondent banks and at the district Federal Reserve Bank
- cash items in the process of collection (funds about to be credited to the bank through the check collection process)

NEW CURRENCY TO DETER COUNTERFEITING

During the late 1990s, the Federal Reserve began issuing redesigned currency, the first major change in U.S. currency since 1928. The new currency incorporates several new security features to make the bills exceedingly difficult to counterfeit. At the same time, the redesigned bills preserve much of the traditional appearance of America's currency.

Security features in the new bills include the following:

- The presidential portrait is enlarged by 50 percent and moved three-quarters of an inch to the left to make room for a nonphotocopiable watermark that matches the portrait.
- A plastic-like thread, imprinted with the bill's denomination and the letters USA, is vertically embedded in each note and the imprints are visible only under certain light.
- Small, plastic-like disks are embedded in the paper of the bill but the image of these disks will not show up if photocopied.
- An additional line around the portrait reads "The United States of America" but in type so small that the line appears as a solid line except when magnified. If a genuine bill is photocopied, that line will appear as a solid line on the copy.

Only about 0.5 percent of all U.S. currency in circulation is estimated to be counterfeit. However, the massive increase in the amount of U.S. currency circulating in foreign countries in recent years and the availability of advanced photocopy and printing technology raised U.S. government concerns over the potential for counterfeiting, particularly by foreign governments or state-sponsored terrorist groups hostile to the United States. To meet this counterfeiting threat, the United States intends to make additional periodic design and security-enhancing changes to America's currency in the 2000s.

The new $100 bill.
*Photo courtesy of the
U.S. Treasury.*

Managing cash assets is an important area of bank operations. Primary reserves are the assets that a bank relies on as its first source of liquidity to meet depositors' demand claims. A bank's primary reserves generally exceed the reserves required to meet the Federal Reserve's reserve requirements, because only vault cash and a bank's deposits at a Federal Reserve bank can meet reserve requirements. Banks that choose not to maintain deposits at a Federal Reserve bank are allowed to keep their required reserves in a pass-through account at another bank if that bank redeposits an equivalent amount at a Federal Reserve bank.

Effectively managing cash assets is important to bank profitability. Idle cash is not an earning asset, and excess vault cash held in each branch of a multibranch bank, represents lost opportunities for revenue. Excess cash balances also present day-to-day management problems related to lack of appropriate storage space and adequate security. On the other hand, when cash is deposited in a correspondent account or in an account at a Reserve bank, it becomes a working asset. It can be used either to earn a return, if invested, or to settle other transactions, such as check collection or electronic funds transfers.

Too little vault cash also may prove costly to a bank. Transportation costs for special deliveries of cash from correspondents or the district Federal Reserve Bank are expensive. Moreover, customer relations may deteriorate if depositors are denied the exact currency mix they request in transactions at tellers' windows.

CHECK COLLECTION

The check collection process is the single largest operational activity of banks (see exhibit 6.2 on the following page). A check is legally a promise to pay. However, operationally it is an instruction form that tells the bank to transfer money balances from one account on its books either to cash or to another account on its books, or to collect funds from an account at another bank for credit to an account on its books.

The check-processing operations of all banks are structured to conform to the following practices:

• Payment by check generally depends on the physical transfer of the check itself, not just the information on the check.

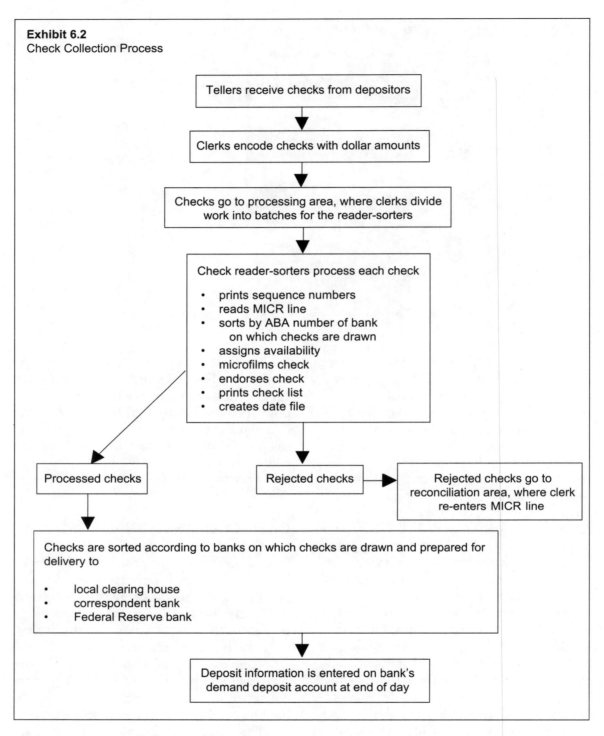

Exhibit 6.2
Check Collection Process

Tellers receive checks from depositors

↓

Clerks encode checks with dollar amounts

↓

Checks go to processing area, where clerks divide work into batches for the reader-sorters

↓

Check reader-sorters process each check

- prints sequence numbers
- reads MICR line
- sorts by ABA number of bank on which checks are drawn
- assigns availability
- microfilms check
- endorses check
- prints check list
- creates date file

Processed checks

Rejected checks → Rejected checks go to reconciliation area, where clerk re-enters MICR line

Checks are sorted according to banks on which checks are drawn and prepared for delivery to

- local clearing house
- correspondent bank
- Federal Reserve bank

↓

Deposit information is entered on bank's demand deposit account at end of day

- Check processing requires gathering different elements of payment information, acting in accordance with this information, and transporting checks between depositing and paying banks.
- Transferring funds by check is provisional, not final, and is subject to the paying bank's not returning the check and the availability of funds in the check writer's account.
- The check collection process can be used to return items that are not payable.

Exhibit 6.3
MICR Encoding

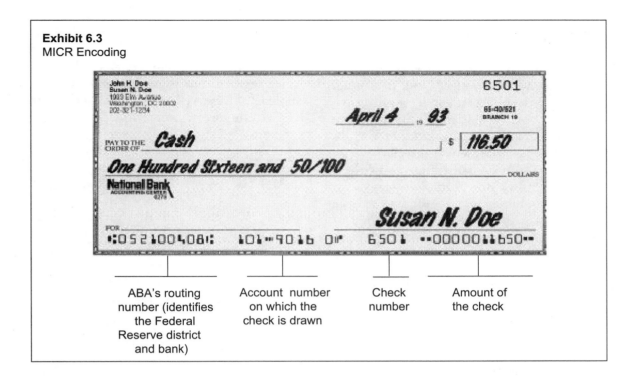

ABA's routing number (identifies the Federal Reserve district and bank)

Account number on which the check is drawn

Check number

Amount of the check

CHECK INFORMATION PROCESSING

Information on a check includes particular instructions that a bank must follow to collect funds for its customers. Today machines process virtually all checks; thus, instruction codes allow high-speed, check-sorting machines to read and sort properly the tens of thousands of checks that banks receive from depositors each day. These codes, called **magnetic ink character recognition** (MICR) symbols, appear across the bottom of all checks (see exhibit 6.3).

MICR encoding shows the check writer's account number, the check number, and the dollar amount of the check; the check routing procedure (including the Federal Reserve district, clearance through a head office, branch office, or special arrangement, and immediate or deferred credit); the bank's identifying number; and a number to verify routing accuracy.

MICR encoding allows banks to automate their accounting systems for credit and debit posting to individual accounts. In these computerized systems, reader-sorters register MICR data on checks, sort them, and produce a magnetic tape that holds a record of each transaction. A sequential list of each account number affected, the dollar amount of every transaction posted to each account, and a code to indicate whether the posting is a debit or a credit is registered on the tape. The number and frequency of tape runs depend on the bank's size and its volume of check transactions.

Once a final tape has been prepared, the bank enters the data on the tape into its master files. The computer updates the file for each account to reflect the current day's debits and credits as registered on the tape. A new closing balance is computed for each account, and the sum of these balances becomes the demand deposit total that appears in the bank's daily statement. In addition, a new master file for the next day's transaction activity is generated.

The computerization of deposit accounting has allowed banks to cope with a growing volume of checks while reducing costs and improving back-office operating efficiency.

CHECK COLLECTION OPTIONS

Once the information on a check has been registered and interpreted, bank personnel must select the quickest and least expensive option for collecting each check. In theory a bank that receives a check drawn on any other bank could present it directly to that bank for payment. Such direct-send collection might work, for example, if only two banks existed in a given region and people or businesses that had accounts at one of those banks wrote nearly all checks received by either bank. Direct-send collection does occur to a limited extent in the U.S. banking system, but it is generally far too costly and time-consuming for banks to present checks separately to numerous other banks.

Smaller banks clear checks through larger regional banks, which, in turn, rely on Federal Reserve banks and local clearing houses for check collection (see exhibit 6.4 below).

ON-US ITEMS

Nearly 30 percent of all checks received by banks are cleared internally; that is, they are deposited in the same bank on which they are drawn and are collected through internal adjustments to the bank's books. These **on-us items** are presented by

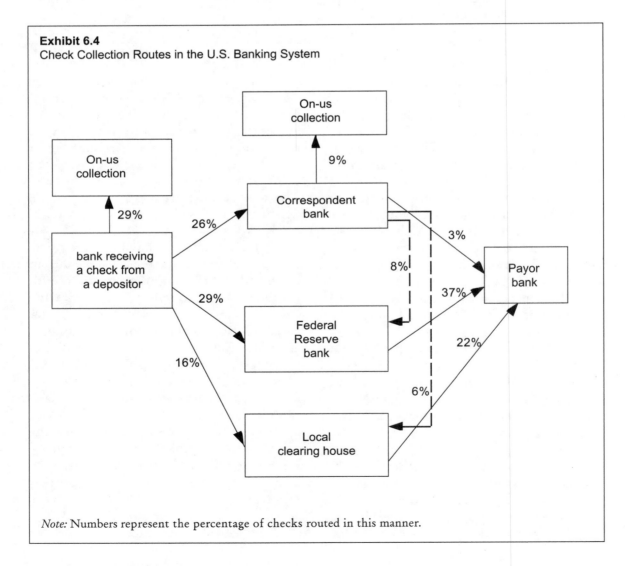

Exhibit 6.4
Check Collection Routes in the U.S. Banking System

Note: Numbers represent the percentage of checks routed in this manner.

depositors who want to cash checks drawn on their own accounts or who want to deposit checks drawn on the same bank by another account holder. Banks typically run all checks received from depositors through reader-sorter processing machines to segregate on-us checks, which are then handled as internal credit and debit adjustments. The check writer's account is reduced by the amount of the check, and the depositor's account is credited with a like amount.

LOCAL CLEARING HOUSES

Approximately 16 percent of all checks are cleared through local clearing houses or clearing arrangements. A **clearing house** arrangement involves banks in a given area that regularly receive large numbers of deposited checks drawn on each other. Representatives of these banks meet at a central site to exchange and collect payment for local checks. The central site may be a separate physical facility or one of the banks that participates in the arrangement. About 1,500 such clearing house arrangements operate throughout the United States. Collection is made by **netting** the amounts presented by the banks against one another. Netting means that each bank that pays more transfers only the differential. By contrast, settlement through major regional clearing houses is made against accounts that participating banks maintain at Federal Reserve banks.

By using clearing houses, banks avoid the expense of transporting checks to numerous other banks and the expense of maintaining separate accounts at many banks (see exhibit 6.5).

CORRESPONDENT BANKS

About 26 percent of checks received by banks are forwarded to correspondent banks for check collection. Typically, smaller banks that do not own reader-sorters and those banks that do not have direct account relationships with the Federal Reserve maintain accounts with correspondents for check collection and other services.

When a correspondent bank receives a batch of checks from a respondent bank, the check collection process can take one of two different routes.

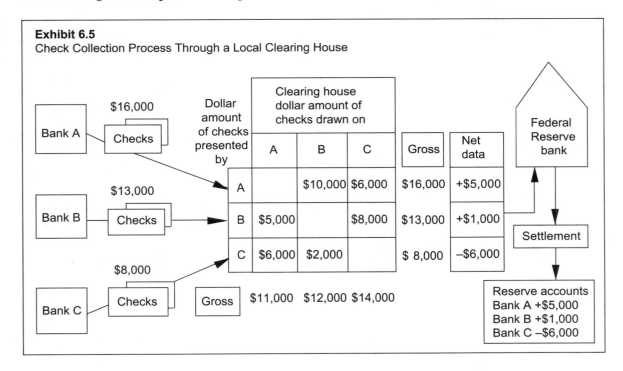

Exhibit 6.5
Check Collection Process Through a Local Clearing House

1. If checks are drawn on another bank that maintains an account with the correspondent, the correspondent transfers deposit credit from one account to another account on its books.
2. If presented checks are drawn on a bank that does not have an account with the correspondent, the respondent's account is credited for the amount of the check and the correspondent bank sends the check either to a local clearing house or to a Federal Reserve bank.

THE FEDERAL RESERVE

Nearly 30 percent of all checks are cleared through Federal Reserve banks. Correspondent banks also rely extensively on the Federal Reserve for interregional collection. The Federal Reserve collects checks by transferring credit balances from one reserve account to another. Individual banks collect on-us checks in a similar way.

For banks that have reserve accounts at different Federal Reserve banks, an extra step is involved. Each Federal Reserve bank maintains an interdistrict settlement account at the Interdistrict Settlement Fund in Washington, D.C. The Interdistrict Settlement Fund handles settlements among Federal Reserve banks. A check presented to a Reserve bank that is drawn on a bank in another Reserve district results in a transfer of interdistrict settlement account balances from one Reserve bank to another.

ELECTRONIC CHECK PRESENTMENT

The clearing and collecting of checks is an expensive process that involves sorting,

---

BANKS' DEMAND DEPOSIT ACCOUNTING UNITS

Most banks have a demand deposit accounting unit that processes and collects check data. The unit

- examines all checks to see if account numbers and dollar amounts are correct
- determines whether any checks should be dishonored, or returned unpaid
- posts all debits and credits to appropriate customer accounts
- prepares insufficient funds reports that indicate, for each account involved, the dollar amount of checks paid and the overdraft that would result if all postings were allowed to stand
- prepares uncollected funds reports that show, for each account, any deposited funds for which credit is being deferred
- reports on all newly opened and closed accounts in which there have been particularly large increases or decreases in balances
- prepares reports of stop payment orders and hold orders
- prepares monthly statements of each account's activity

Posting is the process by which a bank internally pays for a check, debiting the check writer's account, or makes a payment, crediting the depositor's account. This information is used to calculate the bank's end-of-day demand deposit position. Bank management uses both insufficient funds reports and uncollected funds reports to decide whether to pay or return checks.

By systematically processing and collecting check data, demand deposit accounting units enable banks to record inflows and outflows of funds quickly and determine their net funds available for lending or investing. Time is critical because of opportunity cost. At an interest rate of 5 percent, a bank that leaves $1 million idle overnight loses $110 in revenue that it would have earned had it loaned or invested the funds for one day.

processing, and shipping millions of checks each day. To reduce the personnel, equipment, and transportation costs associated with collecting checks, banks, clearing houses and the Federal Reserve have been working to make various aspects of the collection process take place electronically. **Electronic check presentment**, or ECP, sends the MICR information from the check electronically to the paying bank. In the more cost-efficient, truncated form of ECP, the paper check never follows. In the less cost-efficient form of ECP, the paper check is eventually sent to the paying bank. In 2002 about 20 percent of the checks processed by the Federal Reserve banks were presented electronically, either in truncated form or with checks to follow. The Federal Reserve also was testing a program that offers banks digital images of truncated checks over the Internet. Several large banks are participating in this program for checks drawn on corporate accounts.

FLOAT

Float is commonly thought of as the "extra money" created because of the time interval between payment by check and the time the funds are actually debited from the check-writer's account. Another type of float is created by the Federal Reserve, however, when it credits funds to a bank before checks have been collected.

FEDERAL RESERVE FLOAT

The Federal Reserve routinely credits banks for checks they present for payment before the checks are collected from the banks on which they are drawn. The result, Federal Reserve float, means extra reserves exist in the banking system.

Federal Reserve banks follow a three-tier schedule in crediting the accounts of depositing banks for the checks they present. Funds may be credited

- on the same day checks are presented, for checks drawn on banks located in the same city as the Reserve Bank or drawn on the U.S. Treasury
- on the next business day, for checks drawn on banks in nearby cities but not located near a Federal Reserve office
- two business days later, for checks drawn on banks in distant cities

A depositing bank receives credit in accordance with this schedule irrespective of whether the presented checks have actually been processed by the Federal Reserve bank or shipped to the paying bank. As soon as the depositing bank receives credit, the funds can be used to meet reserve requirements, to support new loans, or to make investments. Until the paying bank's account at the Reserve bank is debited, extra reserves (or float) exist on the books of the banking system.

The Federal Reserve's policy of giving quick credit for checks presented for payment provides the nation with a more efficient, speedier check collection system than if Federal Reserve banks credited banks in accordance with actual collection times. The practice eliminates any uncertainty about a depositing bank's usable funds (reserves) and enhances the efficiency of checks as business and consumer payment devices. However, because float adds about $500 million a day in extra reserves to the banking system, it complicates the Federal Reserve's monetary policy control.

TYPES OF FEDERAL RESERVE FLOAT

Federal Reserve float occurs for three reasons, and each reason is associated with a specific type of float, namely

- transportation float
- holdover float
- rejected-items float

Transportation float results from delays in the transport and physical presentment of checks for payment. Bad weather or equipment breakdowns can interfere with carriers' delivery schedules and prevent timely presentment of checks from Reserve banks to paying banks. Holdover float results from processing delays at Federal Reserve banks. For example, computer breakdowns or unexpected surges in check volume sometimes prevent the Federal Reserve from meeting its own delivery deadlines. Rejected-items float can occur if the Reserve banks' sorting machines reject a large number of damaged checks. Because they must be processed manually, some rejected checks may not be processed in time to meet the normal transportation schedules.

Float could be eliminated if the Federal Reserve abandoned its deferred availability schedule and granted credit for deposited checks only after checks had actually been collected. To do so, however, would severely hamper the efficiency of the nation's check collection system.

THE CREATION OF FEDERAL RESERVE FLOAT

The creation of Federal Reserve float can be traced by using T-accounts to show how the books of a Federal Reserve bank and two banks that clear their checks through this Reserve bank are affected.

Assume that on Monday, First Bank presents the Federal Reserve Bank with $10 million in checks drawn on Second Bank. According to the Reserve bank's deferred availability schedule, credit for these checks is posted to First Bank's account on Tuesday, the day after presentment. The Reserve bank's posting on Monday will show an asset increase of $10 million (cash items in the process of collection) offset by a $10 million liability increase (deferred availability items). In effect, the Reserve bank records on its books that it has received $10 million in checks for credit to another bank, is in the process of collecting those checks, and is deferring credit for the checks for one day.

If the Federal Reserve can sort the $10 million in checks presented by First Bank and deliver them to Second Bank by the following day (Tuesday), no float will be created. If, however, the Reserve bank cannot sort and deliver the checks to Second Bank by Tuesday, the delay in delivery creates float.

Suppose a snowstorm prevents carriers from delivering the processed checks to Second Bank until Wednesday. In this case, on Tuesday the books of the Reserve bank will look like the second T-account.

First Bank's account has been credited with $10 million in usable reserve assets

Federal Reserve Bank

Assets		Liabilities	
Cash items in process of collection	+$10,000,000	Account of First Bank	
		Account of Second Bank	
		Deferred availability items	+ $10,000,000

Federal Reserve Bank

Assets		Liabilities	
Cash items in process of collection	+$10,000,000 (Monday)	Account of First Bank	+ $10,000,000 (Tuesday)
		Account of Second Bank	
		Deferred availability items	+ $10,000,000 (Monday) − $10,000,000 (Tuesday)

in accordance with the Reserve bank's deferred availability schedule. The reduction in the deferred availability items account reflects the end of credit deferment. However, because the checks have not yet been received by Second Bank, they are not collected and must still be carried as cash items in the process of collection on the Reserve bank's books. Now $10 million in float, or excess reserves, has been created by the Federal Reserve. In accounting terms, float reflects the difference between the Federal Reserve's cash items in the process of collection (assets) and its deferred availability items (liabilities).

If the checks are presented to Second Bank on Wednesday, the $10 million in float will be eliminated because the Reserve bank then will debit Second Bank's account by $10 million and debit its own cash items account by $10 million. In this way, Federal Reserve float is continually being created and eliminated in the banking system.

EFFECT OF FLOAT ON BANKS INVOLVED

We will now look at how this float affects the other banks involved. First Bank had to wait only one day before it received credit in fully collected funds from the Federal Reserve bank. Thus, on Monday its books showed a $10 million increase in cash items in the process of collection, which offset the $10 million in credit postings it made to depositors' accounts.

Second Bank and its check-writing depositors are the beneficiaries of the $10 million in Federal Reserve float. Because Second Bank's books carried no debits to its account at the Reserve bank or to its depositors' accounts on Tuesday, it had the use of $10 million in reserves for one day longer than scheduled—and its depositors also had the use of their checkbook funds for one day longer.

Had there been no delay in the check collection process, Second Bank would have paid $10 million to First Commercial through an account transfer on the books of the Reserve bank on Tuesday. Instead, because of the delay in its receipt of the $10 million in checks from the Federal Reserve, Second Bank's account balance at the Reserve bank is debited by $10 million on Wednesday. Second Bank then sorts the checks and makes the necessary internal debits to its depositors' (check writers') accounts.

BANK FLOAT AND DELAYED AVAILABILITY

Because the check collection process takes time, checks received from depositors are initially recorded on a bank's books as uncollected (unavailable) funds. This liability posting is offset by an asset posting of an equal dollar amount of cash items in process of collection. The initial posting of a $1,000 deposited check and the subsequent posting after receipt of payment for this check also can be shown using T-accounts.

Initial Posting for a Deposited Check

Assets		Liabilities	
Cash items in process of collection	+ $1,000	Demand deposit (unavailable funds)	+ $1,000

Posting after Collection of a Deposited Check

Assets		Liabilities	
Reserve account at Federal Reserve	+ $1,000	Demand deposits (unavailable funds)	− $1,000
Cash items in process of collection	− $1,000	Demand deposits (usable collected funds)	+ $1,000

Until 1988 no nationwide policy specified when depositors would receive credit for deposited checks. Banks traditionally allowed customers to access funds deposited in their accounts in accordance with the banks' own availability schedules. These schedules varied by bank, by depositor, and by type of deposit. Depositors sometimes were not allowed to use check funds until several days after a check had been deposited. Banks did this to reduce the risk of losses from unpaid, returned checks. If checks were returned unpaid, the banks would not learn of the nonpayment until the checks arrived back at the banks, a process that could take several days. If depositors had already withdrawn the funds credited for the returned checks, the banks would lose money.

During the 1980s, consumer groups complained that banks were unnecessarily and unfairly delaying customers' access to deposited funds. The consumer groups held that most holds were unnecessary, given that only a small percentage of checks were actually returned. Bankers countered that the delays in making funds available to depositors were justified, given the imperfections in the nation's check collection system. Bankers explained that, even though less than 1 percent of checks were returned unpaid, the potential for fraud losses would be significant if the banks were required to release funds before they could learn that a check was not payable. Responding to the debate in 1988, Congress imposed limits on the delays that banks could place on deposited checks.

DELAYED AVAILABILITY STANDARDS

Under the Expedited Funds Availability Act (EFAA, implemented through the Federal Reserve's Regulation CC), banks must generally make funds available for local checks within two business days of deposit and for nonlocal checks within five business days of deposit. In accordance with these delayed availability standards, banks must also grant next-day availability on all government checks, certified checks, and bankers' checks. In addition, the first $100 in deposits in a given day must be made available on the next day. Banks may provide funds earlier than required, and they must disclose their availability schedules to their customers.

In response to the banks' concerns about the risk of loss and fraud associated with providing funds before knowing whether the bank will be paid for the check, Congress included some exceptions to the funds availability schedules. Congress exempted from coverage new accounts, deposit amounts over $5,000, deposits into accounts that customers had repeatedly overdrawn, and checks that a bank had reasonable cause to doubt would be paid. In these cases a bank need not follow the federal funds availability schedule but may have to provide the consumer with a notice of the hold, stating the reason for the hold, its date of expiration, and specifically identifying which items in the deposit are being held.

NEW RETURN-ITEMS PROCEDURES

In 1988 Congress also addressed a fundamental problem that banks faced in the check collection process. If a check was returned unpaid, whether for insufficient funds or other cause, it was routed back the way it came. The check traveled back to each institution that handled it in the forward collection process. While methodical, this process delayed the return of the check to the bank that originally accepted it for deposit. As a result, a depositor's bank often did not know that a check had been dishonored until 10 days to two weeks after the day of deposit.

To address this problem, Congress mandated that the Federal Reserve speed up the return-items process and gave the Federal Reserve broad authority to change the banking system's check collection rules. The Federal Reserve's Regulation CC allows banks to return dishonored checks directly to the bank of first deposit, bypassing all intermediaries. Furthermore, a paying bank that is returning any large-dollar items must notify the depositor's bank in advance. The depositors' bank can then immediately block the withdrawal of funds against the dishonored check.

ELECTRONIC FUNDS TRANSFER SYSTEMS AND SERVICES

Electronic funds transfer (EFT) systems and services have become indispensable to modern-day banking. Banks increasingly use EFT to borrow funds from each other, to invest daily surplus funds, to settle clearing balances in the check collection process, and to provide instantaneous transfer services for depositors. Nevertheless, there is no uniform, nationwide EFT system in America. Rather, there are several wholesale systems that move hundreds of billions of dollars of inter-bank funds each day and several retail systems that provide consumer electronic banking services in selected regions of the country (see exhibit 6.6)

WHOLESALE ELECTRONIC FUNDS TRANSFER SYSTEMS

Banks use two major wholesale EFT systems: Fedwire and CHIPS. The Federal Reserve's funds transfer network, Fedwire, is the main domestic system that banks use to transfer reserve account balances, called federal funds, to one another. Fedwire also is used to transfer third-party payments, which are electronic funds transmitted on behalf of customers. Fedwire provides direct electronic transfer services to banks throughout the United States through in-bank terminal or computer links. About half of the $2.5 trillion in interbank electronic funds transfers made each day occur over Fedwire.

Fedwire is also used to transfer U.S. government and federal agency securities, virtually all of which exist today only in electronic form. In 2002 the Fedwire made 55,000 book-entry securities transfers each day for banks with a total dollar value of $725 billion.

The Clearing House Interbank Payments System, or **CHIPS**, is the focal point for payments in the international dollar market. Each day about 90 percent of all inter-

---

Exhibit 6.6
Payments Handled by Electronic Systems, 2000

Wholesale Payment Systems	Daily Average Volume	Daily Average Value (in trillions)
Fedwire (funds)	357,000	$ 1.1
Fedwire (securities)	55,000	0.725
CHIPS	235,000	1.4

Retail Payment Systems	Annual Transactions (in billions)	Annual Value (in billions)
ATMs	11	$ 762
Debit cards	4	239
Credit cards	18	1,200
ACH	5	16,300

Sources: Federal Reserve, New York Clearing House Association, National Automated Clearing House Association, First Quarter 2002.

national interbank dollar transfers are moved through CHIPS, which translates to about 235,000 daily transfers valued at $1.4 trillion. The New York Clearing House Association operates the system, which links about 100 financial institutions to a central computer. The institutions that belong to CHIPS mostly are branches of foreign banks in New York City and New York's large money center banks.

RETAIL ELECTRONIC FUNDS TRANSFER SERVICES

Retail-oriented electronic funds transfer systems are increasingly changing the way banks provide services. The major retail EFT systems and services are

- automated teller machines (ATMs)
- point-of-sale (POS) terminals and debit cards
- automated clearing house (ACH) services
- telephone bill-paying services
- Internet banking
- electronic bill presentment and payment (EBPP)

AUTOMATED TELLER MACHINES

Automated teller machines are the most widely used retail EFT services offered by banks today. About 250,000 ATMs were being used in 2002. More than half of these ATMs are located off bank premises at convenience stores, gas stations, and shopping malls. Since the 1980s, increasing

---

DAYLIGHT OVERDRAFTS THROUGH EFTs

Transferring funds over Fedwire and CHIPS subjects most large banks to an unusual operational risk. During the course of a day, so much electronic money flows in and out of the nation's large banks so rapidly that, on occasion, some banks pay out more electronic funds than they have on their books. These "daylight overdrafts" typically last for several minutes until incoming electronic funds from other banks provide coverage. But banks are subject to the risk that one bank's inability to make good on its daylight overdrafts could possibly lead to its own failure and to the failure of other banks that received its overdraft electronic funds. Although only a small number of banks incur daylight overdrafts on Fedwire and CHIPS, the dollar value of these overdrafts can routinely top the value of their total assets.

During the 1980s, the Federal Reserve established rules to reduce this risk. Banks that use Fedwire and CHIPS must set a dollar limit on the daylight overdrafts they will accept on behalf of banks or companies for whom they transfer funds. Banks that use CHIPS established additional rules in 1990 to reduce risks in dealing with international interbank transfers. Under these rules, each CHIPS participant must enter into a loss-sharing agreement with the New York Clearing House Association under which it pledges to provide a portion of the funds necessary to make good on all CHIPS transfers if one or more CHIPS participant fails.

To further reduce daylight overdrafts, the Federal Reserve instituted additional risk reduction measures in the 1990s. It imposed a charge (fee) for daylight overdrafts on Fedwire. The intent of the charge was to induce both banks and their corporate customers to alter their electronic payments practices to avoid incurring daylight overdrafts.

Since the mid-1990s, there has been a sharp reduction in daylight overdrafts and a significant change in market payment practices, particularly among government securities dealer firms whose rapid and voluminous purchases and sales of securities each day cause most of the daylight overdrafts on banks' books.

---

numbers of banks have linked their ATMs to those of other banks to form regional, interstate, and national networks. Today most ATM transactions—about 11 billion in 2001—are network transactions made at other banks' ATMs.

The most widely used ATM service allows a depositor to withdraw cash against a checking or savings account. Cash withdrawals accounted for 70 percent of all ATM transactions in 2001. ATMs also allow customers to make deposits to checking and savings accounts, transfer funds between checking and savings accounts, and, in some instances, pay utility bills, or repay installment loans among other features. All of these services are obtainable from ATMs 24 hours a day.

There are two types of ATM fees. The first, a foreign transaction fee, is charged by the bank when their customer uses an ATM not owned by the customer's bank. This charge is intended to cover the fee imposed by the ATM network on the bank. For certain accounts, a few banks charge a smaller fee each time their customer uses one of its own ATMs. The second type of ATM fee is an access fee, which is imposed by the ATM owner on users of the ATM.

Consumer activists complain that these fees are unfair to consumers. However, ATM owners respond that the ability to recover ATM costs encourages deployment of ATMs, increasing consumer convenience.

POINT-OF-SALE TERMINALS AND DEBIT CARDS

Some banks offer point-of-sale (POS) terminals and debit card EFT services. A POS terminal is a minicomputer placed by a bank at a retail site, usually paid for by the merchant. Customers can pay for goods or services at the point-of-sale by using their debit cards. The funds are then electronically debited from the customers' bank accounts and credited to the merchant's account.

During the 1990s, debit card use registered the most rapid growth of any retail EFT service. Today these cards, about 250 million in all, account for about 4 percent of all retail transactions. One factor in the growing popularity of debit cards is that, like ATM transactions, debit card transactions are now made over networks that link a broad, nationwide range of merchants and card-issuing banks. Another factor is the convenience of having both POS and ATM capabilities on a single card. Debit cards also are being distributed by federal and state agencies for use in electronic benefits transfer (EBT) programs.

EBT programs deliver cash entitlement and food assistance benefits to recipients who do not have bank accounts. Recipients use the government-issued debit cards to withdraw cash from designated ATMs or to make food purchases at the POS terminals of designated grocery and convenience stores. In 2001 about 4 million people were enrolled in EBT programs.

AUTOMATED CLEARING HOUSE SERVICES

ACH services enable banks, corporations, and the government to make recurring payments, such as wage and bill payments, in a less expensive and more convenient way than by paper checks. Banks process payment information provided by their customers on their own computers to obtain appropriate credit and debit information. They then forward the payment information to an ACH operator who processes, distributes, and settles the transactions electronically. Currently there are four ACH operators in the United States. The largest is the Federal Reserve, which clears about 80 percent of all ACH transactions.

Like debit card use, ACH use grew rapidly during the 1990s. Still, the share of overall transactions made through ACH remains relatively small, at about 5 percent in 2001.

The most widely used ACH service is the direct deposit transaction. Employees have their salaries, and Social Security recipients their benefits, electronically deposited directly into their checking or savings accounts. Nonetheless, public reluctance to give up paychecks and Social Security checks has held back the growth of corporate and government direct deposit programs. Only half of America's workforce participates in direct payroll deposit. Close to 80 percent of Social Security recipients receive benefits electronically.

Recurring bill payments, mainly for mortgage and utility bills, are the second most used ACH service. However, only about 3 percent of all recurring bills are paid this way.

The federal government has been a major proponent of ACH transactions. Approximately three-quarters of all payroll, benefits, and vendor payments made by the government are made electronically. Also, ACH now is used at merchant locations and at bill collection centers to convert consumers' checks into electronic transactions. A growing number of corporations also are making quarterly tax payments by ACH. All these activities have spurred ACH growth in the early 2000s.

TELEPHONE BILL-PAYING SERVICES

Some banks offer a service that allows customers to make electronic funds transfers through a direct touchtone telephone hookup to their bank's computer. Payments, sorted by the computer, are either credited directly to a merchant's account at the bank or, if the merchant does not have an account there, remitted by mail to the merchant as a banker's check. However, the overall public response to telephone bill-paying has been poor. In 2001, fewer than 500 banks and thrifts offered this service. High transaction charges, concerns over privacy and the security of information provided over the phone, and the awkwardness of providing payment and account data by touching keys on the phone have deterred most bank customers from paying bills by phone.

INTERNET BANKING

Internet banking enables consumers to transmit payment instructions to their banks over the Internet from a personal computer. The bank acts on these payment instructions by transferring funds electronically, or in some instances by bankers' checks, to the appropriate account or institution.

Many banking industry analysts maintain that Internet banking will not take off until personal computer ownership is America is pervasive. The growth in personal computer ownership in the 1990s that was so promising to bankers failed to continue in the 2000s. Today only 60 percent of America's households own a computer. Moreover, only about half of these households have high-speed Internet access, which is seen by industry analysts as an important element in making web-based banking more convenient. The lack of a common electronic payment format and the multitude of different operating systems make standardization difficult, creating significant barriers to broader public use of Internet banking.

ELECTRONIC BILL PRESENTMENT AND PAYMENT

Many bankers believe that electronic bill presentment and payment, or EBPP, will be the breakthrough service that will spark broad use of Internet banking in the 2000s. Under EBPP, major companies present their bills to customers online and customers pay online. However, because EBPP is new, no standard has emerged. Three EBPP systems are currently being marketed: biller direct, consolidator, and portal.

In a biller direct system, the billing firm posts the consumer's bill on the firm's web site. The consumer accesses the site and pays the bill through an ACH transfer or a credit card. The drawback is that the consumer has to visit multiple web sites to pay bills. Billers, however, prefer this system because they retain full control of their customer data and relationship. Utility firms have made use of this system.

In a consolidator system, a third–party presenter, called a consolidator, collects bills from a number of billers and makes them available to consumers on the consolidator's web site.

In a portal system, billers forward their bills to a third-party consolidator who makes them available to consumers by linking to an Internet portal. Consumers go directly to one centralized site, the portal, to pay all of their bills. A bank or an Internet access provider may operate the portal.

Each of these alternative systems reduces statement preparation and postage costs associated with paying bills. These systems also accelerate the receipt of funds by billers. While it is unclear which of these EBPP systems will develop into the dominant system, many bankers believe that EBPP has a future.

Retail EFT Outlook

Retail EFT services have not yet revolutionized the way people and businesses make payments and use banks in the United States. Most bankers realize that a change in the attitude of bank cus-tomers must occur before there is significant behavioral change. They also realize that attitudinal change is likely to occur slowly.

Most bankers see EFT systems as the key to reducing costs associated with check clearing and collection. During the 1980s and 1990s, the costs of maintaining checking accounts and processing checks increased significantly. The application of EFT technology to reduce or eliminate the costly physical handling of paper checks is in the forefront of change in the 2000s. However, various technical, legal, financial, and attitudinal factors stand in the way of more widespread retail use of electronic payments and Internet banking services.

SUMMARY

Banks play a major role in the nation's payments system, both in meeting the public's need for cash and in processing checks and electronic funds transfers. The largest single operational activity of banks is clearing and collecting checks. Check collection involves interpreting the information on checks, acting on the information, and transporting checks to other banks for payment through a local clearing house, a correspondent bank, or the Federal Reserve.

The Federal Reserve follows a fixed schedule for crediting banks for checks they present for payment. Because checks usually are credited before they are collected, extra reserves are created, called Federal Reserve float. In 1987 Congress legislated maximum nationwide delayed availability limits to standardize banks' delayed funds availability schedules.

Banks rely on Fedwire and CHIPS to handle much of their interbank business electronically and to provide instantaneous money transfer services for depositors. Various retail EFT systems exist, including ATM networks and POS/EFT networks. Funds also can be transferred electronically to pay bills and receive deposits using the ACH, telephone, Internet, and electronic bill presentment and payment systems. However, consumer adoption of some of these services has been slow.

REVIEW QUESTIONS

1. Why is it not advantageous for a bank to have cash on hand in excess of its daily needs?
2. What are the three basic ways that interbank checks are collected in the United States? What factors determine a bank's choice of a collection option?
3. Explain how a local clearing house operates and the advantages it offers for clearing checks.

4. What are MICR instructions, what is their significance, and how do banks manage MICR data flow?

5. What is Federal Reserve float, how does it occur, and how does it differ from bank float? In your answer, explain how uncollected funds differ from available funds.

6. Why have retail electronic funds transfer systems and services been slow to develop in the United States?

7. "Within this decade the Internet will revolutionize U.S. banking and payments practices." Do you agree or disagree with this statement? Justify your answer.

ADDITIONAL RESOURCES

"Clicking with Dollars: How Consumers Can Pay for Purchases from e-tailers," in *Economic Review*, Federal Reserve Bank of Kansas City, 2002, 27pp. Discusses the various options consumers have to make payments over the Internet.

Electronic Money, Federal Reserve Bank of Chicago, 1995, 12 pp. Examines retail EFT systems and consumers' responses to them, and explains the rights and responsibilities of consumers and financial institutions when using EFT systems.

Electronic Payment Instrument Study, prepared for the Federal Reserve Retail Payments Office, Dove Consulting, 2001. A study that attempted to measure check volume and assess emerging trends in check payment processes.

Electronic Payments in the U.S. Economy: An Overview, Federal Reserve Bank of Kansas City, Economic Review, 1999, 11pp. Provides an overview of e-payments as they currently exist in the United States.

Federal Reserve Board of Governors Web site, Payment Systems page, at *http://www.federalreserve.gov/paymentsys.htm*. Covers Federal Reserve policy on payment systems and provides information on checks, automated clearing houses, Fedwire and Net settlement.

Federal Reserve Board of Governors, speeches, at *http://www.federalreserve.gov/boarddocs/speeches/*. Contains posted speeches of members of the Federal Reserve Board of Governors; several of the speeches discuss the evolving payment system.

Payment Systems Today, American Bankers Association, 2002. Provides an overview of the major payment systems and related regulations.

Retail Payments in Selected Countries, Bank for International Settlements, 1999. Compares retail payments systems and practices in selected countries.

"The State of Check Payments in the U.S.," The Depository Financial Institution Check Study, research conducted for the Federal Reserve, Global Concepts Payment Systems Consulting, 2001.

Statistics on Payment Systems in the Group of Ten Countries, Bank for International Settlements, 2002. Provides statistics on payments activity in the U.S. and the major industrial countries.

7

THE FEDERAL RESERVE AND OTHER FINANCIAL REGULATORS

LEARNING OBJECTIVES

After studying this chapter, you should be able to

- describe the unique structural characteristics of the quasi-governmental Federal Reserve System
- explain how members of the Board of Governors, members of the Federal Open Market Committee, and directors of the 12 Federal Reserve banks are selected
- cite the major functions of the district Federal Reserve banks
- explain the special functions of the Federal Reserve Bank of New York
- identify the key responsibilities of the Federal Reserve, the Comptroller of the Currency, and the Federal Deposit Insurance Corporation
- define the key terms listed in this chapter

KEY TERMS

Board of Governors
central bank
discount window loans
Federal Deposit Insurance Corporation
Federal Open Market Committee
Federal Reserve bank directors

Federal Reserve membership
fiscal agent
national charter
quasi-governmental
safekeeping
state charter

INTRODUCTION

The Federal Reserve is one of the most important and powerful institutions in the United States. It implements the nation's monetary policy in an attempt to control the cost and availability of money, influencing interest rates and the money supply. However, unlike the central banks of most other industrialized nations, the Federal Reserve is only quasi-governmental.

This chapter examines the Federal Reserve System's unique structure, which includes the Board of Governors, a federal government entity; the 12 Federal Reserve banks, which are private, largely autonomous institutions; and the members of the Federal Reserve, commercial banks. It also presents information about the varied functions of the Federal Reserve, which

- provides payment services for depositories
- serves as the bank for the government
- sets the nation's monetary policy
- regulates banks

The chapter also reviews the other financial institution regulators, which together with the Federal Reserve make up the nation's bank regulatory structure.

You are encouraged to examine Extended Study 4 for a financial profile of the Federal Reserve and a more detailed look at the activities that contribute to its special role in the banking system and the economy. Extended Study 5 presents a brief history of the money and banking system problems that led Congress to establish the Federal Reserve as a central monetary authority in 1913.

A UNIQUE CENTRAL BANK

Every nation has a **central bank**, the bank that is responsible for controlling the national money supply and for serving as the lender of last resort. Like a central government, a central bank distinguishes a nation as a political entity.

The concept of a central bank is not new. The nations of Europe had central banks before the Industrial Revolution. The Bank of Sweden and the Bank of England, two of the world's oldest central banks, were founded in the late 1600s.

Although central banks differ to some extent in structure, function, and economic role, they all share certain common characteristics. A central bank has the sole power to issue a nation's paper currency. It serves as a lender of last resort and thus a source of guaranteed liquidity to banks and other institutions. It acts as the government's bank, marketing the government's debt and acting on behalf of the government to safeguard the value of the nation's money in international trade. It buys and sells the nation's money in foreign exchange markets. A central bank also seeks to control the growth of a nation's money supply to achieve national economic objectives.

The Federal Reserve meets the definition of a central bank, but its structure is fundamentally different from that of other central banks. Most central banks are more closely tied to the executive branches of their governments than is the Federal Reserve. Other central banks are also directly responsible to their governments' treasury or finance ministers.

In contrast to other central banks, the Federal Reserve has a decentralized and **quasi-governmental** structure. Having characteristics of both a private corporation and a government agency, the Federal Reserve can establish the nation's monetary policy separately and independently from the fiscal policies, taxation, and government spending, of the president and the Congress.

The Structure of the Federal Reserve

The structure of the Federal Reserve reflects a legislative compromise over whether

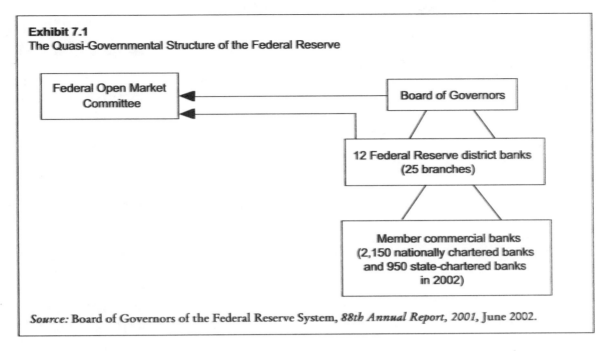

Exhibit 7.1
The Quasi-Governmental Structure of the Federal Reserve

Federal Open Market Committee

Board of Governors

12 Federal Reserve district banks (25 branches)

Member commercial banks (2,150 nationally chartered banks and 950 state-chartered banks in 2002)

Source: Board of Governors of the Federal Reserve System, *88th Annual Report, 2001*, June 2002.

monetary policy power would be centralized or decentralized, be held in public hands or private hands, and be used primarily to meet national needs or regional needs. Its integrated, three-tiered pyramidal structure combines governmental and private features and mandatory and voluntary features (see exhibit 7.1 above).

At the top of the pyramid is the **Board of Governors,** which is an entity of the federal government. This seven-member governing body is primarily responsible for monetary policy, regulation of banks, and broad oversight of the operations of the Federal Reserve banks.

The middle of the pyramid consists of 12 regional Federal Reserve banks, one in each of the nation's 12 Federal Reserve districts. Together, these private corporate entities serve as the nation's central bank.

Off to the side of the pyramid is the 12-member **Federal Open Market Committee** (FOMC), which sets the nation's monetary policy. The FOMC consists of the seven governors plus five Federal Reserve bank presidents.

At the base of the pyramid are the 3,100 commercial banks that are members of the Federal Reserve. **Federal Reserve membership** is required of all nationally chartered banks, whereas state-chartered banks can choose whether or not to become members.

Federal Reserve
Board Room
*Photo courtesy of the
Federal Reserve Board.*

THE BOARD OF GOVERNORS

The Board of Governors is the government component of the Federal Reserve System. The president of the United States appoints the seven governors who compose the board for 14-year nonrenewable terms of office. The Senate must confirm appointments. Like Supreme Court justices, Federal Reserve governors cannot be removed from office at the will of the president, a policy designed to insulate the board from political pressure. Once in office, the governors are expected to make decisions in accordance with the broad national interest, not the partisan interest of the administration that appointed them. The 14-year terms are staggered every two years so that as one governor's term expires a new governor is appointed. This feature ensures that no president can stack the board by making many appointees at one time.

The president also designates which of the seven governors will serve as the chair of the Board of Governors. However, the four-year term of the chairperson does not coincide with the president's term of office. Thus, a newly elected president must wait two years before designating a new chair. In practice, the existing chairperson is invariably redesignated to serve as chairperson for another four years.

The Board of Governors resides in Washington, D.C., and meets formally several times each week to transact its business. It decides matters related to the course of monetary policy as well as on the regulation of banks.

MONETARY POLICY

The seven members of the Board of Governors constitute a majority of the 12-member Federal Open Market Committee (FOMC). The FOMC is the key decision-making body within the Federal Reserve in relation to setting monetary policy. The FOMC meets about once every six weeks to review, evaluate, and (as appropriate) change monetary policy.

The Board of Governors has the sole power to

- determine reserve requirements for the nation's depository institutions
- determine the procedures and conditions under which the 12 Federal Reserve banks can make **discount window loans,** which are loans of reserves to meet temporary liquidity, seasonal, or emergency needs, to depository institutions
- use veto power over interest rates for discount window loans set by the Reserve banks
- set stock market margin requirements on using credit in securities transactions

REGULATION OF THE BANKING SYSTEM

The Board of Governors also supervises and regulates the activities of the Federal Reserve banks, regulates bank holding companies, and issues regulations with which lending institutions must comply in relation to the major federal consumer credit protection laws.

Despite its autonomy, the Board of Governors is accountable to Congress and often has to defend its actions against congressional criticism. However, there is no direct means short of legislation that Congress or the president can employ to change board decisions.

The chairperson of the Board of Governors, considered by many to be the nation's second most powerful government official, meets frequently with the president of the United States and the secretary of the Treasury. The chairperson is involved in all key domestic and international economic policy decisions. On an operational level, board members and staff maintain close working ties with officials and staff of the Treasury Department, the Office of Management and Budget, the Council of Economic

Advisors, and other government agencies. Congress frequently asks the board for its evaluation of economic issues. Board members also frequently testify before congressional committees on pending legislation related to money, banking, or the economy.

FEDERAL RESERVE DISTRICTS

The Federal Reserve Act of 1913 specified that the U.S. central bank would consist of as many as 12 regional central banks. The nation would be divided into Reserve districts, with each district having its own Reserve bank. Power would be decentralized and fragmented to prevent the new central bank from becoming too powerful and dominant over the nation's economic affairs. Also, the U.S. economy of 1913 was far more regionally disparate than it is today. At the time, the Reserve district concept addressed regional development needs and economic interests.

Exhibit 7.2 shows the 12 Federal Reserve districts and the cities where the Reserve banks are headquartered, as well as the locations of the branch banks. The districts vary greatly in size, reflecting the attempt to counterbalance banking power with size of territory.

FEDERAL RESERVE BANKS

The 12 Federal Reserve banks are private corporate entities rather than agencies of the federal government. The Board of Governors broadly supervises their general operations, but their day-to-day central banking activities take place largely independent of board involvement. Moreover, the Reserve banks function as autonomous institutions relative to each other.

The 12 Reserve banks and their 25 branches are the banking service arms of the central bank and are at the center of the nation's payments system (see exhibit 7.3 on the next page). Federal Reserve banks

- hold the reserves of the nation's depository institutions
- lend funds to depositories, acting as lenders of last resort

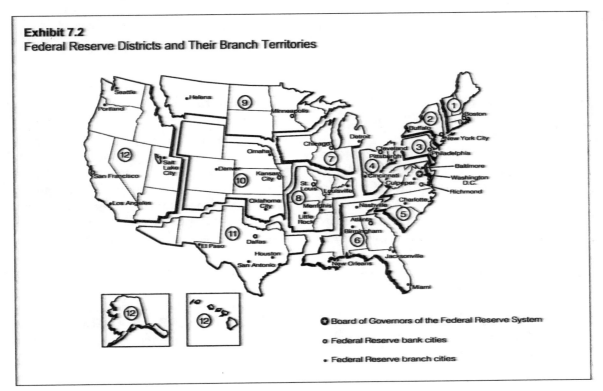

Exhibit 7.2
Federal Reserve Districts and Their Branch Territories

⊕ Board of Governors of the Federal Reserve System

○ Federal Reserve bank cities

• Federal Reserve branch cities

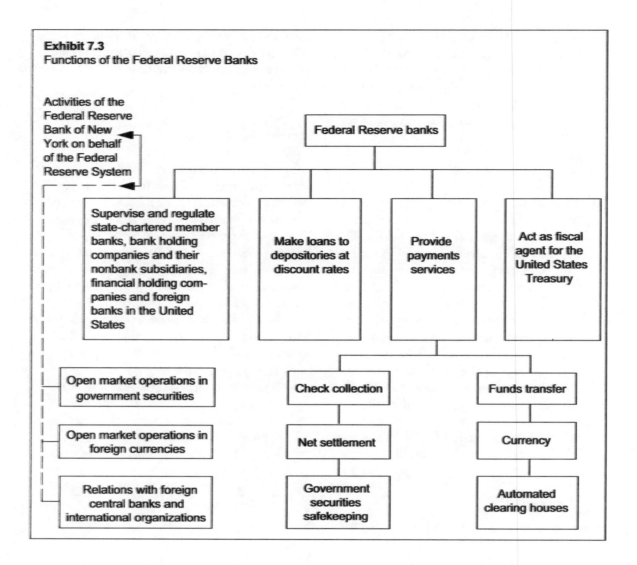

Exhibit 7.3
Functions of the Federal Reserve Banks

Activities of the Federal Reserve Bank of New York on behalf of the Federal Reserve System

Federal Reserve banks

- Supervise and regulate state-chartered member banks, bank holding companies and their nonbank subsidiaries, financial holding companies and foreign banks in the United States
- Make loans to depositories at discount rates
- Provide payments services
- Act as fiscal agent for the United States Treasury

- Open market operations in government securities
- Open market operations in foreign currencies
- Relations with foreign central banks and international organizations

- Check collection
- Net settlement
- Government securities safekeeping

- Funds transfer
- Currency
- Automated clearing houses

- issue the nation's currency and coin
- clear and collect about one-third of the nation's checks
- provide banking services to depository institutions and to the government
- examine state-chartered member banks

The 12 Reserve banks also participate in making monetary policy through the involvement of the five Reserve bank presidents who serve on the FOMC. The Federal Reserve Bank of New York has additional functions in implementing the Federal Reserve's open market operations and in dealing with the central banks of other nations.

SELECTION OF DIRECTORS

In organizing the Reserve banks in 1913, Congress attempted to ensure that central banking power would not rest completely in the hands of bankers, and that regional interests would be considered in central bank decisions. Congress specified that each Reserve bank should have a nine-member board of directors and that six of the directors must be nonbankers.

Federal Reserve bank directors are responsible to the member bank stockholders and to the Board of Governors for the sound management and operation of the Reserve banks (see exhibit 7.4).

For each Federal Reserve bank, the nine-member board of directors consists of three classes of directors (designated A, B, and C). Each class has three directors, who each serve three-year terms.

The six Class A and Class B directors are elected by the District's member commercial banks. Class A directors can be bankers. However, Class B directors cannot be bankers. Thus, although member banks elect the majority of each Reserve bank's nine-member board of directors, no more than three directors may directly represent banking interests.

The Board of Governors appoints class C directors. These individuals cannot be bankers; they typically are educators, lawyers, retired business executives, and leaders of community groups.

DIRECTORS' POWERS

The directors of the Reserve banks primarily serve as information channels among regional business, banking, and other interests and the Washington-based Board of Governors. However, because they appoint the banks' presidents and first vice presidents (subject to the Board of Governors' approval), Reserve bank directors indirectly influence the monetary policy-making process.

Every two weeks, the board of directors of each Reserve bank sets the discount rate for its district. However, the Board of Governors has veto power over any rate change it feels is inconsistent with the needs of the national economy.

RESERVE BANK EARNINGS

The 12 Federal Reserve district banks are profit-making entities, although they are not motivated by profit and do not keep most of their profits. Reserve banks generate profit mainly from the interest they earn on the $550 billion in government securities that constitute the Federal Reserve's open market portfolio. These securities have been purchased by the Reserve banks over the decades in implementing monetary policy. Other earnings are derived from the fees the Federal Reserve charges for clearing checks, electronically transferring funds, and

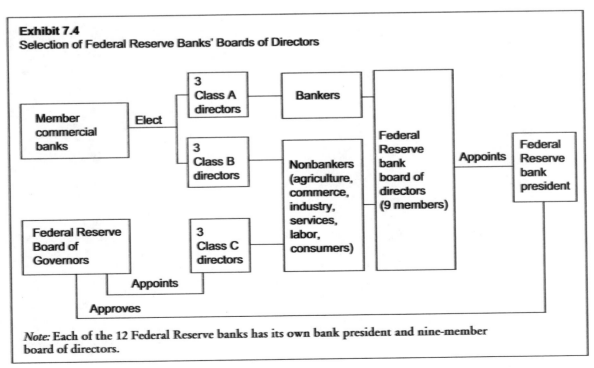

Exhibit 7.4
Selection of Federal Reserve Banks' Boards of Directors

Note: Each of the 12 Federal Reserve banks has its own bank president and nine-member board of directors.

from interest on discount window loans to depositories.

The Reserve banks keep only about 5 percent of the funds they earn. Annual earnings in excess of what the Reserve banks and the Board of Governors need to cover their operating expenses, plus what they need to pay a statutory 6 percent dividend on Federal Reserve bank stock owned by member banks, are returned to the Treasury. The Federal Reserve's ability to fund its own operations helps support its independence.

THE INDEPENDENCE OF THE FEDERAL RESERVE

A major reason why the Federal Reserve is such a powerful central bank is its independence. This independence is rooted in two features of the Federal Reserve's organizational structure, namely

- the 14-year terms of appointment for members of the Board of Governors
- the Federal Reserve's capacity to fund its own operations

Although it is independent, the Federal Reserve is not a separate branch of the U.S. government. It is subject to legislative change at any time and is sensitive to Congressional concerns. Over the decades, Congress generally has been reluctant to modify the Federal Reserve Act in any way that would politicize the Federal Reserve or compromise its independence. During the 1970s, however, Congress did enact legislation to make the Federal Reserve more accountable for its actions. Beginning in the 1970s, Congress required the Board of Governors to report twice each year on

- the Federal Reserve's money-supply growth targets for the coming year
- the central bank's current thinking about the economy's performance
- the Federal Reserve's objectives

Although the legislation that required these reports expired in 2000, the Federal Reserve has voluntarily continued its semi-annual reports to Congress.

During the 1990s, Congress criticized the Federal Reserve for being too secretive in implementing monetary policy and for not providing enough information about the reasons behind monetary policy actions. Six weeks after each FOMC meeting, the Federal Reserve does provide information about its policy deliberations in summary form. Nevertheless, to address this criticism, in 1995 the Federal Reserve agreed to publicly announce after each FOMC meeting whether a decision had been made by the FOMC to tighten or ease monetary policy. In 2002 the Federal Reserve also agreed to immediately disclose how individual FOMC members voted on interest rate decisions.

The Federal Reserve is considered to be among the most independent central banks in the world. However, many economists point to the central banks of Germany and Japan as ideal models for an independent central bank. In both countries, laws have been enacted that specify price stability (no inflation) as the primary objective of the central bank. These laws provide a legal shield against political or special-interest pressures for the German or Japanese central bank to alter its monetary policy. In contrast, because the Federal Reserve can designate its own policy priorities, it is always subject to pressure — from Congress, the president, the media, and special-interest groups—to change its policy.

THE FEDERAL RESERVE BANK OF NEW YORK

The Federal Reserve Bank of New York (FRBNY) plays a unique role in the nation's central banking system (see exhibit 7.3). Its special role reflects its location in the banking and financial center of the world.

The FRBNY is the only district bank authorized to implement open market operations, the Federal Reserve System's primary monetary policy tool. The New York Reserve Bank's trading desk buys and sells government securities in accordance with the general directives of the FOMC on behalf of the entire Federal Reserve System. In addition, the president of the FRBNY is the only Reserve bank president who is a permanent member of the FOMC, traditionally serving as the vice chair of the committee.

The FRBNY also has a unique international role. It acts as the government's and the FOMC's operating arm in the foreign exchange market. It buys and sells foreign currencies in New York to stabilize disorderly exchange market conditions. In addition, it buys and sells U.S. government securities

on behalf of foreign central banks. Since 1924 the FRBNY also has acted as the repository for the world's gold bullion reserves.

THE FEDERAL OPEN MARKET COMMITTEE

The 12-member FOMC makes monetary policy decisions for the Federal Reserve. Its open market operations, which involve the buying and selling of U.S. government securities, determine the cost and availability of money and credit in the U.S. economy.

The FOMC consists of the seven members of the Board of Governors and five Reserve bank presidents (see exhibit 7.5). Of the five Reserve bank presidents, only the president of the Federal Reserve Bank of New York is a permanent member. The four other Reserve bank presidents, who serve one-year terms, are selected in rotation from four regional clusters of the other 11 Reserve banks. The clusters are

- Boston, Philadelphia, and Richmond
- Cleveland and Chicago

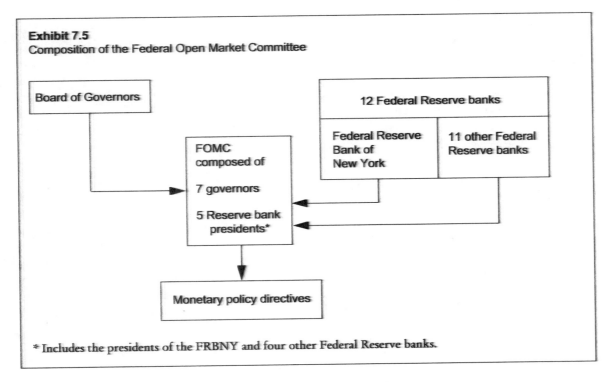

Exhibit 7.5
Composition of the Federal Open Market Committee

Board of Governors

FOMC composed of

7 governors

5 Reserve bank presidents*

12 Federal Reserve banks

Federal Reserve Bank of New York

11 other Federal Reserve banks

Monetary policy directives

* Includes the presidents of the FRBNY and four other Federal Reserve banks.

- Atlanta, St. Louis, and Dallas
- Minneapolis, San Francisco, and Kansas City

No statutory rules govern the FOMC's organization. By tradition, however, the chairperson of the Board of Governors also serves as chairperson of the FOMC and the president of the New York Reserve bank serves as vice chairperson.

The committee formally meets in Washington, D.C., every six weeks or so, but committee members routinely communicate with each other almost daily. If economic or financial conditions warrant action between regular meetings, additional meetings or telephone conferences are held.

At every formal meeting, the committee must vote on a course of action for monetary policy. The committee may vote to

- tighten policy, restricting the availability of money and credit and driving up interest rates
- ease policy, expanding the availability of money and credit and driving down interest rates
- maintain the status quo, leaving the money supply, credit conditions, and interest rates unchanged

This vote governs policy until the next meeting. Committee decisions are incorporated into a policy directive that is forwarded to the Federal Reserve Bank of New York for implementation through its open market operations.

MEMBER BANKS

At the base of the Federal Reserve's pyramidal structure are the member commercial banks. Any bank with a **national charter,** meaning a bank that is licensed to operate by the Office of the Comptroller of the Currency, must be a member of the Federal Reserve. State-chartered banks have the option to become members. The membership option for state-chartered banks reflects Congress's reluctance in 1913 to impose federal law over state-chartered institutions.

Banks that are members of the Federal Reserve must subscribe to stock (agree to purchase securities) in their district Federal Reserve bank in an amount equal to 6 percent of their own capital stock and surplus. Of this amount, 3 percent must be bought; the other 3 percent must remain subject to call for purchase, meaning that the Federal Reserve can require the bank to buy it at some time in the future.

Each year member banks receive a cumulative 6 percent dividend on the stock they have purchased. Stock subscriptions were intended to provide the Reserve banks with their initial working capital. Although the Federal Reserve is self-funding today, stock ownership remains a unique part of the structure of the U.S. central bank.

THE FEDERAL ADVISORY COUNCIL

The Federal Advisory Council, a private advisory group, serves as an information channel for the Federal Reserve. The council consists of 12 members, one appointed by each of the Federal Reserve banks. Members, each of whom serves for one year, are usually leading bankers in their Reserve districts. At least four council meetings are held annually at the Federal Reserve Board offices in Washington, D.C. Additional meetings may be called by the Board of Governors or by the council.

The Federal Advisory Council reviews and discusses operational matters and monetary policy, but does not exert any overt influence on the operations of the Reserve banks or on monetary policy. Rather, its primary role is to transmit bankers' views directly to the Board of Governors and to provide the board with grass-roots information and views about the effects of the Federal Reserve's actions.

FUNCTIONS OF THE FEDERAL RESERVE

The functions of the Federal Reserve can be grouped into three categories: 1) providing payment services for depositories, 2) serving as the government's bank, and 3) setting and implementing monetary policy.

PROVIDING PAYMENT SERVICES FOR DEPOSITORIES

Federal Reserve banks play a major operational role in the nation's payments system by

- issuing the nation's paper currency, also called Federal Reserve notes
- clearing one-third of the nation's checks through an extensive network of branches and regional check-processing centers
- serving as the nation's largest ACH operator
- operating Fedwire, an electronic funds transfer system that moves money and government securities among banks and enables banks to efficiently adjust their reserve balances
- providing **safekeeping,** in the form of protected facilities, for paper securities held by depositories
- collecting interest payments on paper securities held by depositories and crediting payment of matured securities to depositories' reserve accounts

SERVING AS THE GOVERNMENT'S BANK

Federal Reserve banks act as **fiscal agents,** handling government bond payments and other financial matters for the U.S. government. Reserve banks hold and issue new Treasury securities and savings bonds sold by the Treasury to dealers and the public. Banks pay for these securities through transfers of funds over Fedwire. Reserve banks also make periodic interest payments on behalf of the government on outstanding Treasury and federal agency debts, maintain the government's disbursement checking accounts, from which virtually all federal spending and benefits payments are made, and transfer funds between the U.S. government and foreign governments.

SETTING AND IMPLEMENTING MONETARY POLICY

The primary function of the Federal Reserve is to control the nation's supply of money and credit in an attempt to achieve balanced economic growth. Responsibility for formulating monetary policy is shared by the Board of Governors and the Federal Reserve banks. Members of the Board of Governors and Reserve bank presidents jointly control the rate paid on discount window loans and, through their participation on the FOMC, control open market operations.

SUPERVISING AND REGULATING MEMBER BANKS

The Federal Reserve examines state-chartered member banks, bank holding companies and their nonbank subsidiaries, and foreign banks operating in the United States. It also rules on merger and branching applications of state-chartered member banks and permissible activities for bank holding companies. The Federal Reserve must certify, or approve, bank holding companies, securities firms, and insurance companies before they can become financial holding companies. However, the Federal Reserve does not regulate the securities and insurance affiliates of financial holding companies. The Securities and Exchange Commission (SEC), the Commodity Futures Trading Commission, and state insurance commissions regulate such affiliate companies.

An overview of the major functions of each element in the Federal Reserve System appears in exhibit 7.6 on the following page.

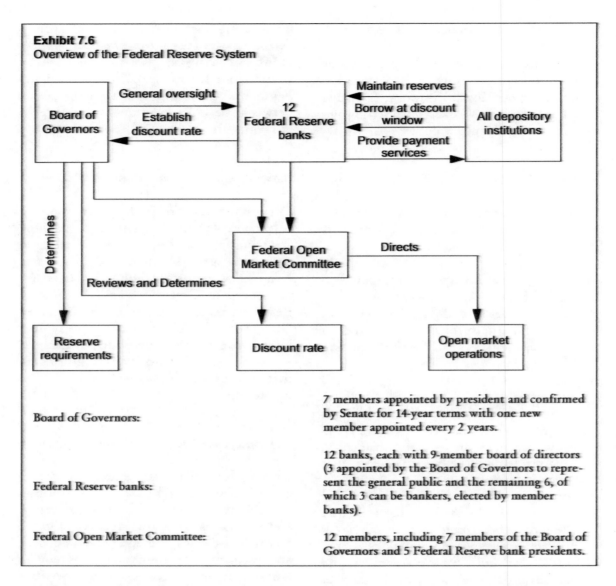

Exhibit 7.6
Overview of the Federal Reserve System

Board of Governors:	7 members appointed by president and confirmed by Senate for 14-year terms with one new member appointed every 2 years.
Federal Reserve banks:	12 banks, each with 9-member board of directors (3 appointed by the Board of Governors to represent the general public and the remaining 6, of which 3 can be bankers, elected by member banks).
Federal Open Market Committee:	12 members, including 7 members of the Board of Governors and 5 Federal Reserve bank presidents.

Although the Federal Reserve is singularly responsible for monetary policy in the United States, regulatory power over the nation's banks is shared with other federal agencies and with state governments.

OTHER FINANCIAL REGULATORS

Banks fall under the jurisdictions of a variety of regulators. Furthermore, most banks are regulated by more than one government agency. The bank's choice of a state or federal charter determines whether its primary regulator will be a state or a federal agency.

Most federal regulation of state-chartered banks is optional. For example, state-chartered banks may become members of the Federal Deposit Insurance Corporation (FDIC), the Federal Reserve or both. Federal Reserve member banks must be FDIC insured, but state-chartered banks that elect FDIC membership need not be members of the Federal Reserve.

In practice, essentially all of the nation's state-chartered commercial banks are FDIC members. These banks are subject to the examinations and administrative rules and regulations of multiple regulatory agencies (see exhibit 7.7).

Exhibit 7.7
Division of Bank Regulatory Responsbilities

Type of Bank	Chartered by	Examined by	Subject to Reserve Requirements Imposed by	Deposits Insured by	Subject to Regulations of	Bank Holding Companies Regulated by
National banks	OCC*	OCC	Fed**	FDIC†	OCC Fed FDIC	Fed State‡
State bank members of Fed	State	Fed State	Fed	FDIC	Fed FDIC State	Fed
State banks *not* Fed members but FDIC insured	State	FDIC State	Fed	FDIC	FDIC State	Fed State
State banks *not* Fed members and *not* FDIC insured	State	State	Fed		State	State

* OCC: Office of the Comptroller of the Currency

** Fed: Federal Reserve

† FDIC: Federal Deposit Insurance Corporation

‡ State: State Banking Departments

STATE BANKING DEPARTMENTS

All states charter commercial banks and some states also charter savings institutions. Three-quarters of the nation's commercial banks are state chartered. A **state charter** is granted after an investigation of the applicants' background and verification that the bank meets the state's capital requirements. State banking departments examine the institutions they charter, rule on their acquisitions and branching applications, and issue advisory opinions on acquisition applications received from bank holding companies. They also examine the branches and agencies of foreign banks operating in their state.

COMPTROLLER OF THE CURRENCY

The Office of the Comptroller of the Currency (OCC) is the unit of the United States Department of the Treasury that charters national banks. All national banks except those in overseas U.S. territories are required to be members of the Federal Reserve System. The OCC also examines national banks and rules on their merger and branching applications.

Federal Deposit Insurance Corporation

For member banks and savings institutions, the **Federal Deposit Insurance Corporation** (FDIC) provides insurance coverage on depositors' accounts up to a certain amount, currently $100,000. The funds for the insurance are held in the FDIC's Bank Insurance Fund (BIF) and its Savings Association Insurance Fund (SAIF). National banks and state-chartered banks that opt for Federal Reserve membership are required to be members of the FDIC. State-chartered commercial and savings banks may elect to be insured.

The FDIC examines state-chartered banks that are FDIC-insured but are not members of the Federal Reserve. It also

- rules on merger and branching applications of state-chartered banks that are not members of the Federal Reserve
- issues advisory opinions on merger applications of Federal Reserve member banks and FDIC-insured, state-chartered nonmember banks
- manages and liquidates assets of failed banks (see exhibit 7.8)

Office of Thrift Supervision

The Office of Thrift Supervision (OTS) charters federal savings and loan associations (S&Ls) and federal savings banks. Although the FDIC examines these institutions and administers the insurance fund for S&Ls, the OTS is responsible for issuing regulations that govern S&Ls and S&L holding companies.

Federal Housing Finance Board

The Federal Housing Finance Board oversees the activities of the 12 regional Federal Home Loan Banks. These banks provide subsidized loans to members of the Federal Home Loan Bank system. Membership in that system is mandatory for S&Ls, and since 1989 has been optional for commercial banks and credit unions that have more than 10 percent of their loans in residential housing.

National Credit Union Administration

The National Credit Union Administration (NCUA) charters federal credit unions and

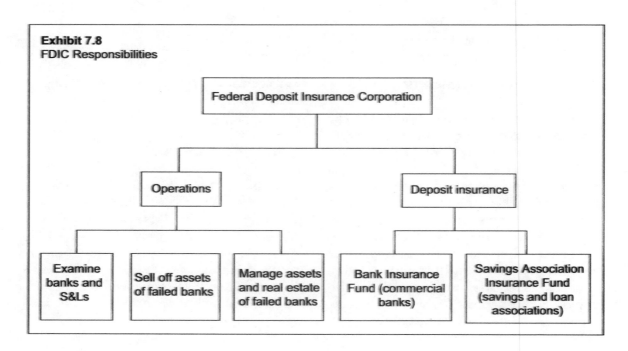

Exhibit 7.8
FDIC Responsibilities

Federal Deposit Insurance Corporation

Operations

Deposit insurance

Examine banks and S&Ls

Sell off assets of failed banks

Manage assets and real estate of failed banks

Bank Insurance Fund (commercial banks)

Savings Association Insurance Fund (savings and loan associations)

FEDERAL RESERVE RESPONSE TO THE SEPTEMBER 11 TERRORIST ATTACKS

The terrorist attacks on New York's World Trade Center on September 11, 2001 destroyed part of the nation's financial markets infrastructure, disrupted communication and transportation systems in and around New York City, and forced major securities dealer firms and banks to shift operations to contingency sites. These developments complicated the trading, clearing, and settlement of financial instruments, including the buying and selling of excess reserves, during the days immediately following the attacks. Fortunately, the Federal Reserve, and particularly the Federal Reserve Bank of New York, was able to respond quickly and effectively to assist the nation's financial system in weathering the crisis.

LIQUIDITY FOR U.S. BANKS

On the day of the attacks, the Federal Reserve immediately assured both domestic and international financial markets that its operations involving check collection, electronic funds and securities transfers, open market purchases, and sales of U.S. government securities continued to function normally, and that the Federal Reserve stood ready to provide needed liquidity to banks. On the day following the attacks, banks borrowed a record $45.5 billion, which they repaid over the next two days.

LIQUIDITY FOR FOREIGN BANKS OPERATING IN THE UNITED STATES

Foreign banks operating in the United States faced strong liquidity needs. The offices of more than 25 foreign banks were destroyed in the attacks. Moreover, many foreign banks with branches in New York City could not present collateral to those branches to secure Federal Reserve discount window loans. In response the Federal Reserve established, for a 30-day period, a $90 billion currency swap arrangement with the European Central Bank and the central banks of the United Kingdom and Canada. The Federal Reserve credited these central banks' accounts with dollars in exchange for an equivalent value of their currency credited the Federal Reserve's account. The central banks used these credits to lend funds to foreign banks in the United States that needed dollars.

CHECK COLLECTION

With air traffic suspended in the days following the attacks, Federal Reserve float rose to a record level, about $30 billion. The Federal Reserve continued to credit the accounts of banks for checks received from them but had no way to present inter-regional checks to the banks on which they were drawn. Float subsided to a more normal level, about $500 million, during the following week as air traffic resumed.

ELECTRONIC FUNDS AND SECURITIES TRANSFERS

To facilitate smooth functioning in federal funds and government securities markets, the Federal Reserve extended Fedwire operating hours for a week after the September 11, 2001, terrorist attacks. The Federal Reserve also suspended its penalty charge on account overdrafts, helped restore computer links between major deal firms and banks in New York City, and helped dealer firms and banks reconcile and settle trading positions.

Continued on next page

CASH

Within days following the September 11 attacks, the Federal Reserve established an overseas cash depot, called a Strategic Inventory Location (SIL). The SIL positioned an inventory of unissued U.S. currency in London to meet the potential cash needs of anxious foreigner who increasingly use dollars in their day-to-day commercial transactions.

MONETARY POLICY

The Federal Reserve did not change monetary policy immediately following the terrorist attacks because the financial markets were too disrupted. However, after one week, the Federal Reserve eased policy. Over the course of subsequent weeks, the economic repercussions of the attacks became clear as consumer spending and capital investment declined and stock and securities prices fell. The Federal Reserve eased policy again. Between mid-September and early November 2001, short-term interest rates were reduced by $1\frac{1}{2}$ percentage points, from 3.5 percent to 2 percent. By early December, the economic shock waves of the September 11 attacks had begun to subside.

EFFECTIVENESS

The Federal Reserve responded effectively to the terrorist attacks of September 11 largely because the Federal Reserve Bank of New York, the main offices of which is located just two block from Ground Zero, was undamaged by the attacks. The New York Reserve Bank's payments service and computer operations, along with about one-third of its staff, are housed in New Jersey and were not directly affected by the attacks.

The financial markets returned to normal operations within weeks of the September 11 attacks, and the economy rebounded by the year's end. In early 2002, Federal Reserve staff were still working with banks to reconstruct check records that had been destroyed on September 11, reconcile account differences, and strengthen contingency communications and computer links among market participants.

---

provides insurance coverage for federal credit unions and state-chartered credit unions that elect insurance. The NCUA also examines all credit unions it insures and acts as the lender of last resort for credit unions.

UNITED STATES DEPARTMENT OF JUSTICE

The United States Department of Justice (DOJ) is part of the executive branch of the U.S. government. The DOJ's antitrust division enforces antitrust laws in connection with bank mergers and bank holding company acquisitions. The DOJ also renders advisory opinions on merger proposals of state-chartered and nationally chartered banks.

FEDERAL FINANCIAL INSTITUTIONS EXAMINATION COUNCIL

The Federal Financial Institutions Examination Council coordinates the independent activities of the federal regulators of financial institutions and assures that their examinations adhere to common standards. Since its establishment by Congress in 1978, the Council has developed a uniform examinations process and a uniform financial institutions rating system. Five agencies comprise the Council: FDIC, OTS, the Federal Reserve Board, OCC, and NCUA.

In general, banks are examined once a year by their primary federal and/or state regulator. The regulatory agencies also review the condition of overseas branches of U.S. banks in conjunction with domestic examinations. Reviews may be conducted on-site or they may be conducted by examining the records of overseas offices maintained at each bank's domestic head office. During the 1980s, the various federal regulatory agencies and a number of states instituted a program of alternate-year examinations. Under this program, federal and state regulators take turns examining state-chartered banks, each examining a given bank every other year.

SUMMARY

The Federal Reserve implements monetary policy through reserve requirements, the discount rate, and open market operations.

The Federal Reserve is a unique quasi-governmental central bank. It consists of 12 regional Reserve banks, which are private corporations nominally owned by member banks and run by boards of directors. The Reserve banks are supervised by a Board of Governors made up of seven officials appointed by the president of the United States. The key monetary policy decision-making entity within the Federal Reserve System is the 12-member Federal Open Market Committee. The committee's operating arm in implementing monetary policy is the Federal Reserve Bank of New York.

The Federal Reserve's major operational functions are to provide payment services to depositories and to act as the banker and fiscal agent of the U.S. Treasury. The Federal Reserve also is a regulator of banks, bank holding companies, and financial holding companies, but it is not the sole bank regulatory authority in the United States. Bank regulation is shared among the states and several federal agencies, most notably the Office of Comptroller of the Currency and the Federal Deposit Insurance Corporation.

REVIEW QUESTIONS

1. Based on the structure of the Federal Reserve, what objectives do you think Congress had when it created the central bank?
2. What specific roles do the FOMC and the Federal Reserve Bank of New York play in the monetary policy process?
3. What are the sources of the Federal Reserve's independence?
4. What characteristics do the 12 Federal Reserve district banks and the Federal Reserve member banks have in common? How do they differ?
5. Who regulates banks in the United States today?

ADDITIONAL RESOURCES

American Bankers Association, at *www.aba.com*. Provides current information on bank regulatory compliance issues.

Board of Governors of the Federal Reserve System, at *www.federalreserve.gov*. Lists the Board of Governors of the Federal Reserve and provides economic data and statistical releases on the Federal Reserve System. Site also includes a search function, which gives access to documents like biographies of governors and presidents, FOMC transcripts, press releases, and statistical releases.

Federal Reserve Bulletin, Board of Governors of the Federal Reserve, monthly publication. Contains FOMC policy directives and reports to Congress, topical articles on banking and economic conditions, and financial and business statistics.

The Federal Reserve System—Purposes and Functions, Board of Governors of the Federal Reserve, 1994, 157 pp. A comprehensive examination of the structure, responsibilities, and operations of the Federal Reserve.

"When it Comes 2 Economic Education, the Federal Reserve is where it's @," at *www.federalreserveeducation.org*. Searchable site explains how the central bank affects the economy through its various operations.

Federal Financial Institutions Examination Council, at *www.ffiec.gov*. Provides current information on how U.S. bank regulatory agencies coordinate their activities.

EXTENDED STUDY 4: THE FEDERAL RESERVE'S STATEMENT OF CONDITION

The Federal Reserve issues a weekly financial profile, or consolidated statement of condition, of the 12 Federal Reserve banks. This statement reflects all of the central bank's activities, as well as its special role in the banking system and the economy as the ultimate source of all money.

The Federal Reserve's statement of condition as of February 2002 is shown on the next page. As you examine this balance sheet, notice that some Federal Reserve assets and liabilities are similar to those of large correspondent banks but others are clearly unique to the central bank. The key difference is the way in which the Federal Reserve acquires assets and liabilities. Each time it obtains an asset, and a corresponding liability, it either creates reserves for banks, which adds to their ability to make loans and create money, or it creates deposits for the Treasury, which adds to the government's ability to spend money.

ASSETS

The combined assets of the Federal Reserve banks in February 2002 totaled $658.1 billion. Of these assets the first two listed, gold certificates and special drawing rights credits, have no counterpart on the commercial bank balance sheet.

GOLD CERTIFICATE ACCOUNT

The Gold Certificate Account is a remnant from earlier decades when Federal Reserve notes issued by the Reserve banks had to be backed by gold. Statutory minimum gold-backing requirements against Federal Reserve notes were abolished in 1968. However, each Reserve bank must still maintain collateral equal to the amount of its Federal Reserve notes outstanding. Although the collateral can be virtually any Reserve bank asset, the Reserve banks continue to pledge their gold certificate credits as collateral against issued notes.

Over the years, the Reserve banks acquired gold certificates (now bookkeeping credits) from the U.S. Treasury. When the Treasury bought gold, it would monetize the gold by issuing gold certificates to the Federal Reserve for an equal amount of dollars credited to its demand deposit account at the Reserve banks. Monetization enabled the Treasury to replenish its checking account without having to borrow or draw on tax receipts. It received dollars created for it by the Federal Reserve. In exchange, the Federal Reserve received gold certificates it could use as backing for its note issues.

Today these gold certificate credits serve primarily as an internal medium of exchange among the Reserve banks. Reserve banks settle daily amounts due each other by transferring gold certificate credits to each other's books through the Interdistrict Settlement Account maintained in Washington, D.C. Because amounts due are settled by increasing or decreasing the gold certificate balances held by each Reserve bank, the gold certificates held by the Federal Reserve are redistributed continually within the system. However, the total remains the same; in recent years, this asset entry on the consolidated statement has rarely, if ever, changed.

Federal Reserve Banks' Consolidated Statement of Condition, February 2002 (in billions)

Assets		Liabilities and Capital Accounts	
		Liabilities	
Gold certificate account	$11.0	Federal Reserve notes	606.9
Special drawing rights certificate		Reserve deposits	20.8
account	2.2	U.S. Treasury account	4.9
Coin	1.1	Foreign government accounts	0.1
Loans	0.1	Other accounts	0.2
U.S. government securities	568.7	Deferred availability cash items	7.5
Repurchase agreements	32.0	Other liabilities and accrued	
Federal agency securities	0.1	dividends	2.4
Cash items in process of collection	7.0	*Total liabilities*	*642.8*
Bank premises	1.5	*Capital accounts*	
Foreign currency assets	15.0	Capital paid in	7.6
Other assets	19.4	Surplus	7.3
		Other capital	0.4
		Total capital accounts	*15.3*
Total assets	658.1	Total liabilities and capital accounts	658.1

Source: Federal Reserve Board, Statistical Release H.4.1(a), February 2002.

SPECIAL DRAWING RIGHTS CERTIFICATE ACCOUNT

Since 1969 the International Monetary Fund (IMF) has administered a treaty-based, internationally accepted medium of exchange on which participating countries have special drawing rights (SDRs). The Federal Reserve's Special Drawing Rights Certificate Account represents the United States' allocation from the IMF. The Federal Reserve banks acquire SDR certificate credits from the U.S. Treasury after it monetizes the SDRs received from the IMF. As with gold monetization, when the Treasury monetizes SDRs it issues certificates, or credits, to the Federal Reserve. In return, the Treasury receives an equivalent amount of dollars posted to its checking account at the Reserve banks.

COIN

This next asset category shows the amount of coin currently on hand in Federal Reserve bank vaults. Coin held by the Reserve banks

is a Federal Reserve asset. This is because all U.S. coinage is issued by the Treasury, which makes it a direct liability of the government and not a liability of the Federal Reserve. The Federal Reserve distributes coin to the nation's banking system in its operational role as the central bank, and it receives excess coin from banks for credit to their accounts at the Federal Reserve.

LOANS

The entry under loans represents outstanding credit extended by Federal Reserve banks to depository institutions at the discount window.

Virtually all discount window loans today are advances. An advance is a loan made on the borrowing bank's own promissory note secured by government securities or other collateral acceptable to the Federal Reserve. In the past, most discount window loans were made against the short-term commercial, industrial, or agricultural paper of a bank's customers; this paper was then rediscounted by the Reserve banks. This past practice was so closely identified with the Federal Reserve that most of the financial press and the academic community still refers to Reserve bank loans as discount window loans, and the Federal Reserve still refers to its interest rate charge for these loans as the discount rate.

Reserve banks sometimes lend money to foreign governments and central banks, and have the power to lend to individuals, partnerships, and corporations under conditions of national economic emergency, although they have never done so.

The System Open Market Account Portfolio

The Federal Reserve Bank of New York purchases U.S. government securities, repurchase agreements, and federal agency securities that appear on the consolidated statement for the System Open Market Account. Ownership of the System Open Market Account portfolio, like ownership of the Gold Certificate Account, is proportionally divided among all the Reserve banks. The exception is securities held under repurchase agreements, which are carried only on the books of the Federal Reserve Bank of New York.

U.S. Government Securities

This asset category represents the Treasury bills, certificates, notes, and bonds the Federal Reserve has bought in the open market from dealers in government securities. It is by far the largest asset category, accounting for more than 85 percent of the Reserve banks' assets in February 2002.

Repurchase agreements

On occasion the Federal Reserve buys government securities from dealers under repurchase agreements, meaning that the dealers agree to repurchase the securities within a short, specified period of time. These agreements are used when the Federal Reserve wants to provide a temporary and self-reversing injection of reserves into the banking system.

Federal Agency Securities

Federal agency securities are issued by agencies of the federal government, excluding the Treasury. Federal agencies established to implement the government's farm and home lending programs generally issue securities to finance their activities. Most of these securities are guaranteed not by the U.S. government, but by the agencies themselves.

Cash Items in Process of Collection

Like all other banks, Federal Reserve banks show cash items in process of collection— that is, checks in the process of being cleared—as a separate asset account. The amount in this category represents the value of all the checks deposited with the Federal Reserve banks for collection and which, on the date of the statement, are still in the process of being collected.

Bank Premises

This balance sheet entry reflects the value of the land, buildings, and equipment of the 12 Federal Reserve banks and their 25 branches.

Foreign Currency Assets

Foreign currency assets are foreign money balances that the Federal Reserve acquires through swap drawings in its international role as the U.S. central bank. In a swap drawing, the Federal Reserve and a foreign central bank exchange, or swap, a predetermined amount of each other's currencies for several months. The exchanged currency is then used in the foreign exchange markets to stabilize exchange rates.

OTHER ASSETS

The Federal Reserve accrues interest on the government securities it owns or is holding under repurchase agreements. It also earns interest on loans made to depository institutions and on foreign currency investments that may have been made in support of its role in stabilizing the value of the dollar in foreign exchange markets. These accumulated interest earnings are recorded as other assets.

LIABILITIES AND CAPITAL ACCOUNTS

As with any balance sheet, the left side of the Federal Reserve banks' consolidated statement of condition must equal the right side; that is, the assets must equal the liabilities plus capital accounts. Many of the liabilities listed on the balance sheet of the Federal Reserve are the same as those of large commercial banks. However, only the Federal Reserve records currency as a liability.

FEDERAL RESERVE NOTES

This entry represents all Federal Reserve notes in circulation, including what is held by the public, banks, and the U.S. Treasury. It serves as a broad gauge on a week-to-week and year-to-year basis of the global economy's preference for U.S. currency.

RESERVE DEPOSITS

This entry is the total amount of reserves that depository institutions maintain at the Reserve banks. All depositories are required to meet the reserve requirements through vault cash or a combination of vault cash and a deposit balance at the Federal Reserve or a pass-through account at a correspondent bank. Most of the nation's small depository institutions meet their reserve requirements with the vault cash they keep in the normal course of business.

U.S. TREASURY ACCOUNT

The U.S. Treasury account is the balance in the general checking account of the Treasury from which virtually all government checks are drawn. In no way is this a measure of the government's entire money holdings. The Treasury maintains the bulk of the government's money in thousands of Treasury tax and loan (TT&L) accounts at banks and thrifts throughout the country. Most tax receipts and funds received from the Treasury's sale of new government securities are deposited into TT&L accounts to minimize the impact of tax collections and Treasury borrowings on bank reserves. When the government needs money to cover anticipated checks, the Treasury transfers funds from its TT&L accounts to its account at the Federal Reserve.

FOREIGN GOVERNMENT ACCOUNTS

Foreign government accounts represent the demand deposit balances that foreign governments and their central banks hold at the Federal Reserve. The Federal Reserve Bank of New York handles transactions involving these accounts for the Federal Reserve System; however, the deposit liabilities are allocated among all the Reserve banks.

OTHER ACCOUNTS

This entry includes several deposit categories. The most important of these are the demand balances of international financial organizations, the special checking accounts of the Treasury used in foreign exchange dealings, and the demand accounts of certain U.S. government agencies.

DEFERRED AVAILABILITY CASH ITEMS

This entry represents the amount of checks and other cash items received by Federal Reserve banks for collection but that will not be credited to the depositing banks' accounts for another one to two days.

OTHER LIABILITIES AND ACCRUED DIVIDENDS

This entry reflects the liabilities that the Federal Reserve is accumulating to pay its statutory dividend on Federal Reserve Bank stock owned by member banks.

CAPITAL ACCOUNTS

The Federal Reserve's capital accounts include capital paid in, surplus, and other capital.

CAPITAL PAID IN

This entry shows the amount that member banks have paid for Federal Reserve banks' capital stock.

SURPLUS

Surplus reflects the earnings that the Federal Reserve is required by law to retain as a reserve against unforeseen losses.

OTHER CAPITAL

Other capital is the amount of earnings for the Federal Reserve since its last payment of dividends to member bank stockholders and its last payment of interest to the Treasury on Federal Reserve notes (the accounting method that is used to transfer earnings to the Treasury).

EXTENDED STUDY 5: ORIGINS OF THE FEDERAL RESERVE

In creating the Federal Reserve System, Congress was attempting to deal with structural defects in the nation's money and banking system that were causing increasing instability in the nation's economy. These defects included an inelastic currency, pyramiding of bank reserves, the lack of a lender of last resort, lack of central supervision of banks, and an inefficient national payments system.

AN INELASTIC CURRENCY

First, the nation lacked a paper currency that could respond to the changing demands of businesses and consumers. The inelasticity of the nation's currency was rooted in the collateral requirements that were imposed on national bank notes, the paper currency that was used from the mid-1860s until the establishment of the Federal Reserve in 1913.

National bank notes were given by the government to nationally chartered banks, which, in turn, issued the notes as their own currency. Because national bank notes had to be fully collateralized by government securities, however, the nation's supply of paper currency depended on the government's debt. The supply of currency expanded and contracted in direct response to changes in the value of government securities in the nation's bond markets rather than in response to the economy's needs. When the government began repaying its Civil War debt by redeeming and retiring securities issued in earlier years, the supply of collateral available for note issuance shrank. This shrank the size of the money supply. The inelasticity meant that the U.S. economy could not adjust to the changing monetary needs and demands of the public

PYRAMIDING OF BANK RESERVES AND LACK OF A LENDER OF LAST RESORT

Another defect in the nation's early banking system was the pyramiding of local banks' reserves into a few of the nation's money center banks. This phenomenon left local banks with insufficient liquidity in times of stress. Banks also lacked a lender of last resort—a source of guaranteed liquidity that they could tap when they needed money.

Because the banking system's reserves were dispersed throughout the country, they could not be quickly transferred to banks in regions that might be under liquidity pressure. In the absence of a lender of last resort, banks were susceptible to cumulative pressures that often led to bank panics.

The Bank Panic of 1907 precipitated establishment of the Federal Reserve. It was a typical bank panic in all but its severity. When New York City banks did not have enough funds to honor reserve claims from their small bank correspondents, they quickly called in loans made to brokers and dealers. Broker and dealer firms, in turn, sold stocks and bonds to raise money to repay their loans. The ensuing selling frenzy on Wall Street drove down the prices of securities, making it impossible for some firms to make repayment. The defaulting brokers and dealers, in turn, brought down a number of banks with them. Moreover, as New Yorkers learned of the plight of brokers and banks, many panicked and withdrew their funds from sound banks, thereby adding to the illiquidity of the banking system.

LACK OF CENTRAL SUPERVISION OF BANKS

Another problem was the lack of uniform protection for the public's bank deposits. The nation's banking system was governed by banking laws and regulations that had been developed along separate federal and state lines. As a result of this decentralized supervision of banks, there was no mechanism for uniformly protecting the public's bank deposits on a nationwide basis.

AN INEFFICIENT NATIONAL PAYMENTS SYSTEM

A final problem that needed to be resolved was the lack of an efficient national payments system. Checkbook money could not be transferred quickly or easily from one part of the country to another. No nationwide system existed for clearing and collecting checks. The result was that banks relied on a number of inefficient practices to collect inter-regional checks. Such practices included exchange charges, circuitous routing, non-par checking, using uncollected funds as reserves, and the proliferation of compensating balances.

EXCHANGE CHARGES

Some banks imposed an exchange charge on checks presented for payment by out-of-town banks. The charge covered the costs incurred in shipping gold or cash to pay for checks, the normal banking practice before the Federal Reserve was created.

CIRCUITOUS ROUTING

To avoid exchange charges, banks frequently sent checks on long, circuitous collection routes across the country. Final payment took an exceedingly long time and banks had no direct way for banks to return dishonored items.

NON-PAR CHECKING

Exchange charges for out-of-town checks meant that checks were credited to depositors' accounts at less than par, or face, value. Because of this practice, out-of-town checks often were not accepted in commercial dealings. Business firms typically required payment of bills either in currency or with a local check.

Uncollected Funds as Reserves

Correspondent banks receiving checks deposited by respondent banks for collection credited their respondents' accounts immediately, even though the checks could not be collected for a number of days. Because these accounts made up a substantial portion of the legal reserves of the nation's respondent banks, the practice resulted in reserves (at that time designed to ensure bank safety and liquidity) being held largely in uncollected funds.

Compensating Balances to Collect Checks at Par

In an attempt to receive full face value for deposited checks, banks often fragmented their reserve deposits, maintaining many different correspondent account balances at banks in different banking regions. This practice damaged bank liquidity and grew exceedingly costly as check usage proliferated.

The Central Banking Solution

The Bank Panic of 1907 motivated Congress to establish a national monetary commission to study the defects in the U.S. money and banking system and to propose a solution. The Aldrich Commission's recommended solution was a central bank controlled by bankers. President Woodrow Wilson made some key modifications to the recommended proposal, most notably adding a government-appointed Board of Governors with supervisory and administrative oversight of the central bank. As amended, the plan became the Federal Reserve Act of 1913.

8

BANK LEGISLATION AND REGULATION

LEARNING OBJECTIVES

After studying this chapter, you should be able to

- explain the major goals of bank regulation
- explain the differences between unit banking and dual banking
- name the significant changes in banking brought about by federal legislation during the 1980s and 1990s
- identify the major consumer regulations and the procedures generally followed by bank examiners to determine regulatory compliance with the Community Reinvestment Act
- define the key terms listed in this chapter

KEY TERMS

bank regulation
bank supervision
Community Reinvestment Act
correspondent banking

purchase and assumption procedures
redlining
respondent banks
thrifts

INTRODUCTION

In the U.S. banking system, the federal government and state governments share regulatory power. This chapter examines this dual bank regulatory structure and the major principles, laws, and regulations that set the boundaries for the business of banking. It first looks at the public policy goals of bank regulation and then introduces seven laws that significantly reshaped banking during the 1980s and 1990s. They are the

- Monetary Control Act of 1980
- Garn-St Germain Act of 1982
- Competitive Equality Banking Act of 1987
- Financial Institutions Reform, Recovery and Enforcement Act of 1989
- Federal Deposit Insurance Corporation Improvement Act of 1991
- Interstate Banking and Branching Efficiency Act of 1994
- Gramm-Leach-Bliley Act of 1999

Finally, the chapter summarizes the major banking regulations and reviews the role of bank examinations in effecting regulatory compliance.

For a more detailed discussion of the major historical developments that have shaped government regulation of U.S. banks and the current examinations and rating process, you are encouraged to examine Extended Study 6.

REGULATORY GOALS AND THE STRUCTURE OF BANKING

Bank regulation is the implementation of banking laws through government-issued rules and directives. **Bank supervision** is the enforcement of those rules and directives through bank examinations and the off-site analysis of data and information on banking performance and practice.

The federal government's major goal in regulating banks is to protect banks, their depositors, and the communities in which they operate from bank failures. To comply with federal regulations, banks must operate prudently, maintain sufficient access to liquidity, manage assets and liabilities wisely to minimize risk of failure and monetary loss for depositors, and prevent a loss of public confidence in the safety and soundness of the banking system.

Another federal regulatory goal is promoting competition in banking. Banks must adhere to uniform rules in advertising, marketing, and offering new deposits. Banks also must not become so large that only a few banks dominate the industry.

Given banks' power to create new money when they make loans, the government also sees potential for anticompetitive abuse in other markets. In an unregulated environment, for example, banks could acquire manufacturing subsidiaries and drive out competition in those industries by supplying subsidiaries with low-cost loans. To prevent this from happening, the government has regulated banks within a narrow business context, as extenders of credit primarily to businesses and, until 1980, as exclusive acceptors of demand deposits.

The federal government also seeks to use regulation to

- protect bank owners from management fraud
- prevent management from placing depositors' funds in unsafe loans and investments
- protect consumers of bank credit and services from discrimination, deception, and abuse of their rights

Since the 1930s, these goals have been pursued and achieved through a system of shared regulation and supervision among different federal agencies and the states (see exhibits 8.1 and 8.2). Indeed, many different government agencies have regulatory responsibility over banks' activities. This regulatory structure encompasses dual banking, unit banking, and correspondent banking.

Exhibit 8.1
Current Bank Regulatory Structure

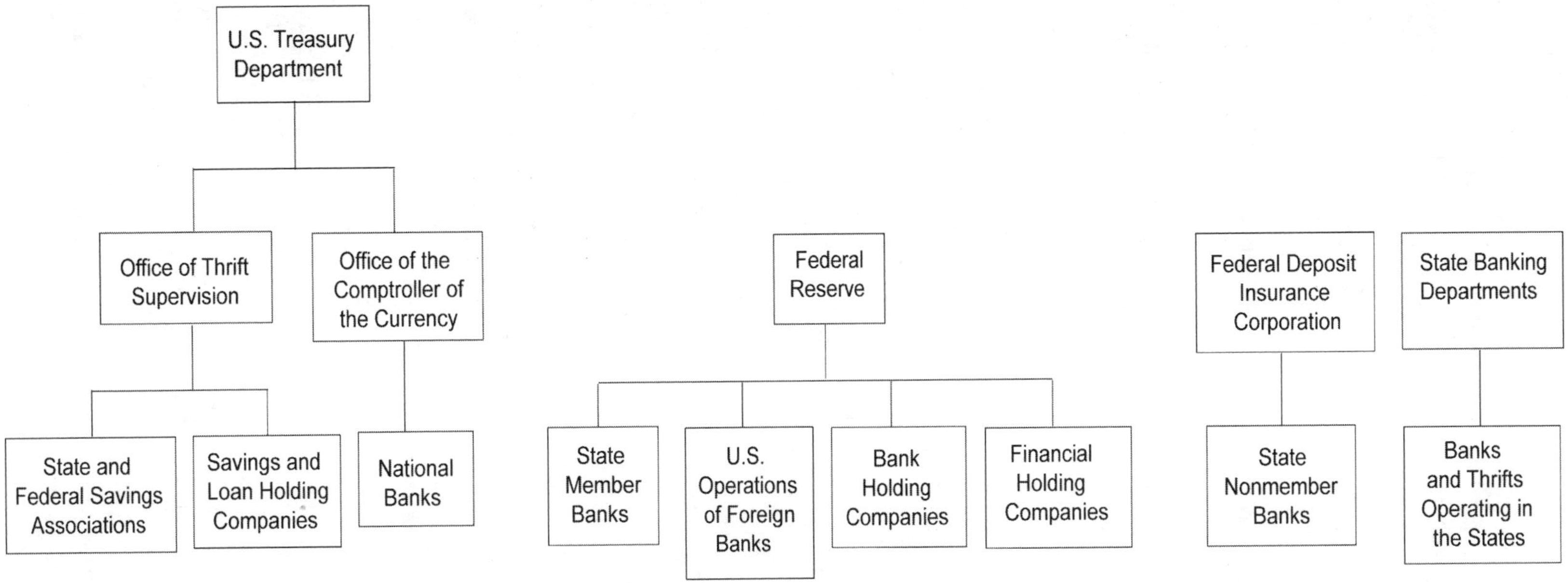

DUAL BANKING

Dual banking refers to the system under which banks are chartered. A bank may be chartered either by the federal government through the Office of the Comptroller of the Currency (OCC) or by the state in which it is domiciled through the state banking department. Banks can choose whether they want to be chartered, and thus regulated, under federal or state law. Banks also may alter their choice at any time by changing their charters. The federal government and the state in which the bank is located may share regulatory control and bank examinations.

Bankers, regulators, and economists have debated the public benefits and costs of this unique dual banking system for years. Opponents of dual banking argue that it does not benefit the public. They argue that the lack of uniformity among state banking laws is disruptive in today's increasingly interstate banking environment. Further, they contend that only the resources of the federal government can ensure well-trained bank examiners. They see dual federal and state examinations as a waste of time and money. Moreover, they claim, the dual banking system enables the banking industry to take advantage of potential competition between federal regulators and state regulators. For example, regulators may compete to attract new bank charters or to retain existing ones by offering loose regulation that is not in the public interest.

Proponents of dual banking argue that dual regulation embodies the same principle of checks and balances that underlies our nation's structure of government. Because a bank can choose a state or federal charter and change its charter at any time, the potential for abusive actions or poor performance by either the federal or state regulatory agencies is checked.

Proponents of dual banking further contend that the system enables state governments to apply banking rules and regulations that more closely relate to the needs and concerns of local communities and their depositors. They also believe that healthy competition among chartering authorities stimulates banking innovation and allows for experimentation at the state level without national disruption of the banking system. Exclusive federal control of bank chartering, they argue, would not guarantee better banking regulation.

UNIT BANKING

Unit banking, a system of thousands of small, single-office banks, historically characterized the U.S. banking industry. Until the 1980s, state and federal laws and regulations severely limited banks' ability to branch, merge, or expand business activities interstate. Most states tightly restricted bank branching. They either permitted branching only within a limited geographic area surrounding a bank's head office or completely prohibited branching within the state.

During the 1980s, however, most states began to liberalize their statewide branching laws and in 1994, federal law, which had prohibited interstate branching, was changed to allow for nationwide banking and branching. Although unit banks remain, unit banking is no longer a requirement in any U.S. locality.

Long-standing prohibitions on branching and limitations on mergers held the U.S. banking industry back from following the historical pattern of consolidation in many U.S. industries. In many industries, such as the steel and automobile manufacturing industries, small firms have been consolidated into a few industrial giants that developed mass-marketing strategies for selling nationally available products and services. In banking, the pattern was different. During the 1920s and 1930s, bank failures caused a sharp reduction in the number of banks in the United States; but from the 1940s to the mid-1980s, the number of banks remained fairly constant, at about 14,000. Since then, bank failures and mergers have pruned the industry to approximately

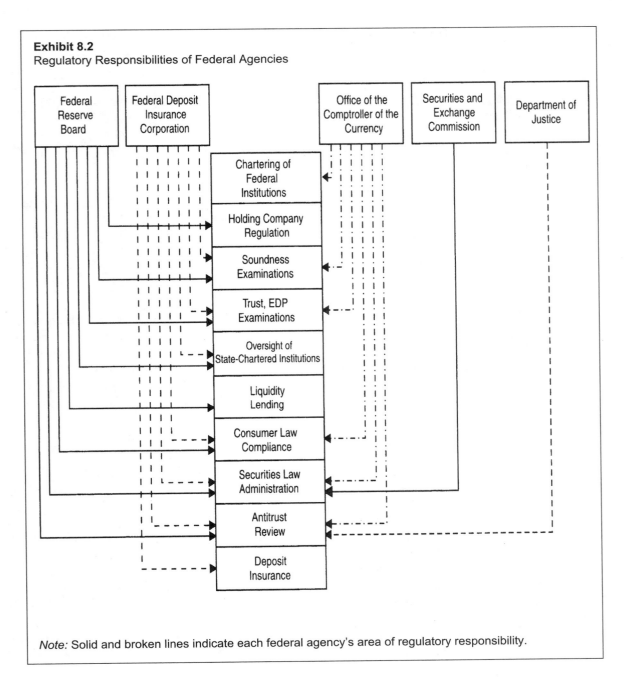

Exhibit 8.2
Regulatory Responsibilities of Federal Agencies

Federal Reserve Board

Federal Deposit Insurance Corporation

Office of the Comptroller of the Currency

Securities and Exchange Commission

Department of Justice

- Chartering of Federal Institutions
- Holding Company Regulation
- Soundness Examinations
- Trust, EDP Examinations
- Oversight of State-Chartered Institutions
- Liquidity Lending
- Consumer Law Compliance
- Securities Law Administration
- Antitrust Review
- Deposit Insurance

Note: Solid and broken lines indicate each federal agency's area of regulatory responsibility.

8,400 banks. By 2001 about 30 percent of FDIC-insured commercial banks, or fewer than 2,500 institutions, were unit banks.

CORRESPONDENT BANKING

The historical limitations on branching and interstate banking restricted the size and scope of bank markets in the United States.

Banks adapted to these restrictions by developing extensive **correspondent banking** relationships. A correspondent bank holds account balances of other banks and provides or sells services to these other, usually smaller, banks through these accounts. Banks that buy the services of correspondent banks are called **respondent banks.**

Today correspondent banks typically provide respondent banks with the following banking and payments services:

- check collection
- loan participation
- backup lines of customer credit
- issuance of dividend checks to respondents' stockholders
- maintenance of dividend reinvestment programs for respondents' stockholders
- investment advice
- analysis of respondents' operating problems
- third-party cash management services, which make optimal use of available cash, for resale

Respondent banks pay for correspondent services either directly, through a fee, or indirectly, by maintaining a required minimum account balance with the correspondent.

RECENT BANKING LEGISLATION

Numerous laws and regulations govern most aspects of banking operations and business activities. To achieve the government's public policy goals, bank legislation and regulation have focused on preventive measures. For example, bank merger and acquisition activities have traditionally been restricted to prevent banks from becoming so large they reduce competition. Through legislation and regulation, the federal government and state governments

- control the terms and conditions under which banks obtain and use assets and liabilities
- insure bank depositors against loss
- fix capital requirements
- establish liquidity, solvency, and profitability guidelines
- outline a code of rights for consumers
- prohibit banks from engaging in unfair or discriminatory practices

Recent federal legislation has profoundly changed banking. During the 1980s and 1990s, Congress enacted laws to

- promote more competition between banks and other financial institutions (Monetary Control Act, 1980)
- allow banks and **thrifts,** which are savings institutions such as savings banks, savings and loan associations, and credit unions, to offer new products (Garn-St Germain Act, 1982)
- deal with the crisis of a failing savings and loan (S&L) industry (Competitive Equality in Banking Act, 1987; Financial Institutions Reform, Recovery and Enforcement Act, 1989)
- protect a dwindling Federal Deposit Insurance Corporation (FDIC) insurance fund (Federal Deposit Insurance Corporation Improvement Act, 1991)
- allow banks to branch across the country (Interstate Banking and Branching Efficiency Act, 1994)
- enable banks, insurance companies, and securities firms to affiliate into single companies (Gramm-Leach-Bliley Act, 1999)

An overview of each of these laws follows.

MONETARY CONTROL ACT

Legislated in 1980, the Monetary Control Act gradually phased out interest rate ceilings on time and savings deposits at banks and thrifts (through Regulation Q) from 1981 to 1986. It also increased FDIC insurance coverage on all deposits to $100,000 for each account and allowed banks and thrifts to offer interest-bearing checking accounts. Mutual savings banks were authorized to obtain a new federal charter that allowed them broader powers to provide more services and to compete with commercial banks. Savings and loan associations and credit unions were given more powers as well. Previously, these thrift institutions had been limited primarily to mortgage and mortgage-related lending.

The Monetary Control Act also extended the Federal Reserve's reserve requirements to all depository institutions, significantly strengthening the Federal Reserve's control over the banking system's creation of money through lending. The act also granted open access to Federal Reserve loans and payments services to all depository institutions.

Congress required the Federal Reserve to price its services explicitly and to make them available to all depository institutions at a uniform price and terms. The act specified that the Federal Reserve, in setting its fees, had to consider all of its direct and indirect costs.

GARN-ST GERMAIN ACT

In 1982 the Garn-St Germain Act substantially expanded thrifts' lending powers. It authorized banks and thrifts to offer money market deposit accounts (MMDAs) to enable them to better compete with existing money market funds. The act also provided support to the struggling S&L industry by permitting banks to purchase failing thrifts across state lines and giving the purchasing banks financial assistance to do so.

COMPETITIVE EQUALITY BANKING ACT

Passed in 1987, the Competitive Equality Banking Act was prompted by a number of troublesome issues that had emerged earlier in the decade. The most prominent issue was the insolvency of the Federal Savings and Loan Insurance Corporation (FSLIC), the agency that at that time insured S&L depositors. The act gave the FSLIC nearly $11 billion to shore up its insurance fund.

The act also closed the consumer bank or nonbank bank loophole in the Bank Holding Company Act, which had inadvertently allowed nonfinancial corporations to own and operate banks. The 1987 act redefined a bank as any institution insured by the FDIC. However, Congress grandfathered those nonbank banks already in operation prior to 1987.

A section of the Competitive Equality Banking Act called the Expedited Funds Availability Act established maximum check-hold periods for banks and required the Federal Reserve to change check collection procedures to speed the return of dishonored checks to a depositor's bank.

FINANCIAL INSTITUTIONS REFORM, RECOVERY, AND ENFORCEMENT ACT

Passed in 1989, the Financial Institutions Reform, Recovery, and Enforcement Act (FIRREA) was designed primarily to address problems that had emerged during the 1980s in the S&L industry and the S&L insurance system. The act provided $50 billion in taxpayer funds to close failed S&Ls and established the Resolution Trust Corporation (RTC) under the management of the FDIC, to administer the funds. FIRREA also restructured the deposit insurance funds for both banks and S&Ls, creating the Bank Insurance Fund (BIF) and Savings Association Insurance Fund (SAIF) as separate funds under the FDIC's control.

Congress established a new Office of Thrift Supervision (OTS) within the U.S. Department of the Treasury to charter and regulate federally chartered S&Ls. It also tightened restrictions on S&L activities, and raised S&L capital requirements to increase safety and soundness within the S&L industry.

FEDERAL DEPOSIT INSURANCE CORPORATION IMPROVEMENT ACT

In 1991 Congress passed the Federal Deposit Insurance Corporation Improvement Act (FDICIA) to provide new funding for the depleted federal deposit insurance fund, to impose risk-based deposit insurance premiums, and to restrict some of the FDIC's policies and actions.

FEDERAL DEPOSIT INSURANCE FUND

The FDIC was created in 1933 following the failures of more than 9,100 banks between 1930 and 1933. The major functions of the FDIC were to protect depositors, especially small depositors, against loss; to bolster public confidence in banks; and to prevent runs—mass customer withdrawals driven by fear of loss—against banks.

The FDIC was immediately successful: runs against banks stopped and bank failures rapidly declined. As seen in exhibit 8.3, bank failures remained low for most of the next 50 years.

During the 1980s, bank failures soared as the quality of bank assets deteriorated and capital levels plummeted as a result of bad loans. For the first time in its history, the FDIC suffered major losses as it paid out funds to insured depositors at closed banks and provided financial assistance to banks that were purchasing the assets and liabilities of failing banks and thrifts.

Between 1985 and 1992, approximately 1,100 banks failed. These failures did not impair public confidence in banking or trigger wide-spread deposit withdrawals, but they did impair the solvency of the federal deposit insurance fund. FDICIA gave the FDIC $75 billion in new borrowing authority to increase the depleted fund: $30 billion could be borrowed from the Treasury and $45 billion could be borrowed by issuing marketable securities. The FDIC, never had to use this new borrowing authority, however, because failures of banks and thrifts declined dramatically after 1992 (see exhibit 8.3).

DEPOSIT INSURANCE PREMIUMS

Until FDICIA the premiums for FDIC insurance had been based on a bank's deposit size. The more deposits a bank had, the higher the premium. This assessment method had long been a source of contention among bankers. Many bankers argued that basing deposit insurance premiums on a bank's size was inconsistent with the principle that insurance premiums should relate to risk. They further contended that size-based premiums were unfair to most large banks, which were statistically more likely to be fiscally sound. Small banks, which paid less, tended to fail at a greater rate than large banks.

FDICIA changed the way the FDIC assesses banks for deposit insurance by link-ing premiums to risk. Under the risk-based premium system, each bank and thrift's insurance rate was dependent on the amount of capital it holds (a proxy for risk) and the FDIC's assessment of its financial condition.

FDIC POLICIES AND ACTIONS

The FDIC can respond to a failed bank in one of five ways. It can

- pay out insurance to the bank's depositors in an outright payoff
- allow a sound bank to buy selected assets and assume the liabilities of the failed bank, through a procedure called a purchase and assumption
- sell all of the bank's assets and its insured liabilities to a sound bank in a whole bank purchase
- take over the bank and operate it in an attempt to nurse it back to fiscal health, called open bank assistance
- declare that all of the bank's deposits, regardless of amount totals, will be accorded insurance protection because the bank is "too big to fail"

In an outright payoff, the FDIC closes the failed bank, pays off the insured depositors, and then liquidates the assets of the bank, distributing the proceeds to the failed bank's creditors and to uninsured depositors.

In a **purchase and assumption procedure,** the bidding banks are permitted to designate to the FDIC those assets of the failed bank they are willing to buy. The FDIC retains assets not selected (principally loans).

Exhibit 8.3
Failures of FDIC-Insured Banks, 1936 to First Quarter 2002

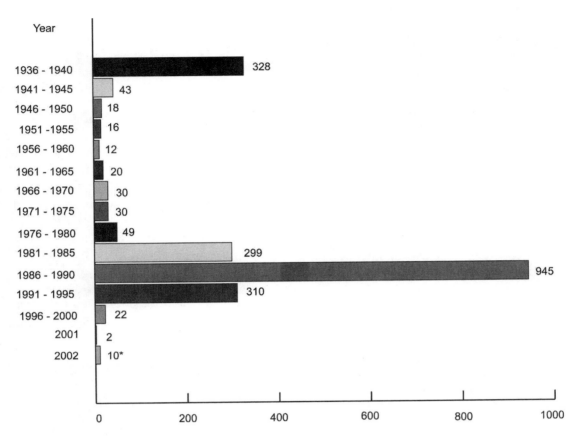

Year

1936 - 1940	328
1941 - 1945	43
1946 - 1950	18
1951 -1955	16
1956 - 1960	12
1961 - 1965	20
1966 - 1970	30
1971 - 1975	30
1976 - 1980	49
1981 - 1985	299
1986 - 1990	945
1991 - 1995	310
1996 - 2000	22
2001	2
2002	10*

0   200   400   600   800   1000

* First half of 2002.
Source: Federal Deposit Insurance Corporation web site for Historical Statistics on Banking, Bank and Thrift Failures, *www2.fdic.gov,* updated as of July 18, 2002.

The purchasing bank assumes all the liabilities of the failed bank, effectively keeping the failed bank open. However, because the liabilities of the failed bank exceed the value of the assets selected by the purchasing bank, the FDIC makes up the difference with a cash payment to the purchasing bank.

Under the whole bank purchase approach, sound banks are asked to bid for all of the assets and the insured deposits of the failed bank. The purchasing bank assumes only insured liabilities, which effectively keeps the failed bank open but shifts potential FDIC losses to uninsured depositors.

Open bank assistance may be used if sound banks are unwilling or unable to bid for the failed bank, and if the bank's closing would require too large a payout from the insurance fund.

When the FDIC declares that all of a bank's deposits will be accorded insurance protection regardless of amount totals, it does so to protect financial markets and the economy from the potential destabilization that could result from the massive losses uninsured depositors would suffer were a large bank to fail.

As bank failures began to increase in the late 1980s, the FDIC's extensive reliance on the purchase and assumption approach for dealing with failed banks, and its application of the too-big-to-fail doctrine drew strong criticism from many bankers and members of Congress. Critics argued that by not allowing some banks to fail, the FDIC effectively provided de facto insurance for all depositors, creditors, and stockholders of these banks. They also asserted that by taking this approach the FDIC eliminated the market discipline to limit risk that uninsured depositors, mainly large corporations, would otherwise exert on bank owners and managers. A further contention was that liberal use of the too-big-to-fail doctrine encouraged risk-averse depositors to maintain accounts only at large banks.

Congress agreed with these arguments. FDICIA encouraged the FDIC to use the whole bank purchase as its principal approach for dealing with failed banks and restricted the FDIC's application of its too-big-to-fail doctrine. Today, the FDIC can use the too-big-to-fail approach only if a large bank failure would directly threaten the stability of the financial system and if the Federal Reserve, the Treasury, and the president approve the action.

DEPOSIT INSURANCE COVERAGE

During the 1980s, many thrifts relied on brokered certificates of deposit as a means of acquiring large amounts of funds from outside their market areas. The thrifts used these funds for high-risk loans and investments. To end this practice, FDICIA eliminated insurance coverage on brokered deposits for all banks and thrifts except for those with the highest capital ratings. Congress made no changes in basic coverage.

Today deposits at banks and thrifts are insured up to $100,000 per person at each bank or thrift where a person has an account.

FDIC REFORM

In 2002 Congress was considering several bills that would make fundamental changes in the federal deposit insurance program. However, bankers were divided in their support for FDIC reform. Among the changes Congress was considering were

- an increase in the deposit insurance limit from $100,000 to $130,000 per account
- insurance coverage on 80 percent of the deposits of state and local governments up to $5 million
- merging the BIF and the SAIF
- eliminating the ceiling on the size of the deposit insurance fund
- giving banks rebates for part of the premiums paid into the deposit insurance fund in the 1990s

Opponents of an increase in the deposit insurance limit contended that such an increase would induce bankers to take greater risks in their lending and investment activities because fewer of the bank's depositors would be exposed to risk. Opponents of 80 percent coverage argued that such coverage would also generate risk by encouraging municipal governments to seek out banks that paid the highest deposit rates without regard to the banks' fiscal health.

Proponents of merging the BIF and SAIF contended that a single, large insurance fund would be stronger than two separate funds. Currently the deposit insurance funds are considered full when they hold amounts of money equal to 1.25 percent of insured deposits. When this capacity is reached, deposit insurance premiums temporarily cease. One reform suggestion has been to eliminate the ceiling or increase the ratio. Opponents have charged that doing this would result in premium increases for all banks. Finally, the proponents of rebates see them as providing a needed financial offset for new premiums likely to be imposed on banks in the years ahead.

Insurance coverage can be increased at a single bank for account holders who establish an IRA or Keogh account. Retirement accounts are insured separately. Accounts established by depositors in the names and Social Security numbers of their spouses or children also are covered separately, as are joint accounts among family members or business partners.

INTERSTATE BANKING AND BRANCHING EFFICIENCY ACT

In 1994 the Interstate Banking and Branching Efficiency Act established a common legal framework for interstate banking and branching throughout the United States. Beginning in 1997, it authorized companies that own controlling interest in one or more banks to buy banks in any state and allowed these bank holding companies to consolidate their interstate banks into branch networks. It also authorized individual banks to branch interstate by merging with other banks across state lines.

The three-year lag between the 1994 enactment and 1997 effective date of the interstate banking law was designed to give states time to opt out of interstate branching. Only two states, Texas and Montana, decided to not to participate in interstate branching.

GRAMM-LEACH-BLILEY ACT

This act, passed in 1999, authorized banks and other financial service companies to establish financial holding companies (FHCs). FHCs are corporations that can own both banks and other companies that provide insurance, securities, and specialized financial services. Gramm-Leach-Bliley also gave the Federal Reserve regulatory responsibility for FHCs, with authority to approve new FHC financial activities. In essence, the Gramm-Leach-Bliley Act repealed the Glass-Steagall Act of 1933.

The Glass-Steagall Act separated commercial banking from investment banking so that commercial banks could no longer underwrite securities or act as securities brokers. During the 1980s and 1990s, however, banks and brokerage firms increasingly breached the Glass-Steagall wall with the assistance of liberal rulings from federal regulators. The U.S. Supreme Court, in separate rulings, upheld each regulatory authorization.

In the 1980s, the OCC authorized national banks to establish brokerage subsidiaries and the FDIC authorized its members to form securities service subsidiaries. In 1983 the Federal Reserve permitted one of the nation's largest bank holding companies, the Bank of America, to acquire Charles Schwab, the nation's largest discount brokerage firm. In the 1990s, the OCC began to allow banks to underwrite collateralized mortgage obligations. The Federal Reserve authorized bank holding companies to sell mutual funds through subsidiaries and to underwrite corporate stocks and bonds provided the revenue the subsidiary derived from this activity was no more than 25 percent of its total revenue.

In enacting Gramm-Leach-Bliley, Congress recognized that the differences between financial institutions and their product offerings had all but disappeared in the changing competitive and regulatory environment of the 1980s and 1990s and that sufficient regulatory protection existed at the federal and state level to allow banks and other financial institutions to affiliate with one another.

CONSUMER PROTECTION LEGISLATION

Before 1968 little, if any, federal law protected consumers in their dealings with banks and other financial institutions. Indeed, consumer protection was primarily a state responsibility. Most states, for example, prohibited usurious interest rates and set ceiling rates on loans to consumers.

The 1968 Consumer Credit Protection Act, of which Title I is the Truth in Lending Act, was the federal watershed. The purpose of the act was to require all lenders to make meaningful disclosure of their credit and leasing terms to enable consumers to compare the various terms available. Lenders were required to provide consumer borrowers with specific written information on the cost of credit, especially the two most important measures of the cost: the finance charge, which is the amount of money paid to obtain credit, and the annual percentage rate, which is the finance charge expressed as an annual percentage of the funds borrowed. The annual percentage rate allows a comparison of credit costs regardless of the dollar amount of the costs or the length of time over which payments are made.

After 1968 Congress significantly expanded the Truth in Lending Act and enacted other statutes to require disclosure of still more information to depositors and borrowers, and to curb various unfair and deceptive lending practices. Of all these statutes, the Community Reinvestment Act has generated the most disagreement among bankers, regulators, and consumer groups.

COMMUNITY REINVESTMENT ACT

Congress passed the **Community Reinvestment Act** (CRA) in 1977 to encourage local banks to grant more credit to residents in low- and moderate-income areas. The act requires federal banking regulators to encourage banks to help meet the credit needs of the communities from which they obtain deposits. Congress wanted to make banks more responsive to the deterioration of housing in the nation's inner cities. They also wanted to prevent further deterioration in those areas by ensuring that individuals

---

CONSUMER PROTECTION LAWS

Since the late 1960s, Congress has enacted a broad range of laws to protect consumers in their financial transactions with banks. These laws include the

- Truth in Lending Act
- Fair Housing Act
- Fair Credit Reporting Act
- Flood Disaster Protection Act
- Equal Credit Opportunity Act
- Fair Credit Billing Act
- Real Estate Settlement Procedures Act
- Home Mortgage Disclosure Act
- Consumer Leasing Act
- Community Reinvestment Act
- Fair Debt Collection Practices Act
- Electronic Funds Transfer Act
- Right to Financial Privacy Act
- Federal Trade Commission Improvement Act
- Expedited Funds Availability Act
- Fair Credit and Charge Card Disclosure Act
- Home Equity Loan Consumer Protection Act
- Women's Business Ownership Act
- Truth in Savings Act
- Bank Sales of Insurance Act
- Financial Privacy Act

and small businesses in the inner cities could obtain funds for housing and commercial purposes. In so doing, Congress brought national attention to the issue of **redlining,** which is the illegal practice of excluding certain geographic areas from eligibility for mortgage loans without regard to the creditworthiness of each mortgage applicant and property.

The CRA provides that bank regulatory examinations must include an assessment of the bank's record in meeting the credit needs of its entire community, including low- and moderate-income areas. It also requires federal regulatory agencies to consider a bank's total community record when deciding whether to grant approval for new branches, mergers, or holding company acquisitions of banks.

Congress left it to the federal banking agencies to define the term *community* as used in the CRA. Congress also delegated to the Federal Reserve Board the tasks of setting specific standards for determining whether a depository was serving the credit needs of its community and what evidence the federal regulatory agencies should evaluate in assessing a depository's past record.

When the CRA was enacted, many community groups in major cities interpreted the new law to mean that banks must allocate a portion of their locally obtained funds to local mortgage lending. Bank regulators did not support this interpretation, but in the 1980s bank examiners began to emphasize checking banks' CRA compliance. Concerns over possible adverse action by the regulators, such as denials of mergers, acquisitions, or branch applications, prompted many banks to expand their lending to low- and moderate-income segments of their communities.

In 1989 Congress passed the Financial Institutions Reform, Recovery, and Enforcement Act (FIRREA). FIRREA required that banks' compliance examination ratings be made public. Congress reasoned that disclosure would be publicly embarrassing for noncompliant banks and would prompt corrective actions. Through 2002, however,

few banks and thrifts have been embarrassed, as most disclosed ratings have been favorable to the banks.

CRA COMPLIANCE

Banks, consumer activists, and regulators have faced two major sources of contention over CRA compliance. These areas of disagreement involve

- allegations of racial discrimination in granting mortgages
- the criteria regulators use for evaluating compliance

DISCRIMINATION IN MORTGAGE LENDING

Since the 1970s, banks with offices in large cities have been required to report annually on the mortgages they make in each neighborhood in which they have offices. Almost from the outset, differences of opinion emerged about the meaning of the mortgage data being reported by the major banks.

Although the data seemed to show that minority areas were receiving significantly fewer mortgages than nonminority areas, banks contended that the data did not adequately reflect the creditworthiness of the applicants, the relative demand for mortgages in different neighborhoods, and the physical condition of the houses in question.

During the 1980s, Congress expanded the scope of required information to include applicants' annual income, race, and sex. The new reporting requirements covered both mortgages denied and mortgages granted. It was thought that this new information would reveal patterns that might indicate a lack of sufficient mortgage credit to inner-city areas.

The changes in reporting and the evaluation of mortgage data gathered during the 1990s shifted attention away from the adequacy of mortgage credit in inner-city areas and toward discrimination against individual mortgage applicants. The new data showed that most mortgage applicants were being approved for credit, but that approval rates varied considerably by race, ethnic status, and income. The data also showed that minority applicants tended to be turned down for mortgages about twice as frequently as nonminority applicants.

CRITERIA FOR EVALUATING CRA COMPLIANCE

Community groups expressed increasing dissatisfaction in the 1990s with regulators' evaluations of banks' CRA compliance. The basic complaint was that regulators were giving too much weight to banks' efforts to meet community credit needs and too little weight to actual results. Banks, in turn, expressed increasing frustration with the lack of quantifiable standards or criteria that regulators could use to assess CRA compliance.

In 1997 the regulators introduced new compliance criteria. Under the new criteria, banks must meet community credit needs through a combination of consumer loans, residential mortgages, small business loans, and loans to community development associations.

Banks are examined in one of three ways, depending on their size and choice. Banks may be examined through

- a streamlined examination
- a self-developed strategic plan
- a full examination that is based on a series of lending, investment, and service tests

Only small banks are eligible for the streamlined examination option. Under this option, the CRA assessment focuses only on the credit needs of the bank's service area and the distribution of the bank's loans to individuals and businesses of different incomes.

Any bank can choose to be evaluated based on its own strategic plan for meeting community credit needs. The bank's plan must incorporate the views of residents of the bank's service area and must have precise, measurable lending and investment goals.

Large banks that do not choose to be evaluated on the basis of a strategic plan are subject to various lending, investment, and service tests. For example, the lending test focuses on the geographic distribution of the bank's loans. The investment test assesses the nature of the bank's community-based investments. In testing a bank's commitment to service, examiners look at the bank's distribution of branches and automated teller machines (ATMs) in low- and moderate-income areas and the range of its service offerings in these communities.

COMPLIANCE EXAMINATIONS

Consumer compliance examinations are conducted by bank examiners who are specially trained to review consumer protection law compliance. All federal bank regulatory agencies operate under a common set of guidelines to ensure uniform enforcement.

Bank examiners follow a detailed examination checklist and each consumer law is covered by a series of procedures for detecting and correcting violations. A compliance examination typically involves the following steps:

- a review of the consumer complaints to note any areas of the bank's operations that may present a problem
- an onsite review of the bank's lending forms, credit applications, and disclosure statements
- a review of a statistical sample of the bank's installment loan files to ensure that the bank is correctly calculating its annual percentage rates and properly disclosing credit costs
- a review of a sample of the bank's mortgage files and accepted and rejected mortgage applications for compliance with CRA and to determine whether they show any pattern of discrimination or

deviation from the bank's established lending policy

- a discussion with bank management of all matters of concern noted by the examiner
- a written report of the examination sent to the bank with a request that management respond to the report and comment on how any violations will be corrected

If a violation is discovered through investigation of a specific consumer complaint, the bank must take corrective action on the complainant's behalf and establish policies to prevent future violations.

BANKING REGULATIONS

Banking regulations are the rules, procedures, and requirements that implement banking laws. All federal and state bank regulatory agencies issue regulations to the depository institutions they supervise.

In 2002 there were 30 Federal Reserve regulations, each carrying a different letter designation: A through Z, AA, BB, CC, DD, and EE (see exhibit 8.4 on the following page). Currently there is no Regulation R. The 30 Federal Reserve regulations, which cover a broad range of compliance areas, can be grouped into the following five categories:

- monetary policy
- bank safety and soundness
- international banking and the activities of bank holding companies
- activities of Federal Reserve banks and Federal Reserve membership
- consumer protection

REGULATIONS ON MONETARY POLICY

Monetary policy regulations enable the Federal Reserve to manage the nation's money and credit supply in line with economic objectives. These regulations govern

- loans to depositories

- reserve requirements
- margin credit

Regulation A establishes the conditions and terms under which Federal Reserve banks lend funds to depositories at the discount window. Regulation A was the first regulation issued by the Federal Reserve in 1914.

Regulation D establishes reserve requirements for all depository institutions. The regulation defines liabilities subject to reserve requirements and specifies the percentages of required reserves that must be applied to these liabilities. It also defines the three types of assets that depositories use to meet reserve requirements: vault cash, balances maintained directly on the books of a Federal Reserve bank, and balances maintained at another institution in a pass-through reserve account. The regulation explains how depositories are to compute and maintain their required reserves and prescribes the penalties for reserve deficiencies. It also establishes procedures and rules for depositories that want to maintain pass-through reserve accounts.

Three regulations cover margin credit extended to finance securities transactions. Regulation T governs credit extensions made by securities brokers and dealers. Regulation U limits the amount of credit a bank can extend for purchasing and carrying margin securities if the credit is secured directly or indirectly by stock. Regulation X sets out rules for extending credit to those purchasing or carrying securities.

REGULATIONS ON BANK SAFETY AND SOUNDNESS

A number of banking regulations are designed to ensure the financial well being and security of banks. These regulations address

- limitations on interbank liabilities
- conflicts of interest

Exhibit 8.4
Categories of Federal Reserve Regulations

Monetary Policy

Regulation
A	Loans to depositories
D	Reserve requirements
T, U, X	Credit by banks, by brokers and dealers, and by others; rules for margin borrowers

Bank Safety and Soundness

Regulation
F	Limitations on interbank liabilities
L	Restrictions on interlocking directorates in banking
O	Loans to officers, directors, and stockholders
Q	Interest on demand deposits prohibition
W	Transactions between banks and their affiliates (proposed)

International Banking and Bank Holding Companies

Regulation
K	Activities of U.S. banks overseas and U.S. operations of foreign banks
Y	Activities of bank holding companies

Federal Reserve Membership and Reserve Banks' Procedures

Regulation
EE	Payments under netting agreements among banks
H	Membership requirements for state-chartered banks
I	Stock ownership requirements for banks joining the Federal Reserve system
J	Check-processing and Electronic Funds Transfer (EFT) procedures
N	Reserve banks' relations with foreign banks and governments
S	Reimbursement for providing customers' banking records to government

Consumer Protection

Regulation
AA	Consumer complaint procedures concerning unfair or deceptive practices
B	Equal credit opportunity
BB	Community reinvestment
C	Home mortgage disclosure
CC	Availability of deposited check funds
DD	Truth in Savings
E	Electronic funds transfers
G	Disclosure and reporting of Community Reinvestment Act related agreements
M	Consumer leasing
P	Privacy of Consumer Financial Information
V	Fair Credit Reporting (proposed)
Z	Truth in Lending

- interest on deposits
- transactions between banks and affiliates

Regulation F establishes standards to limit the risks banks face when they lend funds to other banks. Regulation L prevents conflicts of interest or collusion among banks by prohibiting interlocking directorates. In an interlocking directorate, a board member simultaneously serves on the boards of more than one bank. Regulation L also prohibits officers and employees of member banks from simultaneous involvement with other banks. Regulation O prohibits member banks from extending credit to their own officers, directors, and stockholders

Regulation Q prohibits paying interest on demand deposits, defines the term *interest*, and indicates the prohibitions. From 1933 to 1986, Regulation Q set the maximum interest rates banks could pay on time and savings deposits. Since 1986 banks have been allowed to establish the interest rates they will pay on time and savings deposits.

Regulation W is a proposed regulation that would combine existing restrictions on transactions between banks and their affiliates with Federal Reserve Board interpretations and exemptions.

REGULATIONS ON INTERNATIONAL BANKS AND BANK HOLDING COMPANY ACTIVITIES

Regulation K and Regulation Y govern the activities of international banks and bank holding companies. Regulation K defines the allowable activities and operations of U.S. banking organizations overseas and the operations of foreign banks in the United States. Regulation Y governs the bank and nonbank expansion of bank holding companies, the divestiture of impermissible nonbank interests, the acquisition of a bank by individuals, and the establishment and activities of financial holding companies.

REGULATIONS ON ACTIVITIES OF RESERVE BANKS AND FEDERAL RESERVE MEMBERSHIP

Regulations on Reserve bank activities and Federal Reserve membership are broad ranging. They include

- netting arrangements
- federal reserve membership
- federal reserve check processing and funds transfer procedures

- relations with foreign banks and governments
- financial records

Regulation EE defines the terms and conditions under which selected financial institutions can engage in netting arrangements. Netting arrangements are contracts in which the institutions agree to pay or receive net amounts rather than gross amounts due.

Regulation H defines membership requirements for state-chartered banks that opt to join the Federal Reserve and establishes the capital-to-asset ratios state-chartered member banks must maintain. Regulation H also prescribes real estate lending and appraisal standards, sets out requirements concerning bank security procedures, and establishes rules governing banks' ownership or control of financial subsidiaries. Regulation I details the stock subscription requirements for banks joining the Federal Reserve.

Regulation J establishes procedures and rules under which the Federal Reserve banks process checks and transfer funds electronically over Fedwire. Federal Reserve banks issue operating circulars governing the specific procedures and practices that depository institutions must follow if they use the Federal Reserve's check collection service. One important circular is a time schedule that specifies when checks received by a Federal Reserve bank can be counted by the sending bank as part of its reserves, at which point they become available for use by the sender. Reserve banks give either immediate or deferred credit in accordance with the Federal Reserve's deferred availability schedule.

Regulation J also explains the procedures banks must follow for the return of checks and provides rules for funds transfers. Because Fedwire transfers involve the near-instantaneous transfer and settlement of debit and credit balances on the books of Federal Reserve banks, they are more like cash transactions than check transactions. Thus, the rules and procedures governing electronic funds transfers reflect this difference.

Regulation N specifies the relationships and transactions that the 12 Reserve banks may have with foreign banks and governments and describes the role taken by the Board of Governors in these relationships and transactions. Regulation S establishes procedures and conditions under which financial institutions can be reimbursed for providing financial records to a federal agency.

REGULATIONS ON CONSUMER PROTECTION

The greatest number of banking regulations deals with consumer protection issues. These regulations are complex, cover numerous areas of concern, and are described here only briefly. The regulations discussed here address

- availability of deposited check funds
- consumer complaint procedures concerning unfair or deceptive practices
- consumer lending
- community reinvestment
- electronic funds transfers
- equal credit opportunity
- fair credit reporting
- financial privacy
- home mortgage disclosures
- truth in lending
- truth in savings

Regulation AA prohibits certain acts and practices with regard to consumer credit and establishes complaint procedures for consumers who believe a state-chartered member bank has engaged in unfair or deceptive practices. It also allows the Federal Reserve board to define to banks unfair and deceptive practices.

Regulation B prohibits lenders from discriminating against credit applicants on the basis of age, race, color, religion, national origin, sex, marital status, or receipt of income from public assistance programs. It also establishes guidelines for banks when evaluating credit information.

Regulation BB, which implements the Community Reinvestment Act, specifies the procedures under which state member banks will be evaluated as to whether they are helping to meet the credit needs of their communities.

Regulation C requires that depositories making mortgage loans disclose annually the locations of the property to which their mortgage loans relate, as well as such information as the race or national origin, gender, and income of the mortgage holders, and the types of mortgage loans made.

Regulation CC places specific limits on the length of time that banks may place holds on checks deposited by customers before funds can be withdrawn. Regulation CC implements the Expedited Funds Availability Act (EFAA) and also governs disclosure requirements pertaining to funds availability. Notably, the provisions of Regulation CC govern all checks, not just those collected through the Federal Reserve System.

Regulation DD implements the Truth in Savings Act. The act requires depository institutions to disclose the deposit interest rates (based on the annual percentage yield), fees, and other conditions that apply to their deposit accounts so that consumers can more easily shop for the best selections. The regulation applies to account opening materials as well as advertisements.

Regulation E establishes the rights, liabilities, and responsibilities of consumers and financial institutions using electronic funds transfer (EFT) services. For example, it limits a consumer's liability for unauthorized electronic funds transfers to $50 or less if consumers make prompt notification. It also requires that consumers be given a written, easily understood statement of the terms and conditions of the electronic funds transfer service contracted for, including information on any service charges, rights to stop payment, and the circumstances under which the financial institution would disclose to a third party information about a consumer's EFT account activity.

Regulation G implements provisions of the Gramm-Leach-Bliley Act that require public disclosure of agreements between banks, their affiliates, and others made in fulfillment of CRA requirements.

Regulation M implements the consumer leasing portions of the Truth in Lending Act, specifying disclosure terms in leasing arrangements. The Fair Credit Reporting Act is designed to ensure the accuracy of consumer reports and ensure that reports are only provided when appropriate. It also addresses when consumer information can be shared among bank affiliates. Proposed Regulation V would interpret the notification provisions of the Fair Credit Reporting Act related to sharing consumer information among bank affiliates.

Regulation P implements the provisions of the Gramm-Leach-Bliley Act that limit how financial institutions may share non-public personal information with unaffiliated third parties. Regulation Z establishes extensive disclosure requirements for banks and consumer credit lenders, and establishes procedures for computing the costs of credit and resolving billing errors.

SUMMARY

The bank regulatory structure that has evolved in the United States has as its principal goal the safety and soundness of banks. This goal has been pursued over the decades through bank regulation and bank supervision. Over time, America's banking and regulatory structure have evolved three unique features:

- a dual banking system, in which banks may be chartered by either a state or federal government
- unit banking, which is characterized by the presence of thousands of small, single-office banks
- extensive correspondent relationships, in which larger banks hold account balances and provide check collection and other services to respondent banks

The structure of the U.S. banking industry underwent dramatic change during the 1980s and 1990s. Major banking laws provided much of the impetus for this change. The Monetary Control Act modified the banking regulatory structure by subjecting all depositories to the Federal Reserve's reserve requirements. It also authorized all depository institutions to offer interest-earning checking accounts. The Garn-St Germain Act authorized banks to offer money market deposit accounts in competition with money market funds, and broadened the powers of the bank regulatory agencies to assist failing depositories. The Competitive Equality Banking Act, which gave increased authority to the FDIC, established maximum check-hold periods for banks.

The Financial Institutions Reform, Recovery, and Enforcement Act restructured the deposit insurance system and established the Office of Thrift Supervision. The Federal Deposit Insurance Corporation Improvement Act provided new funding for the FDIC. The Interstate Banking and Branching Efficiency Act eliminated restrictions on interstate bank acquisitions and made interstate branching possible on a nationwide basis. The Gramm-Leach-Bliley Act authorized financial holding companies to engage in banking, insurance, and securities trading under one corporate umbrella.

Federal Reserve regulations that govern virtually every aspect of a bank's activities exemplify the rules, procedures, and requirements that state and federal bank regulators issue to banks to implement banking laws. Since the late 1960s, a wide range of consumer protection laws has been enacted by Congress and implemented by the Federal Reserve. Special regulatory compliance examinations help ensure that consumers receive understandable information about the terms and conditions of their accounts and that they are treated fairly

REVIEW QUESTIONS

1. In what way does the regulation of banks differ from the regulation of other business firms, such as automobile manufacturing companies?
2. Does it make a difference whether a new bank obtains a national or a state charter?
3. Explain the difference between dual banking and unit banking.
4. Bankers, regulators, and economists have long debated the public benefits and costs of a dual banking system. What are the arguments for and against dual banking?
5. Cite two major changes in banking brought about by the Gramm-Leach-Bliley Act of 1999.
6. What major improvements to banking regulation did Congress make in the Federal Deposit Insurance Corporation Improvement Act of 1991? What further changes in the deposit insurance program were considered in the early 2000s?

ADDITIONAL RESOURCES

American Bankers Association, at *www. aba.com*. Provides current information on bank regulatory compliance issues.

Banking Institutions and Their Regulators, Federal Reserve Bank of New York, 1997, pamphlet. A fold-out matrix that shows the regulatory responsibilities of state and federal authorities for different banking institutions.

Federal Reserve Bank of New York, at *www.ny.frb.org/pihome/regs/html*. Provides information and descriptions of Federal Reserve regulations.

FRBNY Guide to Federal Reserve Regulations, Federal Reserve Bank of New York, 1999, 13 pp. Explains each of the Federal Reserve's regulations.

Office of the Comptroller of the Currency (OCC), at *www.occ.treas.gov*. Provides information about the OCC's criteria for evaluating banks' compliance with CRA regulations.

Reference Guide to Regulatory Compliance, by Kathlyn L. Farrell, American Bankers Association, 2002. Provides a detailed outline of the various regulations important to banking by bank functions, including consumer lending, deposit operations, safety and soundness, information reporting, bank safety and soundness, and social responsibility.

U.S. Financial Regulators, at *www. ncua.gov/other/financial.htm*. Lists all the government regulatory agencies and provides links to their home pages.

EXTENDED STUDY 6: THE EVOLUTION OF BANK REGULATION

Political issues have long shaped the course of bank regulation in the United States. Early Americans disagreed about the need for national banks in their developing economy. Because this issue was never resolved, early banking was left to develop along private and state-regulated lines. Most citizens believed the new federal government should not participate in banking activities; others saw national banks as providing a means for the new government to finance itself.

THE NATION'S FIRST CENTRAL BANKS

The nation's early experiences with banking reflected these political crosscurrents. In 1781 a reluctant Continental Congress chartered the Bank of North America to finance the military operations of the newly formed federal government. Ten years later, Congress granted a 20-year charter to the First Bank of the United States. Although the bank was successful as a business and fostered economic growth, its charter was not renewed in 1811. The public felt that a central bank gave the federal government too much power.

In 1816 Congress chartered the Second Bank of the United States, which served as both a government bank and a private bank.

As a government institution, the Second Bank of the United States promoted the safety and soundness of banking by regularly presenting for redemption into gold and silver specie the bank notes of state-chartered banks suspected of over issuing currency. This practice forced state banks to keep an adequate supply of specie on hand and limited the amount of notes they could issue. As a private bank, the Second Bank made loans and investments, accepted deposits, issued bank notes, and maintained 25 branches across the country.

In 1819 the Supreme Court ruled that the national bank was constitutional. Still, many opponents, including state-chartered banks, merchants, farmers, and politicians, viewed it as too powerful an institution for a market economy and a political democracy. Thus, the charter of the Second Bank of the United States was allowed to expire in 1836.

THE FREE BANKING ERA

From 1837 to 1863, banking in the United States was largely free from any federal regulation. This 26-year period became known as the Free Banking Era.

Banking services provided by the Second Bank had been so extensive that most states recognized the need to establish new banking offices to fill the void created by its closing. However, most states had complex, time-consuming procedures that required an act of the state legislature to grant a bank charter. Many states chartered banks only for specific public-good purposes, such as helping to finance a railroad or a bridge. In other states, chartering decisions were often politically motivated.

During the Free Banking Era, states began to reform their bank-chartering systems so that new banks could be established quickly and the public could be assured of a stable banking environment and a safe currency. Most states attempted to achieve these goals by enacting free banking laws. These laws allowed anyone to operate a bank provided all notes issued by the bank were collateralized by state bonds deposited at the state auditor's office. In addition, all notes had to be redeemable on demand, at face value, in gold or silver specie. The failure of a bank to redeem a note presented for payment would result in the closing of the bank and the liquidation of the bank's assets to pay off all noteholders.

The absence of ongoing federal government regulation during the Free Banking Era led to a spate of bank closings in state after state. Many bank failures grew out of the fraudulent over issue of paper currency. Dishonest bankers formed wildcat banks, named for their remote geographic locations. These banks over issued currency in communities far from their head offices, expecting that because of their remote locations few notes would be presented for redemption. These wildcat bankers profited by quickly closing the banks after all notes were circulated and absconding with the bank's gold and silver coin.

Most bank failures during the Free Banking Era were due to substantial declines in the prices of state bonds rather than to banker fraud. State bonds made up the bulk of most banks' investment portfolios. Thus, when bond prices fell, state banks faced severe capital losses. These bookkeeping losses made depositors anxious and led to runs on banks. During these runs, if all depositors' demands for specie redemption could not be honored, the banks were forced to close.

THE NATIONAL BANKING SYSTEM

During the 1860s, the federal government was faced with the pressing demands of financing the Civil War. The government responded by creating a new currency and a system of nationally chartered banks licensed to operate by the newly formed Office of the Comptroller of the Currency (OCC).

To raise money to finance the union army, a plan was devised whereby the federal government would offer a new type of banking license known as a federal, or national, charter. A bank with a national charter could issue a new form of currency, national bank notes. For each note issued, however, the bank was required to hold a slightly larger dollar value of government securities as collateral. The banks would purchase the securities directly from the U.S. Treasury in exchange for gold and silver specie. In effect, then, the government would receive money assets (gold and silver) in return for its liabilities (government securities).

To enhance the prospects of success for the new national banks, a tax was imposed on state bank notes. The tax was designed to eliminate the competition between state bank notes and national bank notes. Congress gradually increased this tax until state-chartered banks ended the practice of issuing currency.

During the decades of dual banking between the Civil War and the start of World War I, no uniform code of bank regulations ensured protection of the public's money. Only nationally chartered banks were subject to stiff capital requirements, lending limits, and examinations by the Comptroller of the Currency. State-chartered banks were subject to differing state rules and regulations and, in many states, risky bank loans, inadequate bank capital, and no reserve requirements. Without central regulation banking practices involving operations such as check collection and correspondent accounts developed privately and beyond the scope of national regulation.

THE ESTABLISHMENT OF FEDERAL REGULATORY OVERSIGHT

In response to the serious money and banking problems that arose under the fledgling dual banking system, Congress in 1913 established the Federal Reserve as the nation's central bank. One of the Federal Reserve's basic missions was to improve the supervision of banking in the United States.

The Federal Reserve has sought to fulfill this mandate in various ways, including

- issuing regulations that outline the boundaries and procedures of acceptable banking practice
- monitoring the safety and soundness of banks by analyzing data and information submitted by banks directly or indirectly through other government agencies
- routinely examining banks for compliance with banking laws, regulations, and procedures
- deciding, since the late 1950s, which nonbank activities bank holding companies can engage in
- issuing, since the late 1960s, rules for most federal consumer credit regulations

During the Great Depression of the 1930s, nearly one-third of the nation's banks failed. The massive failures prompted Congress to recognize the need for additional banking regulation. In 1933 Congress created the Federal Deposit Insurance Corporation (FDIC) to help stabilize the banking system and protect depositors against loss. Shortly thereafter, the FDIC became the federal supervisory authority over state-chartered banks that were not members of the Federal Reserve System. Since then, the FDIC has become closely associated with the chartering process because obtaining deposit insurance has become a necessary requirement for most banks.

THE EXAMINATIONS PROCESS AND RATING SYSTEM

The object of examining and rating banks is to ensure that the banks comply with laws and regulations and to assess each bank's financial health on a regular basis.

Bank examiners rely on the CAMELS rating system for assessing a bank's condition. CAMELS is an acronym for six important criteria: capital, assets, management, earnings, liquidity, and sensitivity to market risk. These six criteria must be evaluated and scored before an examiner can assign an overall rating to a bank's financial health. Examiners rank a bank's performance against each criterion on a scale of 1 to 5, with 1 as the highest rating and 5 as the lowest. A composite rating is then derived for the bank.

The first five criteria were established in 1978. In 1997 sensitivity to market risk was added as the sixth criterion. For this criterion, a bank is rated on how well positioned it is to handle changes in interest rates.

All banks must satisfy certain minimum capital requirements, generally expressed as a fixed percentage of capital to total assets of the bank. During the 1990s, capital adequacy requirements were tightened with the introduction of multiple-tiered risk-based capital-to-asset ratios. In evaluating the quality of a bank's loan and investment assets, bank examiners must determine the expected ability of borrowers to make scheduled interest payments and repay principal. Banks are required to set aside funds as loan-loss reserves to cover potential losses.

A bank's management is rated on its technical competence, leadership, and administrative ability. Examiners also take into account the quality of the bank's internal controls, operating procedures, and lending and investment policies. Earnings generally are rated against the bank's capacity to cover potential losses and meet its capital requirement. A bank's liquidity refers to its ability to readily convert assets into cash to meet depositors' claims. Examiners rate this ability primarily in relation to the volatility of a bank's deposits and the bank's reliance on borrowings.

The regulatory agencies consider banks with a composite CAMELS rating of 1 or 2 to be fundamentally sound. They are generally permitted to operate without any restrictions. A bank that receives a 3 rating is considered weaker than desired, or below average. These banks typically are given specific instructions on how to address their deficiencies. Banks that receive CAMELS ratings of 4 or 5 are considered problem banks with severe weaknesses that could readily bring them to insolvency. These banks are placed under close surveillance, usually issued directives restricting their activities, and generally required to take immediate corrective actions.

A bank's CAMELS rating is confidential and is provided only to the bank's senior management. However, in its periodic reports to Congress on the health of the U.S. banking system, the FDIC usually discloses the number of problem banks it is actively monitoring and the number of banks in each ratings category. In 2001 about 95 banks were identified as problem banks. More than 90 percent of the nation's banks were rated 1 or 2.

9

MONETARY THEORY

LEARNING OBJECTIVES

After studying this chapter, you should be able to

- explain the quantity theory of money and Fisher's equation of exchange
- identify the basic elements of Keynesian income-expenditure theory
- enumerate the basic principles of monetarism
- list the key determinants of income, interest rates, investment spending, and output, and the interrelationships among them
- explain the concepts of marginal efficiency of investment and liquidity preference
- summarize how monetary policy is carried out in the economy
- define the key terms listed in this chapter

KEY TERMS

aggregate demand
consumption
consumption function
elasticity
equilibrium
government spending
investment

liquidity preference theory
marginal efficiency of investment
opportunity cost
speculative demand
total spending
velocity of money
wealth effect

INTRODUCTION

Monetary theory seeks to explain the role money plays in determining levels of employment, production, income, and prices. This chapter examines the structure and precepts of two bodies of monetary theory: Keynesian theory and monetarism. Keynesian theory is named for the British economist John Maynard Keynes. An important assertion of Keynesian theory is that the relationship between income and spending determines short-run economic activity. Monetarism is associated with the American economist Milton Friedman. An important assertion of monetarism is that changes in the quantity of money are the most important influence on economic activity.

Understanding the differences between these theories is important because Keynesian theorists and monetarists often disagree on how money and monetary policy work in the economy. In particular they disagree about whether monetary policy should be easy or tight at any given time.

The chapter's review of monetary theory purposely accentuates the differences between Keynesian theory and monetarism. The primary disagreement between the two schools of thought centers on the importance of the money supply as a cause of economic change. In the extreme, monetarism contends that the money supply is the only causal factor that matters in the economy. In contrast, Keynesian theory contends that the money supply matters very little.

Most economists today consider themselves neither Keynesians nor monetarists. Instead, they accept and synthesize the general principles and much of the analysis of both bodies of theory. Most economists today take an eclectic view of money's role in the economy, considering the money supply one of several important factors that cause economic change.

Large firms drew the weekly payroll from the Reichsbank in Berlin (1923). *Photo courtesy of AP/Wide World.*

To explain economic relationships or processes, economists often develop models that focus only on essential cause-and-effect connections. Such models may be expressed in words, through mathematical equations, or through graphs. This chapter presents some of the important models used by Keynesians and monetarists.

THE QUANTITY THEORY OF MONEY

The origins of monetary theory can be traced to the eighteenth-century quantity theory of money. At that time, economists believed in a direct and proportional relationship between the quantity of money and the level of prices in the economy. They held that an increase in the quantity of money causes an increase in the price level, just as a decrease in the quantity of money causes a decline in the price level.

This crude quantity theory was detailed in 1911 by the American economist and mathematician Irving Fisher (1867–1947). In examining the causes of business cycles, Fisher hypothesized a more sophisticated link between the quantity of money and prices through an equation of exchange.

FISHER'S EQUATION OF EXCHANGE

Fisher's equation of exchange states that, at any given time, the quantity of money in circulation multiplied by **the velocity of money** (meaning the average number of times each unit of money is spent) equals the average price of all goods and services sold multiplied by the volume of transactions or total quantity of goods sold.

Fisher's equation of exchange may be expressed as

$$MV = PT \text{ or } MV = PQ$$

where M stands for the quantity of money in circulation, V stands for the velocity of money, P stands for the average price of all

goods and services sold, T stands for the volume of transactions, and Q stands for the total quantity of goods sold.

In essence the Fisher equation says that the total amount of money spent on goods and services in the economy must equal the total amount of money received from the sale of those goods and services. The relevance and practical application of the equation becomes clear on examining the nature of the assumptions behind each of its components.

Fisher assumed that in the real world V and T are constant. That is, the rate at which the public spends money is relatively stable, and the volume of the economy's transactions is relatively fixed. Fisher also assumed that the economy's transactions are fixed because the economy always tends to operate at full employment. Under his assumptions, if the money supply doubles, the level of prices will double. Conversely, if the money supply is halved, prices will be halved.

Fisher believed that this direct and proportional relationship between the quantity of money and the level of prices helped explain business cycles. He thought that business cycles were caused by imbalances in the quantity of money and by the response of consumers and businesses to an environment of too much or too little money.

Fisher lacked the economic data to substantiate his theory. Moreover, his assumption that the economy always tends to operate at full employment was invalid. Economists now recognize that the economy does not maintain equilibrium at full employment. A fixed level of transactions and a fixed quantity of goods and services cannot be assumed.

Economists also recognize that the velocity of money is not a constant. However, velocity can still be treated as a constant for analytic and model-building purposes because, from month to month and year to year, it fluctuates over a very narrow and statistically predictable range.

The Fisher Equation and Monetary Policy

If Fisher's assumptions are modified to specify constant velocity but not an economy at full-employment equilibrium, the equation of exchange offers a policy guide for monetary control. If the economy is experiencing recession and unemployment, an increase in the quantity of money can be expected to spark increased production and employment. If the economy is experiencing inflation, a reduction in the quantity of money can be expected to stop the rise in prices.

During a recession, an increase in the money supply multiplied by a constant velocity of money theoretically will lead to an increase in money received. As producers see demand for their goods rise because of increased consumer spending, they will expand output by recalling laid-off workers and putting machines back on the production line. It is unlikely that producers will immediately increase prices, however, because to do so would be inconsistent with their attempts to profit as much as possible in the face of expanding demand.

Conversely, during a period of inflation, a reduction in money multiplied by a constant velocity theoretically will cause a reduction in money received. Producers should lower prices in response to falling demand for their goods and services. In reality, however, some producers would likely respond in this way, but many would respond by simply cutting production and releasing workers.

The price of an item reflects the sum of all the costs incurred in producing the item, including wages, rents, interest, and profits. Therefore, a reduction in prices can be sustained only if corresponding cost reductions occur. Wages, rents, and interest are largely contractual costs, so a reduction in prices effectively means a cut in profits, which many firms are loath to accept. In some cases, producers may even raise prices in the face of declining sales in response to contractually incurred costs, such as annual wage increases required under union contracts. Nonetheless, over time, a sustained reduction in money will generate a slowing in production and, in some industries, a decline in prices.

KEYNESIAN THEORY

Keynesian theory is based on the writings and teachings of the twentieth-century British economist John Maynard Keynes (1883–1946). His 1936 book, *The General Theory of Employment, Interest, and Money*, established the analytic framework on which most of the governments of the industrial world today structure their monetary and fiscal policies.

Economists before Keynes believed that, left to itself without active government or central bank involvement, the economy would always fully employ the nation's labor and capital resources and maintain its own balance, or **equilibrium.** These economists maintained that any economic condition that threatened to disrupt the balance of the economy would quickly be nullified by increases or decreases in wages and interest rates as the economy sought to reestablish equilibrium.

Keynes argued that the notion of economic equilibrium was no longer valid in the depression environment of the 1930s. He further maintained that reductions in wages and interest rates could not, of themselves, ensure full employment. Keynes believed that full employment could be ensured only when total income balanced total spending.

Total spending, also called **aggregate demand,** can be expressed as

$$C + I + G$$

where *C* represents **consumption,** meaning spending by consumers; *I* represents **investment,** meaning spending by business on equipment and raw materials; and *G* represents **government spending,** meaning spending by the federal government.

Keynes reasoned that wage reductions, even if they were possible in a highly unionized economy, might not increase employment. Workers might simply spend less, driving down sales and production even more. Keynes also maintained that interest rates did not reflect the price that banks had to pay to entice people to save. Rather, he claimed, interest rates reflected the price that banks had to pay to entice people to give up their preference for liquid money assets. Banks would have difficulty attracting funds if interest rates fell below a level at which people preferred to keep their assets liquid. Accordingly, if people began to save more, the increase in savings would not necessarily lead to lower interest rates and more investment spending. Instead, total demand for goods might fall, along with employment and investment, until the volume of savings balanced the volume of investment spending. The economy would reach equilibrium, but not at full employment. Rather, the economy would be in a state of balanced stagnation with a high level of unemployment.

Keynes's solution, based on his theoretical analysis, was to drive total spending back up to the level at which all workers would be employed. To accomplish this, he said, the government had to make up for the shortfalls in consumer spending and business investment by increasing its own spending. Government spending would have to increase whenever the public tended to save more and consume less than the amount being invested by business. However, the government could not finance this compensatory spending by increasing taxes. Raising taxes would effectively increase consumer savings and reduce consumer spending, thus aggravating the economic imbalance. To avoid this trap, the government would have to finance its additional spending by borrowing, or running a budgetary deficit.

KEYNESIAN RELATIONSHIPS

Keynesian theory, known today as income-expenditure theory, is premised on three fundamental economic relationships:

$$Y = C + I + G;$$
$$Y = C + S; \text{ and}$$
$$S = I + G.$$

Y = C + I + G

The first Keynesian relationship holds that total production and total income always equals total spending:

$$Y = C + I + G.$$

In this equation, Y stands for total production and total income. Once again, C represents consumption; I represents investment; and G represents government spending.

Another way to state this relationship is to say that aggregate demand, the sum of all consumption, investment, and government spending, always equals aggregate supply (also called total production). The relationship is based on the idea that everything produced in the economy is always bought. Unsold merchandise becomes part of business inventories and is counted as part of investment.

For ease of analysis, total production and total income are considered synonymous. Economists use these simplified relationships to examine and relate elements in the national income accounts. For example, the equation $Y = C + I + G$ can be used to relate gross domestic product, which is the total value of all new production, to personal income. A further simplification can be used to examine relationships assuming no foreign spending in the United States and no U.S. sales abroad.

Y = C + S

The second Keynesian relationship holds that all income is either spent on goods and services or saved:

$$Y = C + S.$$

Again, Y stands for total production and total income and C stands for consumption. Here, S represents savings. Again, for ease of analysis, it is assumed that no income is paid in taxes to the government.

S = I + G

In theory, when the third Keynesian relationship becomes self-sustaining, the economy attains equilibrium, a state of balance between aggregate demand and aggregate supply. Specifically, the economy reaches equilibrium when the levels of investment and government spending being added to the economy's level of consumption exactly offset the level of savings, which is the income consumers are not using to buy goods and services. In the equation $S = I + G$, the S represents savings, I represents investment, and G represents government spending.

ATTAINING EQUILIBRIUM

These three relationships hold true for an economy at any point in time. They are axioms that establish a foundation for understanding how changes in income, spending, and savings affect economic relationships. The concept of *equilibrium* is important in each of the relationships. The term connotes a state of temporary balance that already has occurred. In Keynesian models, the economy may be operating well above or below its capacity, even to the point of recession or inflation, and still be in equilibrium. However, the ideal economic condition, toward which monetary and fiscal policy are directed, is a state of sustained equilibrium at full employment.

Keynesian income-expenditure theory essentially asserts that the interaction of aggregate supply and aggregate demand determines the level of economic activity. Equilibrium exists when no shortages or excesses of spending exist relative to output; aggregate demand then equals aggregate supply. Policymakers are challenged to generate economic conditions in which supply and demand can balance while the economy fully uses all of its productive resources. Keynesian analysis thus emphasizes how and why consumption, investment, and government spending respond to change, holding that the determinants of total income are the key to effective policy control (see exhibit 9.1).

CONSUMPTION AND SAVINGS

The level of disposable personal income is the most important determinant of consumer spending and personal savings. Increased income leads to increased spending as people seek to improve their living standards, and to increased savings as people seek to build wealth.

Statistical evidence strongly supports a direct relationship between income level and consumption. However, economists have come to recognize that other factors also greatly affect consumer spending behavior. These factors include expectations about future income and prices, the value of specific financial assets, and the availability of goods and services for spending.

Assuming that these factors remain stable, however, the relationship between income and consumption is expressed as follows: as incomes increase, individuals spend more, but their consumption expenditures represent proportionally less of their total income.

For analysis and model building, consumption behavior is expressed as a **consumption function,** or consumption schedule (see exhibit 9.2 on the following page). This basic Keynesian model illustrates how much consumers will spend at every

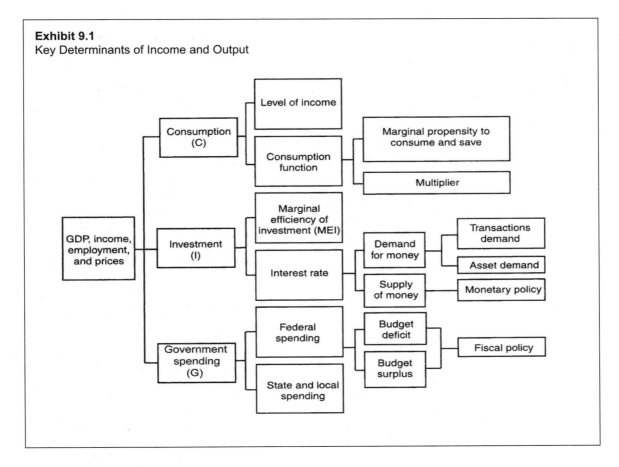

Exhibit 9.1
Key Determinants of Income and Output

level of income, with other factors remaining stable. The 45-degree line dissecting this model provides a visual guidepost that shows all the points of equilibrium *(E)* between spending and income. The consumption function is the base on which all further Keynesian analysis builds.

The slope, or curvature, of the consumption function *(C)* reflects the premise that as income initially increases, most of the increase will be consumed. Nonetheless, some of the increased income will be saved. As income continues to increase, a smaller and smaller proportion of the increase will go to consumption, while more will go to savings.

INVESTMENT SPENDING

The primary determinant of the level of investment spending in the economy is the interest rate. Businesses compare the

expected rate of return on a prospective investment against the cost of obtaining funds to make the investment or against the opportunity cost of using internal funds to make the investment. **Opportunity cost** refers to benefits that are foregone by choosing one alternative over another. Businesses invest as long as the return exceeds the rate of interest they must pay, and businesses continue to invest until the expected return on the last investment dollar equals the interest rate. If the interest rate declines, investment projects with lower expected returns become profitable. As a result, investments will increase. If the interest rate rises, investment projects must offer higher returns to make continued investments profitable. If some investments fail to yield that higher return, investments will likely decrease.

Because investment spending is not related primarily to the level of income, its introduction to the Keynesian model is

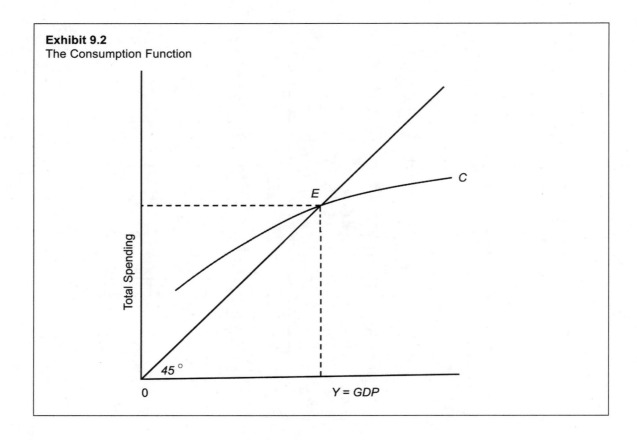

Exhibit 9.2
The Consumption Function

Total Spending (vertical axis)

E

C

45°

0

Y = GDP

treated as an autonomous or separate add-on level of spending. Assuming a given interest rate, the amount of investment spending that would be generated at that interest rate will prevail at all levels of income. Thus, the *C + I* schedule, which is the sum of consumption and investment spending, retains the same curvature as the *C* schedule (see exhibit 9.3).

The *C + I* schedule intersects the 45-degree line well to the right of the *C* schedule, thus increasing equilibrium income and output from *E* to *E'*. The economy also is generating a level of savings that equals the level of investment spending at *E'*. Savings is the difference between income *(Y)* and consumption *(C)*. On the model, it is the difference between the consumption schedule and the 45-degree line. At *E'*, the level of savings or money not being used to buy output is offset by the level of investment spending, which is money entering the production and income stream from an outside source.

Assume that the economy, although in equilibrium, is not at full employment. Specifically, actual consumption and investment spending and saving are less than what is necessary to sustain full use of the economy's capital and labor resources (see exhibit 9.4).

The ideal Keynesian economic environment would be one in which *C + I* intersect the 45-degree line at *E''*, the economy's full-employment capacity point. For that to occur, however, the consumption function *(C)*, the investment function *(I)*, or both would have to increase, shifting upward on the graph.

When Keynes developed his theories in the 1930s, he saw a depression-era economy in which there were few, if any, prospects that consumption or investment spending could be increased to move the economy to full employment.

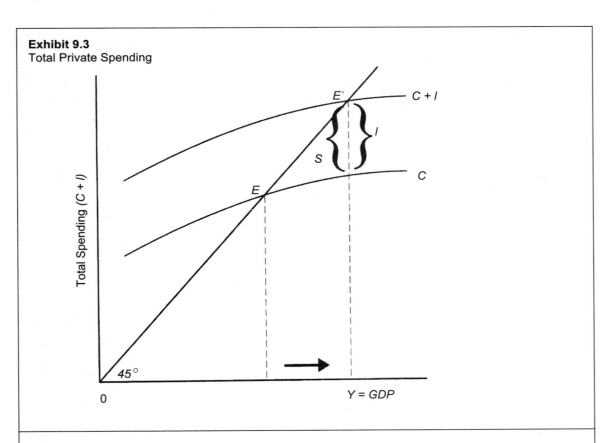

Exhibit 9.3
Total Private Spending

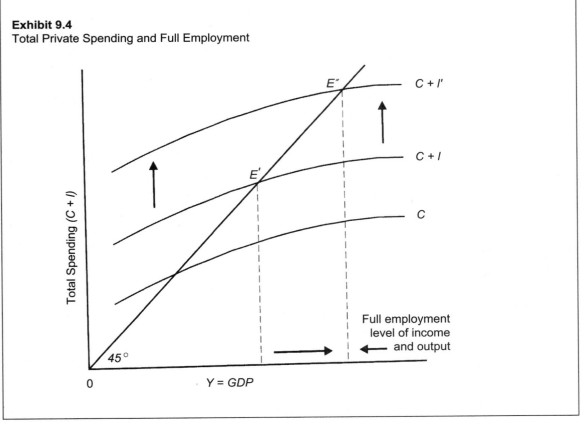

Exhibit 9.4
Total Private Spending and Full Employment

Government Spending

For John Maynard Keynes, the answer to a stable economy was a second source of autonomous spending: government spending. The government could move the economy to full employment by increasing its spending sufficiently to compensate for the shortfall in both consumption and investment spending (see exhibit 9.5).

Introducing government spending *(G)* to the model raises the overall level of spending so that at $C + I + G$, the economy is now at equilibrium and full employment. At *E,* the level of savings equals the level of investment spending and government spending. In effect, autonomous spending now offsets the drain on the economy's income and consumption caused by savings.

The Marginal Efficiency of Investment

An important premise of Keynesian theory is that a change in interest rates will change the level of investment spending in the economy. In any economy, at any time, a range of investment opportunities will generate inordinately high returns and be profitable under almost any circumstances. However, the profitability of most investment opportunities is uncertain, depending on the costs of making the investment relative to the expected return. The **marginal efficiency of investment** (MEI) curve attempts to demonstrate the relationship between the costs of making investments and their expected returns. It is this relationship, according to Keynes, that determines the level of investment spending.

The vertical axis of the model in exhibit 9.6 shows investment returns. The horizontal axis shows the corresponding levels of investment spending that would generate the returns cited on the vertical axis.

In this model, business firms would obtain a 20 percent return on the first $5 billion invested in the economy. If $10 billion were invested, businesses would obtain returns of only 15 percent. Obviously, businesses would prefer to obtain a 20 percent return on every dollar invested,

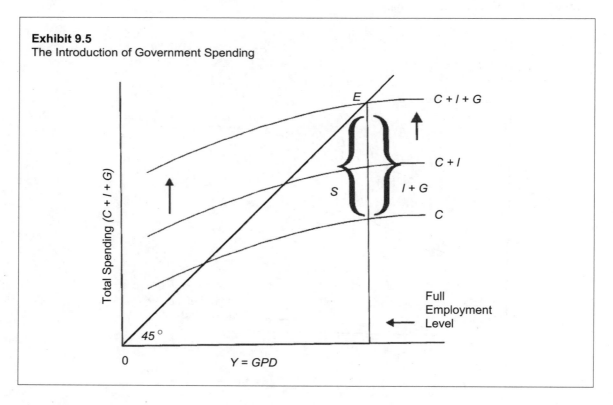

Exhibit 9.5
The Introduction of Government Spending

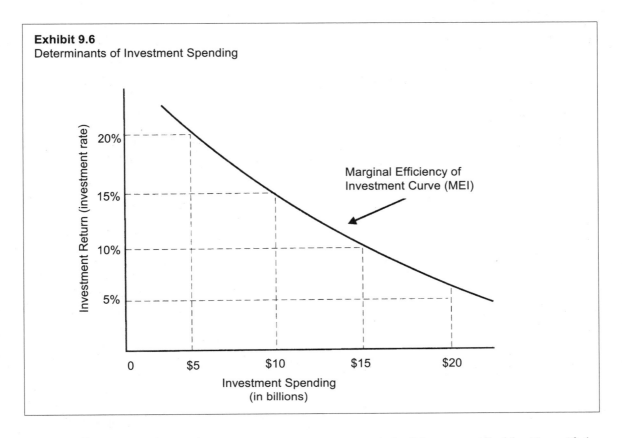

Exhibit 9.6
Determinants of Investment Spending

Marginal Efficiency of
Investment Curve (MEI)

Investment Return (investment rate)

Investment Spending
(in billions)

but the high-return investment opportunities are limited. The high-return investment opportunities are chosen first; then the next best opportunities, and so forth. As the more profitable opportunities become exhausted, lesser opportunities present themselves in descending order, until opportunities paying only 5 percent are available at the $20 billion investment level.

How much business firms will actually invest, however, is determined not by the rate of return of the investment but by its profitability. In exhibit 9.6, $15 billion would be invested at an investment return of 10 percent. However, if interest rates were to rise to 15 percent, many opportunities that had been profitable, such as those paying returns of more than 10 percent but less than 15 percent, suddenly would become unprofitable. The opportunities themselves would not change, but the costs of making the investment would change. For example, if a business firm must pay 15 percent on a loan to obtain a 12 percent return on its use of the loan proceeds, the 12 percent

"opportunity" is not profitable. Even if the firm has the money in hand, it might prefer to place the funds in a relatively safe certificate of deposit or money market instrument rather than make a more costly or risky investment.

FACTORS THAT INFLUENCE THE MEI CURVE

The MEI curve represents the investment preferences of the business community. Although changes in interest rates cause increases or decreases in the level of investment spending, shown as movements up or down the MEI curve, some important determinants affect the preference curve position of the MEI. These determinants cause the curve to shift to the right, to show an increase, or shift to the left, to show a decrease. The shifts of the MEI curve thus show how these determinants independently affect investment spending (see exhibit 9.7 on the following page).

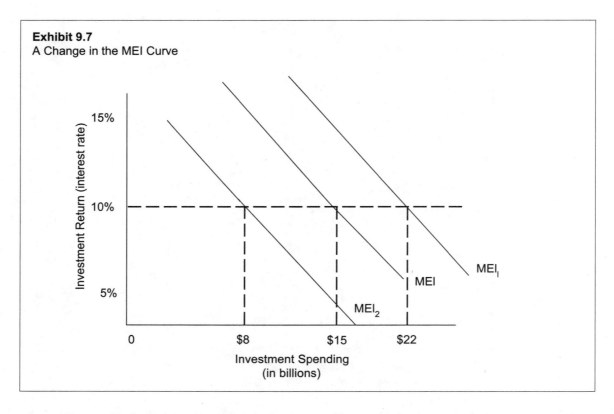

Exhibit 9.7
A Change in the MEI Curve

Investment Return (interest rate)

15%

10%

5%

0 $8 $15 $22

MEI₁

MEI

MEI₂

Investment Spending (in billions)

Business preferences for investment spending will likely change whenever a change occurs in the business community's expectations about investment income or when a basic change occurs in investment costs.

Factors that can shift the MEI to the right include

- introduction of new technology
- increases in profit expectations

Factors that can shift MEI to the left include

- increases in utility cost
- increases in the price of capital goods
- a recession

MONETARY POLICY IMPLICATIONS OF THE MEI CURVE

The monetary policy implications of a shift in the MEI curve are profound. For example, an increase in interest rates designed to blunt inflation by reducing investment spending easily can be nullified if inflationary expectations shift the MEI curve to the right. A decrease in interest rates designed to move the economy out of recession by generating more investment spending may have little, if any, effect if bleak business expectations about future sales shift the MEI curve to the left.

The elasticity of the MEI curve can affect monetary policy substantially. **Elasticity** of the MEI curve, which is shown in the slope of the curve, reflects to the degree of responsiveness of investment spending to a change in interest rates. A steep, almost vertical, MEI curve indicates little responsiveness, or inelasticity. A broad, almost flat, MEI curve indicates substantial responsiveness, or elasticity.

If the economy's MEI curve is highly inelastic, monetary policy must bring about a large change in interest rates to generate even a small change in investment spending. If the MEI curve is highly elastic, even a small change in interest rates will generate enormous changes in the level of investment spending. Unfortunately, economists are unsure what factors affect the elasticity of the MEI curve in the U.S. economy. Because of this lack of certainty, interest rate changes made in accordance with the Federal Reserve's monetary policy may precipitate too little change or too much change in investment spending.

INTEREST RATE THEORY

The interest rate is a crucial element in Keynesian theory. The interest rate not only determines investment spending, it is the primary channel through which changes in monetary policy affect income and output.

DEMAND FOR MONEY

Keynes's theory of interest, known as the **liquidity preference theory,** is predicated on the assumption that people prefer to hold money rather than less liquid assets. Interest, then, is the price that banks and others must pay to get people to give up this preference. The concept of liquidity preference is based on three separate money demand motives: transactions demand, precautionary demand, and speculative demand. The total demand for money in the economy is the sum of these demands.

TRANSACTIONS DEMAND

The transactions demand motive simply means that most people prefer to hold some liquid balances as convenience money to meet daily and weekly spending needs. The amount of money people hold for transactions relates directly to their income level, which is the key determinant of consumer spending. The higher the level of income, the more transactions balances people will hold for convenience spending and other purposes.

PRECAUTIONARY DEMAND

Many people prefer to keep some additional money in liquid form in order to cover unforeseen contingencies. This preference is called precautionary demand. The funds that are thus held act as an emergency liquidity reserve to meet unexpected spending needs or to withstand an unanticipated decline or delay in expected income.

SPECULATIVE DEMAND

Some people prefer to keep additional money balances available in order to speculate about future interest rates and the value of interest-earning assets, such as securities. In theory, this speculative demand leads people to hold more money when interest rates are low and bond prices are high in order to avoid capital losses when interest rates rise. Conversely, speculative demand leads people to hold less money when interest rates are high and bond prices are low in order to capture capital gains when interest rates fall.

The price of securities is inversely related to their investment yield, or interest return. Therefore, a purchase of securities followed by a rise in interest rates would generate a capital loss when the securities were sold. A purchase followed by a fall in interest rates would generate a capital gain when the securities were sold. However, it is exceedingly difficult to know exactly when interest rates will begin to rise or fall. Thus, the **speculative demand** motive represents the demand for money balances by individuals who remain uncertain about the future course of interest rates. They are speculating that by waiting with cash balances, they will be in a better position to gain when they ultimately purchase financial assets.

TOTAL DEMAND FOR MONEY

The total demand for money is the sum of transaction demand, precautionary demand, and speculative demand for money. Total demand is determined by the level of income, expressed as transactions and precautionary demand, plus the interest rate, expressed as speculative demand. For modeling purposes, total demand for money can be represented as a downward-sloping curve called the liquidity preference curve (see exhibit 9.8).

For purposes of analysis, the money supply is assumed to be fixed at any given time, as determined by monetary policy. Graphically, the money supply can be represented by a straight vertical line. The interaction of the money supply with the demand for money can be shown as the intersection of the money supply line with the liquidity preference curve. It is this interaction that determines the equilibrium interest rate, *E*. The Keynesian model suggests that at the level of income assumed, the public is willing to hold the quantity of money available only at the equilibrium interest rate.

THE EFFECT OF A CHANGE IN LIQUIDITY PREFERENCE

Exhibit 9.8 demonstrates what happens when the public's demand for money changes. If the public increases its demand for money, shifting the liquidity preference curve to the right, the interest rate rises (arrow 1). A decrease in the demand for money likewise causes the interest rate to fall. If the Federal Reserve increases the supply of money, shifting the money supply line to the right (arrow 2), the interest rate will fall (arrow 3). Likewise, a decrease in the money supply will cause the interest rate to rise.

MONETARISM

During the 1950s and 1960s, American economist Milton Friedman produced the

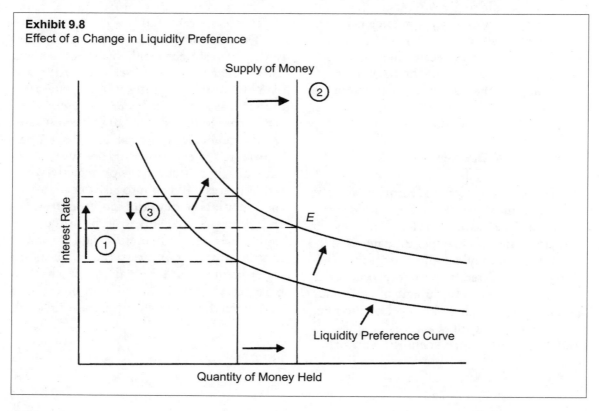

Exhibit 9.8
Effect of a Change in Liquidity Preference

body of economic theory known today as monetarism. Friedman adapted the quantity theory of money and Fisher's equation of exchange to the modern economy. He also provided considerable statistical support that money is the most important determinant of economic activity. Friedman did this by using national income accounts data that had not been developed when Fisher postulated his equation of exchange.

Friedman disagreed with the Keynesian idea that the key relationship in the economy is the relationship between total income and total spending. According to Friedman, the more important relationship is the one between total income and the quantity of money the public prefers to hold. Friedman contends that the public's preference, or demand, for money is relatively stable and predictable. Thus, if the actual amount of money available in the economy differs from what the public wants to hold, consumers and businesses will adjust their spending until they hold money balances in accordance with their preferences.

If the economy has too much money, people and businesses seek to adjust their portfolios by converting excess money holdings into goods and financial assets until they have the balance of money, goods, and financial assets they prefer. If the economy has too little money, people and businesses seek to adjust their portfolios by holding down spending on goods, selling financial assets, and otherwise building up money balances to match their preferences. These portfolio adjustments continue until the public's preferences for money match the actual amount of money available.

Imagine that people all over the country suddenly receive checks for $1 million. Most of them probably have too much money; that is, they have an excess of liquid funds relative to their holdings of goods and financial assets. According to monetarism, they will react by adjusting their personal portfolios to reduce the excess liquidity. Because many people are doing this at the same time, intense competition for available goods and financial assets soon develops, driving up prices. As prices rise, people discover that they must hold more money balances simply to match the purchasing power that they had before they received that $1 million windfall. Inflation effectively ends the adjustment process.

Now assume that, instead of receiving $1 million, everyone's workweek and paycheck are halved. Now people have too little money. They will likely respond by stretching every available dollar, slowing down their rate of spending, and perhaps by selling some financial assets to increase their money balances. This means less income for producers and sellers of goods, however. These producers and sellers will, in turn, begin to stretch every available profit, interest, and rent dollar. Eventually, these cumulative adjustments send the economy into a recession.

THE BASIC TENETS OF MONETARISM

Milton Friedman and other monetarists developed a broad body of economic theory that has tended to refute Keynesian contentions about how the economy works. Although monetarists hold varying opinions about some of the principles and precepts of monetarism, they tend to agree on certain general tenets about the money supply and the economy. Monetarists usually agree that

- the money supply is the single most important determinant of gross domestic product (GDP)
- changes in the money supply cause changes in income and output
- changes in the money supply affect total spending
- increases in the money supply can lead to increases in interest rates
- monetary policy should be structured to generate a small but constant annual rate of money supply growth

Monetarists contend that the money supply is the single most important determinant of the level of GDP. Although many factors affect production, employment, and prices, monetarists believe that a change in the growth of the money supply is the principal determinant of the economy's current level of production and employment and the major determinant of both the current and future level of prices.

Monetarists acknowledge that long-term GDP growth will be determined by technology, productivity, and the quantity and quality of the nation's productive resources. However, they maintain that money supply growth must be properly controlled to ensure reasonable stability in present employment and prices.

Milton Friedman and other monetarists have collected a considerable body of data that they contend demonstrates that changes in money supply causes changes in GDP. They assert that a causal relationship exists between changes in money supply and changes in income and output. Over long periods of time, however, most changes in money supply cause changes in prices. These causal relationships are based on the stability and predictability of the velocity of money.

An examination of M1 velocity from 1910 to 2000 shows several different velocity trends (see exhibit 9.9). These trends clearly indicate that the velocity of money is not constant over long periods of time. Nonetheless, to support their contention monetarists point to the reasonable predictability of money velocity on a year-to-year basis within each of these periods.

Monetarists also contend that changes in money supply change total spending in the economy. This occurs through adjustments that consumers and businesses make in their holdings of financial and nonfinancial assets. Monetarists believe that holders of excess money balances will spend the excess on goods and financial assets in order to regain a preferred balance among their money, financial assets, and goods. Consequently, money supply changes affect a broader range of financial assets and interest rates than Keynesian theory suggests.

Under Keynesian theory, increases in money supply should lead to lower interest rates, which reduce borrowing costs and increase bank lending and business investment spending. Monetarists disagree, arguing that increases in money supply can lead to increases in interest rates. Although increases in the money supply initially cause interest rates to decline, as consumers and businesses begin to spend their excess liquidity and generate new income for others, the demand for money is forced up and interest rates begin to rise. Furthermore, they claim, increases in money supply fuel market expectations of continued inflation. Lenders add an inflationary premium to real interest rates in order to protect themselves against the anticipated loss of purchasing power of the money they expect to receive in repayments over time. Taking these various factors into consideration, monetarists conclude that upward pressure on interest rates tends to exceed downward pressure when the money supply is increased, resulting in a net increase in interest rates.

Because of this effect, monetarists caution that interest rates should not be used as operating targets for monetary policy. Further, they say that the Federal Reserve should not rely on any interest rate as an operating target. Instead, they contend, the Federal Reserve should concentrate on controlling the money supply.

In practice, the Federal Reserve relies on a short-term interest rate, the federal funds rate, as a key operating target. The central bank perceives increases in the federal funds rate as an indicator of a tight monetary policy. Monetarists, on the other hand, would interpret rising interest rates fueled by money supply growth as indicators of an easy monetary policy that suggests further inflation.

Monetarists recommend structuring monetary policy to generate a constant 3 percent to 5 percent annual rate of money supply growth. Although they are sure that

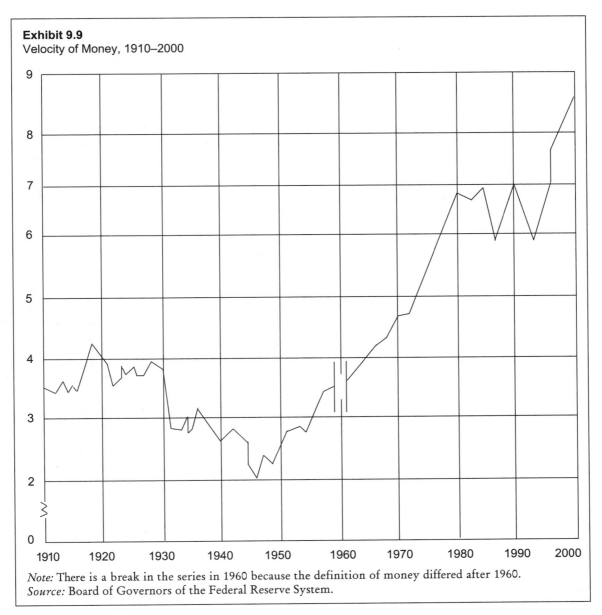

Exhibit 9.9
Velocity of Money, 1910–2000

Note: There is a break in the series in 1960 because the definition of money differed after 1960.
Source: Board of Governors of the Federal Reserve System.

changes in money supply cause changes in income and output, they are unsure precisely how long it takes those changes to affect the economy. Milton Friedman maintains that the time lag between a money supply cause and an economic effect may be 18 months or longer. Most monetarists believe the lag time is shorter, about 6 months. These differing opinions reflect various interpretations of the wide time variations found in the data that link money supply changes to GDP changes.

Because the time lags are variable and seemingly unpredictable, monetarists contend that monetary policy should be structured to generate a constant 3 percent to 5 percent annual rate of money supply growth. They would have the Federal Reserve end its attempts at structuring an easy or tight monetary policy to counter recession or inflation, respectively.

A constant rate of money supply growth of 3 percent to 5 percent per year would match the long-term annual growth rate of the U.S. economy. By providing the economy with 3 percent to 5 percent more money each year, monetarists argue, just enough new money would be assured for balanced, sustainable real growth. Monetarists contend that the Federal Reserve's discretionary, or counter-cyclical, approach to monetary policy tends to destabilize the economy. They maintain that the Federal Reserve worsens the economy's inflations and recessions by failing to appreciate the unpredictable time lags between money supply changes and economic changes. As a result, the Federal Reserve tends to overreact when the economy fails to respond to tighter or easier monetary policy. This overreaction invariably provides the economy with too much easing or too much restraint at the wrong time, thereby exacerbating inflation or recession.

EFFECTS OF MONETARY POLICY

Money supply changes certainly affect the cost of capital and the availability of credit. However, most economists believe that monetary policy also affects the economy by changing the public's perception of its financial wealth. Economists call this latter phenomenon the wealth effect.

COST OF CAPITAL

Tighter money leads to a smaller supply of bank reserves; easier money expands the supply of reserves. When the federal funds rate is higher, banks tend to offset the higher cost of maintaining their reserves by charging higher interest rates on loans. As interest rates rise, some potential business borrowers cannot afford the extra interest cost. When reserves cost less, banks reduce their interest rates on loans, which induces some potential business borrowers to take loans. In effect, higher interest rates raise the cost of capital (investments), while lower interest rates reduce the cost of capital.

As firms cut back or expand their investment spending, their actions influence the economy. Reduced business investment means reduced income and spending by companies that would have received orders for new capital equipment. Increased business investment means increased income for these companies.

AVAILABILITY OF CREDIT

Some of the effects of monetary policy are transmitted through the behavior of lenders. During a period of tight money, some banks are unable to obtain the reserves they need to fund all loan requests. Thus, banks may seek to ration customer credit. Typically, they make funds available first to their most valued customers: those with long-standing relationships and good loan repayment histories. Next in line are customers with relatively weaker credit standings, collateral, and credit repayment histories. Rationing credit often involves imposing more stringent collateral requirements and higher compensating balances on loans, and denying new credit requests. These rationing actions result in some business borrowers obtaining less credit than they had expected or perhaps receiving no credit at all. As a result, the level of investment spending in the economy declines.

During periods when the Federal Reserve eases monetary policy, banks tend to exhibit more liberal and expansive lending behavior.

THE WEALTH EFFECT

The **wealth effect** refers to the effect perceived changes in the public's financial wealth has on spending and savings behavior. In other words, a change in the public's perception of its financial wealth will cause a change in spending and saving.

The public's reactions are rooted in the balance the public tries to maintain between holdings of money and financial assets. When this balance is upset, either by monetary policy or by such nonpolicy occurrences as changes in stock market or real estate values, the public responds.

Monetary policy changes the value of financial assets by driving up or driving down interest rates. When interest rates increase, securities prices decline, generating wealth losses for people and financial institutions. When interest rates decline, securities prices increase, adding to the public's financial wealth. These changes in wealth are then manifested in increased or reduced spending. During the 1990s, monetary ease, coupled with the explosive growth of stock values driven largely by technology stocks, induced large increases in consumer and business spending and a sharp decline in the savings rate.

SUMMARY

Monetary theory provides an essential foundation for monetary policy even though economists do not agree on all of the cause-and-effect relationships among the economic variables on which it is built.

Monetarists maintain that the quantity theory of money is an applicable guide for structuring monetary policy. Monetarists claim that a direct, causal relationship exists between money and gross domestic product (GDP), because changes in the velocity of money are relatively stable and predictable. On the basis of these two premises, monetarists contend that the Federal Reserve can best control the economy by providing a constant 3 percent to 5 percent annual rate of money supply growth.

Nonmonetarists argue that the velocity of money is not stable and that the Federal Reserve's provision of money supply growth must be flexible. Moreover, Keynesian theory maintains that monetary policy works by affecting the cost as well as the supply of available money. Interest rate changes affect borrowers, lenders, and the public's financial wealth, generating changes in business investment and public consumption levels. In turn, business investment and public consumption alter the economy's level of income and output.

Most economists and policymakers take an eclectic approach to monetary theory. The difficulty in achieving and maintaining full employment, price stability, and economic growth has led to an ongoing re-evaluation of the theoretical underpinnings of monetary policy and modifications in policy strategies.

REVIEW QUESTIONS

1. Briefly explain the quantity theory of money and Fisher's equation of exchange.
2. An important condition for Keynesian equilibrium is $S = I + G$. Why?
3. What are the determinants of total demand for money? What would happen to demand if there were a massive increase in banks' issuance and the public's use of credit cards?
4. In implementing monetary policy, why does it matter whether the marginal efficiency of investment (MEI) curve or the liquidity preference curve is highly elastic or highly inelastic?
5. What are the major differences between monetarism and Keynesian theory?
6. Why do monetarists contend that the only appropriate monetary policy is a constant 3 percent to 5 percent annual growth in the money supply?

ADDITIONAL RESOURCES

American Bankers Association, at *www. aba.com.* Web site of the American Bankers Association; provides current information on the economy and analysis by top bank economists.

Economics for Financial Services Providers, by Jon A. Hooks, Ph.D., American Bankers Association, 1999. An ABA textbook on economics written for financial services providers.

Economic Review, Federal Reserve Bank of San Francisco, quarterly publication. Contains technical articles relating economic theory to current policy issues.

Economic Trends, Federal Reserve Bank of Cleveland, monthly publication. Charts the latest economic statistics and briefly discusses the current state of the economy.

"Essential Principles of Economics: A Hypermedia Text" (chapter summary) at *http://william-king.www.drexel.edu/top/ prin/txt/equil/sum.html.* Discusses the Keynesian theory of economics.

Review, Federal Reserve Bank of St. Louis, bi-monthly journal. Contains articles about national and international economic developments, monetary theory, and current research.

10

POLICY GOALS AND THE FINANCIAL SYSTEM

LEARNING OBJECTIVES

After studying this chapter, you should be able to

- explain full employment, the unemployment rate, and the types of unemployment that exist in our economy
- describe demand-pull, cost-push, and scarcity-induced inflation, and explain the wage-price spiral
- explain how consumers, businesses, and financial institutions respond differently to anticipated and unanticipated inflation
- explain the relevance of trade-off, or Phillips curve, analysis
- list the key factors that determine U.S. productivity growth
- cite the various approaches taken by bank management that improved productivity in the 1990s
- define the key terms listed in this chapter

KEY TERMS

consumer price index
hidden unemployment
income effect
non-accelerating-inflation rate
  of unemployment
Phillips curve

price stability
productivity
supply-chain management
wage-price spiral
wealth effect

INTRODUCTION

The nation's economic objectives are full employment, price stability, and economic growth. In this chapter, we'll examine these three goals and the problems policymakers face in reducing the unemployment rate, fighting inflation, and increasing U.S. productivity. The United States has never achieved full employment, price stability, and economic growth simultaneously. Some economists believe that attaining any one or two of the goals may be possible only at the expense of one or more of the others. This chapter examines each of these major economic objectives, along with some of the trade-offs involved in achieving them.

To provide insight into the challenges confronting policymakers, the chapter explores the changing U.S. labor force and the increasingly structural nature of U.S. unemployment. Sources of inflation and problems in measuring inflation also are examined.

Many economists contend that increasing productivity is the only way that the United States can achieve its economic goals. The chapter ends with an examination of the

reasons for U.S. productivity growth and how banks have been increasing productivity.

FULL EMPLOYMENT

Full employment is reached when all of a nation's productive resources, both capital and labor, are in full use. In practical terms, full employment is associated more with labor than with capital. Full employment has come to mean a condition in which all but a reasonable percentage of the nation's labor force is employed.

No absolute measure constitutes full employment or, conversely, reasonable unemployment. The unemployment rate is defined as the percentage of the labor force that is unemployed and looking for work. Concepts of reasonable joblessness in the U.S. economy have changed over time. During the 1980s, when unemployment averaged more than 6 percent of the labor force, a 5 percent unemployment rate was considered the short-term full employment goal. In the late 1990s, with employment having fallen below 4.5 percent, a 4 percent unemployment rate was a reasonable short-term goal (see exhibits 10.1 and 10.2). Since

Exhibit 10.1
Unemployment Rate, 1910–2001

Percent of labor force

Source: Bureau of Labor Statistics.

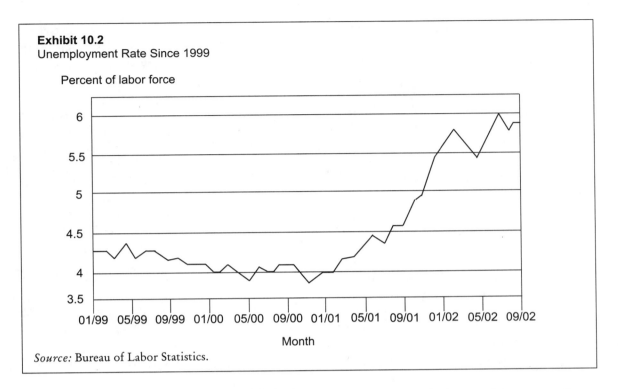

Exhibit 10.2
Unemployment Rate Since 1999

Percent of labor force

Source: Bureau of Labor Statistics.

1946, when full employment was established as a national goal, the United States has been able to attain this goal only for brief periods—in the early 1950s, in the late 1960s, and in 2000.

Exhibit 10.1 shows the nation's unemployment performance from 1910 to 2001. In 1933, with the U.S. economy in the depths of the Great Depression, the U.S. unemployment rate reached a record high of 24.9 percent. Just 11 years later, in 1944, with its economy operating at wartime, full-production capacity, the United States registered its lowest unemployment rate ever of 1.2 percent.

To understand why the nation's idea of reasonable unemployment changes over time and why sustaining full employment has been difficult, we must first understand the economic factors from which the national unemployment rate is derived.

UNEMPLOYMENT RATE

The U.S. unemployment rate represents the percentage of the U.S. population, age 16 years old or older, that is either employed or without a job but seeking one. Some adults, such as full-time students, full-time homemakers, retired persons, and unemployed persons who are not looking for work, are not counted as part of the labor force. In 2002 the nation's labor force totaled 143 million people, including 2 million members of the armed forces. An additional 70 million nonworking adults were excluded from the count because they fell in the categories noted above.

The unemployment rate is determined by taking the number of unemployed people in the labor force—about 7.7 million people in early 2002—as a percentage of the entire labor force. The U.S. unemployment rate in September 2002 was 5.6 percent.

Increases in the unemployment rate reflect an inability to obtain jobs among people who

- lose their jobs
- voluntarily leave their jobs
- return to the labor force after having worked previously
- enter the labor force for the first time

During the early 2000s, about three-fifths of the nation's unemployed persons had lost their jobs because of corporate downsizing and slow economic growth in the wake of the 2001 recession. In the previous decade, however, about two-thirds of unemployed persons were either new entrants to the labor force or persons who were re-entering the labor force. New entrants to the labor force typically include teenagers who have never worked before and immigrants. Re-entrants to the labor force often include early retirees who are seeking to supplement their income or women who are seeking to return to work after rearing children.

A rising unemployment rate does not necessarily indicate that workers are being laid off, and a falling unemployment rate does not necessarily indicate that laid-off workers are being recalled. The unemployment rate can increase if there is an expansion in the number of people seeking work and can decline if job seekers stop looking for work.

CHANGING U.S. LABOR FORCE

During the 1980s and 1990s, the U.S. economy created enough new jobs to sharply expand employment and reduce the unemployment rate. More than 30 million new jobs were created and the unemployment rate was halved from 8 percent to 4 percent over this 20-year period.

The U.S. economy's record of job creation in the 1980s and 1990s was unmatched by that of other industrial countries. The unprecedented employment that was generated, however, masked structural changes in America's workforce and the nature of unemployment. A large percentage of job seekers during this period were women re-entering the work force, teenagers who had never worked before, and displaced workers who had lost a job because of corporate downsizing, foreign competition, or technological changes. Many of these job seekers found only low-paying

jobs or were forced to work part-time because full-time work was unavailable. In 2001 nearly 4 million workers held jobs in this latter category, which economists classify as **hidden unemployment.**

During the 1980s and 1990s, virtually all new jobs in the U.S. economy came from small- and medium-size businesses. These employers were primarily service firms, such as restaurants and fast-food chains, hospitals and other medical care facilities, retail stores, regional airlines, management consultant firms, financial institutions, and public utilities. Meanwhile, the nation's large corporations, primarily in the manufacturing sector, lost nearly 5 million jobs. Federal government employment levels remained essentially flat during this period. Today more than 75 percent of the nation's workforce is in service sector occupations; about 15 percent of workers hold manufacturing jobs.

THEORIES OF UNEMPLOYMENT

In an effort to understand why unemployment exists, economists have identified several different kinds of unemployment: frictional unemployment, seasonal unemployment, cyclical unemployment, and structural unemployment.

FRICTIONAL UNEMPLOYMENT

In our market economy, workers are free to change jobs and move from one part of the country to another. Because of this, a segment of the labor force at any given time will be in the process of voluntarily changing jobs. Typically, these workers seek higher wages, better working conditions, or advancement opportunities. This kind of joblessness, which is both temporary and voluntary, is referred to as frictional unemployment. It is considered an inherent characteristic of a market economy. In 2002, for example, more than 10 percent of the nation's unemployed persons had voluntarily left jobs and had not yet found other employment.

SEASONAL UNEMPLOYMENT

During the course of a year, some industries typically experience pronounced swings in business activity and employment because of changes in weather, consumer demand, or production style. Seasonal unemployment is common in retailing, clothing, auto manufacturing, farming, and construction, for example. At particular times of the year, workers are temporarily laid off in response to changes in production and demand.

CYCLICAL UNEMPLOYMENT

A recession, characterized by a decline in the gross domestic product (GDP), usually is accompanied by an increase in cyclical unemployment. Workers laid off because of an economic downturn normally are called back when the economy begins to move to the recovery phase of the business cycle. Economists believe cyclical unemployment can be treated by stimulative monetary and fiscal policies designed to boost aggregate demand or total spending, speed up the economy's recovery phase, and drive down unemployment.

STRUCTURAL UNEMPLOYMENT

Many unemployed persons lack the education and skills to fill available jobs. Other unemployed persons have been displaced from a job by new work processes, new technology, or foreign competition. These latter reasons for unemployment are directly related to the structure of the U.S. economy.

Structural unemployment typically varies greatly among regions of the country and among occupations and industries. During the 1990s, for example, the economy underwent a profound restructuring that saw a substantial decline in occupations such as secretaries, telephone operators, supervisors, assemblers, and packagers, and unemployment was particularly high among blue-collar workers and among middle-aged workers 35 to 54 years old, the age group most affected by corporate downsizing and restructuring. At the same time, demand for computer programmers, brokers, accountants, teachers, and sales personnel increased. Unemployment was virtually nonexistent among professionals, managers, and administrators. College-educated workers had the lowest unemployment rate.

Many economists contend that structural unemployment results mostly from a mismatch between the labor skills required by U.S. employers and the labor skills, or lack thereof, of the unemployed. The mismatch arises from changes in technology, competitive international relationships, demand for certain products, or in the proportion of different skill groups in the population. During the 1980s, for example, an influx of unskilled teenagers entered the labor force, contributing to structural unemployment.

Economists further contend that policies directed at stimulating aggregate demand will not reduce structural unemployment. Only a policy aimed at preparing unemployed persons to fill available job openings will substantially reduce the unemployment rate.

The increasingly structural nature of U.S. unemployment has caused economists to re-examine traditional theories of unemployment and propose alternatives to conventional monetary and fiscal policies to reduce joblessness.

PROPOSALS TO REDUCE STRUCTURAL UNEMPLOYMENT

Proposals to reduce structural unemployment are directed at a broad range of sources, or causes, of structural joblessness. These causes include

- technological and competitive displacement
- teenage job needs
- re-entry into the work force
- lack of skills and education

The problems of displaced workers have led economists and others to call for government protection against foreign competition through measures such as

- import quotas that limit the amount or value of foreign goods that can be brought into this country
- local content laws that require a fixed percentage of the components of U.S.-manufactured items to be made in the United States
- federal subsidies to industries that have high levels of unemployment

To boost work opportunities for teenagers, some economists propose suspending or substantially reducing the federal minimum wage for teenagers. Other economists and union leaders argue that doing this would undermine adult minimum wage rates and fail to address the underlying problem, teenagers' lack of skills and education to meet current job demands.

Many potential workers lack relevant information about the wages, working conditions, and job opportunities available to them. Job seekers must take time to investigate job prospects and in some cases wait for better job offers. Thus, some unemployment periods may represent an investment in time made by workers seeking the right jobs. Measures or programs that speed the job-finding process by providing accurate information and quickly matching potential workers to job vacancies might reduce unemployment numbers.

Some structural unemployment persists because the supply of workers with limited skills and education exceeds the demand for such workers at prevailing wage rates.

Measures or programs that provide adult education, skill development, or job training might help bridge this gap.

PRICE STABILITY

The economic goal of **price stability** is achieved in an inflation-free economy when consumers and businesses stop basing their financial decisions on expectations of continued inflation. During inflationary periods, the prices of all goods and services increase and the value of money declines. During inflation-free periods, prices and the value of money remain stable, creating price stability. From 1950 to 1965, the nation achieved price stability. From 1966 through 1980, however, price increases accelerated, averaging about 6 percent each year and reaching double digits at the beginning of the 1980s. During the 1980s and 1990s, price increases slowed, until inflation ended in the early 2000s (see exhibit 10.3). For most of this 20-year period, the nation's monetary policy primarily focused on stopping inflation.

Improvements in the quality of U.S. goods and services add, on average, about 1 percent to 2 percent to the nation's price structure each year. These increases do not reduce the purchasing power of money because consumers obtain equivalent value for their somewhat more expensive purchases in terms of better or more useful goods. Thus, economists do not count these productive increases as inflation.

CONSUMER PRICE INDEX

The **consumer price index (CPI)** is the most widely reported and generally accepted measure of inflation in the United States. The CPI, which measures the cost of a hypothetical basket of goods and services purchased by consumers, is calculated each month by the Bureau of Labor Statistics (BLS), an independent agency within the U.S. Department of Labor.

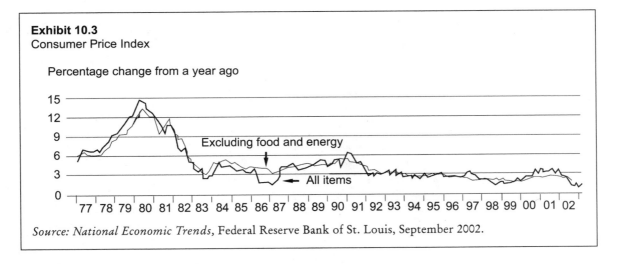

Exhibit 10.3
Consumer Price Index

Percentage change from a year ago

Source: *National Economic Trends,* Federal Reserve Bank of St. Louis, September 2002.

The market basket of goods and services used to calculate the CPI encompasses thousands of different goods and services, each weighted by the item's relative proportion in the market basket. The market basket is updated every 10 years. Exhibit 10.4 on the following page shows the current composition of the CPI market basket.

When preparing the monthly CPI, the BLS calculates price changes for the items in the market basket. The algebraic sum of these price changes, weighted by each item's relative proportion in the market basket, indicates whether consumer prices have increased, decreased, or remained unchanged during the previous month.

To most Americans, this index indicates the degree of inflation in the U.S. economy. The index actually overstates the rate of inflation, because immediate changes in spending behavior in response to price changes are not factored into the CPI calculation. For example, if the price of steak goes up during the month, many consumers likely will switch from steak to lower-priced chicken or fish. As a result, consumers are not as affected by the increase in steak prices as the price increase might suggest.

The CPI also does not measure the effect new products and services have on consumer spending behavior. The cellular phone is an example of a popular product that was not in the market basket of goods

and services during the 1990s. If cellular phones and cellular service charges had been included in the market basket, the declining prices for these products in the 1990s would have offset some of the increases recorded in the prices of other goods and services, thereby reducing the overall measure of inflation.

The failure of the CPI to adequately measure quality improvements in goods and services is another source of overstatement in the index. When the price of an item increases, a decision must be made whether the price increase has been caused by inflation or by an improvement in quality. These decisions often are difficult to make.

The accuracy of the CPI is an issue for more than economists. The government uses the CPI to adjust numerous federal programs, such as Social Security, federal employee pensions, and the standard deduction allowance for federal income taxes. If Congress were to reduce the CPI adjustment to offset overstatements, government tax revenues would be higher and government outlays lower.

SOURCES OF INFLATION

Economists classify inflation according to its source: demand-pull, cost-push, or scarcity-induced.

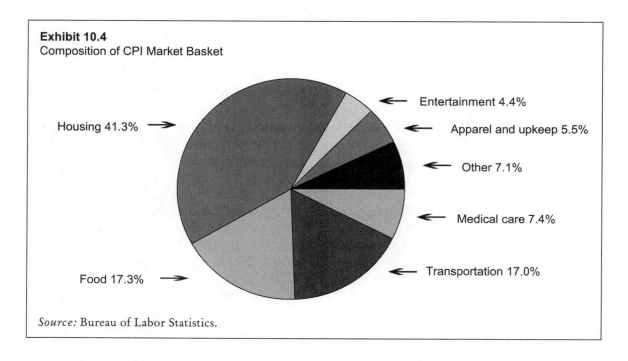

Exhibit 10.4
Composition of CPI Market Basket

Housing 41.3%

Entertainment 4.4%

Apparel and upkeep 5.5%

Other 7.1%

Medical care 7.4%

Transportation 17.0%

Food 17.3%

Source: Bureau of Labor Statistics.

DEMAND-PULL INFLATION

In demand-pull inflation, excess demand causes prices to rise. Demand-pull inflation occurs when the total demand of consumers, businesses, and government exceeds the supply of goods and services available. The demand, expressed as spending, generates competitive pressures that pull up prices.

A rapid growth in the nation's money supply typically increases total demand faster than goods can be made available. As a result, some economists characterize demand-pull inflation as a condition in which too much money chases too few goods.

COST-PUSH INFLATION

In cost-push inflation, prices are pushed up by producers who offset increases in their production costs by marking up prices and passing costs on to consumers. As demand-pull pressures drive up prices, workers press for higher wages to compensate for their loss of purchasing power. If they succeed in obtaining higher wages, they drive up production costs. Producers push up prices to offset these cost increases and protect profit margins. Prices are ratcheted up through this **wage-price spiral,** leading to increasingly higher rates of inflation.

SCARCITY-INDUCED INFLATION

With scarcity-induced inflation, prices rise because of a shortage of key commodities or goods. Shortages may result from natural causes or from governmental actions. For example, in the 1970s, a worldwide drought created a scarcity of wheat and grain that drove up food prices. A famous example of governmentally induced scarcity occurred in 1973, when the Organization of Oil Producing Countries (OPEC) placed limits on world oil supplies. This action led to a five-fold increase in the price of U.S. gasoline, aggravating U.S. inflation.

ANTICIPATED AND UNANTICIPATED INFLATION

The nation's experience with inflation in the 1970s caused economists to modify some of their theories about consumer and business responses to rising prices. Because inflation reduces the purchasing power of money, the longer money is held and not spent, the less value it has for both consumers and businesses. Thus, one theory maintained that consumers speed up their spending and reduce their savings during inflationary periods in order to obtain the maximum purchasing power for their income. Similarly, businesses are expected to speed up investment spending during inflationary periods.

Economists now recognize that consumers and businesses react differently to unanticipated inflation than they do to anticipated inflation. When consumers and businesses correctly anticipate price increases, they behave according to conventional theory by increasing their spending and investment. Consumers and businesses respond more defensively, however, when inflation is unexpected or when the degree of inflation is greater than expected. This was the case in the 1970s, when the U.S. economy was hit with unexpected increases in energy prices.

EFFECTS OF INFLATION

Inflation reduces the purchasing power of all money, though its effects on consumers, businesses, and governments are borne unevenly. This unevenness adds an important social and political dimension to the problem of inflation. The following are some of the ways that inflation may differently affect various groups.

INCOME EFFECT

Inflation redistributes income from persons with fixed or slowly increasing incomes, such as retired pensioners and government employees, to those whose incomes rise rapidly, such as self-employed professionals and union workers covered by contracts with built-in cost-of-living adjustments. This phenomenon is referred to as the **income effect** of inflation.

WEALTH EFFECT

Rising prices also redistribute wealth from creditors and savers to debtors. Economists call this phenomenon the **wealth effect.**

Banks and other financial institutions that lend long-term money at fixed interest rates lose money during inflationary periods because they are repaid in dollars that have less purchasing power than those they originally loaned. Debtors, on the other hand, gain money because they repay borrowed funds with money that is worth less than the money they originally borrowed.

PROFILE OF INFLATION

Inflation ravaged the U.S. economy from the late 1960s to the early 1980s. This longest and most severe inflation in the nation's history originated with the demand-pull pressures of the mid-1960s, when the government increased its social service spending to fight a war on poverty in the United States and its military spending to fight the war in Vietnam. Cost-push pressures in the late 1960s carried inflation into the 1970s. Prices also were driven up during the 1970s by scarcity-induced inflation, caused by shortages of important food crops and imported oil.

A highly restrictive monetary policy, a severe recession in 1981 to 1982, and a world oil glut that caused oil prices to decline broke the nation's inflationary spiral. During the 1980s, inflation decelerated. A renewed commitment by the Federal Reserve to achieve price stability in the 1990s helped trigger a further deceleration. In the early 2000s, annual consumer price increases averaged less than 2 percent.

Savers who receive fixed rates of return on their funds, such as persons with traditional savings accounts, lose money if the interest they receive is lower than the inflation rate. Over the course of a year experiencing 5 percent inflation, for example, the funds in a 2 percent savings account would lose 3 percent in purchasing power.

As noted previously, the redistribution of wealth generated by inflation occurs mainly when inflation is unanticipated. If inflation is fully and correctly anticipated, banks and other lenders typically add an inflation premium to the interest rate they charge. The inflation premium compensates for purchasing power losses over the length of the loan. Correctly forecasting the inflation rate over long periods is difficult, however. Many banks now seek to protect themselves against unexpected inflation by lending long-term money at rates that change monthly or quarterly instead of at fixed rates. Nonetheless, interest rate ceilings on consumer loans and mortgages sometimes limit the ability of lenders to factor in inflation premiums on these types of loans.

TAX EFFECT

Under the federal income tax structure and the structure of many state income taxes, inflation acts as a form of tax increase for wage earners. This phenomenon reflects the fact that rising prices typically are accompanied by rising wages. Increased wages tend to push income earners into higher tax brackets, however, generally requiring that a larger proportion of the wage gain be paid in taxes.

PROFITS ILLUSION EFFECT

Inflation creates an illusion of profit gains for businesses in two ways. Inflation

- drives up the value of inventories and capital

- generates bookkeeping profits on inventory valuation and capital depreciation

Because inventory and depreciation profits do not consider replacement costs, however, these bookkeeping profits can grossly exaggerate a company's real earnings and lead to faulty planning and decision-making.

Assume, for example, that an automobile manufacturer builds a $20,000 car in January. The $20,000 price reflects the cost of materials, labor, profit, and all the other costs of building the car. In December the car is still at the plant waiting to be shipped to a dealer. During the intervening 12 months, however, materials prices and autoworkers' wages have increased by 10 percent. As a result, cars now are selling for $22,000, but because the car built in January only cost $20,000 to produce, the auto company's books now show $2,000 in added inventory profit. The additional profit is an illusion, however, because the replacement cost of the car—what it would cost to produce another, similar car—is now $22,000.

INTERNATIONAL COMPETITIVENESS EFFECT

Inflation in the United States also drives up the price of domestic goods relative to goods made in other countries. As U.S. goods become more expensive, foreigners reduce their orders and buy equivalent goods made elsewhere. At the same time, U.S. producers and consumers step up their own purchases of lower-priced foreign goods. The result of this inflation-induced surge in imports and the slowing of exports is an erosion of the U.S. trade position.

WINNERS AND LOSERS EFFECT

National statistics mask the most insidious of inflation's effects on the economy by creating specific winners and losers. This is because the specific impact of inflation on any individual is a function of that person's age, job, family status, region of residence, buying and investment habits, and other factors. Inflation redistributes income and wealth in an uneven way. It tends to generate both winners and losers, which, in turn, tends to aggravate social and political tensions and erode social values.

TRADE-OFF DILEMMA

Many economists contend that an inverse relationship exists between inflation and unemployment; that is, the inflation rate can be reduced only at the expense of a higher rate of unemployment, and unemployment can be reduced only at the expense of a higher rate of inflation. New Zealand economist Alban W. Phillips first proposed the trade-off relationship between inflation and unemployment in the 1950s. Phillips formulated the trade-off contention based on his studies of wages, prices, and unemployment in England. This inverse relationship is referred to as the Phillips, or trade-off, curve.

The **Phillips curve** reflects the various combinations of inflation and unemployment that coexist during a given period by demonstrating that higher unemployment typically accompanies lower inflation and that lower unemployment typically accompanies higher inflation. In exhibit 10.5, for example, the Phillips curve (P) reflects the relationship between inflation and unemployment during the 1960s. A shifting of the Phillips curve to the right *(P₁)* reflects increased trade-off costs that most economists believe occurred in the 1970s.

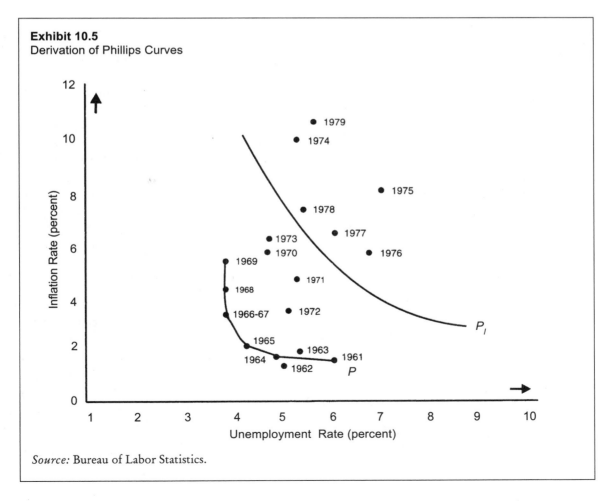

Exhibit 10.5
Derivation of Phillips Curves

Source: Bureau of Labor Statistics.

During the 1980s, the Phillips curve shifted further to the right, reflecting a worsening trade-off. In the 1990s, however, unemployment and inflation both declined substantially, generating a leftward shift in the Phillips curve and raising questions among economists about the validity of the Phillips curve analysis.

CAUSES OF THE INFLATION-UNEMPLOYMENT TRADE-OFF

Most economists attribute the behavior of the U.S. economy's inflation-unemployment relationship during the 1980s to four factors: price rigidity, wage rigidity, structural changes in the labor force, and government policies.

PRICE RIGIDITY

Most American markets are not highly competitive. In important industries, such as automobiles and appliances, two or three large firms have come to dominate the entire market. The size and market share of these few companies give them the power to set prices. As a result, the prices of some U.S. goods don't decline even when demand slows. The failure of prices to respond to market conditions perpetuates inflation.

WAGE RIGIDITY

Most union contracts are negotiated to cover a three-year period. Unions seek wage-increase agreements that include current productivity gains, expected productivity gains, and anticipated purchasing power losses due to projected inflation, and that offset current purchasing power losses due to inflation. Because wage increases in union contracts are legally binding for three years, most businesses cannot reduce wages unilaterally when demand for their goods falls.

STRUCTURAL CHANGES IN THE LABOR FORCE

Advances in technology and intense competition from foreign manufacturers displace many workers whose skills are no longer in demand. Workers with specialized skills may be forced to seek employment as unskilled workers, either permanently or temporarily while they retrain. In either case, the economy's overall need for unskilled workers has declined because U.S. production has shifted toward goods and services that require technological skills or professional training and education.

GOVERNMENT POLICIES

Many federal government regulations contribute to price and wage rigidity. The minimum-wage law, import quotas on cars, tariffs, and price supports all put a floor under prices and wages.

CHANGES IN THE TRADE-OFF

Economists contend that the substantial decline in both unemployment and prices that occurred in the 1990s reflects profound changes in government policies, the composition of the labor force, and the competitive relationships that softened wage and price rigidity. These changes include deregulation, union givebacks, declines in jobless benefits, declines in teenage job seekers, and foreign competition.

DEREGULATION

The government's deregulation of numerous industries, such as trucking, airlines, communications, and securities, put pressure on businesses to rein in operating costs. These pressures led firms to make fewer concessions to union demands and to hire more nonunion workers. Competition spurred by deregulation also drove wage concessions granted to producers by both union and nonunion workers.

Union Givebacks

Unions traditionally have shown a strong reluctance to accept reduced wages or benefits when the firms or industries they deal with face a slump in business or strong competitive challenges. Unions have been more willing to accept layoffs and unemployment for some of their members. With foreign competition, increased plant closings, and domestic deregulation, however, many unions have accepted reduced wages and benefits in order to protect jobs by safeguarding the continued profitability of unionized employers.

Declines in Jobless Benefits

Revenue-strained states and the federal government have tightened eligibility rules for unemployment insurance benefits. The ensuing decline in jobless benefits has induced many laid-off workers to accept alternative, lower-paying jobs more quickly or to negotiate a lower wage with their previous employer in order to be rehired.

Declines in Teenage Job Seekers

The number of teenage job seekers declined during the 1990s. The result was that there were fewer hard-to-employ teenagers in the labor force. A shortage of teenagers was expected to continue during the 2000s.

Foreign Competition

Concerns over business loss to foreign competition motivate many U.S. producers to keep domestic price increases small.

Base Rate Employment and Zero Inflation

Some economists contend that the relationship between inflation and unemployment is not an inverse one. Instead, they claim, the economy can reduce inflation to zero and reduce unemployment to its base rate at the same time. Zero inflation is the point at which the inflation rate is so low that economic and financial decision-makers no longer take it into account.

The concept of a base unemployment rate implies the existence of a point beyond which the economy cannot absorb additional unemployed workers. Workers unemployed when the base unemployment level is reached are either frictionally unemployed or structurally unemployed.

Economists believe that the problem of base unemployment cannot be addressed through stimulative monetary and fiscal policies. They contend that any attempt to do so would immediately stimulate cost-push inflation. For this reason, the base unemployment rate often is referred to as the **non-accelerating-inflation rate of unemployment** (NAIRU). Economists further contend that when inflationary expectations end, inflation can be reduced to zero without increasing unemployment. Some economists, however, remain convinced that policymakers still face a trade-off dilemma when implementing monetary and fiscal policy.

ECONOMIC GROWTH

Economic growth, as measured by annual increases in real GDP, is the third key economic goal of U.S. policymakers. Economists contend that for the United States to sustain annual increases in real GDP over time the nation's two other key economic objectives—full employment, and price stability—must be reached first. A fully employed economy means that the country is efficiently using its labor and capital resources. An economy with stable prices also generates efficiency by reducing investment and spending uncertainty. Both of these conditions are necessary for the United States to sustain economic growth.

During the 1970s and 1980s, the U.S. economy grew at a slower rate than that of most other industrial nations (see exhibit 10.6). During the 1990s, however, U.S. growth accelerated and surpassed that of Europe and Japan. As exhibit 10.7 shows, America's growth surge in the 1990s was concentrated in the second half of the decade. This growth spurt gave rise to the view among many economists that the United States had established a new economy that was built on information technology, strong productivity growth, and a booming stock market.

PRODUCTIVITY: THE KEY TO ECONOMIC GROWTH

Economists are focusing more and more on **productivity,** the output per hour worked, as the key to the economy's growth performance. The slow growth of the U.S. economy during the 1980s is attributed largely to the decade's meager 1.4 percent productivity growth per year. In contrast, the strong growth of the economy from 1995 to 2000 is attributed to that period's productivity growth surge of 2.5 percent per year. If that productivity growth rate were to continue unabated, economists estimate that U.S. living standards would double in less than 30 years.

REASONS FOR PRODUCTIVITY GROWTH

Economists do not know exactly why U.S. productivity growth surged in the 1990s. It is likely that no single reason can explain this performance. The growth in U.S. productivity has generally been attributed to high-tech capital investments, the effective use of information technology, qualitative improvements in technology, and foreign competition.

HIGH-TECH CAPITAL INVESTMENTS

In recent decades, U.S. producers have had to invest in information technology to remain competitive. That investment, coupled with falling prices for hardware and software, led to faster rates of investment spending and an increase in the U.S. capital-to-labor ratio. As a result, the average U.S. worker had more and better machines and tools to work with at the end of the 1990s than when the decade began.

EFFECTIVE USE OF INFORMATION TECHNOLOGY

Computers and the use of information technology led to fundamental improvements in the way all businesses operated. One example, applicable to the wholesale and

Exhibit 10.6
Comparative Growth Rates, Selected Countries and Decades (percent per year)

Country	Per Capita GDP		
	1970s	1980s	1990s
Asia*	5.9	6.6	4.4
Japan	3.3	3.5	0.9
Europe**	2.5	2.1	1.6
United States	2.1	1.8	2.2

*   Hong Kong, Singapore, South Korea, Taiwan, Thailand.
** Austria, Belgium, Denmark, Finland, France, Germany, Ireland, Italy, Netherlands, Norway, Portugal, Spain, Sweden, Switzerland, United Kingdom.
Source: Economic Policy for the Information Economy, Federal Reserve Bank of Kansas City, 2001.

Exhibit 10.7
U.S. Economic Growth (percent per year)

Period	Real GDP Growth	Real GDP Per Capita Growth	Average Unemployment	Average Core Inflation*
1970 to 1990	2.9	1.0	7.0	5.9
1990 to 2000	3.2	2.2	5.6	2.4
1990 to 1995	2.4	1.3	6.6	3.0
1995 to 2000	4.1	3.2	4.6	1.7

* Excludes food and energy prices.
Sources: Bureau of Economic Analysis, Bureau of Labor Statistics.

retail trades, is **supply-chain management.** This computer-based process enables a seller to track and control ordering, invoicing, loading, and shipping activities. By reducing errors, eliminating paperwork, and avoiding costly fluctuations in production and inventories, supply-chain management improved efficiency and productivity in these industries, which registered the strongest productivity growth in the 1990s (see exhibit 10.8).

QUALITATIVE IMPROVEMENTS IN TECHNOLOGY

The accelerated pace of innovation and technological change in the 1990s contributed to productivity growth. U.S. industries were presented with computer hardware and software that was more powerful, functional, and less expensive than the technology that had been available earlier in the decade.

FOREIGN COMPETITION

Many U.S. businesses were forced by foreign competition to modernize their plants, scrap obsolete equipment, close old factories, and cut production costs by laying off workers. As a result, productivity in manufacturing grew at rates well above the national average (see exhibit 10.8).

Many economists believe that increasing productivity is the only way the U.S. can achieve its economic objectives. Increases

in pay are not inflationary if matched by gains in productivity. Moreover, producers do not have to resort to higher prices to increase revenues if workers can generate increases in output per hours worked. In the final analysis, increasing productivity may be the necessary precondition for achieving price stability and full employment, as well as sustained economic growth.

PRODUCTIVITY IN BANKING

When productivity does not increase, rising production costs invariably lead to higher prices or lower profits. Static productivity poses a particular problem for banks. Rising production costs cannot easily be passed on to consumer and corporate depositors in the

Exhibit 10.8
Annual Productivity Growth in Selected U.S. Industries, 1995–1999 (in percent)

Manufacturing	4.34
Mining	4.06
Agriculture	1.18
Transportation	1.72
Wholesale trade	7.84
Retail trade	4.93
Construction	(0.89)
Finance	6.76
Personal services	1.09
Business services	1.69
Health services	(1.06)

Source: Council of Economic Advisers, 2001.

form of higher prices. Banks are limited by law to maximum charges they can impose on portions of their earning assets, particularly consumer loans. Banking products and services also are highly competitive, so loan or service charges that rise too rapidly in relation to charges imposed by competitors can cause a bank to lose customers.

During the 1990s, banks' operating management focused on reducing labor costs and improving worker productivity. Improving productivity in any service industry is difficult, however, because service industries do not readily lend themselves to the operating efficiencies generated through automation. In addition, measurement of productivity in service industries can be a complicated matter.

PRODUCTIVITY MEASUREMENTS

Many banking jobs involve analytical, administrative, and managerial tasks for which quality or productivity can be difficult to measure. Thus, economists rely on productivity proxies to measure banks' output.

Economists measure banks' deposit activities by counting the number of checks, deposits, and withdrawals banks post. Banks' trust activities are measured by counting the number of accounts managed. Loan activities are measured by the number of new loans made. No weight is given to the dollar value of the transactions and accounts banks handle.

Most economists maintain that were dollar value included in measurements of bank productivity, the measures would show strong, steady increases. Nonetheless, they note that the numbers still would not adequately measure the efficiency of bank employees or the quality of their work.

In recent years, most banks have significantly increased back office and data processing productivity. Technology has improved the speed and accuracy with which money and data are transferred

between banks and, more importantly, between different units within a bank.

For some banks, however, the overall quality of their deposit-related services has declined, the costs of increased technical staff and computer consultants have been high, and their organizational and management structures have failed to adapt effectively to automated processes. These banks have not been able to obtain maximum productivity benefits.

PRODUCTIVITY PROGRAMS

Traditional productivity theory attributes gains in output per hours worked to factors that assist workers in producing more. Modern productivity theory, however, has focused increasingly on worker attitudes and worklife quality as factors that stimulate or constrain worker output. Many banks have begun to rely on productivity programs that seek to raise the level of employee job satisfaction to increase productivity. Productivity programs typically

- involve employees in management decisions that affect their jobs
- provide challenging work that allows for the development of skills and abilities
- link compensation more closely to accomplishment
- give due recognition for work done well

OTHER APPROACHES

From 1985 to 2000, bank productivity increased, on average, by 2.8 percent per year. In contrast, during the preceding 15-year period banking productivity grew by only 0.7 percent annually. The strong growth in banking productivity pre-dates the mid-1990s surge in nationwide productivity that economists associate with the new economy and its extensive reliance on information technology. Banking productivity performance has been attributed to a number of factors, including

- substituting capital for labor
- changing service delivery systems
- shifting the skill mix of bank staff
- adapting work processes to new technology
- shifting to self-service banking

CAPITAL FOR LABOR

Banks substituted capital equipment for labor, spurred by advances in computer and telecommunications technology, well before the new economy. Increasing the amount of capital available to aid workers and the quality of the capital itself are core factors that drive productivity growth.

NEW SERVICE DELIVERY SYSTEMS

During the 1980s and 1990s, banks deployed new, less labor-intensive service delivery systems that boosted productivity. These systems included automated teller machines (ATMs), centralized customer calling centers, point-of-sale (POS) and debit systems, and new, smaller branches in America's 24-hour supermarkets.

SKILL MIX OF BANK STAFF

Banks were able to generate faster productivity growth than the economy as a whole. They were able to shift their staffing composition to higher-skilled, higher-paid, and more productive workers who could work extensively with technology and software to process work. This shift began about a decade before the new economy.

WORK PROCESSES ADAPTED TO NEW TECHNOLOGY

Banks adapted their back office operations to computer technology, and in the 1990s, to a number of front office processes as well. Today many banks make loan decisions using computer software that enables them to assess risks more accurately and make decisions more quickly. Some banks are experimenting with new, more sophisticated computer programs for evaluating complex loans. Recent studies indicate that this approach to lending both increases productivity and reduces a bank's loan losses more effectively than does reliance on the instincts of loan officers.

SELF-SERVICE BANKING

Many banks successfully encouraged customers to do more of the work associated with banking themselves. They did this by emphasizing the convenience to customers of using

- automated phone services
- deposit-drop machines
- automated teller machines
- direct deposits
- automated bill paying services

SUMMARY

The nation's three primary economic objectives are full employment, price stability, and economic growth. Full employment is an elusive goal in part because a segment of America's unemployed workers lack the specific education and skills necessary to fill available jobs or who have been displaced from jobs by new technology or foreign competition.

Maintaining an inflation-free economy that also has no inflationary expectations also is difficult. Moreover, because inflation's effects are borne unevenly the harm that inflation inflicts adds a social and political dimension to the problems it causes. Inflation redistributes income and wealth, creates illusory inventory profits for businesses, and reduces international competitiveness.

Many economists contend that a trade-off relationship exists between inflation and unemployment. This relationship, which can be illustrated using a Phillips curve, provides policymakers with an unresolved dilemma.

America's ability to achieve its economic growth goals relates directly to its ability to increase productivity. Without increased productivity, rising production costs invariably lead to rising prices. Therefore, the need to increase productivity has become a major goal for most banks today.

REVIEW QUESTIONS

1. How can unemployment and employment increase concurrently? How is the unemployment rate determined?
2. Economists subdivide inflation into three primary types, attributed to different sources. What are the three main types of inflation? The wage-price spiral often is referred to as the glue that binds these sources of inflation together. Why do you think the wage-price spiral would be referred to this way?
3. How does inflation affect the redistribution of income and wealth?
4. Why would an unanticipated inflation rate of 5 percent be more harmful to banks than a correctly anticipated inflation rate of 10 percent?
5. What factors determine national productivity? What measures have banks employed to increase productivity?

ADDITIONAL RESOURCES

Bureau of Labor Statistics, at *http://stats.bls.gov*. Offers information on economic statistics on a variety of topics, such as industry and geographical statistics, current economic news releases, and current publications and research papers.

Federal Reserve Bank of San Francisco, at *www.sf.frb.org*. Provides access to Federal Reserve Bank of San Francisco research articles on inflation, unemployment, productivity, and other economic topics that routinely appear in the banks' Economic Letter.

Labor Markets, at *www.clev.frb.org/Research/index.htm#pubs*. Provides monthly publications, including information on the labor market.

National Bureau of Economic Research, at *www.nber.org*. Provides information, research, and data on employment; prices; and other U.S. economy performance measures.

Reducing Unemployment: Current Issues and Policy Options, Federal Reserve Bank of Kansas City, 1995. Examines the causes of unemployment and options for reducing the U.S. unemployment rate.

11

MONETARY POLICY AND TOOLS

LEARNING OBJECTIVES

After studying this chapter, you should be able to

- distinguish between general and selective monetary policy tools
- describe how the discount rate is used as a monetary tool
- cite the three ways reserve requirements can be used to control the creation of money
- explain how open market operations work and how primary dealer firms are used to implement monetary policy
- cite the key measures used as operational targets in monetary policy strategy
- explain the difference between dynamic and defensive open market operations, and why and how the Federal Reserve uses defensive open market operations
- cite the major factors, other than monetary policy, that affect reserves in the banking system
- define the key terms listed in this chapter

KEY TERMS

computation period
discount rate
federal funds rate
margin
margin requirements
national economic objectives

open market
repurchase agreements
reservable liabilities
short-term adjustment credit
Treasury tax and loan accounts

INTRODUCTION

U.S. monetary policy seeks to control the cost and availability of money and credit to achieve specific economic objectives. The basic monetary policy tools wielded by the Federal Reserve are the discount rate, reserve requirements, and open-market operations. Monetary tools change the amount or composition of bank reserves, the money supply, and the level of interest rates. These changes directly affect banks' lending activities and business spending patterns.

This chapter examines how the nation's monetary policy tools work and the strengths and weaknesses of those tools. It also presents the key factors that affect their use in fighting recession or inflation. Next, the chapter turns to an examination of monetary policy strategy. This strategy sets long-term objectives for employment, price stability, and economic growth by meeting short-term operational targets, generally for bank reserves and the federal funds rate. In theory, if these targets are hit the economy should be positioned to meet the Federal Reserve's long-term objectives.

The Federal Reserve's strategy for implementing monetary policy involves both dynamic and defensive open-market operations. Both types of operations are examined in this chapter. Buying and selling of government securities to counter recession, contain inflation, or promote balanced economic growth characterize the Federal Reserve's dynamic open market operations. Buying and selling of government securities to offset or nullify undesired day-to-day changes in bank reserves and money supply characterize the Federal Reserve's defensive open market operations. The chapter also looks at the major nonpolicy factors that cause such changes, namely, the public's handling of cash, the level of Federal Reserve float, and the actions of the U.S. Treasury.

Recent years have brought profound changes to the Federal Reserve's policies on discount window lending, which involves loans of reserves to banks. For additional information on the evolution of the discount window, you are encouraged to examine Extended Study 7.

MONETARY POLICY TOOLS

Monetary policy tools are classified as either general or selective in their application and effect on the economy. General monetary policy tools seek to control the total quantity, availability, or cost of money throughout the economy without regard to the purpose of the funds. These policy instruments typically work by increasing or decreasing bank reserves. Selective monetary policy tools focus on a specific financial market or component of total credit, such as stock market lending, consumer credit, or real estate. These tools attempt to control the cost or flow of funds only in selected sectors of the economy.

The Federal Reserve's administration of monetary policy and its use of monetary policy tools are general rather than specific. U.S. monetary policy is directed toward the total economy and broad national economic goals. Under this general approach, decisions about which applicants are granted credit and at what price, or interest rate, are decided in the marketplace rather than by the central bank.

Central banks in other countries use selective policy tools far more often than does the Federal Reserve. Many foreign countries direct their monetary policy toward specific sectors or industries to promote social objectives and industrial growth. In some countries, central banks lend money to government units for public projects, invest central bank funds in private companies, and make loans to favored industries at below-market rates.

In contrast, the Federal Reserve relies primarily on one general monetary policy tool to achieve U.S. economic objectives: open market operations. The Federal Reserve buys and sells U.S. government securities,

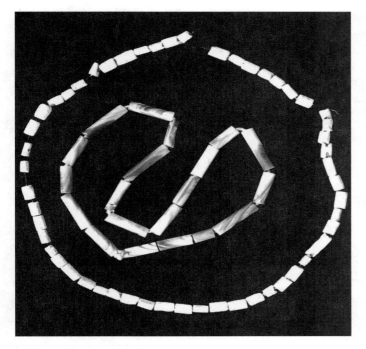

Wampum, a Native American money, fashioned into a belt. *Photo courtesy of the Smithsonian Institution, NNC, Douglas Mudd.*

thereby increasing or decreasing bank reserves and the nation's money supply. In this way the Federal Reserve seeks to move the economy in an appropriate direction at an appropriate speed.

Before looking at open-market operations in more detail, it is helpful to examine the Federal Reserve's two less-frequently used general monetary policy tools: the discount rate and reserve requirements.

DISCOUNT RATE

The **discount rate** is the interest rate that Federal Reserve banks charge commercial banks and other depository institutions that borrow reserves. An increase in this basic cost of reserves acts as a powerful deterrent to depositories' borrowings from the Federal Reserve. Conversely, a decrease in the rate stimulates banks' borrowing from the Federal Reserve and the subsequent loans that the banks make to private borrowers. In theory, by raising or lowering the discount rate, the Federal Reserve can reduce or expand business lending and investment spending in the economy. A change in the discount rate also can serve as an announcement to

the banking community and the public that the Federal Reserve is changing the monetary policy.

In practice, however, discount rate changes typically are made as a secondary measure, to support monetary policy changes implemented through open market operations. The Federal Reserve uses the federal funds rate rather than the discount rate to guide its open market operations. The **federal funds rate** is the interest rate banks charge one another for overnight reserve loans.

CRITERIA FOR FEDERAL RESERVE LENDING

The Federal Reserve has established three sets of criteria for lending reserves to depositories: short-term adjustment credit, seasonal credit, and extended credit.

SHORT-TERM ADJUSTMENT CREDIT

The Federal Reserve lends reserves to depositories to meet short-term liquidity needs. Most of the Federal Reserve's lending is **short-term adjustment credit.**

The nation's large banks do most of the borrowing from the Federal Reserve's discount window, but they borrow only for a day or two at a time. On the other hand, small banks tend to borrow less frequently, but they typically borrow funds for a week or longer.

SEASONAL CREDIT

The Federal Reserve also lends reserves to small- and medium-size depositories that experience strong seasonal disturbances in deposit and loan flows. Many banks in agricultural and resort communities are subject to seasonal variations that affect their reserve positions for 90 days or more at a time. A two- or three-day loan from the Federal Reserve would not address the problems or needs of these banks. Thus, the Federal Reserve has established seasonal borrowing criteria to help banks in these circumstances. Few banks qualify for these loans; of those that do, few use the seasonal borrowing option.

EXTENDED CREDIT

The Federal Reserve also lends reserves to depositories in its capacity as the nation's lender of last resort. Loans are made as a last resort when exceptional circumstances, such as a sustained run-off of deposits or a spate of unforeseen loan losses, threaten an individual depository with failure due to illiquidity. Extended credit, called emergency lending, is very rare. When the Federal Reserve must act as a lender of last resort, the situation usually makes national headlines.

In 1991 Congress amended the Federal Reserve Act to discourage the Federal Reserve from prolonged lending of reserves to banks likely to fail. Congress was concerned that Federal Reserve loans to such banks might lead to increased losses to the Federal Deposit Insurance Corporation (FDIC) because the funds that a failed bank owes the Federal Reserve, like other insured deposits, become the financial obligations of the FDIC.

To address this concern, Congress made the Federal Reserve financially liable for any FDIC losses attributable to Federal Reserve loans used to keep failing banks open longer than necessary. Since 1994, when the amendment went into effect, the Federal Reserve has issued its own rules that put time limits on its emergency extensions of credit. These time limits range from five days for banks faced with imminent failure, to two months for banks in critical financial difficulty.

DISCOUNT WINDOW SAFETY VALVE

The Federal Reserve primarily uses the discount rate and discount window reserve loans as safety valves for individual banks that are experiencing reserve pressure. These safety valves enable banks to obtain reserves for one or two days until they can make broader adjustments to the mix of their assets and liabilities and bring their reserves in balance with their deposits.

Small banks generally receive easier access to this kind of adjustment credit than large banks. Large banks typically have access to a broad range of alternative funding sources. The discount rate also is set below other short-term interest rates, principally the federal funds rate. The goal is to ease the cost burden on the borrowing banks, relieving stress from insufficient reserves and providing additional liquidity.

The Federal Reserve tries to maintain a narrow spread between its discount rate and the generally higher federal funds rate. A narrow spread ensures that, if market rates rise, solvent banks will not abuse the discount window as a source of cheap reserves. A narrow spread also ensures that, if market rates fall, the role of the safety valve will be maintained. Thus, the Federal Reserve initiates discount rate changes to align the discount rate with changes in the federal funds rate. Recall that the Federal Reserve sets the federal funds rate through its open-market operations.

Federal Reserve banks administer discount window lending to ensure that borrowed reserves are used in a manner consistent with the safety-valve approach. Reserve banks ask borrowing institutions the reason for each discount window loan request, review changes in the institution's weekly financial statement, and review the overall record of the institution's past discount window use. Reserve banks use one or more of the following criteria to evaluate whether borrowed reserves are being misused:

- frequency of discount window borrowing
- number of consecutive weeks an institution has borrowed, even if the borrowing was only for one day during a given week
- borrower's pattern of discount window use over moving periods of 13 weeks or longer
- amount borrowed as a percentage of total deposits

- amount borrowed as a percentage of required reserves
- repetitive patterns of borrowing, such as continuous weekend or every-other-week borrowings

RESERVE REQUIREMENTS

Changing the reserve requirements is the single most powerful monetary policy tool a central bank can use to control its nation's money supply. The power of this tool lies in its double impact, with both short- and long-term effects on the money supply. Initially, a change to reserve requirements alters only the composition or allocation of required and excess reserves in the banking system. Over time, however, a change in reserve requirements results in greater or smaller demand deposit expansion in the banking system. Consequently, the change affects the growth of the money supply in the economy.

For example, if the reserve requirement is 10 percent against demand deposits and just one bank has $100,000 in excess reserves, the banking system as a whole

---

CLOSING THE DISCOUNT WINDOW SAFETY VALVE

In mid-2002 the Federal Reserve issued a proposal that would fundamentally change the way banks can use the discount window. Under the Federal Reserve's proposal

- all discount window loans made to meet banks' short-term liquidity needs would be priced 1 percentage point above the federal funds rate
- banks would be allowed to borrow short-term credit without restrictions; indeed banks could even loan their borrowed funds to other banks
- any discount window loans made to meet banks' extended credit needs would be priced 1.5 percentage points above the federal funds rate

The proposal, which was issued to elicit banker comments on the changes, is aimed at reducing banks' reluctance to borrow from the Federal Reserve by eliminating restrictions. It also is intended to blunt spikes in the federal funds rate by reducing banks' dependence on federal funds when they need additional reserves.

If the proposed changes are put in place, the Federal Reserve's long-standing safety valve approach to discount window lending would end. The imposition of above-market interest rates for short-term discount window loans, however, would bring Federal Reserve lending practices in line with those followed by most other central banks.

theoretically could create $1 million in demand deposits through the multiple expansion process. Now assume that the Federal Reserve changes the reserve requirement. Consider the following scenarios:

- If the requirement is raised to 20 percent, the banking system's ability to create new demand deposits would fall to $500,000.
- If the requirement is reduced to 5 percent, the banking system's demand deposit expansion potential would increase to $2 million.

Because reserve requirements affect banks and the money supply so strongly, the Federal Reserve rarely changes them. When it does change reserve requirements, the Federal Reserve deliberately makes the changes small, such as one or two percentage points, to blunt the impact.

POWER TO CHANGE RESERVE REQUIREMENTS

During the 1930s, the Federal Reserve Board was given the power to change reserve requirement percentages, but only within ranges established by Congress. The Monetary Control Act of 1980 established a new system of reserve requirements for all depository institutions that was based on two tiers of percentages. The first tier applied to small banks; the second, to large banks. The act gave the Federal Reserve authority to change requirements on transaction accounts on the second tier within a range of 8 percent to 14 percent. The Board of Governors also can change reserve requirements on business time deposits within a range of 0 percent to 9 percent. The percentages in effect as of 2003 are shown in exhibit 11.1.

SUPPLEMENTAL RESERVE REQUIREMENTS

The Federal Reserve Board of Governors also can impose a supplemental reserve requirement of up to 4 percent on transaction accounts. If the Board were to use this power, the supplemental reserves would earn a market interest rate. To date, the Board of Governors has never used this power.

EXTRAORDINARY RESERVE REQUIREMENTS

If the Federal Reserve determines that extraordinary circumstances exist, the Board of Governors also may impose reserve requirements on any liability for six months.

RESERVE REQUIREMENTS AS A POLICY TOOL

The Federal Reserve has never used changes in reserve requirement percentages as a primary monetary policy tool for fighting inflation or recession because the effect of such changes is too blunt, powerful, and long-lasting. Changes in reserve requirements also have been thought to cause excessive administrative difficulties and high implementation costs for smaller banks.

Since 1980 the Federal Reserve has changed the reserve requirement on transaction accounts only once. In 1992 it reduced the requirement on transaction accounts in the second tier from 12 percent to 10 percent. This converted more than $8 billion in required reserves to excess reserves. The reduction was made to reduce banks' funding costs, thereby strengthening their balance sheets and positioning them to make more loans. Assuming a money expansion coefficient of 10, an $8 billion increase in excess reserves could, in theory, generate $80 billion in new loans and demand deposits in the banking system.

RESERVE ASSETS AND RESERVABLE LIABILITIES

At present only vault cash, reserve account balances, or pass-through account balances at a correspondent bank may be used to meet reserve requirements. But the Federal Reserve has the authority to change the kind

The Federal Reserve's reserve requirements apply to all commercial banks and thrift institutions whether or not they are members of the Federal Reserve.

*Deposits Subject to Reserve Requirements**	*Reserve Requirement*
Net transaction accounts**	
$0 million to $6.0 million	0% of amount
More than $6.0 million and up to $42.1 million	3% of amount***
More than $42.1 million	10% of amount

* In 2003 there were no reserve requirements against time and savings deposits or other non-transaction account liabilities. From 1980 to 1990, however, there were 3 percent reserve requirements on both short-term (less than 18 months) business time deposits and Eurodollar borrowings (borrowings by U.S. banks from banking offices in other countries). From 1980 to 1983, there had also been a 3 percent reserve requirement on long-term (more than 18 months) business time deposits; that requirement was reduced to 0 in 1983.

** Transaction accounts consist of demand deposits, NOW accounts, share draft accounts, automatic transfer service accounts, and any other accounts or deposits from which payments or transfers may be made. (Money market deposit accounts, however, are not classified as transaction accounts.) In calculating required reserves, banks can subtract from their total of transaction accounts the amount of cash items (checks) in the process of collection and deposits of other banks on their books. Banks also can subtract $6.0 million from their reservable liabilities.

*** The breakpoint between the 3 percent and 10 percent reserve requirement on transaction accounts is indexed. Each year the Board of Governors is required to increase (or decrease) the breakpoint by 80 percent of the growth (or decline) in transaction accounts during the prior year. The Monetary Control Act of 1980 established a $25 million baseline. In 2003 the breakpoint was set at $42.1 million.

Source: Federal Reserve Bulletin, October 2002.

of assets depository institutions can use to meet reserve requirements and the liabilities that are subject to reserve requirements, so it can use reserve requirements to implement monetary policy in two other ways.

If the Federal Reserve were to classify government securities held by banks as additional eligible or legal reserve assets, total reserves would increase immediately. If the Federal Reserve were to remove vault cash from its list of legal reserve assets, total reserves would immediately diminish.

The Federal Reserve also can redefine **reservable liabilities,** which are liabilities that are subject to reserve requirements. A new definition would not increase or decrease total reserves, but would signifi-

cantly change the amount of required and excess reserves in the banking system. For example, if the Federal Reserve added federal funds borrowings to the list of reservable liabilities, banks would have to come up with more required reserves to cover their federal funds liabilities.

In 1992 the Federal Reserve used its definitional ability to close loopholes that some banks had used to avoid reserve requirements during the 1980s. For example, the Federal Reserve tightened its definition of transaction accounts to include time deposit sweep accounts from which banks transfer idle balances in corporate transaction accounts into seven-day certificates of deposit at the end of each day. The Federal

Reserve made these newly defined transaction accounts subject to 1992's applicable 3 percent and 10 percent reserve requirement.

REQUIRED RESERVE CALCULATIONS

The Federal Reserve also sets the rules governing how banks calculate their reserve requirements. For example, large depository institutions must compute their required reserves once every two weeks. The calculations are based on the institution's daily average deposit balances during a 14-day **computation period.** The computation period ends every second Monday. Small depositories with net transaction account deposits of less than $6.0 million, however, are exempt from maintaining and reporting required reserves as of 2003.

The Federal Reserve's rules mean that large banks can be in a deep reserve deficit on any given day during the 14-day computation period as long as they balance those deficits with reserve surpluses of like amounts on other days. Depositories are allowed to carry a reserve deficit or surplus of up to $50,000 or 4 percent of required reserves, whichever is the larger amount, into the next maintenance period. Banks must cover a reserve deficit, however, with a surplus of like amount in the following period. Similarly, a bank with a surplus in a given period can generate a deficit of like amount in the next period without being penalized.

OPEN MARKET OPERATIONS

The Federal Reserve's open market operations involve the purchasing and selling of government securities. These operations are the most important policy tool used by the Federal Reserve. When selling securities from its System Open Market Account portfolio, the Federal Reserve takes reserves out of the banking system, thereby restricting the ability of banks to make loans and investments. When buying securities, the Federal Reserve adds new reserves to the banking system, thereby expanding banks' lending and investing capabilities.

For example, when the Federal Reserve buys $1 million of securities in the open market from a dealer firm, it pays for the securities with an electronic funds transfer (EFT) to the dealer firm's account at the local bank. The result of this EFT is an increase of $1 million in bank reserves, which are held temporarily at the dealer's bank and reflect credit for the account of the selling dealers firm. The funds transfer process also generates a $1 million increase in the money supply. The effect of the $1 million EFT is illustrated in exhibit 11.2.

When the Federal Reserve Bank of New York sells securities from the System Open Market Account bank, reserves and the money supply are reduced. The Federal Reserve Bank receives an EFT from the dealer's firm, drawn on the firm's bank. Posting this transfer results in a reduction to the dealer bank's reserve account of $1 million. At the same time, the dealer's bank reduces the dealer firm's checking account to reflect the EFT (see exhibit 11.3).

If the dealer's bank had $1 million in excess reserves before the Federal Reserve's open market sale, it would now discover it had temporarily lost its lending capability. If it had no excess reserves, the bank would be placed in a temporary reserve deficiency. Either circumstance would likely cause the bank to

- borrow reserves in the federal funds market
- sell securities from its investment portfolio
- make some other asset or liability adjustment to enable the bank to achieve the reserve requirement balance or to enable it to continue to make loans

SECONDARY EFFECTS OF OPEN MARKET OPERATIONS

Federal Reserve purchases of government securities in the open market drive up the

Exhibit 11.2
Federal Reserve Purchase of Securities

Federal Reserve Bank of New York		Dealer's Bank	
Assets	Liabilities	Assets	Liabilities
System open-market account +$1 million	Reserve account of dealer's bank + $1 million	Reserve account + $1 million	Demand deposit of dealer firm + $1 million

Government Securities Dealer Firm		
Assets		Liabilities
Checking account at bank	+ $1 million	
Securities held	- $1 million	

The dealer's bank must hold some of its new reserves as required reserves against the dealer's new $1 million deposit. However, the bulk of the reserves can be used to fund new loans and create new money. If a 10 percent reserve requirement is assumed, then the banking system, through the multiple expansion process, could in theory generate $9 million in new deposits from a base of $1 million in total deposits (and $900,000 in excess reserves).

price of securities. Because securities prices and their investment yields, or interest rates, are inversely related, an increase in securities prices drives down interest rates. At the same time, the Federal Reserve's open market purchase adds to reserves, which further drives down interest rates. If the increase in the supply of reserves is not offset by an increase in demand for reserves by banks, it also should help to drive down interest rates. As interest rates fall and securities prices rise,

the value of securities in banks' investment portfolios increases.

Federal Reserve sales of securities from the System Open Market Account portfolio drive down the price of securities and drive up interest rates. Because of the inverse relationship between securities prices and interest rates, a reduction in securities prices also drives up interest rates. As interest rates rise and securities prices fall, the value of securities in banks' portfolios declines.

Exhibit 11.3
Federal Reserve Sale of Securities

Federal Reserve Bank of New York		Dealer's Bank	
Assets	Liabilities	Assets	Liabilities
System open market account - $1 million	Reserve account of dealer's bank - $1 million	Reserve account - $1 million	Demand deposit of dealer firm - $1 million

Government Securities Dealer Firm		
Assets		Liabilities
Checking account at bank	- $1 million	
Securities held	+ $1 million	

THE OPEN MARKET

The Federal Reserve conducts its open market operations with a vast portfolio of U.S. securities it has acquired over the decades in implementing monetary policy.

When conducting open market operations, the Federal Reserve works exclusively through the trading desk of the Federal Reserve Bank of New York (FRBNY) and transacts business with a small group of dealer firms called primary dealers. These dealers in government securities, most of which are headquartered in New York City, constitute the **open market** (see exhibit 11.4).

Some open market dealer firms are the autonomous dealer departments of the nation's large money center banks. Most dealer firms, however, are not associated with banks. To do business with the Federal Reserve in the open market, a dealer firm first must demonstrate that it has adequate capital and that it already has handled substantial business volume over a protracted

---

Exhibit 11.4
Open Market Dealer Firms

ABN AMRO Incorporated
BNP Paribas Securities Corp.
Banc of America Securities LLC
Banc One Capital Markets, Inc.
Barclays Capital Inc.
Bear, Stearns & Co., Inc.
CIBC World Markets Corp.
Credit Suisse First Boston Corporation
Daiwa Securities America Inc.
Deutsche Banc Alex. Brown Inc.
Dresdner Kleinwort Wasserstein Securities LLC.
Goldman, Sachs & Co.
Greenwich Capital Markets, Inc.
HSBC Securities (USA) Inc.
J.P. Morgan Securities, Inc.
Lehman Brothers Inc.
Merrill Lynch Government Securities Inc.
Mizuho Securities USA
Morgan Stanley & Co. Incorporated
Nomura Securities International, Inc.
Salomon Smith Barney Inc.
UBS Warburg LLC

Source: Federal Reserve Bank of New York, April 2002.

---

period of time. It then must be prepared to submit reports of its trading activities and positions to the FRBNY.

The primary dealer market is critical to the efficient implementation of open market operations. By working through dealers, the Federal Reserve ensures that its purchases and sales of government securities increase or decrease bank reserves. For example, banks typically would be reluctant to part with the reserves needed to fund high-earning loans by purchasing securities from the Federal Reserve. Banks have no control over the actions of their dealer firm depositors, however; thus, the dealers that buy securities from the Federal Reserve expedite the reduction in reserves that banks themselves may have been unprepared to accept.

Dealer firms are motivated by profit, so their willingness to buy from or sell to the Federal Reserve is based on price and marketability, not concerns over the availability of reserves. On the other hand, the Federal Reserve's trading desk is not motivated by profit. The Federal Reserve seeks to increase or reduce bank reserves and the money supply in accordance with Federal Open Market Committee (FOMC) policy directives established to achieve national economic goals. If needed, the Federal Reserve will take a loss on an open market transaction to achieve its monetary policy goals. The Federal Reserve can sell securities from its portfolio to reduce bank reserves at a price low enough to entice the most reluctant of dealer buyers. To increase bank reserves, the Federal Reserve also can buy securities at a price high enough to obtain the securities inventories of the most reluctant dealer sellers.

EFFECT OF OPEN MARKET OPERATIONS

Open market transactions take place in New York, but the effect of open market operations on bank reserves, money supply, and interest rates is nationwide. This is because banks throughout the country are

The Changing Open Market

Since the mid-1980s, the open market has undergone two significant changes. It has

- taken on a decidedly international character
- become substantially smaller

FOREIGN-OWNED DEALER FIRMS

About one-third of the primary dealer firms that constitute the open market today are owned by foreign organizations. These firms account for about one-third of open market trading volume. This change in the composition of the open market reflects the increasing importance and volume of investments by foreigners in U.S. government securities and it was accompanied by some controversy.

During the late 1980s, despite strong congressional sentiment favoring restrictions, the Federal Reserve accepted four Japanese firms as primary dealers in the open market. Both the House and Senate passed bills to deny Japanese companies status as primary dealers until Japan reciprocated with U.S. firms. The Federal Reserve, however, contended that the Japanese dealer firms, like other domestic and foreign dealers in the open market, had met all Federal Reserve standards for trading as primary dealers. Thus, their participation was consistent with the long-established policy of equal regulatory treatment for domestic and foreign institutions competing in the United States.

In 1988 Congress passed the Primary Dealers Act based on the principle of reciprocal regulatory treatment for foreign dealer firms competing in the U.S. government securities market. Since then the Federal Reserve has adopted a policy consistent with this legislation. Primary dealer status cannot be granted to any foreign-owned dealer firm unless its home country provides similar competitive opportunities to U.S. companies.

A SMALLER OPEN MARKET

The number of government securities dealer firms that constitute the open market has been declining for more than a decade. Today only 22 firms interact with the Federal Reserve; less than half the 46 firms designated dealer firms that traded in the late 1980s. The reasons for the decline are varied but include

- mergers between banks and securities firms that have reduced the number of securities dealers in the market
- absence of profit from buying or selling securities from or to the Federal Reserve and selling or buying them on the secondary market, largely because of the very small margin between the buying and selling price for U.S. government securities in the market
- costs that open market dealer firms incur when holding positions, or inventories, in U.S. government securities

The shrinkage of the open market has not disturbed the effectiveness of open market operations. Indeed, to foster its operational efficiency, the FRBNY has traditionally dealt with only small numbers of dealers on a day-to-day basis. In 2001 five dealer firms handled more than half of the year's open-market operations, with an average daily dollar volume of $272 billion.

linked to each other through extensive correspondent relationships and through the highly efficient nationwide federal funds market.

When the Federal Reserve sells securities to open market dealer firms, the dealers typically finance their daily activities and inventories with funds borrowed daily from the nation's large money center banks located in New York, Chicago, and San Francisco. These banks generally purchase federal funds daily, in part to accommodate their dealer customers. The source of these federal funds is banks from all over the country.

Suppose, for example, that a bank in Montana with $1 million in excess reserves and no borrowers sells those reserves in the nationwide federal funds market. A New York money market bank buys the reserves to fund a loan to an open market dealer customer. After the dealer purchases the Federal Reserve's securities, the dealer's checking account balance decreases, as do the reserves held by the New York money market bank. Yet, in effect, those reserves came from Montana.

When the Federal Reserve buys securities from open market dealers, the dealers' checking account balances increase, as do the reserves held by the dealers' banks. Both the dealers and their banks have to repay yesterday's loans, however. As those loans are repaid, banks in all parts of the country, such as the Montana bank just cited, experience increases in their reserve accounts.

The lending and borrowing relationship between banks and dealers and the lending and borrowing relationship between small banks and big banks in the federal funds market transmit the effect of open market operations to bank reserves, the money supply, and interest rates in all corners of the banking system.

OPEN MARKET OPERATIONS AS A MONETARY TOOL

General reliance on open market operations as the primary monetary policy tool did not begin until 1951. That year the Federal Reserve and the Treasury agreed that monetary policy no longer need be directed toward maintaining rigidly stable interest rates on Treasury securities. This agreement, called the Accord of 1951, ended the fixed interest rate policy the Federal Reserve had introduced in 1941, which had enabled the Treasury to finance World War II borrowings at low cost.

With the requirement to maintain fixed interest rates removed, the Federal Reserve could use open market operations to expand or contract bank reserves and decrease or increase interest rates. It also began to use open market operations on a day-to-day basis to offset undesired changes in bank reserves resulting from nonpolicy factors, such as Treasury borrowing activities and changes in the public's holdings of cash.

SELECTIVE CONTROLS

Although the Federal Reserve's use of monetary policy tools is essentially general in nature, it occasionally has used selective controls to influence the cost or flow of funds in specific sectors of the economy. Central banks in many other countries use selective controls routinely. In the United States, selective monetary policy controls usually involve a tightening or relaxing of required down payments or maturity terms for a particular class of loans. Such controls alter the amount of funds being loaned for a particular purpose without changing the level of bank reserves or the availability of bank credit in the economy as a whole.

MARGIN REQUIREMENTS

The Securities Exchange Act of 1934 gave the Federal Reserve Board power to establish margin requirements on loans made for purchasing or carrying securities. A **margin** is the difference, or spread, between the market value of securities used as collateral for a loan, or used for the purpose of purchasing stock, and the amount of the loan granted. A **margin requirement** sets the maximum margin in percentage terms.

Margin requirements are implemented through Federal Reserve regulations T, U, and X. The requirements were established to prevent excessive stock market speculation by controlling the credit used for stock purchases. Today's 50-percent margin requirement means that only 50 percent of the value of the securities used as collateral can be borrowed. In effect, the margin requirement represents the percentage of the loan down payment the borrower must have in cash.

Since the 1930s, economists have been unable to find evidence of a relationship between stock market margin requirements and the levels of prices, employment, or output in the economy. Moreover, some economists question whether margin requirements, by themselves, can control stock market speculation. They argue that two factors limit the influence of margin requirements on speculation; namely, that

- some lenders are not subject to margin requirements
- speculation-motivated borrowers can deny intent, pledge other assets as collateral for loans, and then buy stocks anyway

In addition, there is some question about whether or not margin requirements are needed for every stock market-related loan. Indeed, in the 1990s Congress reduced the scope of the Federal Reserve's authority to set margins on certain loans to registered broker-dealer firms.

MONETARY POLICY DECISION-MAKING PROCESS

The Federal Open Market Committee (FOMC) meets in Washington, D.C. every six weeks or so to set monetary policy. At these meetings, fundamental decisions are made regarding whether monetary policy should be structured to stimulate, restrain, or maintain the current status of the economy. The decisions are embodied in a policy directive sent to the open market trading desk of the FRBNY. This directive specifies the ultimate goals of monetary policy as well as the Federal Reserve's interest rate, through the federal funds rate, reserve growth, and other targets.

At each FOMC meeting, the seven members of the Federal Reserve Board of Governors and the five Reserve bank presidents that comprise the committee review the current status of the economy, examine a range of economic forecasts and projections, and discuss which of the following three policy alternatives to implement:

- easier monetary policy, which is characterized by a speedup in reserve and money supply growth and by declining interest rates
- tighter monetary policy, which is characterized by a slowdown in reserve and money supply growth and by rising interest rates
- stable monetary policy, which is characterized by no change in the pace of reserve and money supply growth and no change in the level of interest rates

Each policy alternative is examined in the context of the economy's current condition and the likely future course of output, employment, and inflation. The FOMC reviews a range of economic indicators, forecasts, and projections as it attempts to gauge the economic implications of each policy alternative.

Most FOMC directives call for a stable monetary policy. One reason for this is the complexity of the economy. Monetary policy changes do not begin to affect the economy until months after implementation. Therefore, sufficient time must be allowed to see if a policy change is generating the desired results. Another reason for a generally stable monetary policy is the nature of the business cycle. Business activity tends to expand and contract over long cycles. Changing the monetary policy each month would be inconsistent with these cyclical business patterns.

NATIONAL ECONOMIC OBJECTIVES

The Federal Reserve's monetary policy strategy is designed to achieve the broad **national economic objectives** of price stability, full employment, and economic growth. A Federal Reserve policy directive does not set specific numerical targets for the ultimate goals of its policy, such as prices, the unemployment rate, and real growth in the gross domestic product (GDP). Rather, the directive sets short-term targets for the cost and availability of money.

OPERATING TARGETS

The Federal Reserve directs its open market operations to achieve specific short-term operational goals. The most important of these goals are week-to-week growth in bank reserves and a daily federal funds rate that is consistent with the needs of the economy. If these short-term targets are met, the economic results will show in various measures that the Federal Reserve uses as gauges or intermediate targets for guiding monetary policy. These measures include

- real interest rates, which are nominal interest rates minus the rate of inflation
- unemployment rate
- nominal and real GDP growth
- commodity prices
- price, or value, of the dollar in foreign exchange markets

- inflation expectation surveys
- money supply growth

Economists believe that measures such as these provide a good indication of the future course of output, employment, and inflation.

The FOMC uses the federal funds rate as its key operational target. Setting and monitoring the target typically involves a series of steps similar to the following list.

- Assume that the FOMC believes a federal funds rate of 3 percent would be most appropriate on a day-to-day basis for achieving the FOMC's economic objectives.
- The FOMC asks the manager of the New York trading desk to monitor the federal funds rate against this target.
- The FOMC reviews the target at each FOMC meeting and makes changes, if appropriate. Levels of reserves in the nation's banking system may need to be adjusted to keep the federal funds rate close to the FOMC-specified target rate.
- Because adjustments to reserve levels may cause them to grow at a rate that is incompatible with the Federal Reserve's current strategy, reserve conditions are monitored after each adjustment to be sure the adjustments are working as planned.
- Between committee meetings, if it appears that reserve conditions have become incompatible with the federal funds rate target, the FOMC chairperson will typically call a special meeting or hold a conference call with FOMC members to discuss what policy option to take.

As long as interbank transactions generate a federal funds rate close to the target, the trading desk will not alter the prevailing balance between the supply of, and demand for, bank reserves. As data on the intermediate gauges and short-term target measures become available on a daily, weekly, and monthly basis, decisions are made about whether changes in open market tactics or policies are warranted. Even if reserves are held on target on a short-term basis, however, interest rates, money supply growth, or any of the other intermediate measures could be driven significantly off course because of the nonpolicy factors that affect these measures.

DYNAMIC OPEN MARKET OPERATIONS

Economists characterize open market operations as being offensive or defensive. Dynamic open market operations are designed to achieve broad economic objectives, such as countering recession, containing inflation, or promoting balanced economic growth. Economists say that when the Federal Reserve buys and sells securities to advance its strategy it is acting dynamically or on the offensive, to try to change bank reserves to implement monetary policy.

DEFENSIVE OPEN MARKET OPERATIONS

Defensive open market operations occur when the Federal Reserve buys and sells securities to offset or nullify a range of factors that change bank reserves on a day-to-day basis. On an operational level, the Federal Reserve integrates its defensive open market operations with its dynamic, offensive operations to form a comprehensive monetary policy implementation strategy.

FACTORS THAT CHANGE BANK RESERVES

Several major factors may increase or decrease the level of bank reserves from one day to the next, often in unpredictable ways. These factors include

- the public's handling of cash and deposit funds
- the daily level of Federal Reserve float
- actions of the U.S. Treasury

The public's changing preferences for holding currency is the most significant nonpolicy factor that affects reserves. If people withdraw more cash from banks than they deposit, the banking system loses reserves. Depositors who move funds between types of accounts or between small and large banks also change the amount of required and excess reserves in the banking system because reserve requirements only apply to transaction accounts and reserve requirements differ for large and small banks.

Bank reserves also are reduced when the public moves funds into and out of institutions not subject to the Federal Reserve's reserve requirements, such as money market funds and brokerage firms. Conversely, an outflow of funds from brokerage accounts and money market funds to bank deposit accounts increases reserves.

Changes in the daily level of the Federal Reserve float, which often result from uncontrollable delays in the check collection process, also affect reserve levels. An increase in float adds reserves to the banking system; a decrease reduces reserves.

Actions taken by the U.S. Treasury also can increase or decrease the level of reserves. Such actions may include

- managing the government's tax receipts and expenditures
- issuing new securities to finance spending or to repay maturing debt
- monetizing gold or special drawing rights

Exhibit 11.5 illustrates the major factors that affect bank reserves, including actions that are the direct result of monetary policy.

DEFENSIVE OPEN MARKET TECHNIQUES

Repurchase agreements, also called repos, and matched sale-purchase transactions, or reverse repos, are the Federal Reserve's two primary defensive open market techniques. Both repos and reverse repos involve the temporary purchase or sale of Treasury securities by the Federal Reserve. These transactions have a short-term, self-reversing effect on bank reserves; they first supply reserves and then absorb them, or vice versa.

In a repo transaction, the New York trading desk buys a government security from a dealer firm, which agrees to repurchase the security for its original price plus an agreed-upon rate within a specified period. The time period can be up to 15 days, but usually is 1 to 7 days. When buying a security under a repo agreement, the payment from the trading desk to the dealer firm results in a credit to the reserve account of the bank in which the dealer firm has its account. The credit increases the bank's reserves. When the dealer firm repurchases the security, the dealer firm's bank experiences a reduction in reserves.

Matched sale-purchase transactions, or reverse repos, have the opposite effect on bank reserves. They first withdraw and then return reserves to the banking system. In a matched transaction, the New York trading desk executes two transactions simultaneously for different delivery dates. The trading desk sells securities to open market dealers, while simultaneously buying the same obligations for delivery, usually one to seven days later. The buying dealers pay for their purchases immediately, thereby reducing bank reserves. When the Federal Reserve pays for its repurchase of the securities on the agreed delivery date, reserves are injected back into the banking system.

APPLICATIONS OF DEFENSIVE STRATEGY

The three most significant nonpolicy factors to which the Fed responds are the public's

Exhibit 11.5
Major Factors Affecting Bank Reserves

Source of Change	Change in Banking System's Total Reserves		
	Increase	Decrease	No Effect
Public Actions			
Withdrawing cash from banks		X	
Depositing cash for credit to demand and time accounts	X		
Transferring funds from demand deposits to time deposit accounts			X*
Treasury Actions			
Transferring Treasury tax and loan (TT&L) funds into Federal Reserve disbursement accounts		X	
Monetizing gold bullion or SDR certificates (and spending monetized funds)	X		
Borrowing money by selling new Treasury bills to dealer firms			X**
Other Actions			
A decrease in Federal Reserve float		X	
A decrease in foreign balances at Federal Reserve banks	X		
Monetary Policy Actions			
Purchasing open market securities	X		
Selling open market securities		X	
Lending through the discount window to depositories	X		
Increasing reserve requirements			X***
Reducing reserve requirements			X***

* Increases excess reserves because there are no reserve requirements against time deposits.

** Does not change reserves because the funds used to buy the Treasury securities are deposited in TT&L accounts. However, there is an "economic" effect in that the Treasury now has money to spend that dealers were previously holding out of the spending stream.

*** Changes excess reserves but does to change total reserves.

use of currency, changing levels of Federal Reserve float, and actions taken by the U.S. Treasury. These three factors, and the Federal Reserve's defensive strategy responses to them, bear closer examination.

CURRENCY

Because the cash held by banks is part of total reserves, withdrawals of cash from the banking system by the public decrease bank reserves. Conversely, deposits of cash by individuals and businesses into their checking and time accounts increase bank reserves.

The public's behavior with cash is far from random. Cash tends to flow out of banks, draining reserves, on Thursdays and Fridays, particularly before three-day holiday weekends when individuals increase their holdings of convenience money. Cash tends to flow back to banks, increasing reserves, on Mondays and Tuesdays, when merchants deposit cash receipts from weekend sales. Currency also tends to flow out of banks during the first half of every month as end-of-month paychecks and Social Security checks are cashed.

The Federal Reserve uses defensive open market operations to offset the effect of cash on bank reserves on a day-to-day basis. The Federal Reserve's cash defense is most intense between late November and early January. Early in this six- to eight-week holiday season, the public typically withdraws a large amount of cash from the banking system. In 2001–2002 the amount was $7 billion.

As money is spent or given as gifts and gratuities, this cash flows back into the banking system. Without open market operations, and assuming no offsetting reserve inflows from nonpolicy sources, the banking system would lose an inordinate amount of reserves during late November and early December. This reserve drain would not only drive up the cost of reserves and short-term interest rates, but also could make credit unavailable for many businesses that would need short-term bank loans to finance inventories during the holiday season. Conversely, the infusion of reserves in late December and early January from cash deposits likely would drive down interest rates and might lead to an overexpansion of bank lending.

The Federal Reserve uses defensive open market operations to try to prevent this seasonal fluctuation in reserves. During late November and early December, when banks are losing reserves, the Federal Reserve provides new, offsetting reserves by buying securities. In late December and early January, as banks are regaining reserves through cash deposits, the Federal Reserve sells securities to drain off excess reserves. The net effect of both the public's cash behavior and the Federal Reserve's defensive open market operations is to stabilize bank reserves.

The relatively predictable nature of consumers' cash behavior makes the Federal Reserve's defensive actions easier. Repetitive behavior can be anticipated with reasonable accuracy, based on statistical data, and factored into each day's defensive strategy. The public's short-term cash behavior has become less predictable in recent years, however. The amount of currency in circulation more than doubled from the 1970s to the 1990s. During the same period, there was a commensurate increase in the weekly variability of the public's cash holdings, from $500 million to about $1 billion. For all these reasons, currency is now the largest single nonpolicy factor affecting bank reserves.

FEDERAL RESERVE FLOAT

The daily level of the Federal Reserve float is another nonpolicy factor compensated for by the Federal Reserve's defensive strategies. Federal Reserve float is the name given to the extra reserves that exist in the banking system because the Federal Reserve credits banks for deposited checks before the checks are actually collected. Changes in the daily level of float cause bank reserves to increase or decrease. Because these changes can be both substantial and unpredictable, the Federal Reserve factors float changes into its defensive open market operations strategy. An increase in float is counteracted with an equivalent dollar-value sale of open market securities; a reduction in float is countered with an equivalent purchase of securities.

Offsetting the level of float in the banking system is not a problem. It is difficult, however, to predict the level of daily float because it often rises and falls in response to uncontrollable factors. During winter months, for example, bad weather may delay interregional check couriers from presenting checks to banks on which they are drawn.

ACTIONS TAKEN BY THE U.S. TREASURY

The activities of the U.S. Treasury constitute the third principal nonpolicy factor to which the Federal Reserve responds with defensive open market operations. The Treasury's tax collecting, borrowing, and spending activities, along with decisions about whether to use the central bank or private banks to deposit and withdraw the government's funds, all can affect bank reserves. If the Treasury's balances at Federal Reserve banks increase from tax receipts or borrowings, for example, bank reserves decline. If the Treasury's balances at Federal Reserve banks decrease because of government spending, bank reserves expand.

TREASURY TAX AND LOAN ACCOUNTS

The Treasury uses a special system of deposits called **Treasury tax and loan (TT&L) accounts** at most commercial banks in the country to minimize the affect of Treasury's actions on bank reserves and monetary policy control. All federal tax receipts, which are mainly payroll tax withholdings, and funds received from the sale of bonds are deposited in these accounts. Banks that hold TT&L accounts must post collateral, including various government securities, to cover the funds in the accounts. The Treasury also maintains accounts at each Federal Reserve bank. All government disbursements, such as Social Security payments and the civil service payroll, are made from these accounts. As funds are needed to cover disbursements, the Treasury transfers its deposits from the TT&L accounts at commercial banks to the disbursement accounts at the Federal Reserve banks.

The Treasury has two types of TT&L accounts: the remittance option account and the note option account. Thus banks are offered a choice of account relationships. Under the remittance option account, banks can hold TT&L funds for one day before transferring the funds to the Treasury's disbursement account at the district Reserve bank. Banks choosing this option are not required to pay for the TT&L funds. Under the note option account, banks can hold TT&L funds for extended periods of time, but they must buy or borrow the funds from the Treasury under an open-end note arrangement. The interest rate payable to the Treasury under the note arrangement is one-quarter of a percentage point below the average federal funds rate for the period during which the TT&L funds are held.

Banks holding TT&L funds pay the Treasury an investment return if they have chosen the note option. At the same time, the Treasury pays fees to the banks that provide TT&L account-related services.

CORPORATE TAX PAYMENTS

Corporate tax payments collected by the U.S. Treasury also affect bank reserves and money supply growth, and are another factor the Federal Reserve must take into account in its defensive open market operations. Assume that U.S. corporations pay their quarterly taxes to the Internal Revenue Service with $5 billion in checks written on their demand deposit accounts at the nation's banks. Because the Treasury deposits these checks in TT&L accounts at commercial banks the reserves remain unchanged.

Because all Treasury disbursements are made from the Treasury's accounts at the Federal Reserve, the $5 billion on account at banks must be transferred into the Federal Reserve banks. Because of this transfer process, the banking system's reserves temporarily decline by $5 billion.

The reserve decline is likely to be short-lived, however, because as soon as Social Security recipients deposit the Treasury's checks, bank reserves increase to their previous level. The money supply also returns to its original level because the government is no longer holding the $5 billion in corporate tax payments.

In some cases, the decrease in reserves caused by the Treasury's TT&L transfers might threaten to cause a significant deviation in the Federal Reserve's growth-target trend for reserves. Usually, the Federal Reserve does not wait for the expected rebound in reserves due several days later when Social Security recipients deposit their checks. Instead, it uses its defensive open market operations to offset the deviation and keep reserves on track.

SUMMARY

The Federal Reserve can use three general policy instruments to implement monetary policy: the discount rate, reserve requirements, and open market operations. Theoretically, changing the discount rate can depress or stimulate bank borrowings from the Federal Reserve and banks' subsequent lending. Reserve requirement changes, the most powerful monetary tool, alter the composition of required and excess reserves in the banking system and change the banking coefficient of demand deposit expansion for the future. Open market operations are the central bank's principal policy tool. Federal Reserve purchases of government securities in the open market add reserves to the banking system; sales from the Federal Reserve's portfolio reduce reserves.

Open market operations, which are carried out by the New York trading desk, follow policy directives set approximately every six weeks by the Federal Open Market Committee. These directives establish broad economic policy goals, along with operational, short-term targets linked to intermediate, long-term financial and economic measures.

Numerous factors other than monetary policy can change the level and growth of bank reserves. From the public's use of cash to changes in the level of Federal Reserve float and the way the U.S. Treasury manages the government's tax collections and disbursements, all can affect bank reserves. The Federal Reserve uses defensive open market operations on a daily basis to offset or nullify changes in reserves that, if unchecked, would push reserve growth off target.

REVIEW QUESTIONS

1. How are the discount rate and discount window lending used as a monetary policy tool?
2. Whenever the Federal Reserve buys or sells anything, bank reserves and the money supply change. Why, then, does the Federal Reserve limit its buying and selling to government securities in the open market?
3. Changing reserve requirement percentages is one way the Federal Reserve can use reserve requirements as a monetary policy tool. What are the two other ways?
4. The Federal Reserve's monetary policy strategy involves the setting of short-term operational targets to achieve long-term national economic objectives. Why does the Federal Reserve do this?
5. How do dynamic and defensive open market operations differ? How can you tell whether the Federal Reserve's open market operations have been dynamic or defensive in any given week?
6. Assume that the Federal Reserve is on target for reserve growth. What nonpolicy factors might cause reserve growth to go off target?
7. What is the purpose of Treasury tax and loan (TT&L) accounts? How do the remittance and note option accounts work? How do they affect bank reserves?

ADDITIONAL RESOURCES

"Conducting Monetary Policy without Government Debt: The Fed's Early Years," *Review,* Federal Reserve Bank of St. Louis, May-June 2002, 14 pp. Discusses how the Federal Reserve implemented monetary policy in the 1920s and 1930s and the Federal Reserve's failure to respond vigorously to the Great Depression.

Federal Open Market Committee, Board of Governors of the Federal Reserve, 1994, pamphlet. Explains the structure and role of the FOMC.

"Financial Innovation and Monetary Transmission," *Economic Policy Review*, Federal Reserve Bank of New York, May 2002, 289 pp. Proceedings of a conference on the transmission of monetary policy and the response of various economic sectors to monetary easing and tightening.

Monetary Policy Objectives, Board of Governors of the Federal Reserve, semiannual publication. Report to Congress on monetary policy.

"When it Comes 2 Economic Education, the Federal Reserve is where it's @", Web-page article at www.federalreserve education.org. Searchable site explains how the central bank affects the economy through its conduct of monetary policy.

Woodrow: Federal Reserve Bank of Minneapolis. Web site at http://woodrow.mpls.frb.fed.us/info/policy/fomc.cfm. Provides information about the Federal Open Market Committee.

U.S. Monetary Policy and Financial Markets, Federal Reserve Bank of New York, 1990, 23 pp. An in-depth description of how monetary policy is developed and the techniques used by the Federal Reserve to implement policy.

EXTENDED STUDY 7: EVOLUTION OF THE DISCOUNT WINDOW AND THE DISCOUNT RATE

When the Federal Reserve was established in 1913, the discount rate was the only monetary policy tool authorized by Congress. The economy of 1913 was very different from today's economy, as was economists' and bankers' understanding of the workings of the economy and the role of the central bank. Until the 1930s, the Federal Reserve operated passively, responding to changes in the economy's monetary needs but not actively promoting such changes. The central bank's role was guided by the automatic, self-regulating principles of a doctrine known as the *real bills* or *commercial loan theory*. This doctrine maintained that the economy would balance itself automatically if the nation's supply of money were pegged to short-term, 90-day, self-liquidating inventory or to commercial loans made by banks to business and agriculture.

COMMERCIAL LOAN THEORY

The commercial loan theory convinced member banks to deposit their reserves with the Federal Reserve banks. The Federal Reserve banks then gave member banks access to credit through discount window loans. The Reserve banks' exclusive power to issue paper currency was limited by collateral requirements, also called backing requirements, which were tied to the Reserve banks' discount window loans.

When banks reached their lending capacity and had no excess reserves against which new loans could be made, they obtained additional reserves from Reserve banks by borrowing at the discount window. To obtain credit from the Reserve banks, however, member commercial banks had to present eligible paper for rediscounting. Eligible paper consisted only of the short-term loans banks had made to businesses and farmers to enable them to buy or manufacture inventories. This narrow definition of eligible paper was based on the belief that only short-term inventory loans were truly supportive of economic growth, and that only a growing economy needed additional money.

By making loans to member banks through the discount window, Federal Reserve banks obtained the member banks' short-term loan paper, essentially the private IOUs of the banks' customers. This paper was essential for issuing Federal Reserve notes because, under the Federal Reserve Act, Federal Reserve notes had to be backed by 40 percent gold and 100 percent eligible paper. Thus, the supply of paper currency also was linked to the growth of the economy.

According to the commercial loan theory, in a growing economy the demand for short-term inventory loans should be strong and banks should be active lenders. As banks rediscounted customers' commercial paper at Federal Reserve banks' discount windows, they received additional reserves against which they could expand loans. Meanwhile, the Federal Reserve received additional collateral against which it could issue currency. A growing economy called for more money, and the commercial loan theory seemed to provide the mechanism for supplying it.

EFFECTS OF RECESSION AND INFLATION

The commercial loan theory was based on the false premise that short-term commercial loans, also called real bills, were always self-liquidating. A business that borrowed from a bank for 90 days to build up its inventories was expected to be in a position to repay the bank as soon as it sold the inventories. Inventories themselves served as collateral for the original loans. Things did not always work as expected, however. When the economy moved into a recession and the demand for goods and services slumped, so did the demand for loans. Corporations that had borrowed often found themselves unable to sell enough of their inventories to repay their loans. Defaulted loans created liquidity problems for banks, but banks that lacked additional eligible paper could not obtain funds from the Federal Reserve. Thus, in times of recession, the commercial loan theory exacerbated economic contraction and illiquidity for banks.

The commercial loan theory also failed during periods of inflation. Businesses found that with rising prices the money value of their inventories also rose, enabling them to borrow more from banks. Rising inventory values allowed banks to obtain more reserves from the Federal Reserve against their inflated loans and gave the Federal Reserve additional collateral for expanded currency issuance. Thus, when prices were

rising rapidly, the Federal Reserve's adherence to the commercial loan theory added to inflation. Its adherence to the strictures of this theory helps explain why the Federal Reserve could not cope with the collapse of the economy and the banking system in the early 1930s.

REGIONAL DISCOUNT RATES

As envisioned in 1913, the commercial loan theory was to be complemented by different discount rates in each of the 12 Federal Reserve districts. Thus, each Reserve bank could pursue a separate monetary policy to accommodate its region's economic needs. In theory, if developing industry in the South needed easier credit, the Federal Reserve banks of Atlanta and Richmond could set a low discount rate, which would influence other lending rates in the region to remain low. At the same time, if business expansion in the Northeast threatened to generate inflation, the Federal Reserve banks of New York, Philadelphia, and Boston could set a high discount rate, which would keep loan rates high in those areas, blunting excess lending and the subsequent business spending pressure.

This theory quickly yielded to the reality that money and credit respect only interest rate differentials and profit incentives, not district boundaries. With no impediments to the flow of money among districts, borrowers in the Northeast, where interest rates were high, could shift loan demand to correspondents in the South, where interest rates were low. In time, as money shifted from the South to the Northeast, the depletion of the money supply in the South would cause interest rates to rise while the expansion of the money supply in the Northeast would cause interest rates to fall. These back-and-forth adjustments would continue until a national equilibrium interest rate was reached. The power of the Reserve banks' directors to set the discount rate in their districts is the only remaining vestige of this early approach to regional monetary policy.

12

FISCAL POLICY AND DEBT MANAGEMENT POLICY

LEARNING OBJECTIVES

After studying this chapter, you should be able to

- cite the ways that fiscal policy can be used to counter inflation and recession
- describe the federal budget process
- summarize the problems the economy faces if federal debt growth accelerates
- explain how debt management, wage-price controls, and indexation work
- describe the balance of payments and its component measures
- define the key terms listed in this chapter

KEY TERMS

country risk
federal budget deficit
federal debt
foreign exchange
full-employment budgeting
gold tranche

inflation hedging
international reserves
nondiscretionary government spending
special drawing rights
tax-based income policy

INTRODUCTION

Fiscal policy uses a government's spending and taxation to achieve specific economic goals. Debt management involves actions taken by a government to change the composition of its national debt. Balance of payments management involves actions taken to balance international transactions to achieve economic goals. In the United States, fiscal policy is the responsibility of Congress and the president; debt and balance of payments management are responsibilities of the U.S. Treasury.

This chapter examines how the nation's processes for fiscal policy, debt management, and balance of payments management work. It discusses key factors that affect their use in fighting recession or inflation. It also reviews national debt ownership and the components of the nation's balance of payments to understand the scope of financial interactions between the United States and other countries.

The U.S. government also has used other programs to counter inflation. Some of these programs are wage-price controls, which are government-imposed limits on wage and price increases, and indexation, which is reflected in the cost of living escalator clauses in all money payment contracts. These programs are reviewed as well.

FISCAL POLICY TOOLS

Federal spending and taxation are the two fiscal policy tools on which the federal government relies to change the pace and direction of the economy. In theory, if the economy is slipping into a recession, the federal government can increase its spending and reduce taxes. If the economy is expanding rapidly and inflationary pressures are building, the federal government can reduce its spending and increase taxes.

In practice, however, the government's ability to use fiscal policy to deal with recessionary and inflationary pressures faces several limitations. One of these limitations

stems from the lengthy political process involved in changing federal spending programs or tax laws (see exhibit 12.1).

The second limitation relates to the automatic nature of much of the government's spending. Over the decades, about two-thirds of the government's expenditures have become **nondiscretionary government spending.** These are bills that the government is obligated to pay, mostly entitlements such as Social Security and interest on the federal debt. Nondiscretionary government spending is not immediately subject to the control of Congress or the president.

A third limitation is the general reluctance of Congress and the president to raise taxes to fight inflation because most voters would not readily accept such an action. The lack of political support for anti-inflation tax increases is based, in part, on the public's perception that the federal income tax structure favors both low-income and wealthy households. The public believes that any increase would be disproportionately borne by middle-income earners. Primarily for these reasons, the record of U.S. fiscal policy in countering inflation has been poor.

All government spending is funded from either tax receipts or borrowing. If the government finances increased spending by raising taxes, the money is merely transferred from the private sector to the public sector; thus, total spending typically does not increase. In essence, the increase in government spending is offset by a decrease in consumer spending. Likewise, if the government reduces its spending and reduces taxes, consumer spending is likely to increase, with the result that total spending remains unchanged.

If, however, the government increases its spending by borrowing, total spending increases. If the economy is operating at full capacity, an increase in government spending can overstimulate the economy into inflation. This occurs because federal spending in excess of tax receipts requires substantial federal borrowings. These

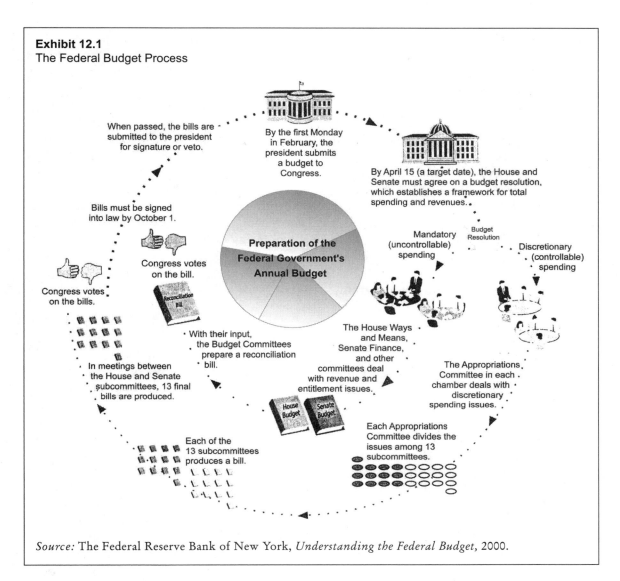

Exhibit 12.1
The Federal Budget Process

When passed, the bills are submitted to the president for signature or veto.

By the first Monday in February, the president submits a budget to Congress.

By April 15 (a target date), the House and Senate must agree on a budget resolution, which establishes a framework for total spending and revenues.

Bills must be signed into law by October 1.

Congress votes on the bill.

Preparation of the Federal Government's Annual Budget

Mandatory (uncontrollable) spending

Budget Resolution

Discretionary (controllable) spending

Congress votes on the bills.

With their input, the Budget Committees prepare a reconciliation bill.

The House Ways and Means, Senate Finance, and other committees deal with revenue and entitlement issues.

The Appropriations Committee in each chamber deals with discretionary spending issues.

In meetings between the House and Senate subcommittees, 13 final bills are produced.

Each of the 13 subcommittees produces a bill.

Each Appropriations Committee divides the issues among 13 subcommittees.

Source: The Federal Reserve Bank of New York, *Understanding the Federal Budget,* 2000.

borrowings put pressure on the Federal Reserve to provide ample reserves and money supply growth so that banks have sufficient funds to lend to the dealer purchasers of the government's increasing debt issues. This interrelationship between fiscal and monetary processes contributed to the inflation that plagued the U.S. economy during the 1970s and early 1980s.

THE FEDERAL BUDGET

Any imbalance between what the federal government spends and what it collects in tax revenues appears as either a federal

budget surplus, which results from an excess of tax revenues, or a **federal budget deficit,** which results from an excess of government spending. A budget deficit represents the amount of money the federal government has to borrow by selling new Treasury securities to fund its current spending.

During a recession, the government spends more as part of fiscal policy in order to boost total spending in the economy and counter the recession. Because tax revenues typically fall during a recession, the increased government spending generates a budget deficit. During an inflationary period, fiscal policy calls for a reduction in government spending to restrain overall demand for goods and services in the economy. Because tax revenues generally increase during periods of inflation, a decrease in government spending normally generates a budgetary surplus.

Since the 1930s, when fiscal policy was introduced to stimulate total spending, the federal budget has been increasingly structured to automatically stabilize the economy against severe downturns in the business cycle. One way this has been accomplished is through built-in spending programs designed to provide people with a base level of income and subsequent spending power.

Many of these government programs, such as unemployment insurance, are triggered by the downturn itself. As a recession deepens and worker layoffs mount, the number of people collecting unemployment insurance increases, as does the total dollar amount spent by the government to support the unemployment insurance bills of the states.

The federal income tax also is designed to stabilize the economy. The federal tax structure automatically counters inflation and recession by taking in more tax dollars when incomes rise, as with inflation, and taking in fewer dollars when incomes decline, as with a recession. Typically, in times of inflation nominal incomes rise, although the purchasing power value of these incomes may not increase at all. Over time, the nominal income gains put people into higher tax brackets.

The concept of automatic stabilization has, on occasion, been tried in federal budgeting. **Full-employment budgeting** is an approach that builds from an estimate of the total amount of tax revenues the government would receive were the economy operating at full productive capacity and full labor employment. Government spending is pegged to this estimated full-employment tax revenue level. In theory, any deficit created by the pegged spending level provides the appropriate degree of stimulus necessary to propel the economy toward its full-employment level.

Theoretically, if the economy is at full employment, government spending and tax revenues will balance and no deficit will be created.

Since they were introduced in the 1930s, the nation's automatic stabilizers have tended to blunt the severity of the economy's business-cycle downturns. Some studies indicate that, on average, the stabilizers have reduced the severity of U.S. recessions by about one-third. Automatic stabilizers, however, have proved less successful in countering inflation.

THE FEDERAL DEBT

The **federal debt,** also called the national debt, is the total of all past federal deficits, which is the total of all outstanding bills, notes, and bonds owed by the federal government Before fiscal policy was used to achieve economic goals, the government ran few, if any, budgetary deficits. Several deficits were incurred in the nation's early history to finance wars, but surpluses in later years offset most of these. The introduction of fiscal policy to stimulate total spending during the Great Depression of the 1930s resulted in 10 consecutive annual deficits. These deficits, coupled with government borrowing during World War II, boosted the federal debt to about 115 percent of gross domestic product (GDP) by 1945 (see exhibit 12.2).

During the 1950s and 1960s, the government ran small but persistent annual budget deficits, and the national debt slowly continued to grow. Because the economy grew even faster, however, the ratio of federal debt to GDP steadily declined. A declining ratio of federal debt to GDP is a favorable sign of the economy's capacity to absorb debt.

By the beginning of the 1980s, however, the ratio of federal debt to GDP began to steadily increase. A recession, coupled with a substantial tax cut, lowered tax revenues while government spending continued to increase. The federal budget began the 1990s

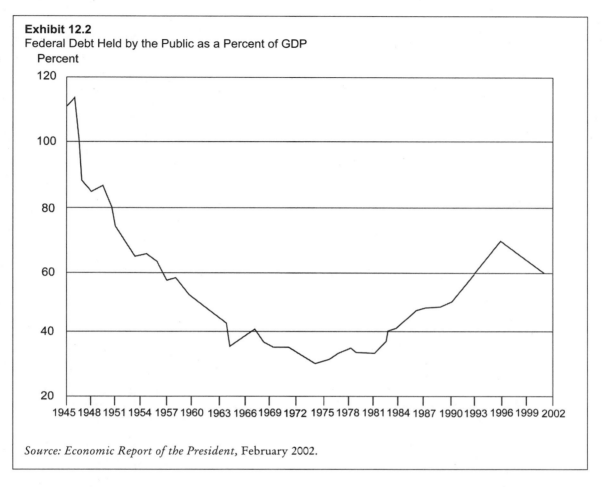

Exhibit 12.2
Federal Debt Held by the Public as a Percent of GDP

Source: Economic Report of the President, February 2002.

in deficit, but generated surpluses at the end of the decade. Government spending cuts on defense programs and discretionary programs, an increase in taxes, and lower interest rates on government borrowings were largely responsible for the surpluses. Since the mid-1990s, the ratio of federal debt to GDP has fallen to about 60 percent, but the federal debt itself has grown to more than $5.8 trillion.

PROFILE OF FEDERAL DEBT HOLDERS

Nearly half of the federal government's debt is owed to private investors; the other half is owed to various federal agencies, government trust funds, and the Federal Reserve. The largest private holders of the government's debt are foreign governments, whose proportions of ownership have increased steadily since the late 1980s (see exhibit 12.3 on the following page). As of 2002, foreign governments own 43 percent of the government's debt. This foreign ownership has generated growing concern among many U.S. economists. Federal debt owed to financial institutions, state and local governments, and individuals, when paid off, transfers income within the United States, from the government to the private sector. Interest payments on debt also transfer income within the economy. Federal debt owed to foreign governments, when paid off, transfers income and purchasing power abroad, a trend that carries the potential for reducing U.S. income and consumption. The payment of interest on debt held by foreigners also transfers income abroad.

The explosion of federal debt in recent decades, coupled with high interest rates during the 1980s, generated sharp growth

Exhibit 12.3
Holders of the Federal Debt, 2002

	Amount (in billions)	Percent of Total Held by Private Investors
Net federal debt	$ 3,381	
Held by Federal Reserve	568	
Held by private investors	2,813	
State and local governments*	395	14%
Banks	198	7
Mutual funds	378	13
Insurance companies	98	3
Private pension funds	360	13
Individuals	189	7
Foreign**	1,195	43
	2,813	100

* Includes pension plans.
** Primarily foreign governments.
Source: Federal Reserve Board, *Flow of Funds Accounts of the United States,* and U.S. Department of the Treasury, *Treasury Bulletin,* June 2002.

in the interest payments that the federal government must make to debt holders (see exhibit 12.4). Lower interest rates during the 1990s, federal budget surpluses, and reduced borrowings helped reduce interest on the debt to about 12 percent of federal outlays, or $215 billion, in 2000. Nonetheless, the government's interest payments today exceed every component of government spending except for defense, Social Security, and Medicare.

CONCERNS ABOUT FEDERAL DEFICITS AND DEBT

Most economists believe that keeping the federal budget in surplus and reducing the federal debt are necessary preconditions for keeping interest rates low and freeing more of the government's revenue for discretionary uses. If, however, the federal budget begins to register annual deficits in the mid-2000s, and the growth of the federal debt begins to accelerate, the economy will be confronted with three economic problems: competition for tax revenues, competition

Exhibit 12.4
Interest on the Federal Debt

	Amount (in billions)	Percent of Total Federal Spending
1980	$ 63	11%
1985	153	16
1990	202	16
1995	240	15
2000	215	12

Source: Budget of the U.S. Government, fiscal year 2001.

for available credit, and increased foreign claims on U.S. output and resources.

COMPETITION FOR TAX REVENUES

The more tax revenue the government must allocate to pay interest on the debt, the less tax revenue is available to fund existing government programs, finance new programs, or fund tax cuts.

COMPETITION FOR AVAILABLE CREDIT

Federal budget deficits must be financed with government borrowings. The larger these borrowings, the smaller the supply of credit available to the business and consumer sectors. Government borrowings not only crowd out private-sector borrowings, leading to smaller business investment spending for new factories and equipment, but they also drive up interest rates. This is particularly true if the markets perceive the government's borrowings as financing inflationary government spending.

INCREASED FOREIGN CLAIMS ON U.S. OUTPUT AND RESOURCES

If foreign investors continue to maintain their preferences for holding U.S. government securities, an increased federal debt will lead to an increase in the amounts held by foreigners. Although foreigners have shown no hesitancy in holding U.S. government securities as long-term investments, these holdings, nonetheless, represent a claim on U.S. goods and services. If foreigners used their investment dollars to buy U.S. goods and services instead of U.S. government securities, a smaller proportion of the nation's output would be available to meet domestic demand.

U.S. GOVERNMENT'S RESPONSE

During the 1980s, a major focus of the national debate on the economy's performance was how to reduce the size of the government's annual budget deficits and the growth of the federal debt. This debate resulted in federal legislation in the 1980s and 1990s that put in place measures to reverse the pattern of federal deficits and growing debt.

In 1985 Congress set annual targets for deficit reductions through 1991 and required the government's budgets to meet those targets. If the president and the Congress could not agree on spending cuts and tax increases to bring projected annual deficits to the targets, across-the-board cuts would be imposed automatically to bring the deficits down. The government's deficit projection targets, however, assumed that federal tax revenues would grow substantially in the late 1980s. Because this did not happen, the United States was left with large deficits.

In 1990 Congress placed spending limits on defense and other discretionary spending and imposed automatic spending cuts. These spending limits reduced the deficit by nearly $500 billion through 1995. Congress also required that any new spending would have to specify the source of the funds for the spending. This program also failed to substantially slow the growth of the federal debt, however.

One reason the federal debt continued to grow was that federal outlays for entitlement programs, such as Social Security and Medicare, were not cut enough to stop their growth. During the early 1990s, large automatic increases in spending for Medicaid and Medicare took place. Another reason the program failed was the unexpectedly slow growth of the economy in the early 1990s, which held actual increases in tax revenues well below initial congressional projections.

In 1993 Congress passed another five-year plan of tax increases and spending cuts aimed at reducing the debt by about $500 billion. Personal and corporate tax rates were increased, taxes were added on Social Security benefits and gasoline, and spending cuts were authorized for medical care, federal pensions, and many other areas. A freeze was imposed on discretionary spending. This program helped reduce the size of the government's budget deficits in the mid-1990s.

In 1997 Congress put in place an additional deficit reduction program that sought to build on the two previous plans adopted earlier in the decade. This program was relatively modest because there was not much deficit left to reduce. Most of the work of eliminating the deficit had already been accomplished because of the strong recovery of the U.S. economy from the 1990 recession and the prior deficit reduction measures.

In theory, the deficit reduction measures of the 1990s, which reduced government spending and increased taxes, should have contracted the economy. The Federal Reserve's efforts to keep interest rates relatively low early in the decade are seen by most economists as having successfully offset this contraction.

FISCAL OUTLOOK FOR THE MID-2000s

The fiscal outlook for the mid-2000s prepared by the Congressional Budget Office forecasts renewed budget deficits and federal debt growth caused by

- the weak performance of the stock market in 2001 and 2002, coupled with a mild recession in 2001, which is expected to hold down capital gains, income, and corporate profit tax revenues during the early 2000s
- a major tax cut passed by Congress in 2001, which is expected to hold down overall tax revenue growth during the mid-2000s
- projected increases in discretionary spending for both defense and non-defense outlays during the early 2000s
- a sharp increase in nondiscretionary spending during the mid-2000s, with Social Security and Medicare outlays expected to soar as America's population ages
- increased federal interest payments as the federal debt grows throughout the decade

DEBT MANAGEMENT

The U.S. Treasury's debt management actions can affect interest rates and financial market conditions. The Treasury can take these actions, which involve the control of maturities and the timing of issuance of new government securities, to change the structure or composition of the national debt. These actions can be used as a tool to counter recession or contain inflation.

To meet the government's short-term financing needs or to replace maturing government securities, the Treasury can choose to issue short-term, intermediate, or long-term securities. These decisions, as well as decisions about the frequency of financing new or replacement issues, can cause interest rates to rise or fall.

If the Treasury wants to use debt management as a tool to fight recession or long-term inflation, it can restrict its issuance to short-term securities.

RECESSION

If the Treasury issued only short-term securities, it would change the composition of the federal debt. Such a restricted issue would affect total spending in the economy by changing the liquidity of consumers, businesses, and banks. By issuing short-term debt, the Treasury would add to the market's supply of these instruments, thereby driving down their price and raising short-term interest rates. Because of this increase in supply, however, consumers, businesses, and banks would find themselves in an unbalanced financial asset position. To regain balance, they would need to buy long-term bonds, which would result in a decline in long-term interest rates. The economic effect of the decline in long-term interest rates would be to stimulate the economy.

INFLATION

By replacing maturing short-term securities, such as 120-day T-bills, with long-term securities, such as 10-year bonds, during inflation, the Treasury could both drive down the price of long-term securities and raise yields, and drive up the price of short-term securities, thereby lowering yields. In doing so, the Treasury would replace liquid near-money substitutes with less liquid financial assets. Consumers, businesses, and banks seeking to maintain their prior levels of liquidity would need to compensate by holding more money and near-money balances, thereby shifting some potential spending funds into financial assets.

Lengthening the maturity structure of the federal debt also could reduce spending by diverting some consumer and business spending into the higher yielding long-term government securities. Thus, issuing only long-term debt during inflation would act as a restraint on total spending.

Economists are unsure how effective such debt management strategies would be in actually countering recession or inflation because the Treasury has chosen not to use debt management as a fiscal tool. Rather, the Treasury's primary motivation in using debt management is simply to keep the government's interest costs as low as possible. Indeed, because its decisions can have a major effect on financial markets and the economy, the Treasury coordinates its debt management actions with the daily open market operations of the Federal Reserve.

Treasury officials participate in a daily early-morning conference call with the New York trading desk. The Federal Reserve's defensive strategy for that day is reviewed, and matters related to the timing, size, and maturity of new issues of Treasury securities are discussed. The Federal Reserve factors the Treasury's debt management actions into its day-to-day defensive open market operations.

BALANCE OF PAYMENTS MANAGEMENT

The U.S. balance of payments is a statistical record of the money value of all transactions that occurred between the United States and the rest of the world during a given year. It serves as a measure of our performance in the world economy, and also as a record of our financial interactions with other countries. The government uses the balance of payments as a management guide for advancing the nation's economic objectives.

When calculating the U.S. balance of payments, all outflows of money are recorded as payments and all inflows of money are recorded as receipts. Outflows include all funds paid for imports of goods and services or paid in the course of making foreign investments, making loans, or providing aid to other countries. Inflows include all funds taken in from exports to other countries, sales of financial assets or property to overseas purchasers, and repayments of foreign loans. The difference between all international payments and all international receipts constitutes the balance of payments.

BALANCE MEASURES

The balance of payments is composed of five balance measures, each of which focuses analytical attention on a different aspect of the nation's international activity (see exhibit 12.5).

BALANCE OF TRADE

The balance of trade is the difference in value between exports and imports of goods. If a country exports more merchandise than it imports, it is said to have a balance of trade surplus, or a favorable balance of trade. If a country imports more goods than it exports, it is said to have a balance of trade deficit, or an unfavorable balance of trade.

In many countries, merchandise trade is the primary component of the balance of payments. In the United States, merchandise trade represents only about half of the nation's total balance of payments. Most U.S. merchandise imports consist of petroleum products, computer hardware, foods and beverages, and automobiles, the latter coming mostly from Japan. Most U.S. merchandise exports consist of grains, computer software, chemicals, civilian aircraft, and auto parts and engines, with the latter being sent mostly to Canada.

From 1870 to 1970, the United States almost always exported more than it imported. Since the mid-1970s, however, the United States has registered increasingly larger annual trade deficits. In 2000 the trade deficit exceeded $450 billion, the largest annual U.S. trade deficit on record.

BALANCE ON GOODS AND SERVICES

The balance on goods and services measures merchandise trade plus the export and import of services. Services include such diverse activities as transportation and tourism; consultancy; banking and insurance; and transactions such as royalties and license fees. Also included in the service count are U.S. earnings on investments abroad and payments of earnings on foreign investments.

In the United States, service exports traditionally have exceeded service imports. U.S. earnings abroad from direct investments, such as holdings of foreign factories and property, and from portfolio investments, such as holdings of foreign stocks and bonds, more than offset deficits in tourism and military expenditures. For the first time in more than 50 years, beginning in the late 1990s, payments to foreigners on investments in the United States began to exceed U.S. receipts on foreign investment. Other net service income, which comes mostly from consultancy and financial services, continues to

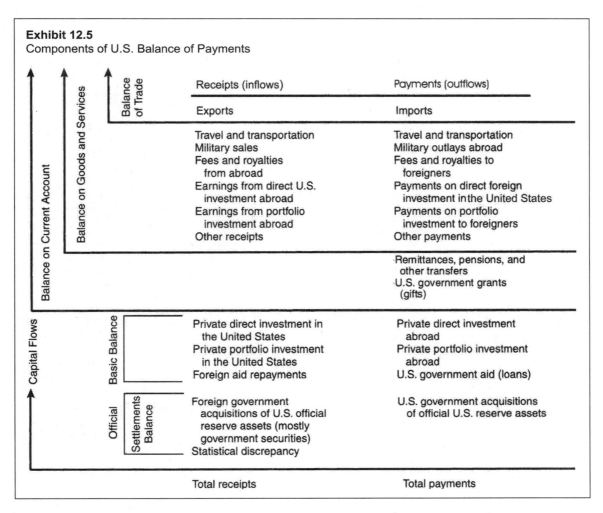

Exhibit 12.5
Components of U.S. Balance of Payments

	Receipts (inflows)	Payments (outflows)
Balance of Trade	Exports	Imports
Balance on Goods and Services	Travel and transportation Military sales Fees and royalties from abroad Earnings from direct U.S. investment abroad Earnings from portfolio investment abroad Other receipts	Travel and transportation Military outlays abroad Fees and royalties to foreigners Payments on direct foreign investment in the United States Payments on portfolio investment to foreigners Other payments
Balance on Current Account		Remittances, pensions, and other transfers U.S. government grants (gifts)
Basic Balance (Capital Flows)	Private direct investment in the United States Private portfolio investment in the United States Foreign aid repayments	Private direct investment abroad Private portfolio investment abroad U.S. government aid (loans)
Official Settlements Balance	Foreign government acquisitions of U.S. official reserve assets (mostly government securities) Statistical discrepancy	U.S. government acquisitions of official U.S. reserve assets
	Total receipts	Total payments

remain strong, however, providing some degree of offset.

BALANCE ON CURRENT ACCOUNT

The balance on current account measures the difference between receipts from and payments to foreign countries for goods, services, income, and unilateral transfers. Unilateral transfers are private gifts to foreigners and grants-in-aid to foreign governments, other than military grants. During the late 1990s, unilateral transfers from private U.S. citizens and the U.S. government to foreigners averaged about $45 billion each year.

The current account balance measures all the ongoing transactions between the United States and other countries that result in an international transfer of money; it does not, however, reflect inflows or outflows of capital. A current account in surplus reflects a situation in which the United States is able to more than pay for external purchases out of current income. A current account in deficit reflects a situation in which the United States must finance external purchases from borrowings. Since the mid-1980s, the United States has become a net borrower from, rather than a net lender to, foreign countries (see exhibit 12.6 on the next page).

Current account deficits or surpluses capture the positive or negative contribution of foreigners to domestic aggregate demand. The current account measure provides only a partial picture of the U.S. economy's international performance, however, because it fails to take into account capital flowing into or out of the United States.

Exhibit 12.6
U.S. Balance of Payments Performance, 1970–2000 (in billions; negative reflects deficit)

Year	Trade	Goods and Services	Current Account
1970	2.6	5.6	2.3
1975	9.0	22.9	18.2
1980	-25.3	8.3	1.5
1985	-124.4	-102.7	-117.7
1990	-108.7	-78.2	-99.3
1995	-173.4	-105.1	-148.1
2000	-452.2	-375.7	-444.7

Source: U.S. Department of Commerce, Bureau of Economic Analysis, *Survey of Current Business,* May 2002 and "U.S. International Transactions," *Federal Reserve Bulletin,* May 2002.

Inflows and outflows of capital are measured in the basic balance and in the official settlements balance. These inflows and outflows can completely offset a current account deficit or surplus and can profoundly affect the domestic economy.

CAPITAL FLOWS—BASIC BALANCE

The basic balance registers U.S. investment abroad and foreign investment in the United States. U.S. investment abroad is called capital outflow; foreign investment in the United States is called capital inflow. Since the late 1980s, more capital has flowed into the United States annually than has flowed out. Foreign capital inflows to the United States are predominantly portfolio investments, meaning purchases of U.S. government securities, corporate bonds and corporate stock in non-controllable amounts. The foreign capital inflow reflects

- the diversity of financial investment opportunities in the U.S. financial market, a diversity that no other country can match
- the low rate of inflation in the United States, the growth of the U.S. economy, and the stock market boom of the late 1990s
- relatively high rates of return on U.S. portfolio investments, coupled with low **country risk,** which is the risk that

political or financial instability in a country will jeopardize an investment

Country risk is high in many countries, but market interest rates in these countries do not always accurately reflect this risk. When country risk occurs, as it did during the 1990s in Eastern Europe, Asia, and South America, funds from these countries have tended to flow into the United States, even though interest rates in the United States may actually be lower.

CAPITAL FLOWS—OFFICIAL SETTLEMENTS BALANCE

The official settlements balance measures the change in holdings of international reserve assets of the United States. This balance gauges the strength of the U.S. dollar in the world's markets.

A country generates a balance of payments deficit when it spends more abroad than it takes in from abroad. To finance any deficit, a nation must either draw on its accumulated wealth or borrow. When a nation with a balance of payments deficit chooses not to or cannot borrow, it must draw on the wealth of its international reserves.

International reserves consist of four types of financial assets that governments throughout the world have agreed to accept from each other in payment or settlement of debt. These assets are

- gold
- special drawing rights (SDRs)
- gold tranche
- foreign exchange

GOLD

By international agreement, gold dealings among governments are transacted at the official U.S. government gold price of $42.22 an ounce rather than at market prices. Since the 1970s, market prices for gold have ranged well above this official gold price, however, so countries do not normally settle balance of payments deficits with payments in gold.

SPECIAL DRAWING RIGHTS

Special drawing rights (SDRs) are money balances that are created by the International Monetary Fund (IMF) and allocated to participating member countries. IMF members may use SDRs to settle the financial claims of other member nations.

GOLD TRANCHE

IMF member nations have automatic borrowing privileges at the IMF. The credit line thus maintained is called a **gold tranche,** and it can be counted as part of a member nation's international reserve assets.

FOREIGN EXCHANGE

Foreign exchange is the supply of the world's major trading currencies, which are primarily U.S. dollars, euros, and Japanese yen. Because foreign exchange accounts for most nations' international reserve assets, balance of payments deficits typically are paid with foreign currencies. Foreign

governments tend to purchase U.S. government securities with the dollars they acquire in settlement.

CONCERNS ABOUT BALANCE OF PAYMENTS PERFORMANCE

The deterioration of the U.S. balance of payments during the 1980s and 1990s resulted from huge increases in U.S. imports coupled with weak demand for U.S. exports. The slowdown in export growth in the 1980s mostly reflected the weakened competitiveness of important U.S. industries, such as the steel and auto industries. During the 1990s, a major factor affecting the balance of payments was the slumping economic status of key U.S. trading partners, such as Germany and Japan. Foreign capital inflows during the 1980s and 1990s offset much of the impact of America's deteriorated trade position.

Some economists contend that the rapid rise in U.S. imports helped economies abroad and enhanced the export earnings of developing countries. U.S. reliance on low-priced imports also was an important factor in holding down U.S. inflation. Moreover, the inflows of foreign capital that offset the nation's large current account deficits enabled the United States to finance large federal budget deficits at lower interest rates than otherwise would have prevailed.

Other economists point out that the United States paid a high price for these benefits. The growth in U.S. imports during the 1980s and 1990s led to a profusion of U.S. dollars in foreign hands. Foreigners used these dollars to acquire vast quantities of U.S. corporate stocks and bonds, Treasury securities, real estate, manufacturing firms, and bank loans. This massive accumulation of U.S. assets by foreigners shifted the status of the United States from the world's largest creditor nation to the world's largest debtor nation. The result of this change was that the United States has had to use a growing portion of its domestic income to pay foreigners on their accumulated investments in the United States—a trend that could, in time, reduce U.S. living standards.

RESTORING BALANCE

In the 1990s, U.S. fiscal policy came to place high priority on

- reducing the balance of payments deficit
- reducing America's need to import capital
- restoring the balance between U.S. exports and imports

The policy approaches that could reduce the payments deficit and restore balance are fraught with risks, however.

LIMIT IMPORTS

Placing a quantitative or dollar-value limit on goods and services entering the United States could damage the U.S. economy. American consumers and businesses would be hurt because of America's heavy dependence on imported oil and foreign sources of supply for machinery, equipment, and parts. The American automobile industry, for example, imports engines, bearings, tires, and other key components for most U.S.-produced cars. If foreign car imports are restricted, thereby increasing demand for U.S. cars, the demand for the foreign components needed to produce those domestic cars also increases. The inability to obtain foreign parts or sufficient quantities of imported oil could lead to economic dislocations, such as worker lay-offs and a sharp increase in oil prices.

A more selective approach, such as the tariff the United States imposed on imported steel in 2002, benefits workers and producers in the affected industry, but does so at the expense of U.S. consumers who then pay higher prices. If such restrictions are sufficiently broad-based, ensuing price increases can trigger inflation. Export industries also can be hurt if other countries retaliate against U.S. policy by imposing their own restrictions on imports to their countries from the United States.

RESTRICT CAPITAL INFLOWS

Any move to limit capital inflows to the United States, assuming no expansion in U.S. monetary policy, likely would result in a rise in real interest rates, leading to dislocations in America's financial market. Furthermore, direct capital controls are inconsistent with free-market precepts and would be administratively difficult to implement, monitor, and enforce.

PURSUE COORDINATED FISCAL POLICIES WITH IMPORTANT TRADE PARTNERS

The United States' major trade partners are Japan, Germany, Canada, and Mexico. If these nation's economies could be made to grow faster than the U.S. economy, it is likely that their demand for U.S. goods would increase. In response to the increased demand, U.S. exports would increase faster than U.S. imports, which would improve the U.S. trade balance. It is unlikely, however, that foreign governments would implement fiscal policies that were expansive to the point of overstimulating their economies and risking inflation.

A prolonged slowdown in the growth of the U.S. economy, such as might happen in a severe recession, also would improve the U.S. trade position by reducing domestic demand for imports. It is unlikely, however, that U.S. fiscal policymakers would seek to create a recession as a means to improve trade; a recession also would generate unacceptable rates of unemployment.

WAGE-PRICE CONTROLS

Wage-price controls are government-imposed regulations that attempt to limit wage and price increases. Some economists advocate their use as a less socially costly and more effective means of curbing inflation than monetary and fiscal restraint.

One proposed use of wage-price controls calls for all annual wage increases and cost-of-living adjustments to be pegged to an inflation projection made by the government for the coming year. Under this proposal, all unions would be required to negotiate wages at the time the projection is made. All government cost-of-living adjustments, such as those made for Social Security payments, also would be made at the time of the projection.

Another long-standing proposal calls for the government to implement a policy to enforce wage-price moderation. Under such a **tax-based income policy,** corporate taxes would increase automatically for companies when their annual wage or price increases exceeds the year's inflation rate. Taxes would automatically decline for companies when their annual wage or price increases are less than the year's inflation rate.

Those in favor of wage-price controls believe that structural changes in the U.S. economy over the last three decades have made wages and prices difficult to restrain through conventional monetary and fiscal policy. They cite the power of the nation's large unions and large industrial firms to set wages and prices as much as three years in advance as a key reason why monetary and fiscal policy cannot control cost-push inflation. Proponents of wage-price controls see them as possibly the only effective way to prevent cost-push inflation before it starts.

Wage-price control advocates also contend that anti-inflationary monetary and fiscal restraint invariably leads to rising unemployment. Proponents believe that such controls would enable the Federal Reserve and the government to avoid this trade-off and implement milder and more evenhanded restraints.

Opponents of wage-price controls argue that such controls contradict the freedom of choice basic to American society. They claim that government regulation of wages and prices distorts private decisions about how to allocate resources. Opponents of wage-price controls also claim that economic inefficiency and market dislocations occur when prices and the profit motive are not allowed to determine the balance between supply and demand.

Opponents of wage-price controls also argue that it would be impossible to impose such a program without having important information leak prematurely to the press and the public. Such information leaks could negate the effectiveness of any such program, they contend, because anticipatory price and wage increases made before the onset of controls could easily negate the anti-inflation impact of the controls.

Finally, opponents of wage-price controls contend that such controls are largely unenforceable. They observe that, apart from the highly visible prices of large firms and the wages negotiated by major unions, it would be exceedingly difficult, if not impossible, to monitor compliance. Opponents question whether the nation's 10 million small businesses and self-employed workers would adhere to such controls. In addition, they note, myriad personal transactions, ranging from doctors' fees to tips on restaurant meals, would largely fall beyond the scope of even the most comprehensive controls program. Moreover, the reasonable and fair administration of a national controls program would require a vast and costly bureaucracy of government examiners, monitors, administrators, and analysts.

INDEXATION

Some economists see indexation as the preferred long-term answer to dealing with inflation in the U.S. economy. Indexation involves the systematic use of cost-of-living escalator clauses in all money-payment contracts.

Under a national program of indexation, all wages, rents, interest payments, profits, taxes, and transfer payments would be tied to cost-of-living escalators so that all monies paid and received would increase proportionally with increases in prices. A 10 percent increase in the price index during the year, for example, would result in a 10 percent increase in wages, rents, interest, profits, taxes, and transfer payments. Indexation would offset any loss in the purchasing power of money with an equivalent increase in the amount of money. Thus, inflation would not result in a redistribution of income or wealth or lead to dislocations in consumer and business spending, savings, and investment patterns. Moreover, because indexation would produce no winners or losers, the government could employ stringent anti-inflation policies with broad political and social support.

A substantial degree of indexation already exists in the U.S. economy. More than 70 million Americans receive at least some part of their income in indexed form (see exhibit 12.7).

Adherents of indexation contend that applying the system nationwide would bring about a more equitable economy because the benefits and burdens of inflation would be borne evenly by everyone. They also claim that indexation would eliminate any business and union incentives to foster inflationary price and wage actions. In addition, it would eliminate consumer and business **inflation hedging,** or the buying up of such nonproductive assets as gold and art objects, which distorts the economy's investment and savings flows.

Opponents of indexation maintain that such a system would institutionalize rather than eliminate inflation. They contend that in an indexed economy, because there are no inflation losers, no social or political pressures would emanate from business or consumer groups for the government to stop inflation. Thus, the government probably would pursue expansionary and stimulative economic objectives. To illustrate this contention, opponents of indexation point to the experience of other countries that employ indexation.

Opponents further contend that a system of national indexation would nullify the benefits of indexation now in place in the U.S. economy for Social Security recipients and other groups that traditionally lose income and wealth during inflation. Because all income earners would receive the same cost-of-living adjustments, each person's relative economic position in the economy would remain frozen. Thus, Social Security recipients would fare as poorly as they had before the indexation of their benefits, which Congress enacted in the 1970s as a means of improving their relative position in an inflationary economy.

Development of any national indexation program faces certain technical problems. These problems include

- the choice of an appropriate index measure
- the treatment of existing payment contracts

Exhibit 12.7 Indexation in the U.S. Economy		
Taxes	*Fully Indexed Programs*	*Private Sector*
• Tax bracket break points	• Social Security	• Rents
• Personal exemption and standard deduction	• Railroad retirement	• Employee compensation
• Earned income tax credit	• Supplemental security income	• Alimony and child-support payments
• Limit on itemized deductions	• Veterans' compensation	
• Pension contribution limits	• Federal military and civilian employee pensions	
• Excess pension distribution tax	• The official poverty line	

Most broad national measures of inflation are based on averages. The consumer price index (CPI) is but one example. Using such a measure as the basis for adjusting incomes likely would generate inequities. Using such a measure as the basis for adjusting incomes likely would generate inequities. For example, people living in high-cost areas would be undercompensated, but those living in low-cost areas would be overcompensated.

Similarly, inequities would result from any attempt to adapt payment contracts made before indexation to the new system. For example, long-term corporate and government bond holders would clearly be at a disadvantage were they locked into non-indexed contractual obligations in an indexed economy. On the other hand, holders of fixed-rate mortgages clearly would be at a disadvantage if their contracts were converted into indexed obligations in a fully indexed economy.

BALANCING FISCAL AND MONETARY POLICY

No single component or tool of fiscal policy, debt management, or balance of payments management is strong enough to control the economy. Containing inflation and countering recession are best accomplished when fiscal policy and monetary policy work in the same direction. The need for balance between monetary policy and fiscal policy is rooted in the different ways the policy tools work and how each policy's strengths offset the other's weaknesses in the economy (see exhibit 12.8).

Exhibit 12.8
Fiscal Policy–Monetary Policy Comparison

	Fiscal Policy	Monetary Policy
Determined by	President of the United States Congress of the United States	Federal Reserve
Tools	Government spending Federal taxes	Reserve requirements Discount rate Open market operations
Use of tools to counter inflation	Increase taxes Reduce government spending	Increase discount rate Raise reserve requirements Sell government securities from open market portfolio
Use of tools to counter recession	Reduce taxes Increase government spending	Reduce discount rate Lower reserve requirements Buy government securities in open market
Initial impact of use of tools	Increase or decrease in consumer take-home pay Increase or decrease in corporate earnings	Increase or decrease in interest rates Increase or decrease in money-supply growth
Major strengths	No operational lag; direct impact on income and spending	No administrative lag; can be implemented immediately
Major weaknesses	Long administrative lag linked to legislative, political process	Largely dependent on bank lending, business/consumer borrowing behavior Indeterminate, possibly long, operational lag

SUMMARY

The federal government relies on government spending and taxing powers as its primary fiscal policy instruments for changing the pace and direction of the economy. An increase in government spending and a reduction in federal taxes act as a strong anti-recessionary stimulus to the economy; a reduction in government spending and an increase in federal taxes act as a powerful anti-inflationary restraint. Fiscal policy has limitations, however, because of the lengthy process required to change federal spending programs or tax laws and the nondiscretionary nature of many government outlays.

Most economists see keeping the federal budget in surplus and reducing the national debt as a critical long-term challenge for the U.S. economy. If fiscal policymakers cannot accomplish these goals, the economy will face increasing competition over limited tax revenues and available credit, and the U.S. standard of living could be affected by increased foreign claims on U.S. output and resources.

The government can use other economic tools to counter recession or contain inflation. One tool is debt management, the actions the U.S. Treasury could take to change the structure and composition of the national debt. These changes can affect interest rates and generate liquidity imbalances that, when corrected, can move the economy out of recession or inflation. Another tool is balance of payments management, the actions that the government can take to ensure a balance in the financial interactions between the United States and the rest of the world. Additional tools the government has used include wage-price controls and indexation, which have been applied to prevent and/or minimize the harmful effects of inflation. Given the competing strengths, weaknesses, and effects of the various fiscal and monetary tools available, most economists agree that using a complementary blend of fiscal and monetary policy is the most effective way to guide the economy's pace and direction.

REVIEW QUESTIONS

1. Outline an appropriate anti-inflationary policy that uses the three monetary and two fiscal policy tools in a complementary way.
2. Why is fiscal policy difficult to implement?
3. What are the three problems that the economy faces if federal debt growth accelerates?
4. How would debt management work if the U.S. Treasury chose to use this power to counter recession or inflation?
5. Explain the relevance of the following balance of payments measures: balance of trade, balance on current account, and official settlements balance.
6. Define wage-price controls and indexation and explain at least one argument for and against each.

ADDITIONAL RESOURCES

"A Citizen's Guide to the Federal Budget," at *www.access.gpo.gov/usbudget/fy2001/guide03.html*. Provides a detailed exposition of the federal budget process; how the federal budget is prepared and the steps that need to be taken before an annual budget becomes law.

"ABA Bank Economist Outlook," at *www.aba.com/Industry+Issues/BankEconomistOutlook.htm*. Provides current economic news, economic data, FOMC activities, articles by bank economists.

The Brookings Institution, at *www.brook.edu/pub/bpea/summ1st.html*. Provides a summary of articles on fiscal policy drawn from presentations made at a Brookings Institute conference on the economy.

Congressional Budget Office, at *www.cbo.gov.* Provides the current fiscal year's budget and economic outlook, a 10-year forecast of U.S. government surpluses or deficits, and a broad range of tax revenue and government expenditure statistics.

International Monetary Fund, at *www.imf.org.* Includes information about the different member countries.

Economics for Financial Service Providers, Jon. A. Hooks, Ph.D., American Bankers Association, 1999. An ABA textbook on economics written for financial services providers.

Public Debt: Private Asset, Federal Reserve Bank of Chicago, 2001, 8pp. Describes the mechanics of government borrowing.

Understanding the Federal Budget, Federal Reserve Bank of New York, 2001, 16 pp. Describes issues surrounding the national debt.

EXERCISE 4: ECONOMIC POLICY PROBLEMS

Write the word *inflation* next to the options appropriate for curbing inflation, and write the word *recession* next to those options appropriate for stopping recession.

1. _____ increasing reserve requirements

2. _____ decreasing reserve requirements

3. _____ buying government securities

4. _____ selling government securities

5. _____ lowering the discount rate

6. _____ raising the discount rate

7. _____ raising taxes

8. _____ lowering taxes

9. _____ increasing government spending

10. _____ reducing government spending

For items 11, 12, and 13, indicate whether total spending would increase, decrease, or remain the same, by writing *I, D,* or *S* next to the statement.

11. _____ Increased government spending is financed by increased taxation.

12. _____ Increased government spending is financed by increased borrowing.

13. _____ Government spending and taxation are reduced.

13

THE ROLE OF BANKS IN INTERNATIONAL TRADE AND INVESTMENT

LEARNING OBJECTIVES

After studying this chapter, you should be able to

- explain how foreign exchange rates are determined and how the foreign exchange market operates
- cite how banks can protect market participants against changes in exchange rates through forward purchase and sale contracts
- describe the key payment and credit instruments used in international trade
- explain why foreign banks seek to operate in the U.S. market
- discuss how foreign banks are regulated in the United States
- define the key terms listed in this chapter

KEY TERMS

bankers' acceptance
cable transfer
euro
export draft
forward purchase contract

forward exchange option
letter of credit
reciprocity
vehicle money

INTRODUCTION

World trade and investment require that banks be able to buy, sell, and transfer foreign currencies internationally on a moment's notice. Banks also provide short-term and long-term financing necessary for effective trade. Banks absorb the risk in international financial transactions by offering market participants foreign exchange purchases and sales for future delivery. This chapter explores the important roles of the U.S. dollar and U.S. banks in international trade and investment. The chapter also looks at foreign exchange rates, the foreign exchange market, and the principal international payment and credit instruments.

It concludes by focusing on foreign banking in the United States and how foreign banks are regulated. This discussion highlights the changing competitive and regulatory environment affecting international banking.

THE U.S. DOLLAR IN THE WORLD ECONOMY

The U.S. dollar is the world's predominant **vehicle money.** That is, the U.S. dollar is the money used by the world's traders and investors in international dealings. The dollar's transcendent role in the world's economy stems from several characteristics of the U.S. economy and financial system.

The United States offers other nations the largest supply of goods and services in the world. According to recent International Monetary Fund data, America produces nearly two-fifths of the gross domestic product (GDP) of the world's industrialized economies and is the world's largest importer and exporter nation. Foreign businesses and consumers that want to purchase U.S. goods and services typically have to pay American suppliers with U.S. dollars. Today little, if any, trade between nations is done by exchanging one good for another.

The United States also offers international traders, investors, and financial institutions the world's largest investment market, with credit instruments covering the entire risk and liquidity spectrum.

The United States also enjoys tremendous political and economic stability, which has generated worldwide confidence in the integrity of the dollar as a medium of exchange and store of value.

FOREIGN EXCHANGE

Foreign exchange consists of foreign currencies, foreign deposit balances in commercial banks, and credit instruments used in trade, such as letters of credit, bankers' acceptances, and bills of exchange, also known as **export drafts.** To U.S. importers and exporters, all monies other than U.S. dollars are foreign exchange. For Japanese importers and exporters, U.S. dollars and all monies other than yen are foreign exchanges. Most of the world's international trade is transacted in U.S. dollars, even when U.S. importers or exporters are not involved. Moreover, most of the world's foreign exchange consists only of the monies of the leading industrial nations, including

- U.S. dollars
- British pounds
- Japanese yen
- European euros

The **euro** is the recently adopted common money of Austria, Belgium, Finland, France, Germany, Greece, Ireland, Italy, Luxembourg, Netherlands, Portugal, and Spain.

FOREIGN EXCHANGE RATES

A foreign exchange rate is the price of one nation's money in terms of another nation's money. Exchange rates are expressed in two ways:

- in terms of how much foreign money can be exchanged for one unit of domestic money
- in terms of how much domestic money can be exchanged for one unit of foreign money

For example, the exchange rate between the U.S. dollar and the euro can be expressed as U.S. $1.00 = 1.15 euros, or 1 euro = U.S. $0.87.

Exchange rates provide a measure of relative value by indicating how many units of one nation's money must be exchanged for one unit of another. In theory, an exchange rate equates the purchasing power value of two different monies. For example, if exchange rates were U.S. $1.00 = 2 British pounds and U.S. $1.00 = 100 Japanese yen, this would mean that 1 British pound would command the equivalent of $0.50 worth of purchasing power in London whereas 1 yen would command the equivalent of only $0.01 of purchasing power in Tokyo.

This example makes it appear that the pound is expensive and the yen inexpensive. This is not the case, however, when prices and costs in England and Japan are matched up. A production worker in Liverpool may receive a weekly wage of 800 pounds, whereas the same job may command 40,000 yen in Kyoto. Both salaries might represent the equivalent of U.S. $400 in purchasing

---

THE EURO

During the 1990s, many of the nations of Europe adopted a plan to establish a single European currency and a single European central bank. The plan was seen as a way to integrate the separate economies of Europe into one system and, in so doing, establish the basis for the future political integration of Europe's countries into one nation.

The plan was adopted by a formal treaty known as the 1991 Maastricht Treaty of European Union. Under this plan, a single European currency, to be called the euro, would reflect the relative weight or value of each European nation's currency. Weights would be based on the size of each nation's economy.

The euro was initially introduced in 1999 as a unit of account for denominating financial asset values and commercial transactions across Europe. Euro currency and coin became the single currency in 2002 after a brief period when the new currency co-circulated with the older domestic currencies of the nations involved. The national monies of the participating European nations, including the German Deutschemark, French franc, and Italian lira, ceased to be legal tender and today no longer exist.

Under the new system, a European central bank manages the euro and is responsible for a common European monetary policy. The countries in the European union no longer conduct their own independent monetary policy. While each country retains control over its own fiscal policy, it cannot change the money supply or change the exchange rate to pursue national economic goals. Moreover, the participating countries are obligated to meet various monetary and fiscal goals to ensure that they keep inflation rates, interest rates, and government budget deficits low.

Not all of the European countries participate in the euro system. Currently 12 member states of the European Union participate in the common currency. They are Austria, Belgium, France, Finland, Germany, Greece, Ireland, Italy, Luxembourg, Portugal, Spain, and the Netherlands. Fearing a possible loss of independence, Denmark, Sweden, and the United Kingdom (which includes Great Britain and Northern Ireland) have opted to retain their individual currencies.

power in their respective countries. Remember that exchange rates reflect the relative purchasing power of various currencies.

Exchange rates are established by supply and demand and, like stock prices, can change periodically throughout the day. They are published daily in the financial press. Banks and dealers normally quote exchange rates to the hundredth or thousandth of a U.S. cent because daily exchange rates typically change in these increments.

EXCHANGE RATE DETERMINATION

Although the purchasing power of money establishes the theoretical basis for determining exchange rates, the interaction between the supply and demand of a nation's money in the foreign exchange market is the real determinant.

For example, assume that the price of 1 euro is U.S. $0.50 ($1.00 will buy 2 euro) and a U.S. importer wants to buy a shipment of French wine that costs 20,000 euro. In order to pay for the wine, the U.S. importer will have to sell $10,000 to buy 20,000 euro for immediate, or spot, delivery. If U.S. demand for euro equals European demand for dollars, the exchange rate will stay at $1.00 for 2 euro. If the American demand for European goods increases and American importers need more euro, with all other supply and demand factors remaining unchanged, the dollar price of euro may be bid up to $1.20 for 2 euro. U.S. importers then would have to pay $12,000, instead of $10,000, for 20,000 euro.

FACTORS THAT INFLUENCE EXCHANGE RATES

Exchange rates are influenced by long-term factors that affect the supply of, and demand for, a nation's money in foreign exchange markets. These factors include

- a nation's domestic inflation rate relative to that of its major trade partners, with a

high inflation rate reducing market demand for the nation's currency
- new technology only available from other countries, with such an occurrence increasing market demand for foreign exchange
- domestic political and economic instability, which can cause the selling of domestic money for foreign money, thereby increasing demand for foreign exchange and driving down the nation's exchange rate

Two additional factors influence exchange rates: a nation's balance of payments position and government intervention. If a nation has a balance of payments deficit, market forces could cause the nation's exchange rate to fall as foreign holders of the money sell it in the foreign exchange market. Conversely, a nation with a payments surplus could experience an increase in its exchange rate as domestic holders sell their excess foreign exchange

The international financial system created in 1944 for the post-World War II global economy was built on the premise that foreign governments would buy and sell foreign exchange. The United States would meet the world's demand for dollars through annual balance of payments deficits generated by U.S. imports, overseas investments, and foreign aid. The United States also would manage the system as a kind of global central bank. Annual U.S. balance of payments deficits mean that more dollars have flowed out of the United States during the year than have flowed in from abroad. Foreign holders of excess dollars bring settlement to the year's balance of payments deficits by either

- buying U.S. financial assets with their excess dollars, or
- selling the dollars in the foreign exchange market for their own money

When dollars are sold, the sales invariably drive down the price of the dollar in foreign exchange markets. The sales also drive up the price of other monies, often above the level that foreign governments have established as being consistent with their domestic and external economic goals. When this occurs, governments intervene in the foreign exchange markets, selling their own money to drive down its price through the purchase of dollars.

The intervention does not eliminate the excess dollars generated by the U.S. balance of payments deficit. It merely transfers the ownership of the excess dollars from private foreign hands, such as corporations and banks, to foreign governments and central banks. Governments typically hold the excess dollars either by purchasing U.S. financial assets or by holding them as part of their nation's international reserves, which are the financial assets that governments throughout the world agree to accept from each other in payment or settlement of debt.

Day-to-day exchange rate fluctuations typically reflect seasonal and temporary factors more than they reflect long-term factors. For example, exports of goods may cluster at certain times of the year, or a nation may receive large payments from corporations sending profits back to their home countries. The bulges in receipts typically strengthen the price of that nation's money in the foreign exchange market if incoming payments are exchanged for domestic money. Conversely, a seasonal burst of imports, or outgoing payments to another country, typically will weaken the price of a nation's money.

Because the U.S. dollar is the standard for defining exchange rates and the world's vehicle money, a change in the price of any money means an equal and opposite change in the price of the dollar. These price changes can mean the difference between profit and loss on any given international trade or investment transaction. This element of risk, present in international commercial dealings, doesn't exist in domestic dealings. Banks play an essential role in facilitating international trade and investment by covering the risks inherent in international transactions. They do this through their daily participation in the foreign exchange market.

THE FOREIGN EXCHANGE MARKET

The foreign exchange market is the institutional setting in which buyers and sellers of foreign exchange transact business. These buyers and sellers include importers, exporters, tourists, international investors, speculators, and on occasion, governments. The market consists mainly of major banks and foreign exchange dealer firms in key financial centers such as New York, London, Tokyo, and Singapore. Most transactions are conducted via telephone and cable, by and through commercial banks.

A cluster of foreign banks with offices in New York and a handful of large New York City banks with branches in other countries conduct the bulk of foreign exchange activity. These banks buy and sell foreign exchange, mainly bank deposits, for corporate and individual customers. The large New York City banks that deal in foreign exchange stand ready to buy or sell any major currency on an ongoing basis, and typically offer favorable terms on large transactions.

Most of the nation's smaller banks do not deal directly in the foreign exchange market. Rather, they meet customer demand by buying foreign exchange from or selling it to their correspondent banks.

Large banks and corporations routinely use foreign exchange brokers to handle large transactions. Foreign exchange broker-dealer firms act as intermediaries, matching up banks holding foreign exchange with those seeking foreign exchange. The largest banks often use brokers and dealers, rather than dealing directly with one another, to save time and remain anonymous until a transaction is arranged. Anonymity prevents competing banks from learning one another's exchange operations and positions.

Foreign exchange brokers do not trade on their own account, but merely arrange transactions for a commission. Today more than half the dollar value of foreign exchange transactions involving banks in the United States is channeled through brokers.

The foreign exchange markets' primary function is to facilitate the transfer of purchasing power internationally from one nation's money to another. Another important function of the market, however, is to provide importers and exporters with short-term credit to finance trade. The market also enables traders and investors to minimize the risk that a given foreign trade or investment could be rendered unprofitable because of an unanticipated change in the foreign exchange rate. This risk is protected against with forward purchases and sales.

Forward Exchange Market

Importers can protect themselves against unexpected cost increases like exchange rates changes that occur after a foreign trade has been negotiated and before payment has been made, by making a **forward purchase contract.** Buying forward involves a foreign exchange purchase at an agreed-upon price, although payment is not made until the bank delivers the foreign exchange at some future date.

Depending on one's expectations about exchange rates, forward purchase contracts may be an attractive option. At any given time, some importers of Japanese products may believe that the spot rate for yen will remain unchanged; others may think the rate will drop, and still others may think that the rate will increase. Not everyone needing yen will go into the foreign exchange market to cover their transactions. Normally a U.S. importer of Japanese goods that expects the price of the dollar to increase with respect to the yen will buy forward. If a rate increase is expected, buyers of forward exchange generally will pay slightly more than the spot rate. The premium size varies with the outlook and is reflected in the one-month, three-month, and six-month forward rates quoted by banks. The premium is larger when a substantial rise is expected and smaller when a small increase is expected.

Exporters who believe the exchange rate is likely to go down can cover that risk by arranging to sell forward. Exporters do this by contracting to sell the foreign exchange they expect to receive at the same time they contract with the foreign buyer. When selling forward, the foreign exchange is sold at an agreed-upon price, but delivery is not made until a future date. By selling forward, U.S. exporters can protect themselves against the risk of a decline in the price of the dollar when they actually receive a foreign currency in payment. If the market anticipates that the exchange rate will fall, exporters will have to sell forward at a discount, or below the spot rate. The forward rate quoted by banks reflects this discount.

Most international trade is not covered by buying-forward or selling-forward arrangements. Most exporters and importers either cannot afford or do not choose to

German note for 500 million marks, circa 1919 to 1923. *Photo courtesy of the Library of Congress, Prints and Photographs Division [LC-USZ62-98364].*

allocate funds to cover exchange-rate risk. Moreover, in some nations the demand for imports is so strong that a price hike induced by a fluctuation in the exchange rate would have little adverse effect on purchases of foreign goods. Thus, importers often cover any foreign exchange losses simply by raising their selling prices.

Importers and exporters who participate in buying-forward or selling-forward arrangements transfer their market risk to banks. The charge for absorbing this risk is included in the price of the forward contract. Some banks try to match forward purchase contracts with forward sales contracts to ensure their market position regardless of the direction an exchange rate changes. Other banks fold customer transactions into their own speculative trading positions.

FORWARD EXCHANGE OPTIONS

Many of the nation's large banks offer corporate customers forward exchange options as an alternative to outright forward purchases and sales as a hedge against exchange-rate risk.

A **forward exchange option** is a type of forward purchase contract that may be, but does not need to be, exercised. Again, it is an arrangement to buy or sell foreign exchange at a future date for a price that is set at the time of the contract. Banks charge for options whether or not they are executed. The fee is usually about 1.5 percent to 5 percent of the contract's value, depending on the term of the option. Forward exchange options allow international traders and investors to protect themselves against unfavorable changes in exchange rates while positioning themselves to benefit from favorable changes.

Assume that a U.S. importer contracts to buy British goods worth $3 million at a time when the spot exchange rate is 1.5 pounds to U.S. $1.00. The importer will have to pay 4.5 million pounds to the British exporter when payment comes due in three months. To protect against exchange-rate risk, the importer can purchase a forward exchange option to buy 4.5 million pounds at 1.5 pounds per U.S. $1.00 at a future time.

Assume that the option costs $100,000 and that over the course of the next three months, the price of the pound falls from 1.5 pounds per U.S. $1.00 to 1.25 pounds per U.S. $1.00. If the importer has no forward contract, or has a forward contract that has not been written as an option, the importer would now have to pay $3.6 million, instead of $3 million, to buy 4.5 million pounds. If the importer has purchased a forward exchange option, however, it can exercise the option to buy the 4.5 million pounds at the agreed-upon price of 1.5 pounds per dollar. By exercising the option, the importer saves $500,000, the savings incurred by the hedging action minus the cost of the option ($600,000 – $100,000).

If, on the other hand, the price of the pound increases from 1.5 pounds to 1.75 pounds per U.S. $1.00 over the three-month period, each dollar would buy more pounds. By not exercising the option, the importer can buy 4.5 million pounds for about $2.6 million, instead of $3 million. Not exercising the option allows the importer to take advantage of the change in the foreign exchange rate, which results in a $300,000 savings, the savings from the lower price of the pounds minus the cost of the option ($400,000 – $100,000).

Under a forward contract, the importer is obligated to buy pounds in the foreign exchange market at the agreed-upon price, regardless of what the market does. An option allows the importer to hedge against a possible loss and benefit from a possible gain.

Banks that sell forward exchange options absorb the risk associated with changes in exchange rates. They typically either reflect this absorption of risk in their premium charges on options or attempt to balance purchase options against sale options.

A sharp change in exchange rates can spell the difference between profit and loss for international traders and investors. The greater the opportunity for changes in exchange rates, the greater the degree of risk. High risk either discourages trade or drives prices higher to finance risk coverage. If exchange rates were allowed to fluctuate so widely that market conditions became disorderly, world trade and investment would suffer. Thus, nations have sought to establish ground rules that allow exchange rates to respond to changing supply and demand conditions, yet prevent fluctuations that would discourage trade and investment.

Freely floating exchange rates, which are rates determined solely by supply and demand, rarely have existed in the real world. Before the 1940s, the international financial system operated under a gold standard in which exchange rates were rigidly fixed, varying only within a very narrow range.

From 1944 to 1971, the Bretton Woods Agreement fixed exchange rates. Under this international agreement, nations were obligated to maintain the price, known as *par value*, of their monies in foreign exchange markets within a range of 1 percent above or below the international price registered with the International Monetary Fund (IMF). To maintain par value within this narrow range, nations were required to intervene frequently in the foreign exchange markets against the forces of supply and demand. They bought their national money to drive its price up or sold their national money to drive its price down.

During the 1970s, the fixed exchange rate system based on government intervention in the foreign exchange markets broke down. Since then, the major industrial nations have opted for a looser form of fixed exchange rates called independent floating, while most nations have adopted programs of either managed floating or pegged exchange rates.

- The United States, Britain, Japan, and 45 other countries that practice independent floating allow the market to determine their exchange rate. Government intervention is aimed only at moderating erratic or excessive fluctuations in the exchange rate, not to establish specific exchange rate levels.
- About 25 nations actively intervene in the foreign exchange market to increase or decrease their nation's exchange rates. This managed floating generally is done without predetermined target levels for the exchange-rate increases or decreases.
- Approximately 45 countries peg their exchange rate to that of one or more of their major trade partners. These nations ensure that the price of their currency will fluctuate in tandem with their partners' currency, thereby maintaining the same relative value. Active government intervention is sometimes used to maintain these pegged rates.

INTERNATIONAL PAYMENTS

The principal payment devices used in international trade are the cable transfer and the export draft. Export drafts are also known as bills of exchange.

A **cable transfer** is an order sent by cable from an importer's bank to a foreign bank. The order directs the foreign bank to pay out a specific sum of foreign money to the exporter. A cable transfer results in an immediate transfer of funds. It differs from a bank draft only in that a written check is not issued or mailed.

Assume, for example, that a U.S. importer agrees to purchase British merchandise for 1.5 million pounds at a time when the exchange rate is U.S. $1.00 to 1.5 pounds. The import firm could phone its bank to request that 1.5 million pounds be paid directly to the exporter. The bank would execute the order through a cable transfer to its London branch or correspondent bank to pay the British exporter 1.5 million pounds. The import firm also could request the funds be deposited directly at the exporter's bank in London.

Another way to handle international payments involves an export draft, or bill of exchange. An export draft is the basic financial instrument used in international trade to buy goods or services from abroad. It works similarly to a check in domestic trade, directing that a specified sum of money be paid. In the example above, the importer buys a British pound draft from the bank and mails it to the British exporter directly. A draft is drawn by the importer's bank against foreign exchange balances it holds in a bank abroad, payable at that bank. Payment is made on receipt of the draft document in the case of a sight draft, or within a certain number of days after receipt in the event of a time draft.

Either the cable transfer or the export draft would result in the transfer of funds from a U.S. bank's balance at a London bank to the British exporter's bank account in England. No currency is shipped with either type of transaction.

Most drafts covering exports from the United States are drawn in U.S. dollars, but they may be drawn in other currencies and routed for collection through U.S. banks. Banks act as agents for exporters when dealing with importers' banks because most export drafts specify that the importer's payment be made to the exporter's bank.

Bills of exchange become foreign exchange credit instruments when exporters sell these drafts to local banks for domestic money rather than sending them and waiting for payment in foreign exchange. The purchasing banks either hold the instruments and collect from the importer or sell the instruments to investors to obtain funds immediately.

BANKERS' ACCEPTANCES

When banks substitute their own credit for that of the importer, the drafts become bankers' acceptances. A **bankers' acceptance** is a time draft drawn on and accepted by the bank on which it is drawn. It usually arises in international trade when there is an underlying obligation for a buyer to make payment to a seller at some future time. The bank that accepts the draft assumes the obligation of making payment at maturity on behalf of the buyer or the buyer's bank.

Assume again that a British exporter negotiates the sale of $1 million worth of merchandise to a U.S. importer. Under the conditions of the sale, the U.S. importer has until 30 days after delivery to make payment. The British exporter needs the funds immediately, however, to cover its production and payroll costs. A bankers' acceptance might be the best option.

The British exporter would make an arrangement involving the U.S. importer, the importer's bank, and the exporter's own London bank. The exporter draws up a time draft on the importer's bank stating that certain goods have been shipped to the U.S. company for which U.S. $1 million, or 1.5 million pounds, is payable 30 days after delivery. The exporter then can sell the draft to the London bank for pounds at the spot exchange rate. The London bank, in turn, sends the draft to the importer's bank in New York, where it is accepted.

By accepting the draft, the importer's bank effectively substitutes its own creditworthiness for that of the importer. On acceptance, the draft becomes payable by the New York bank whether or not the importer pays. Depending on the London bank's preference, the New York bank either will sell the acceptance in the secondary market and pay the London bank, or hold the acceptance until it reaches its due date. At that time, the importer pays the New York bank, which in turn, pays the London bank.

In the United States, large banks typically sell bankers' acceptances in the secondary market in $25,000 lots. This practice enables small banks and consumers to invest in these short-term investment instruments. Acceptances carry reasonably competitive yields in comparison with other money market instruments of comparable maturity.

FINANCING EXPORTS AND IMPORTS

In the United States, international trade is financed mainly through bankers' acceptances and bank loans. U.S. bank loans to foreign importers for the purchase of goods and services from U.S. exporters frequently run as long as 5 years, and in special cases, up to 10 years. Loans to U.S. importers typically are short-term loans and working capital loans.

Commercial banks are the main source of credit for exporters and importers in the United States. Finance companies and other specialized institutions finance some international trade.

Additional financing methods include letters of credit, cash deposits in advance, open-account arrangements, and consignment arrangements.

LETTERS OF CREDIT

A **letter of credit** is a declaration by a bank that it will make payments on behalf of a given party under prearranged conditions. The financial instrument substitutes the bank's credit for the company's credit. It is called a letter because it takes the form of a notification to the party likely to receive the payments. Companies ordering goods from foreign suppliers with whom they have no credit relationship frequently use a letter of credit.

An export letter of credit allows exporters to receive rapid payment for internationally traded merchandise. For example, assume that a German importer has negotiated a multimillion-dollar series

of purchases from a U.S. exporter to take place over the coming year. The German importer has arranged with its bank to establish a letter of credit. The importer's bank would instruct its correspondent bank in New York to inform the U.S. exporter that a letter of credit has been established. On presentation of documents that show a shipment has been made, the letter of credit would authorize the exporter to draw drafts on that bank to receive funds. The exporter's bank would act as the collection agent for the draft.

An import letter of credit is the primary method used to finance commodity imports to the United States. Foreign exporters that lack sufficient information about U.S. importers or are unsure of the importer's credit, often specify a letter of credit as a condition of their trade transaction.

In an import letter of credit, the importer's bank establishes the letter of credit and the terms of the arrangement. If the bank requires a guarantee or collateral for the amount it commits to pay under the letter of credit, this requirement is specified in the letter. If funds are to be issued in foreign exchange, this also is specified. Most imports to the United States are settled in dollars. Today, however, a growing number of transactions are being conducted in the currency of the foreign seller.

CASH IN ADVANCE

Cash payments before merchandise is shipped are used when the credit of a foreign importer is doubtful or when unstable political or economic conditions might delay payment from abroad. Although cash-in-advance arrangements afford the exporter the greatest protection, they place the importer at a significant disadvantage. Moreover, in some countries, exchange controls prohibit prepayments. For these reasons, the volume of international trade conducted on a cash-in-advance basis is small.

OPEN ACCOUNT

In an open-account arrangement, the exporter allows the importer to pay for goods at a specified future date, but without any evidence of the negotiable instrument obligation. Exporting on an open-account basis is simple and avoids the finance-related charges connected with other payment arrangements. But enforcing payment of dishonored open-account transactions often requires complicated legal procedures, and in some countries bankers' acceptances and export draft claims take legal precedence over open-account claims. For these reasons, open-account settlement is used primarily when exporters are dealing with internationally established importers or where legal claims are not likely to arise. Multinational corporations' sales of goods to their own foreign subsidiaries, for example, often are made on open accounts.

CONSIGNMENT

Under a consignment arrangement, goods are transferred but not sold to an importer. The exporter retains title to the goods until they are sold to a third party. Again, because no tangible obligation exists with this arrangement, problems can arise when trying to obtain payment if the importer defaults. Consequently, most companies make consignment arrangements only with their own subsidiaries abroad.

FOREIGN BANKING IN THE UNITED STATES

Foreign banks maintain a substantial presence in the United States. In 2001 foreign banks accounted for 10 percent of all U.S. bank deposits and 20 percent of all business loans. More than 50 countries have established hundreds of offices in the United States, and two-thirds of these offices provide full retail and wholesale banking services.

TYPES OF FOREIGN BANKING OFFICES

Most foreign banks in the United States maintain either a branch office or an agency office. A branch is an office of a foreign bank in the United States that accepts domestic deposits. An agency is an office of a foreign bank that cannot accept deposits from U.S. citizens or residents, but otherwise operates as a full-service bank. There are more than 500 branch and agency offices in the United States today.

Foreign banks operate about 100 bank subsidiaries in the United States. Any banking office in the United States that is owned or controlled by a foreign bank holding company is considered a bank subsidiary. U.S. subsidiaries of foreign banks can operate as full-service banks under the same rules and regulations as banks owned by U.S. bank holding companies.

A few foreign banks operate Edge Act corporations in the United States. These offices engage exclusively in international banking and investment business. They can make loans, accept deposits, and provide full banking services, but only if these activities relate to foreign or international transactions. During the early 1980s, many foreign banks opened Edge Act corporations so that they could operate across state boundaries. By the late 1980s, however, most states had liberalized their branching rules, effectively enabling foreign banks to operate interstate branch offices. As a result, most foreign banks opted to close their Edge Act offices and open new branches and agencies to establish a nationwide banking presence.

Foreign banks maintain more than 200 representative offices in the United States. A representative office cannot accept deposits, make loans, or manage investments. However, a representative office does enable a foreign bank to establish a presence in the United States and to promote the bank's services to U.S. customers. For example, a foreign bank's representative office can provide information and handle administrative matters for U.S. residents who may have dealings abroad. Some foreign banks also establish representative offices as a means of assessing whether U.S. market conditions warrant opening a branch or agency in a particular location in the United States.

REASONS FOR MAINTAINING OVERSEAS OFFICES

U.S. and foreign banks establish overseas offices to provide financial services to domestic customers, usually multinational corporations, that have foreign operations. Foreign banks also maintain a substantial U.S. banking presence because of the role of the U.S. dollar in international finance, and the size and prominence of the U.S. economy and financial markets. A related reason is the desire to acquire a dollar base or to better manage the dollar position of the parent bank.

The U.S. dollar is the world's principal currency for international transactions, and about 80 percent of international lending is in U.S. dollars. By holding a substantial dollar base in the United States, foreign banks generally can pay less for dollar funds than if they were acquired on an ad hoc basis from abroad. Thus, foreign banks with a presence in the United States have an advantage over other foreign banks when structuring loan charges to their customers.

Foreign banks also establish offices in the United States to more effectively finance exports by their domestic customers. Foreign banks with a U.S. office can better service their corporate clients when dealing with letters of credit, export drafts, bankers' acceptances, international money transfers, and foreign exchange. Access to the world's largest pool of investment capital and financial instruments enables foreign banks with U.S. offices to provide better investment services to their corporate clients.

In addition, a U.S. banking office enables foreign banks to develop a retail banking business in the world's largest financial market.

Japan and the European countries have established the largest full-service banking presence in the United States. That is not surprising given the large size of Japanese and European banks. Of the 30 largest banks in the world, 17 percent are Japanese banks and 70 percent are European banks (see exhibit 13.1).

FOREIGN BANKS AS U.S. LENDERS

Foreign banks have become major lenders to U.S. business firms largely by purchasing business loans from U.S. banks. During the 1980s, large U.S. banks began selling off substantial portions of their business loan portfolios to boost profits. The major buyers of these loans were foreign banks' U.S. offices. Today the combination of the loan purchases in the 1980s and new loans made in the 1990s have boosted foreign bank holdings of U.S. business loans to 20 percent.

Foreign banks became avid purchasers of U.S. banks' business loans because these loan acquisitions enabled them to quickly build up their loan portfolios with quality assets they would have been unlikely to book on their own. The major purchasers were large Japanese banks in the United States. These large banks, in turn, generally participated, or shared, in the loans they acquired with other, smaller Japanese banks in the United States.

Foreign banks' market share of U.S. business loans understates the importance of foreign lending in this country. Most foreign branches and agencies make a wide variety of loans to U.S. banks and other financial institutions, to securities brokers and dealers, and to individuals. Many foreign banks also make loans to the United States from offshore offices that are not counted in U.S. statistics, such as those located in the Cayman Islands.

Exhibit 13.1
The 30 Largest Banking Companies in the World, 2002 (by geographic grouping)

Company Name	City
European Banks	
Deutsche Bank	Frankfurt
Allianz AG	Munich
UBS AG	Zurich
BNP Paribas	Paris
HSBC Holdings PLC	London
Bayerische Hypo-und Vereinsbanken AG	Munich
ING Group NV	Amsterdam
Credit Suisse Group	Zurich
Royal Bank of Scotland Group PLC	Edinburgh
ABN Amro Holding NV	Amsterdam
Barclays PLC	London
Société Générale	Paris
HBOS PLC	Edinburgh
Commerzbank	Frankfurt
Credit Agricole SA	Paris
Axa	Paris
Fortis	Utrecht
Westdeutsche Landesbank Girozentrate	Dusseldorf
Lloyds TBS Group PLC	London
Rabobank Group	Utrecht
Dexia	Brussels
Japanese Banks	
Mizuho Holdings	Tokyo
Mitsubishi Tokyo Financial Group	Tokyo
UFJ Holdings	Osaka
Sumitomo Mitsui Banking Corp.	Tokyo
Norinchukin Bank	Tokyo
U.S. Banks	
Citigroup Inc.	New York, New York
J.P. Morgan Chase & Co.	New York, New York
Bank of America Corp.	Charlotte, North Carolina
Wachovia	Charlotte, North Carolina

U.S. REGULATION OF FOREIGN BANKS

Foreign banks operating in the United States are subject to federal banking regulation and examination. Since 1978 they also have been accorded national treatment, which means they have the same powers and are subject to the same restrictions as domestic banks. Before 1978 foreign banks in the United States were not subject to most U.S. banking laws and, as a result, had a number of competitive advantages over U.S. banks.

INTERNATIONAL BANKING ACT

The International Banking Act of 1978 ended several years of national debate on the inequities between the treatment of foreign and domestic banks in the United States. The act made a number of major changes. The act

- prohibited any new interstate branching for foreign banks, although it grandfathered those foreign banks that already had branch offices in more than one state

- gave foreign bank agencies and branches the option of giving up their state banking charters and obtaining a federal charter from the Office of the Comptroller of the Currency (OCC)
- imposed the Federal Reserve's reserve requirements on foreign agencies and branches
- required foreign bank branches with retail deposit operations to obtain federal deposit insurance and pay Federal Deposit Insurance Corporation (FDIC) insurance premiums
- subjected foreign banks' non-banking activities to the same restrictions as those applicable to U.S. banks' non-banking activities
- divided the general supervision of foreign banks among the federal regulators

Imposing reserve requirements on foreign banks with U.S. offices was done to both strengthen U.S. monetary policy control and establish competitive equity between domestic banks and foreign banks. Before 1978 the U.S. offices of foreign banks were not subject to reserve requirements, and thus were inherently more profitable than their domestic counterparts.

The most notable restriction on non-banking activities by foreign banks was the prohibition on owning and operating investment banking and securities affiliates. Foreign banks that had established investment and securities affiliates before 1978, however, were not required to divest them.

With regard to supervision, the Federal Reserve was given authority to examine any foreign branch or agency. The Comptroller of the Currency supervises branches or agencies with a federal charter; the FDIC and the states supervise those with FDIC insurance; and the Federal Reserve and the states supervise those without FDIC coverage.

The International Banking Act went a long way toward equalizing the rules under which American banks and the U.S. agencies and branches of foreign banks compete in U.S. banking markets.

FOREIGN BANK SUPERVISION ENHANCEMENT ACT

In 1991 Congress passed the Foreign Bank Supervision Enhancement Act, imposing regulations on foreign banks that wanted to establish banking offices in the United States or expand existing U.S. operations. Foreign banks also were subject to new examination requirements.

Before 1991 foreign banks had only to meet state licensing requirements. Since passage of the Enhancement Act, all foreign banks that want to establish new branches or agencies in the United States must obtain approval from the Federal Reserve. As a condition of approval, the Federal Reserve must determine whether a foreign bank applying to open a new branch or agency is subject to comprehensive global regulation by its home country. If the Federal Reserve finds that home country supervision is not sufficiently broad, the approval is denied. Foreign banks with existing branches and agencies in the United States also are subject to this provision of the act. They, too, must demonstrate that their home country's regulators provide comprehensive supervision. If not, the Federal Reserve is required to close all of their U.S. offices.

The Enhancement Act designates the Federal Reserve as the primary regulator of all foreign bank branches, agencies, subsidiaries, and representative offices in this country. Except for representative offices, each foreign office must be examined at least annually.

POLICY OF RECIPROCITY

The policy of national treatment embodied in the International Banking Act muted, but did not end, the controversy over an alternative policy for regulating foreign banks in the United States. This policy, known as the policy of **reciprocity**, advocates that foreign banks receive the same regulatory treatment that foreign countries adopt for the treatment of U.S. banks. Thus, banks from countries with liberal banking laws would receive liberal treatment in the United States, whereas banks from countries with restrictive laws would be regulated restrictively.

Congress rejected a policy of reciprocity in 1978 because it seemed inconsistent with our government's pro-competitive philosophy. Implementation of such a policy was also seen as impractical. U.S. banks are exposed to such disparate regulatory treatment throughout the world that any reciprocity-based law for foreign banks would lead to a complex body of divergent rules. It also could create competitive inequities between U.S. banks and U.S. offices of foreign banks.

Many developing countries either prohibit foreign bank ownership of indigenous banks or limit a foreign banking presence in their countries. They do this by law, current policy, or administrative practice. For example, Cuba, Ethiopia, Libya, Iraq, and Pakistan prohibit all forms of foreign bank presence or ownership. Syria, Venezuela, and Colombia are countries that permit a foreign banking presence only through a representative office.

Some countries permit foreign control of indigenous banks to varying degrees (see exhibit 13.2 on the following page). Many countries also impose exchange controls that limit or restrict the movement of foreign exchange or domestic funds into or out of the country. Exchange controls tend to benefit domestic banks because they do not need to return earnings or profits to a parent bank in another country.

Countries that do not follow a policy of reciprocity in their dealings with U.S. and other foreign banks make this choice for a number of reasons. Developing countries often seek to protect their fledgling banks against competition from the larger, stronger banks of industrial nations. In theory, such protection gives the developing banks time to establish the necessary operating efficiencies and financial strength to compete. Some countries see any U.S. or foreign banking presence as a political and economic threat to their national sovereignty. Others seek to protect the narrow financial interest of indigenous bankers, who in many countries hold political as well as financial power.

Many industrial countries contend that their restrictions on foreign banks strengthen their domestic monetary policy control and their control over the nation's foreign exchange market and foreign exchange rate. Other countries see foreign banking restrictions as a means of insulating the domestic financial system from any external risks associated with the operations and activities of foreign banking offices.

SUMMARY

U.S. balance of payments deficits result in other nations either holding U.S. dollars or dollar investments or selling dollars for some other money or financial asset. The effects of such settlements are reflected in foreign exchange rates.

In theory, foreign exchange rates equate the relative purchasing power of different monies. In reality, the interaction of currency supply and demand in the foreign exchange market is a powerful determinant of exchange rates. The resulting fluctuations in exchange rates spell the difference between profit and loss for international traders and investors.

Banks provide a way for exporters and importers to protect themselves from exchange rate losses through forward purchase or forward sale contracts and options. As important participants in the world's foreign exchange markets, banks also transfer money internationally and provide importers and exporters with short-term credit. Foreign deposit balances in banks, which can be transferred by cable or export drafts, along with credit instruments provided by banks, such as letters of credit and bankers' acceptances, constitute

Exhibit 13.2
Countries that Permit Foreign Control of Indigenous Banks

Specific Amount of Foreign Participation Allowed by Law	Specific Amount of Foreign Participation Allowed in Practice	No Majority Control and No Specific Maximum
Australia	Bahrain	Central African Republic
Bermuda	Dominican Republic	Cyprus
Burkina Faso	Greece	Egypt
Canada	Iceland	Ireland
Congo	Morocco	Malaysia
Denmark	Oman	Malta
Ecuador	Qatar	Netherlands
Finland	Singapore	Tunisia
Gambia	South Africa	
Japan	United Kingdom	
Nigeria		
Philippines		
South Korea		

No Limit on Foreign Control of Indigenous Banks

Argentina	France	Niger
Austria	Gabon	Panama
Bahamas	Ghana	Paraguay
Barbados	Honduras	Rwanda
Belgium	Hong Kong	Senegal
Belize	Israel	Seychelles
Bolivia	Italy	Sierra Leone
Botswana	Ivory Coast	Spain
Burundi	Jamaica	Sri Lanka
Cameroon	Kenya	Sudan
Cape Verde	Lebanon	Switzerland
Cayman Islands	Luxembourg	Uruguay
Chile	Mali	Germany
Costa Rica	Mauritania	Zaire
Djibouti	Mauritius	Zambia
Fiji	Mozambique	

the principal payment items used in international trade.

Foreign banks maintain a substantial presence in the United States and have acquired a significant share of U.S. deposits and U.S. business loans. The United States follows a policy of equal regulatory treatment for domestic and foreign banks rather than a policy of reciprocity. Foreign banks operating in the United States today are subject to the same regulations and restrictions that apply to U.S. banks. Before 1978, however, foreign banks were not subject to most U.S. banking laws and enjoyed competitive advantages over domestic banks. During the 1990s, Congress imposed stricter federal oversight on foreign bank activities in this country.

REVIEW QUESTIONS

1. How are foreign exchange rates determined? Suggest three factors that would likely increase or decrease supply or demand for U.S. dollars in European exchange markets.

2. What are the three primary functions of the foreign exchange market?
3. Why would a U.S. exporter sell foreign exchange forward? Under what conditions would it be advantageous for a U.S. importer to buy foreign exchange forward?
4. What is a bankers' acceptance? How does a bankers' acceptance differ from a letter of credit?
5. Cite at least three reasons why foreign banks maintain branches, agencies, and other banking offices in the United States.

ADDITIONAL RESOURCES

Bank for International Settlement, at *www.bis.org*. Provides access to the annual report of the Bank for International Settlements, which discusses current international financial market developments.

The Federal Reserve Bank of New York, at *http://www.ny.frb.org/bankinfo/circular/ 10863.html*. Provides the text of Regulation K that governs the international banking operations of U.S. banks and the operations of foreign banks in the United States.

The Foreign Exchange Market in the U.S., Federal Reserve Bank of New York, 1998, 125 pp. Provides an in-depth expedition of the workings of the U.S. foreign exchange market.

Global Banking, American Bankers Association, 1999, textbook. Describes the services and lending practices of international banks.

International Economic Trends, Federal Reserve Bank of St. Louis, quarterly publication. Provides data on U.S. international transactions.

"U.S. International Transactions in 2001," *Federal Reserve Bulletin*, May 2002. Reviews U.S. balance of payments performance in 2001 and prospects for 2002.

ANSWERS TO REVIEW QUESTIONS

CHAPTER 1: MONEY

1. *Briefly describe the three functions of money. Explain which function, if any, holds the greatest importance.*

   Money's basic function is to serve as a medium of exchange: an item that is generally accepted in exchange for goods and services or in the settlement of debt. Money's second function is to serve as a unit of account, a standard of measurement for determining the value of goods and services. Money's third function is to serve as a store of value, a means of holding and accumulating the power to purchase goods and services in the future. To qualify as money, an item first must be accepted generally as a nation's medium of exchange; however, all three functions of money must be met adequately if a chosen from of money is to succeed.

2. *What is the difference between barter and the use of commodity money?*

   In a barter transaction, certain goods and services are accepted in exchange for others based on the mutual needs of the participants. In a commodity money transaction, goods and services can be bought without the necessity of exchanging other goods and services. Commodity money is similar to barter, however, in that the use of commodity money as an exchange medium is based on its inherent value rather than its representational value or national backing.

3. *"Gold as a commodity money would be a poor medium of exchange in today's American economy." Do you agree or disagree? Explain your answer.*

   Gold would be an inefficient and impractical medium of exchange for the millions of transactions involved in today's economy because it is not readily divisible, portable, or easy to protect.

4. *Must fiat money be designated as legal tender by a government in order for it to be generally accepted as a nation's money? Does legal tender status ensure the general acceptability of money? Does government insurance for deposit money affect its acceptability as money? Explain your answers.*

No. For example, in the United States, only coin and currency have legal tender status, but checkable deposits are the preferred means of payment today. While legal tender status is usually necessary for fiat money to be generally accepted by a nation, legal tender status does not guarantee national acceptance. The society must be assured first that the designated money will be a good standard and store of value. Government insurance for deposit money increases its acceptability because it assures the protection of individual deposits up to a certain limit. Deposit insurance, together with government supervision, has supplanted the public's reliance on legal tender status with confidence in the safety and soundness of the United States' banking system.

5. *What are the basic differences between the M1, M2, and M3 measures of money supply?*

Each of these money supply measures is progressively broader in its attempt to count all of the funds the public has immediately available for spending. M1 is the narrowest measure. It counts all mediums of exchange, principally cash, demand deposits, and interest-earning checkable deposits at banks and savings institutions. M2 is a broader measure. It includes all of the items counted in M1, plus near-monies that are close substitutes for money, most notably time and savings deposits at banks and savings institutions. M3 is a still broader measure. It includes all of the monies and near-monies counted in M1 and M2, plus certain highly liquid assets used primarily by big business firms, such as large-denomination certificates of deposit and eurodollar deposits held abroad.

CHAPTER 2: MONEY AND ECONOMIC ACTIVITY

1. *How does the economy benefit when consumers place their savings in banks and other financial intermediaries instead of holding their savings as cash?*

Savings represent a leakage from the economy's circular flow of income and spending. If all savings were held as cash, the economic system might spiral down into a recession; without an infusion of new money, sales would decline, production would be cut, and laid-off workers would spend less. When consumers hold their savings in depositories and investments, banks and other financial intermediaries are able to inject this money back into the economy through loans that enable individuals, businesses, and governments to spend more than they currently have. This keeps the economy in balance.

2. *What functions do financial intermediaries, brokers, and dealers perform that lenders and borrowers could not perform for themselves?*

Financial intermediaries, brokers, and dealers act as middlemen in transactions between lenders and borrowers. By providing established active markets for such transactions, they ensure the rapid and efficient flow of credit throughout the economic sectors of the country.

3. *What would be the economic and financial consequences if consumers and businesses could not obtain credit from financial intermediaries?*

Credit from financial intermediaries enables consumers and businesses to spend more than their current incomes would allow. If purchases had to be financed solely with savings or current income, fewer consumers would be able to buy big-ticket items like cars, houses, or vacations. Businesses would probably be unable to replace obsolete machinery or buy inventories of raw materials needed to sustain high-level production. In short, if consumers and businesses could not obtain credit, the U.S. economy would not grow.

4. *Why does the Federal Reserve focus primarily on controlling commercial bank lending as opposed to other financial intermediary lending?*

The Federal Reserve focuses primarily on controlling commercial bank lending because commercial banks traditionally were the only intermediaries that could create new demand deposit money. The lending process of commercial banks creates an increasing number of demand deposits throughout the economy. By using its monetary policy to influence the amount of money that banks create through lending, the Federal Reserve is able to help prevent the creation of too much money in the economy, which could lead to inflation, or the creation of too little, which could lead to recession.

5. *How and why do rising interest rates differently affect consumer, business, and government borrowers?*

For consumers, rising interest rates mean higher rates on mortgages, auto loans and installment credit. Consumers may find it harder to obtain auto loans and other installment credit because state usury laws limit maximum rates on consumer loans, making it more profitable for lenders to divert available funds to business loans not subject to the usury limits. Faced with higher mortgage rates and difficulty in obtaining installment credit, consumers' purchases of houses, and other big-ticket items decline.

Large corporations tend to be less concerned with rising interest rates because they can finance their capital spending through bond sales or retained earnings, thereby bypassing the banking system. Small or new businesses, however, may find that they cannot afford the higher interest rates on loans.

Rising interest rates affect government entities in a variety of ways. State and local governments, unlike the federal government, are often bound by maximum interest rates or limits to their tax base; therefore, they frequently stay out of the credit markets when money becomes tight.

CHAPTER 3: BANKS AND MONEY CREATION

1. *Explain the use of T-accounts in analyzing the lending process of banks.*

A T-account shows how a single transaction changes a bank's balance sheet without the need to construct a full balance sheet. A T-account shows only the asset or liability account affected by a transaction. Plus or minus signs are used to indicate account increases or decreases. A T-account must balance, with equal pluses (or minuses) on opposite sides, or with offsetting pluses and minuses on the same side. In analyzing commercial bank lending, the T-account shows how cash assets, demand deposits, and required and excess reserves are affected by a loan transaction.

2. *Evaluate this statement: "As my bank's commercial loan officer, I do not create money; I simply lend out the money that depositors have placed in the bank."*

This statement is inaccurate. Commercial loan officers do not lend out depositors' funds; they use depositors' funds as a base on which to create money in the form of a new demand deposit balance for the receiver (business borrower) of the loan. Whenever a bank takes in cash deposits, it must set aside an amount to meet reserve requirements. The bank can then make loans equal to the remainder, called the excess reserves. The bank accepts the borrower's debt obligation as an asset and creates a demand deposit balance in the amount of the loan as a liability. Thus, a new loan increases both the bank's assets and its liabilities.

3. *If there were no reserve requirements, could banks create an infinite amount of demand deposits? Why or why not?*

No. In theory, if a bank were not subject to reserve requirements, it could make new loans and create new demand deposits using every dollar it held as cash assets. However, when the proceeds of these new loans were disbursed and the loan funds were transferred through the check collection process, the bank would lose a dollar in cash assets for every dollar it had created.

Apart from the legal requirement to hold back reserves, banks need to hold a percentage of their assets as cash or on deposit with other banks in order to maintain the liquidity necessary to meet cash withdrawals and pay the claims of other banks presenting depositors' checks for collection. Without setting aside such reserves, banks would soon find themselves without the necessary liquidity to operate as depository institutions.

4. *How can a bank that finds itself with a reserve deficiency obtain new reserves? Would these options work if the entire banking system needed additional reserves? Explain your answers.*

A bank with a reserve deficiency can pursue several options to obtain new reserves. It can borrow federal funds from other banks, borrow from the central bank, sell the government securities it holds as secondary reserve assets in its investment portfolio, call in loans, or make some other adjustment in its assets and liabilities.

However, only one of these options—borrowing from the central bank—would work if the entire banking system needed additional reserves. The other options essentially are adjustments that redistribute an existing reserve deficiency throughout the banking system. In such redistributions, the repayment of bank loans does not result in the making of new loans and the concurrent creation of new demand deposits because the system does not gain any excess reserves. The entire banking system can meet a reserve deficiency only with an infusion of reserves from outside the system, by borrowing from the Federal Reserve.

5. *How do banks use federal funds transactions to adjust their reserves?*

Federal funds are reserves that banks buy from or sell to one another on a daily basis. These transactions are the most popular method used by large banks to obtain needed reserves to fund loans or meet reserve requirements, or to sell reserves in excess of current needs. As banks compete for reserves to expand their own loan and investment portfolios, the cost of federal finds increases. In order to pay the increased cost of borrowing reserves, a bank that wants to expand its earning assets must charge more on loans and earn more on its investments.

EXERCISE 1: MULTIPLE EXPANSION OF BANK DEPOSITS

1. $\dfrac{1}{\text{reserve requirement}} \times$ initial deposit = total deposits.

2. The multiplier, or expansion coefficient, is 12.5.

3. Following is how the chart should be filled in, based on the information for the exercise:

Multiple Expansion of Bank Deposits

Bank Position	New Deposits	New Loans and Investments	Required Reserves
Bank One	$100,000	$92,000	$8,000
Bank Two	92,000	84,640	7,360
Bank Three	84,640	77,869	6,771
Sum of first three banks' deposit expansion	276,640	254,509	22,131
Sum of remaining banks' deposit expansion	973,360	895,491	77,869
Total for banking system	1,250,000	1,150,000	100,000

CHAPTER 4: FINANCIAL MARKETS AND FINANCIAL INTERMEDIARIES

1. *What are the major differences between commercial banks and savings banks, credit unions, and money market funds?*

Commercial banks, savings banks, and credit unions are all depository financial intermediaries, unlike money market funds, which are technically investment companies that purchase securities for individual or institutional investors. Most legal differences between banks and savings institutions have been eliminated and today the business activities and products of commercial banks and savings banks overlap significantly. The primary activities of commercial banks traditionally have been accepting demand deposits and making loans to businesses, thereby creating demand deposit dollars. Savings banks traditionally have held most of their assets in residential mortgage loans.

Credit unions are cooperatives whose members purchase savings shares and can then borrow from the pooled savings of members. Credit unions are considered nonprofits and thus are not subject to most taxes. They have a competitive advantage over banks in lending rates because of this status as well as their low overhead and labor costs.

Money market funds hold a considerable percentage of the funds that flow from consumers and businesses into the financial markets. Money market funds generally offer higher interest rates than banks and thrifts, because they invest in higher-risk investment instruments. Money market funds are mutual fund investment companies specializing in short-term investments, such as certificates of deposit, commercial paper, bankers' acceptances, and U.S. Treasury Bills.

2. *What competitive advantages, if any, do nondepository intermediaries such as Merrill Lynch and General Electric have over commercial banks?*

Nondepository intermediaries whose primary business is not lending or deposit taking are essentially nonfinancial intermediaries. Such businesses have nationwide distribution outlets, which give them greater marketing capabilities than commercial banks. They also are not subject to the same regulations governing lending and investing. Until 1999, when banking law was changed, these intermediaries were able to provide financial services that were restricted for banks. However, the Gramm-Leach-Bliley Act of 1999 allows commercial banks, insurance companies, brokerage firms and securities dealer firms to affiliate under common ownership and offer customers a complete range of financial services.

3. *What are the major types of time deposits offered by commercial banks?*

The major types of time deposits offered by commercial banks include small-denomination certificates of deposit, such as six-month CDs; money market deposits; large-denomination time deposits of $100,000 or more; passbook or statement savings deposits; and IRAs and other retirement accounts.

4. *Explain how a money market deposit account operates.*

Money market deposit accounts (MMDAs) are time deposits on which depositors can make up to six transfers, using three checks and three preauthorized transfers, each month. The accounts carry no minimum maturity, but banks may require seven days' notice of withdrawal. MMDAs are not subject to minimum balance requirements but most require balances from $500 to $2,500. Unlike money market funds, MMDAs are government insured through the Federal Deposit Insurance Corporation.

5. *Cite three changes in the deposit structure or operations of financial intermediaries that occurred during the 1980s.*

One change was that savings banks and savings and loan associations were given the same powers as commercial banks to issue credit cards, to offer NOW accounts, and to make business loans. Another change was that mutual savings banks were given the option of changing from mutual to stock-issuing corporate organizations so that they could raise needed capital and more strongly compete with other financial intermediaries. A third change was the introduction of interest-bearing checking accounts and the rapid growth and popularity of the money market deposit account.

CHAPTER 5: THE BANK AS A BUSINESS FIRM

1. *What major expense items appear on the bank income statement?*

The largest expense item is the interest banks pay on time deposits. Other major expense items appear in the noninterest expense category. These items include salaries and benefits, occupancy expenses, the fees banks pay to other companies for outsourced services and consultants, and merger-related costs. Still another item that can be a major source of expense at times is the loan loss provision. A bank's profitability can be significantly impaired by setting aside large amounts of loan loss reserves against the prospect of future loan losses.

2. *Cite the three largest loan categories on commercial banks' books and two characteristics that differentiate each of those loan categories.*

The three largest loan categories are business loans, real estate loans, and consumer loans. Business loans are typically short-term loans that carry low processing costs and relatively low risk. They can be single-payment or installment loans, secured by collateral or unsecured. Not subject to usury limits in most states, these loans offer considerable pricing flexibility but generally low yields. They may involve loan commitment fees or require compensating balances.

Real estate loans are classified by type of collateral rather than intended purpose. Because they are fully collateralized, they are among the lowest-risk loans. However, the earnings yields on real estate loans are typically lower than the yields on most other loans. Consumer loans, particularly credit card loans, carry relatively greater credit risk than other loans and carry relatively higher processing costs. Because repayment of principal and interest on consumer loans is typically made on a scheduled basis, most consumer loans also generate a predictable cash flow return to the lending bank.

3.   *Why would a business firm pay a loan commitment fee? Why would a bank impose a compensating balance on a loan? Why would a bank participate in a loan with another bank?*

Business firms pay loan commitment fees in exchange for the preauthorization of a loan to be made weeks or months ahead. Preauthorization provides the company with the assurance that credit will be available when the company needs it.

Banks impose compensating balances on loans to increase their profitability; by investing the compensating balances, banks increase their return on the loans. Compensating balances also give banks extra protection in the case of default because existing deposit balances can be used to offset outstanding loan balances.

Loan participations enable smaller banks to undertake loans that otherwise would be too large. Participating banks commit fewer reserves and take on less risk. Also, banks can participate in large loans that would be legally prohibited otherwise. Correspondent banks participate in large business loans as part of their respondent relationships and to diversify their own portfolios.

4.   *Why do banks buy securities? Explain the difference between U.S. Treasury securities, federal agency securities, and municipal obligations.*

Banks buy securities to provide a secondary source of liquidity, to earn interest income and capital gains, and to counterbalance risks taken in bank lending. Bank purchases of local government securities also help to promote account and deposit relationships. Banks also use securities to meet pledging requirements against trust operations and as collateral for government deposits.

U.S. Treasury securities include Treasury bills, notes, and bonds. They are free of credit risk, traded in a large secondary market, and their income is exempt from state and local taxes. Banks use Treasury securities as short-term investments and as a secondary source of liquidity for expected and unexpected demands for funds.

Federal agency obligations are issues of federally owned or sponsored agencies and corporations. They are second only to Treasury securities in safety and marketability, and offer somewhat higher yields. Some provide income free from state and local taxes.

State and local obligations (municipal securities) include short-term tax anticipation notes and tax warrants and long-term bonds issued by state and local governments and their agencies. These obligations are higher in credit risk than Treasury or federal agency securities. Municipal securities pay lower interest returns than other securities, but income earned on these issues is exempt from federal income tax.

5. *What are the objectives of an asset allocation strategy?*

The overall objective of an asset allocation strategy is to expand bank earnings by continually reallocating bank assets. After meeting the bank's operating and fixed-asset expenses, bankers using the asset allocation strategy allocate funds in four ways to achieve various objectives: first to primary reserves in order to meet reserve requirements and daily liquidity needs; next to secondary reserves based on the bank's forecasted loan and deposit growth over the coming year; then to the bank's income account (loan portfolio) to meet all loan demand; and finally to the bank's residual account to make investments in securities.

6. *What is liability management? If you were in charge of liability management at your bank, what sources of managed liabilities would you rely on and why?*

Liability management involves the use of borrowed or purchased money to fund loan and investment growth. Banks using this approach try to fund a desired increase in their assets by increasing their liabilities. If I were in charge of my bank's liability management, I would rely on borrowing federal funds, issuing negotiable certificates of deposit, borrowing Eurodollars, using the proceeds of commercial paper sold by affiliates, engaging in repurchase agreements, and selling loans under repurchase agreements. I would rely on these liabilities because they can be directly controlled by the bank.

7. *What tactics can be used to implement a spread management strategy?*

Maturity matching, duration matching, and variable rate pricing of all loans and deposits are three tactical approaches that a bank can use to match its assets and liabilities for the purpose of maintaining a constant interest rate spread. In maturity matching, bankers attempt to match the maturities of specific deposit liabilities with loan and investment maturities. In duration matching, bankers attempt to match their assets and liabilities based on the average length of time that these items are expected to remain on the balance sheet. In imposing variable rates on both loans and deposits, bankers seek to protect the bank's spread from unexpected interest rate changes. Since both deposit rates and loan charges are increased or decreased in tandem, a bank's interest spread remains constant whether interest rates go up or down.

EXERCISE 2: BALANCE SHEET PROBLEMS

PROBLEM 1

Based on this balance sheet, First Commercial Bank's

1. primary reserves are $10,000 (cash + reserve accounts + correspondent deposits)
2. secondary reserves are $30,000 (securities)
3. total reserves are $8,000 (cash and reserve account)
4. required reserves are $4,000 (10 percent of transaction deposits)

5. earning assets are $70,000 (loans + securities)
6. First Commercial could create $4,000 of new money.
   (total reserves–required reserves)

PROBLEM 2

Based on this balance sheet, National Community's

1. excess reserves are $18,740 (total reserves – required reserves)
2. secondary reserves are $100,000 (federal agency securities)
3. required reserves are $15,260 (10 percent of total transaction deposits: private, bank, and U.S. government)
4. total reserves are $34,000 (vault cash + Federal Reserve balances)
5. earning assets are $370,000 (loans + federal agency securities)

EXERCISE 3: PERFORMANCE RATIO PROBLEM

Based on the balance sheet and the income statement, Second Community Bank's

1. return on assets (net income/assets) is 1.01 percent
2. return on equity (net income/equity) is 14.28 percent
3. ratio of capital to assets (equity/assets) is 7.10 percent
4. ratio of loans to deposits (loans/deposits) is 48.64 percent
5. Interest expenses represent 82.29 percent of Second Community Bank's total operating expenses.
6. Salaries and benefits represent 13.58 percent of Second Community Bank's total operating expenses.
7. Other information needed to assess Second Community Bank's performance is a qualitative evaluation of management performance.

CHAPTER 6: BANK OPERATIONS AND THE PAYMENTS SYSTEM

1. *Why is it not advantageous for a bank to have cash on hand in excess of its daily needs?*

   Although a primary responsibility of banks is satisfying the public's need for cash, a bank that holds excess cash misses revenue opportunities because idle cash earns nothing. Excess cash on hand also presents storage and security problems.

2. *What are the three basic ways that interbank checks are collected in the United States? What factors determine a bank's choice of a collection option?*

   U.S. banks collect interbank checks through local clearing houses, correspondent banks, and the Federal Reserve. Clearing houses are used by banks in a given area that regularly receive checks drawn on each other. The clearing house arrangement cuts the cost of transporting and presenting checks to numerous other banks. Correspondent banks are used for check collection by smaller banks that do not own reader-sorter machines or that do not have direct account relationships with the Federal Reserve. Larger banks and correspondent banks that require interregional collection clear checks directly through Federal Reserve banks. Two major factors determine a bank's collection choice: 1) which option costs the least, and 2) which option results in the quickest credit of the checks presented for collection.

3. *Explain how a local clearing house operates and the advantages it offers for clearing checks.*

In a clearing house arrangement, representatives from participating banks meet at a convenient, usually central, site. There they exchange and collect payment for local checks. Collection is made by netting the amounts presented by each bank against the others. At major regional clearing houses, settlement for the transactions is made against the Federal Reserve accounts of participating banks. The advantage of the clearing house arrangement is that banks need not transport and present checks individually to numerous other banks. This—and the fact that a bank need only maintain one low-balance clearing account for check settlement, as opposed to numerous accounts at several banks—makes the check collection process more efficient and cost-effective.

4. *What are MICR instructions, what is their significance, and how do banks manage MICR data flow?*

MICR instructions are magnetic ink character recognition symbols. MICR instructions appear on the bottom of each check, allowing reader-sorter machines to process checks at high speed. MICR encoding shows the check writer's account number, the check number, the dollar amount of the check; the check routing procedure (including the Federal Reserve district, clearance through a head office, branch office, or special arrangement, and immediate or deferred credit); the bank's identifying number; and a number to verify routing accuracy.

Using MICR instructions allows banks with computerized systems to record data and post credits and debits to individual accounts quickly and efficiently. Magnetic tapes are made of all MICR data at the end of the day. The bank then enters the data into its master files, updating each account's debits and credits for the day and computing a new closing balance. Most banks have demand deposit accounting (DDA) units that centrally manage the bank's MICR data flow.

5. *What is Federal Reserve float, how does it occur, and how does it differ from bank float? In your answer, explain how uncollected funds differ from available funds.*

Federal Reserve float is the extra reserves that exist in the banking system when the Fed credits banks for checks presented but not yet collected. Depending on the paying bank's proximity to a Federal Reserve bank, the account of the depositing bank is credited on the day of presentation or within a maximum of two business days, whether or not the Federal Reserve has processed the checks or has shipped them to the paying bank. The depositing bank can use the funds for reserves or other purposes as soon as its account is credited. Federal Reserve float exists until the paying bank's reserve account is debited.

Bank float represents the funds available to a bank that result from the time lag after a check deposit is credited and the time the depositor is able to use the funds. Uncollected funds are those that have been credited to a depositor's account but that are not yet collected and not available for withdrawal by the depositor. Available funds are those that a depositor can withdraw.

6. *Why have retail electronic funds transfer systems and services been slow to develop in the United States?*

Retail electronic funds transfer (EFT) services have been slow to develop in the United States because

- customers are reluctant to accept new technologies
- customers like the service and the price of the paper-based products that banks offer
- laws and regulations have been slow to adapt to the use of EFTs

Today automated teller machines (ATMs) are widely used and during the 1990s debit card use registered rapid growth. Other electronic services, such as electronic bill presentment and payment (EBPP), are not yet widely used, however, because of several drawbacks. The most notable drawbacks are the lack of one common electronic payment format, and the multitude of different operating and software systems that make standardization difficult.

7. *"Within this decade the Internet will revolutionize U.S. banking and payments practices." Do you agree or disagree with this statement? Justify your answer.*

The Internet will likely have a lasting impact on banking and payment practices, but it may take more than a decade for that impact to be felt. The use of electronic bill presentment and payment (EBPP) services over the Internet grew substantially during the late 1990s, but overall public use of web-based banking services slowed in the early 2000s. Currently only 60 percent of U.S. households own a computer, and only about half of these households have high-speed Internet access. The lack of a common electronic payments format and the multitude of operating and software systems make standardization difficult, which creates barriers to broad public use of such Internet services as EBPP. An even greater barrier is the attitude of bank customers, which must change for Internet banking to succeed. That attitudinal change is likely to occur slowly.

CHAPTER 7: THE FEDERAL RESERVE AND OTHER FINANCIAL REGULATORS

1. *Based on the structure of the Federal Reserve, what objectives do you think Congress had when it created the central bank?*

The Federal Reserve's quasi-governmental, decentralized structure includes government, private, mandatory, and voluntary features in an integrated three-tier pyramid. This structure reflects a desire for a central bank that can make independent policy decisions and that reflects compromises between competing political and economic interests.

The seven-member Board of Governors is a federal government entity with responsibilities for monetary policy, bank supervision and regulation, and broad oversight of Reserve banks. The nature of board appointments is designed to insulate the board from partisan political pressure, enabling the board to make decisions in the national interest.

The 12 district Federal Reserve banks are private and autonomous corporate entities that together make up the central bank. This district structure has two purposes: to decentralize power so that a single central bank can not dominate the nation's economic affairs, and to address disparate regional development needs and economic interests.

The 12-member Federal Open Market Committee sets the nation's monetary policy. Its members are drawn from the Federal Reserve Board of Governors and Reserve bank presidents, which ensures that the decision-making power of the central bank is shared between the private and government sectors and that decisions reflect both regional and national interests.

The members of the Federal Reserve are nationally chartered banks and those state-chartered banks that have chosen to be members. In a political compromise, state-chartered banks were given the option of Federal Reserve membership because Congress was reluctant to impose federal law over state banks. Today monetary policy is channeled through all depository institutions.

2. *What specific roles do the FOMC and the Federal Reserve Bank of New York play in the monetary policy process?*

The 12-member FOMC is the monetary policy decision-making center of the Federal Reserve. The FOMC meets every six weeks or so to review the state of the economy and to vote on whether to tighten or ease the availability of money and credit, or to maintain the status quo. Committee decisions are incorporated into a policy directive that is forwarded to the Federal Reserve Bank of New York for implementation through open market operations.

The Federal Reserve Bank of New York (FRBNY) is the operating arm of the Federal Reserve. In accordance with the FOMC's directives, the FRBNY trading desk buys and sells government securities on behalf of the entire Federal Reserve system. The bank also acts as the government's and FOMC's operating arm in the foreign exchange market by buying and selling foreign currencies in New York to stabilize disorderly exchange market conditions. Its unique role is primarily a result of its location in the banking and financial center of the world.

3. *What are the sources of the Federal Reserve's independence?*

The Federal Reserve's independence is rooted in two features of its organizational structure. The first feature is the 14-year terms of appointment for members of the Board of Governors. The second is the Federal Reserve's capacity to fund its own operations.

The seven members of the Board of Governors are appointed by the president of the United States with the consent of the Senate. Appointed to 14-year terms on a staggered schedule, governors cannot be removed from office or reappointed to another term. The length and staggered nature of the appointments protects against any president stacking the Board of Governors and against governors having partisan loyalties to any one administration. Short of legislation, the president and Congress cannot change Board decisions.

Through its considerable interest earnings, the Federal Reserve is able to fund itself, which frees it from the congressional appropriations process. This freedom insulates the Federal Reserve from potential political or partisan pressure that could be exerted through the budgetary appropriations process.

4. *What characteristics do the 12 Federal Reserve district banks and the Federal Reserve member banks have in common? How do they differ?*

Like Federal Reserve member banks, the 12 district banks are private corporate entities that function as autonomous institutions. Unlike member banks, however, the district Reserve banks hold the banking system's reserves, lend funds only to depositories, issue the nation's currency and coin, and provide banking services only to the government and to depository institutions. District Reserve bank boards also indirectly influence the monetary policy-making process. Consequently, the director selection process and board structure of the district Reserve banks are much more complex than those of member banks. Also unlike member banks, although district Reserve banks are profit-making entities, a sizable portion of their profits is returned to the U.S. Treasury. Other differences are that member banks must subscribe to stock in their district Reserve banks, and member banks may hold national or state charters.

5. *Who regulates banks in the United States today?*

Depending on a bank's charter, a bank is regulated by a state agency, a federal agency, or a combination of state and federal agencies. The current bank regulatory structure includes state banking departments, the Comptroller of the Currency, the Federal Reserve, and the Federal Deposit Insurance Corporation.

CHAPTER 8: BANK LEGISLATION AND REGULATION

1. *In what way does the regulation of banks differ from the regulation of other business firms, such as automobile manufacturing companies?*

The regulation of banks is shaped by certain public policy goals that do not apply to other business firms. Specifically, regulations seek to maintain public confidence in the safety and soundness of the banking system; to protect banks, their depositors, and their communities from bank failures; to foster healthy competition in banking; to protect bank owners from fraud and mismanagement; and to protect bank customers against discrimination or other abuses. Because banks have the power to create money, they are more closely regulated than other private companies.

2. *Does it make a difference whether a new bank obtains a national or a state charter?*

Yes. A bank's choice of charter will determine to what degree the federal or state government will share in the bank's regulatory control and examination. In other words, the charter will determine whether a bank's primary regulator will be a state or a federal agency. Nationally chartered banks must be Federal Reserve members and must be FDIC insured; but state-chartered banks have the option of joining the FDIC and/or the Federal Reserve. The Comptroller of the Currency (OCC) oversees nationally chartered banks; the Federal Reserve focuses on state-chartered member banks; and the FDIC examines state-chartered banks that are FDIC insured but not members of the Federal Reserve. The shared chartering and regulation of banks by both the federal and state governments is the defining characteristic of America's unique dual banking system.

3. *Explain the differences between dual banking and unit banking.*

Dual banking and unit banking are two different aspects of the U.S. banking system. One has to do with regulatory oversight and one has to do with the number and location of bank branches. *Dual banking* refers to the dual regulation of U.S. banks that 1) allows a bank to be chartered either by the federal government, through the OCC, or by the state in which the bank is located and 2) through a series of membership options subjects banks to the regulation of both the federal and the state governments. *Unit banking* refers to the single bank office structure of the U.S. banking industry. This structure has been shaped by federal and state laws that, until the 1990s, severely limited branching, merging and interstate expansion.

4. *Bankers, regulators, and economists have long debated the public benefits and costs of a dual banking system. What are the arguments for and against dual banking?*

The arguments for dual banking are that it reflects the system of checks and balances on which our government is based, allowing banks to counter abusive or inadequate regulatory control by changing their charters at any time. Proponents of dual banking also feel that it allows state governments to regulate banks in ways that more closely reflect the needs and concerns of the banks' local communities and depositors.

The arguments against dual banking are that the lack of uniformity among state banking laws is disruptive to the banking environment. Also, because banks can shop for a charter from state to state, decisions on state chartering may hold the potential for pressure and political favor. Finally, some bankers feel that state governments do not have adequate resources to ensure highly paid and well-trained bank examiners; that dual examinations are a waste of time and money; and that dual regulation enables banks to play off federal and state regulators against each other.

5. *Cite two major changes in banking brought about by the Gramm-Leach-Bliley Act of 1999.*

One change was that banks could establish financial holding companies and through these companies provide insurance securities investment, underwriting, and other financial services that had largely been prohibited to banks since 1933. Another change was that the act gave the Federal Reserve the authority to approve new financial holding company formations and their new activities. The act also allows banks, insurance companies, and brokerage firms to affiliate with one another through the financial holding company organizational structure.

6. *What major improvements to banking regulation did Congress make in the Federal Deposit Insurance Corporation Improvement Act of 1991? What further changes in the deposit insurance program were considered in the early 2000s?*

The improvements included the establishment of a risk-based system for assessing deposit insurance premiums on banks, restrictions on the FDIC's use of its too-big-to-fail doctrine, and the ending of insurance coverage for brokered CDs for all but the most well-capitalized banks.

Among the changes being considered by Congress in the early 2000s are increasing the $100,000 per account deposit insurance limit, providing greater insurance coverage for municipal deposits, merging the separate bank insurance and savings association insurance funds, and eliminating the ceiling on the size of the deposit insurance fund.

CHAPTER 9: MONETARY THEORY

1. *Briefly explain the quantity theory of money and Fisher's equation of exchange.*

The quantity theory of money holds that a direct and proportional causal relationship exists between the quantity of money and prices; an increase in the quantity of money causes an increase in prices; a decrease in the quantity of money causes a decrease in prices.

Fisher's equation of exchange, $MV = PT$ or $MV = PQ$, states that the quantity of money in circulation at any given time multiplied by the velocity of that money equals the average price of all goods and services sold multiplied by the volume of transactions or total quantity of goods sold. In other words, the total amount of money spent on goods and services must equal the total amount of money received from the sale of those goods and services.

2. *An important condition for Keynesian equilibrium is S = I + G. Why?*

When the level of savings in the economy is exactly offset by the level of investment and government spending (that is, when $S = I + G$), the economy will attain equilibrium, a balance between aggregate demand and aggregate supply. If aggregate demand exceeds aggregate supply, goods become scarce; businesses expect higher profits and increase their production, and the GDP increases, producing inflation if the economy is already at full employment. If aggregate supply exceeds aggregate demand, goods remain unsold; businesses reduce output and GDP declines, producing recession if prices do not decline.

3. *What are determinants of total demand for money? What would happen to demand if there were a massive increase in banks' issuance and the public's use of credit cards?*

The total demand for money is determined by the level of income, which affects transactions demand and precautionary demand, and the interest rate, which affects speculative demand. The higher the level of income, the more money people will hold for transactions purposes and precautionary motives. Speculative demand for money is inversely related to interest rates: the higher the rates, the lower the prices of bonds and the smaller the amount of speculative balances held, because most speculative funds have already been used to purchase bonds.

A massive increase in bank issuance and public use of credit cards would indicate a change in the public's liquidity preference. It would presumably lower the transactions and precautionary demands for money, causing interest rates to fall and raising consumption and investment to a higher equilibrium level of income and output.

4. *In implementing monetary policy, why does it matter whether the marginal efficiency of investment (MEI) curve or the liquidity preference curve is highly elastic or highly inelastic?*

If the MEI curve is highly elastic, investment spending is highly responsive to small changes in interest rates; if the curve is inelastic, investment spending is much less responsive to interest rate changes. Thus, in implementing monetary policy, the Federal Reserve would have to bring about a larger change in interest rates to achieve a small change in investment spending if the MEI curve were inelastic. On the other hand, a small change in interest rates brought about by the Fed's monetary policy could lead to very significant changes in the level of investment spending if the MEI curve were highly elastic.

The relative degree of elasticity of the liquidity preference curve similarly reflects the relative degree of change in the level of interest rates that would be brought about by the Fed's changing of the money supply. A highly elastic liquidity preference curve would tend to be associated with great change, whereas an inelastic liquidity preference curve would tend to be associated with little change.

5.   *What are the major differences between monetarism and Keynesian theory?*

Keynesian theory maintains that the most important relationship in the economy is that between total income and total spending. Monetarism maintains that the most important relationship in the economy is that between total income and the quantity of money that the public prefers to hold. Based on this basic difference, monetarists believe that changes in the money supply will cause changes in income and output, changes in the price level over time, and changes in total spending in the economy.

6.   *Why do monetarists contend that the only appropriate monetary policy is a constant 3 to 5 percent annual growth in the money supply?*

Monetarists believe that a constant 3 to 5 percent annual growth in money supply would match the U.S. economy's long-term annual growth rate, and would provide the economy with just enough new money for balanced, sustained growth. They contend that because of the variable and unpredictable time lags between changes in money supply and the consequent changes in income and output, the Fed's countercyclical approach to monetary policy actually destabilizes the economy. They also maintain that the Fed invariably overreacts when the economic response to monetary policy changes is slow. Economists' opinions vary as to the legitimacy of these contentions.

CHAPTER 10: POLICY GOALS AND THE FINANCIAL SYSTEM

1.   *How can unemployment and employment increase concurrently? How is the unemployment rate determined?*

Unemployment and employment can increase concurrently if new entrants or re-entrants to the labor force expand the size of the labor force and some of them obtain jobs while others do not. Even though no existing workers are being laid off and employment is, in fact, increasing, unemployment also is increasing.

The unemployment rate is determined by taking the number of unemployed people in the labor force as a percentage of the total labor force. The labor force is defined as everyone over the age of 16 years who is employed or seeking a job. Persons who are not employed but not seeking a job are not included in the labor force. Thus, the unemployment rate represents the percentage of the U.S. labor force that is not working and is seeking work.

2.   *Economists subdivide inflation into three primary types, attributed to different sources. What are the three main types of inflation? The wage-price spiral often is referred to as the glue that binds the sources of inflation together. Why do you think the wage-price spiral would be referred to this way?*

One type of inflation is demand-pull inflation, in which prices begin to rise because the demand for goods and services exceeds the supply. Demand-pull inflation typically follows rapid growth in the nation's money supply. Another type of inflation is cost-pull inflation, in which producers pass on their increased production costs to consumers in the form of price markups. A third type of inflation is scarcity-induced inflation, in which prices rise as the result of a shortage of key commodities or goods. Scarcity-induced inflation may have natural or artificial causes, including government actions.

In a wage-price spiral, demand-pull pressures pull up prices and workers seek higher wages to counteract their loss of purchasing power. If the higher wages are paid, production costs rise. The increased production costs push prices still higher, because of cost-push inflation. The result is that workers again lose purchasing power and again press for higher wages. If higher wages are obtained, the cycle of higher production costs and cost-push inflation continues.

3. *How does inflation affect the redistribution of income and wealth?*

Inflation redistributes income from individuals with fixed or slow-rising incomes, such as pensioners and government workers, to those whose incomes are rising rapidly or contain cost-of-living adjustments, such as self-employed professionals and some union workers.

Inflation redistributes wealth from creditors and savers to debtors, particularly when the inflation is unanticipated. During an inflationary period, creditors who make longer-term, fixed-rate loans lose money because they are repaid in dollars that have less purchasing value than the dollars originally lent. Savers who use fixed-rate savings instruments lose money if the interest rate they receive on their funds is lower than the inflation rate.

4. *Why would an unanticipated inflation rate of 5 percent be more harmful to banks than a correctly anticipated inflation rate of 10 percent?*

With an anticipated inflation rate, banks and other lenders can compensate for expected purchasing power losses over the life of their loans by adding an inflation premium to the interest rates they charge on loans. If the inflation is unanticipated and if banks hold substantial amounts of fixed-rate loans, they will be repaid in inflated dollars that have less purchasing power than the dollars originally loaned.

5. *What factors determine national productivity? What measures have banks employed to increase productivity?*

The growth in U.S. productivity during the 1990s has generally been attributed to high-tech capital investments, the effective use of information technology, qualitative improvements in technology, and foreign competition.

Even before the national productivity gains of the 1990s, banks had begun to increase their productivity. In recent years, banks have attempted to further increase productivity by

- improving worklife quality to boost employees' motivation and morale
- increasing investments in automation and electronic processing technology in order to substitute capital for labor
- changing service delivery systems to be less dependent on labor

- shifting the skill mix of bank staff to higher-skilled employees who use extensive computer technology and software to process work
- adapting both back office and front office operations to new computer technologies

Banks with heavy retail and consumer businesses also have tried to increase productivity through greater emphasis on self-service banking.

CHAPTER 11: MONETARY POLICY AND TOOLS

1. *How are the discount rate and discount window lending used as a monetary policy tool?*

    Today changes in the discount rate generally support monetary policy changes already made and implemented through open market operations. Discount window lending primarily serves as a safety valve for individual banks that need to borrow reserves for a day or two until they can make other adjustments in their assets and liabilities. Discount window loans are mainly used by smaller banks under reserve stress due to short-term liquidity drains.

2. *Whenever the Federal Reserve buys or sells anything, bank reserves and the money supply change. Why, then, does the Federal Reserve limit its buying and selling to government securities in the open market?*

    The Federal Reserve relies on purchases and sales of government securities because the active market in U.S. government securities, the largest financial asset market in the world, ensures the prompt and efficient implementation of open market operations.
    A bank might be reluctant to alter its reserves through a purchase or sale of government securities in accordance with the Federal Reserve's monetary policy strategy. However, a bank has no control over the deposits it holds for dealer firms. Dealer firms are motivated by profit; thus, dealers can always be induced to accept a transaction if the Federal Reserve offers to sell securities at a low enough price or offers to buy securities at a high enough price. The Federal Reserve might offer to sell securities at a low price in order to reduce bank reserves or buy securities at a high price in order to increase bank reserves.

3. *Changing reserve requirement percentages is one way the Federal Reserve can use reserve requirements as a monetary policy tool. What are the other two ways?*

    The Federal Reserve can reclassify the kinds of eligible assets that depository intuitions can use to meet reserve requirements and can reclassify the kinds of liabilities that are subject to reserve requirements.

4.	*The Federal Reserve's monetary policy strategy involves setting short-term operational targets to achieve long-term national economic objectives. Why does the Federal Reserve do this?*

To reach its long-term (year-to-year) objectives for employment, price stability, and economic growth, the Federal Reserve tries to reach intermediate (quarter-to-quarter) objectives for financial and economic measures over which it has some influence. The Federal Reserve tries to achieve these intermediate objectives by focusing on short-term (week-to-week) operational targets, such as the growth rate of bank reserves and the federal funds rate, which it can control directly.

5.	*How do dynamic and defensive open market operations differ? How can you tell whether the Federal Reserve's open market operations have been dynamic or defensive in any given week?*

Dynamic open market operations involve the Federal Reserve's buying and selling of government securities to counter recession, to contain inflation, or to promote balanced economic growth. Defensive open market operations are made to offset or nullify undesired day-to-day changes in bank reserves and money supply that are unrelated to monetary policy, such as the public's handling of cash, the daily level of Federal Reserve float, and the actions of the U.S. Treasury.

    The Federal Reserve's defensive open market techniques include repurchase agreements and reverse repos, which are temporary purchases or sales of Treasury obligations. These techniques are short-term and self-reversing; they first supply and then absorb reserves, or vice versa.

6.	*Assume that the Federal Reserve is on target for reserve growth. What nonpolicy factors might cause reserve growth to go off target?*

Reserve growth could be driven off target by numerous factors, including

- bank depositors who increase their cash deposits or cash withdrawals (because cash is a component of bank reserves)
- bank depositors who move funds between types of accounts, between small and large banks, or into institutions not controlled by the Federal Reserve (because reserve requirements only apply to transaction accounts, are lower for small banks, and do not apply to non-depository institutions, such as mutual funds)
- an increase or decrease in the daily level of Federal Reserve float
- the U.S. Treasury's management of its tax receipts and spending

7.	*What is the purpose of Treasury tax and loan (TT&L) accounts? How do the remittance and note option accounts work, and how do they affect bank reserves?*

As Treasury balances at Federal Reserve banks increase from tax receipts or borrowings, bank reserves decline. As Treasury balances at Reserve banks decrease because of government spending, bank reserves increase. The purpose of Treasury tax and loan accounts is to minimize the impact of Treasury actions on bank reserves and monetary policy control.

TT&L accounts are accounts maintained at banks for the U.S. Treasury. Federal tax receipts and funds received from bond sales are deposited in TT&Ls. When the Treasury needs funds to meet obligations such as Social Security payments, the civil service payroll, and other government disbursements, it transfers its deposits from TT&Ls at banks to its disbursement accounts at Federal Reserve banks.

Under the remittance option, banks are not required to pay for TT&L deposits (which build up a bank's deposit base and provide for new loans and investments), but they can only hold the funds for one day. Under the note option, banks can hold the funds for extended periods, but they must pay interest on the funds.

CHAPTER 12: FISCAL POLICY AND DEBT MANAGEMENT POLICY

1. *Outline an appropriate anti-inflationary policy that uses the three monetary and two fiscal policy tools in a complementary way.*

The monetary policy tools to fight inflation include increasing the discount rate, raising reserve requirements, and selling government securities from the open market portfolio; the anti-inflationary fiscal policy tools include increasing taxes and reducing government spending.

2. *Why is fiscal policy difficult to implement?*

One reason it is difficult to implement fiscal policy is that changing federal spending or tax laws is a lengthy process. A second reason relates to the nondiscretionary or automatic nature of much of the government's spending and taxation. A third reason is the general reluctance of congress and the president to raise taxes to fight inflation, because such an action would be poorly received by most voters.

Fiscal policy tools and monetary policy tools also work in different ways. Fiscal policy tools affect income, spending, and savings; monetary policy tools affect interest rates, bank reserves, and money supply growth. Monetary and fiscal policy must work together in the same direction to contain inflation or to counter recession.

3. *What are the three problems that the economy faces if federal debt growth accelerates?*

The first problem is contention over tax revenues. The more tax revenues the government has to use to pay interest on the nation's debt, the less money is available to fund existing government programs or finance new ones. The second problem is competition for available credit. The more the federal government has to borrow, the smaller the supply of credit available to the business and consumer sectors. The third problem is increased foreign claims on U.S. output. Foreigners have been holding an increasing proportion of the federal debt. If these foreign holders were to sell their holdings to buy U.S. goods and services, a smaller proportion of the nation's output would be available to meet domestic demand.

4. *How would debt management work if the U.S. Treasury chose to use this power to counter recession or inflation?*

To fight recession, the Treasury could restrict its issuance of new securities to short-term securities only. To fight inflation, the Treasury could limit issuance to long-term securities only.

By issuing only short-term securities, the Treasury would create an imbalance between the types of financial assets the public chooses to hold. The public would respond by buying more long-term bonds, which would drive down long-term interest rates. This interest rate decline would help counter recession by leading to more business borrowing and subsequent capital investment spending.

Issuing only long-term securities during an inflationary period would cause the public to adjust their holdings of financial assets to obtain more liquidity. To do so, the public would shift some potential spending funds into short-term securities. Spending would also be reduced if consumers and businesses diverted some funds into the higher-yielding long-term bonds. Both responses would help counter inflation.

5. *Explain the relevance of the following balance-of-payments measures: balance of trade, balance on current account, and official settlements balance.*

The balance of trade is the difference between a nation's exports and imports of goods. A trade deficit is said to result if a nation imports more goods than it exports; a trade surplus, if it exports more than it imports.

The balance on current account measures all ongoing transactions between the United States and other countries that result in international transfers of money, including the balance on goods and services plus unilateral transfers. This measure is only a partial measure of U.S. international performance because it does not reflect capital inflows and outflows, which can completely offset account deficits or surpluses.

The official settlements balance is part of the capital flows measure, together with the basic balance. The official settlements balance measures the change in holdings of international reserve assets of U.S. and foreign governments during the year.

6. *Define wage-price controls and indexation and explain at least one argument for and against each.*

Wage-price controls are government-imposed regulations that attempt to limit wage and price increases. Proponents of wage-price controls believe that structural changes in the U.S. economy make it difficult to control wages and prices with traditional fiscal and monetary policy. Wage-price controls would prevent cost-push inflation before it starts. Opponents believe that wage-price controls contradict freedom of choice and distort decisions on how to allocate resources. They also believe that by not allowing prices to determine the balance between supply and demand, wage-price controls would lead to inefficiency and market dislocations.

Indexation is the systematic use of cost-of-living escalator clauses in money-payment contracts. Adherents believe that indexation can even out the benefits and burdens of inflation that are borne by different sectors in the economy, eliminate or decrease wage-price spirals, and eliminate distorted investment and savings flows caused by inflation hedging. Opponents argue that indexation does not eliminate inflation because no economic sector would become an inflation loser, and thus no pressure would be put on the government to stop inflation. Opponents also contend that a nationwide indexation program would eliminate the benefits of indexation now in place for Social Security recipients and other groups that traditionally lose income during inflationary periods.

EXERCISE 4: ECONOMIC POLICY PROBLEMS

1. inflation
2. recession
3. recession
4. inflation
5. recession
6. inflation
7. inflation
8. recession
9. recession
10. inflation
11. *S* Increased government spending is financed by increased taxation.
12. *I* Increased government spending is financed by increased borrowing.
13. *S* Government spending and taxation are reduced.

CHAPTER 13: THE ROLE OF BANKS IN INTERNATIONAL TRADE AND INVESTMENT

1. *How are foreign exchange rates determined? Suggest three factors that would likely increase or decrease supply or demand for U.S. dollars in European exchange markets.*

Exchange rates express how much foreign money will exchange for one unit of domestic money, or how much domestic money will exchange for one unit of foreign money.

Although the purchasing power of money establishes the theoretical basis for determining exchange rates, the interaction of supply and demand for a nation's money in the foreign exchange market is the real determinant. One factor that might cause the supply or demand for U.S. dollars to increase or decrease in European exchange markets is the U.S. inflation rate. A high rate, relative to Europe, would reduce European demand for dollars. Another factor is demand for technology that is only available from U.S. producers, which would increase European demand for dollars, as would political and economic instability in European countries. U.S. balance-of-payments deficits could cause the price of the dollar to fall in the exchange markets if holders of surplus dollars sold them for other currencies.

2. *What are the three primary functions of the foreign exchange market?*

The three primary functions of the foreign exchange market are (1) the international transfer of purchasing power from one national money to another; (2) the provision of short-term credit to importers and exporters for the purpose of financing trade; and (3) the provision of forward purchase and sale contracts and options to enable traders and investors to minimize the risk of exchange rate changes in their transactions.

3. *Why would a U.S. exporter sell foreign exchange forward? Under what conditions would it be advantageous for a U.S. importer to buy foreign exchange forward?*

A U.S. exporter might sell foreign exchange forward believing that the exchange rate is likely to go down. By selling forward, the U.S. exporter protects against a possible decline in the dollar's price between the time the exported goods are shipped and the time the exporter receives payment for the goods in a foreign currency. A U.S. importer might buy foreign exchange forward if it anticipated that the dollar's price would increase with respect to foreign monies.

4. *What is a bankers' acceptance? How does a bankers' acceptance differ from a letter of credit?*

A bankers' acceptance is a time draft instrument accepted by and drawn on a bank that substitutes its own credit for that of an importer or buyer. The draft is payable on the due date by the accepting bank whether or not the importer or buyer pays, and thus is readily salable in the secondary market.

A bankers' acceptance is similar to a letter of credit. Again, the financial instrument substitutes the bank's credit for the company's credit and in fact, many bankers' acceptances are created when payment is made by letter of credit. The two instruments differ, however, in that a bankers' acceptance is a form of time draft and a letter of credit is actually a letter, addressed to the party likely to receive the payments. Because of its specificity, companies ordering goods from foreign suppliers with whom they have no credit relationship frequently prefer to use a letter of credit.

5. *Cite at least three reasons why foreign banks maintain branches, agencies, and other banking offices in the United States.*

Foreign banks may maintain U.S. branches, agencies, and other banking offices for any of several reasons, including

- to provide financial services to their domestic customers (mostly multinational corporations) that have foreign operations
- to acquire a dollar base or better manage the dollar position of their parent banks
- to aid their domestic customers in more effective financing of exports of goods to the United States
- to provide better investment services to their corporate clients
- to develop a retail banking business in the world's largest financial market

GLOSSARY

A

agency An office of a foreign bank in the United States that cannot accept deposits from U.S. citizens or residents, but otherwise can operate as a full-service bank.

aggregate demand The sum of all consumption, investment, and government spending (*see* total spending).

anticipated inflation A period or degree of inflation that is fully anticipated by consumers and businesses. If anticipations are correct, consumers and businesses are likely to behave according to conventional theory, speeding up their current spending to beat expected price increases.

asset Any item a bank owes or has owed to it; loans and investments constitute the bulk of most banks' assets.

asset allocation A bank funds management strategy in which funds are assigned to securities and loan asset categories and then reallocated as loan demand changes.

asset sensitive A bank that has more assets than liabilities subject to repricing in a given time period.

Automated Clearing House (ACH) A clearing facility operated for the convenience of banks in a particular region, generally through the regional Federal Reserve bank. Automated clearing houses electronically process interbank credits and debits. They also may handle the automatic deposit of customers' wages, direct deposit of social security payments, and preauthorized payments of bills by banks.

Automatic Transfer Service account (ATS account) An account arrangement in which funds from a time account are automatically transferred into a checking account to cover presented checks.

availability schedule Credit for cash letters (checks) deposited with correspondent banks or with Federal Reserve banks, granted in accordance with an availability schedule that gives banks immediate, one-day or two-day deferred credit, depending on the location of the banks on which the checks are drawn.

B

balance of payments A record of a country's receipts from and payments to foreign countries during a given period.

balance of trade The difference between a nation's exports and imports of goods over a given period.

balance on current account The difference between a nation's international receipts from and payments to foreign countries for goods, services, income and unilateral transfers, such as private gifts to foreigners, and grants-in-aid to foreign governments, other than military grants.

balance sheet A detailed list of assets, liabilities, and owners' equity showing a company's financial position at a specific time. A bank's balance sheet is generally called a statement of condition.

bank *See* commercial bank.

bank float Check funds that have been collected by banks for depositors but are not yet available for depositors' use.

bank holding company (BHC) A company that owns a controlling interest in one or more banks.

Bank Holding Company Act Enacted into law in 1956, the Act sets parameters for regulating bank holding companies and designates the Federal Reserve as the supervisory agency. The Federal Reserve has responsibility for approving new bank holding company activities.

Bank Insurance Fund (BIF) The deposit insurance fund for commercial banks administered by the FDIC.

bank notes Currency issued by a bank. Note issues of commercial banks are no longer circulated.

bank regulation Implementation of banking laws through government-issued rules and directives.

bank supervision The enforcement of banking regulations through continuous on-site examinations and off-site monitoring and analysis of data and information on banks' performance and practices.

bankers' acceptance A time draft drawn on and accepted by the bank on which it was drawn that is used to finance the export, import, shipment, or storage of goods. The bank accepting the draft assumes the obligation of making payment at maturity on behalf of the buyer or the buyer's bank.

barter The trade or exchange of one good for another.

barter economy An economy in which goods and services are traded without the exchange of money.

base rate The bank's starting point to begin negotiations of a specific rate for a specific customer. The base rate usually is derived from one of several commonly used indices, such as the federal funds rate or the London interbank offer rate (LIBOR). *Also see* prime rate.

bill of exchange *See* export draft.

Board of Governors *See* Federal Reserve Board.

borrowed funds All direct or indirect non-deposit liabilities of a bank.

broker (1) A licensed person or firm that buys and sells securities, commodities, property, or other assets for a commission. A broker is an agent, not a principal; a broker does not carry an inventory. (2) A person or firm licensed to sell insurance.

brokered CDs Large denomination ($100,000 or more) certificates of deposit marketed by banks and thrifts to groups of investors through nationwide brokerage firms.

business cycle Short-run fluctuations in the level of economic activity as measured by changes in GDP.

C

cable transfer An order sent by cable from an importer's bank to a foreign bank directing the foreign bank to pay out a specific sum of foreign money to the exporter. Also known as wire transfer.

CAMELS rating system The rating system used by federal and state bank examiners to evaluate a bank's safety and soundness. The system considers six factors (Capital adequacy, Asset quality, Management, Earnings, Liquidity, and Sensitivity to market risk). Numerical ratings applied to these factors are combined into an overall composite rating.

capital account (1) The net worth, capital investment, or owners' equity of an enterprise. The capital account is the difference between an entity's assets and liabilities. (2) The account used to record the flow of long-term investment capital to and from a nation.

capital adequacy standards These are requirements established by major industrial nations primarily for banks involved in international trade, but required of all US banks since 1991. The standards define on a risk basis capital funds as a percentage of bank total assets; essentially, the higher the risk for an asset, the higher the capital requirement. Also known as risk-based capital guidelines.

capital gains The amount by which the proceeds from the sale of capital assets exceed their cost.

capital requirement The amount of capital (funds paid in by stockholders) necessary for a bank to receive a charter.

cash assets The liquid assets banks hold; consists primarily of coin and currency on hand and deposit balances at other banks.

cash items in the process of collection The asset posting that a bank makes on its balance sheet for checks received from depositors for which payment has not been received.

central bank A bank responsible for controlling a country's monetary policy and serving as its lender of last resort. In the United States, the Federal Reserve is the central bank.

check routing symbol A numerical code that facilitates handling and routing checks for collection. The code is the denominator of the fractional number located in the upper right-hand corner of a check; it is reproduced in magnetic ink character recognition (MICR) symbols at the bottom of the check. The first two digits identify the Federal Reserve district in which the drawee bank is located. The third digit designates through whom the check will be cleared, and the fourth indicates whether the check will be credited with immediate or deferred funds.

check truncation The process of electronically capturing the essential information on a conventional paper check and transferring the electronic information, not the paper check, through the clearing system.

clearing house (1) An establishment maintained by financial institutions for settling clearing claims. (2) A place where representatives of banks in the same locality meet daily, or several times daily, to exchange checks on each other and to settle resulting balances.

Clearing House Interbank Payments System (CHIPS) An automated clearing house of the New York Clearing House Association used chiefly for interbank electronic funds transfers for international customers of CHIPS members.

coefficient of demand deposit expansion The multiplier by which the banking system can create deposits. The coefficient is determined by taking the reciprocal of the reserve requirement ratio.

collateral Something of value, such as a car or a house, that a borrower pledges as backing for a loan.

commercial bank A privately owned financial institution that makes business loans, accepts demand deposits, and provides a variety of other financial services.

commercial paper A negotiable, short-term, unsecured promissory note in bearer form issued by businesses to obtain funds.

commodity money A type of money in which the medium of exchange itself is also a useful commodity.

Community Reinvestment Act (CRA) A law passed in 1977 that requires banks to meet the credit needs of the local communities from which they obtain deposits, including the low- and moderate-income sections of those communities.

compensating balances The balances that a customer must keep on deposit with a bank in order to ensure a credit line or loan, to gain unlimited checking privileges, and to offset the bank's expenses in providing various services.

computation period The period over which banks that must maintain reserves compute their required reserves. Large depository institutions compute their required reserves once every two weeks. The computation period ends every second Monday. Small depositories with net transaction account deposits of less than $6.0 million are exempt from maintaining and reporting required reserves as of 2003.

consumer bank *See* nonbank bank.

consumer price index (CPI) An index measuring the cost of a hypothetical basket of goods and services purchased by consumers.

consumption Spending by consumers on goods and services.

consumption function A schedule in the basic Keynesian model, graphically represented as an upward-sloping curve, that illustrates how much consumers will spend at every level of income.

contingent liabilities Liabilities that do not appear on a bank's current balance sheet but are likely to be posted on the balance sheet in the future because of current agreements, such as loan commitments and letters of credit.

correspondent banking A banking system in which larger banks hold account balances of other, usually smaller banks and provide or sell services to those banks through the accounts. The correspondent bank generally receives fees for some of the services it provides to the smaller, respondent banks.

cost-push inflation An inflationary cycle that results from the increasing costs of supplies and labor. These increased costs lead to increased prices for goods. As the cost of living rises, workers demand wage increases and the cycle repeats itself.

country risk The risk that political or financial instability in a country will jeopardize an investment or the ability of borrowers to repay obligations to foreign creditors.

credit card A form of consumer credit known as open-end credit, such as MasterCard and Visa, that allows the cardholder to make purchases from merchants and pay for the purchases by making installment payments to a bank.

credit unions Cooperative organizations of individuals with a common affiliation, such as employment. Credit unions are owned by their members and accept deposits of members in the form of share purchases, pay interest on the shares out of earnings, and primarily provide consumer installment credit to members. Savings banks, savings and loan associations, and credit unions are the nation's savings institutions.

creditworthiness A borrower's ability to obtain credit from lenders, usually based on the amount and quality of the borrower's assets and repayment history.

cyclical unemployment Unemployment generated by worker layoffs caused by a downturn in the business cycle.

D

daylight overdraft A condition during the course of the banking day when a bank pays out more electronic funds than it has on its books.

dealer An individual or firm that buys and resells securities or other assets for profit. A dealer carries an inventory, as distinct from a broker, who does not carry inventory.

dealer firms Firms that buy and sell securities or other assets for profit. Dealers carry an inventory, as distinct from brokerage firms, which do not. The Federal Reserve sells to and buys from primary government securities dealer firms to implement its monetary policy.

dealer market A nationwide telephone market for trading government securities, centered primarily in New York City.

debt management Actions taken to change the structure or composition of the national debt. Debt management includes the control of maturities and timing of the issuance of securities by business or government.

debit card A plastic card that serves as an access device to an electronic funds transfer (EFT) terminal. When used for payments, it immediately transfers funds from the user's account (a debit) to another party.

defensive open market operations The Federal Reserve's buying and selling of government securities in the open market to offset or nullify undesired changes in the growth or level of bank reserves and the money supply caused by such factors as Treasury borrowings or tax payments.

defined-benefit plan A pension plan that makes specific monthly payments to retired employees based on a formula that usually factors in the employee's length of service and earnings.

defined-contribution plan A pension plan that takes in contributions (savings) from employees, which may or may not be matched by employer contributions, and invests the funds into one or more investment alternatives determined by the employee.

delayed availability standards Rules established in the 1987 Expedited Funds Availability Act that stipulate that banks must make funds available for local checks within two business days of deposit and for other checks within five business days of deposit.

demand deposit accounting unit (DDA unit) In most banks, the back-office department (demand deposit accounting unit) that processes each day's check data.

demand deposits Funds that customers may withdraw from banks with no advance notice, usually by writing checks or using automated teller machines. Checking accounts are the most common form of demand deposits.

demand-pull inflation A general rise in the prices of goods and services that results when total demand (consumer, business, and government spending) exceeds the total supply of goods and services available at current prices.

depression A severe, extended recession that includes a precipitous decline in real gross domestic product (GDP). During the Great Depression from 1929 to 1933, for example, real GDP fell by 50 percent.

derivatives Financial investments that derive value from another financial asset that is either underlying the instrument or related to it.

direct send A check collection practice in which a bank that receives a check drawn on another bank presents it directly to that bank for payment.

discount rate The interest rate that Reserve banks charge depositories for loans.

discount window The figurative expression for the Federal Reserve facility for lending reserves to depositories.

discount window loans Reserves lent by the Federal Reserve to depositories to meet temporary liquidity, seasonal or emergency needs.

disintermediation The public's mass withdrawal of deposit balances from banks and thrifts for direct placement into money market investments, such as Treasury bills and mutual funds. This is a reversal of the traditional flow of consumers' funds into financial intermediaries. Disintermediation occurred in the 1960s and 1970s when interest rate ceilings prevented depositories from matching prevailing rates.

disposable personal income A measure of the amount of income people have available for spending and saving after they pay taxes.

dual banking The aspect of the banking system in the United States that allows banks to be chartered either by the state in which it is domiciled or by the federal government through the Office of the Comptroller of the Currency. The side-by-side existence of both state-chartered and nationally chartered banks creates a dual banking system.

dynamic open market relations The use of open market operations to achieve broad economic objectives, such as countering recession, containing inflation, or promoting balanced economic growth. Also known as offensive open market relations.

E

earnings A bank's income or revenue; one of the six criteria used by bank examiners in evaluating a bank's safety and soundness.

earning assets Loans, investments and other interest-bearing (or dividend-bearing) assets.

elasticity The degree of responsiveness of one variable to another, as for example, the responsiveness of investment spending to a change in interest rates.

electronic funds transfer (EFT) An electronically based rather than paper-based means of transferring funds to and from accounts.

electronic check presentment The process whereby a drawee bank debits a payor's account based on magnetic ink character recognition (MICR)-line data captured by the depository bank and transmitted to the drawee bank. In its most efficient form the actual item is never transferred.

equation of exchange *(MV = PT or MV = PQ)* The quantity of money *(M)* multiplied by the velocity of that money *(V)* equals the average price of all goods sold *(P)* multiplied by the volume of transactions *(T)* or the volume of goods sold *(Q)*. The equation of exchange is most closely associated with Yale economist Irving Fisher (1867–1947), and is often referred to as Fisher's equation of exchange.

equilibrium For economic modeling purposes, a condition of economic balance in which aggregate demand and aggregate supply are equal.

euro The common currency of 12 European nations, introduced in 2002 to replace their individual domestic currencies. As of 2002, the 12 members of the European Union were Austria, Belgium, Finland, France, Germany, Greece, Ireland, Italy, Luxembourg, Netherlands, Portugal, and Spain.

eurodollar borrowings A bank's borrowings of dollar-denominated funds on the books of banking offices outside the United States.

excess reserves Funds held by depository institutions in excess of the legal minimum required by the Federal Reserve.

exchange rate The price of one currency relative to another currency.

export draft A check drawn by an importer's bank against foreign exchange balances the bank holds in a bank abroad that are payable at that bank. Also known as a bill of exchange.

F

federal agency securities Debt instruments issued by U.S. government-owned or government-sponsored corporations and agencies, such as the Federal National Mortgage Association (Fannie Mae) and the Government National Mortgage Association (Ginnie Mae).

federal budget deficit A shortfall between the tax revenues collected by the government and the funds spent by the government in a given fiscal year. A budget deficit represents the amount of money the federal government has to borrow by selling new Treasury securities to fund its current spending.

federal debt The total of all past federal deficits indicating the amount of outstanding bills, notes, and bonds owed by the federal government. A budget deficit represents the amount of money the federal government has to borrow by selling new Treasury securities to fund its current spending.

Federal Deposit Insurance Corporation (FDIC) The federal agency that insures depositors' accounts up to a certain amount (currently $100,000) at banks and savings associations. The FDIC is responsible for examining all state-chartered banks that it insures, except those that are members of the Federal Reserve.

federal funds One-day loans from one bank to another. These loans are funds immediately available from reserve accounts at Federal Reserve banks.

federal funds rate The interest rate that banks charge one another for overnight loans of reserve funds.

Federal Open Market Committee (FOMC) A committee of the Federal Reserve that sets monetary policy and issues guidelines for open market operations. The Committee is composed of the seven members of the Federal Reserve's Board of Governors and five Federal Reserve bank presidents.

Federal Reserve bank directors The individuals responsible to the member bank stockholders and the Board of Governors of the Federal Reserve banks for the sound management and operation of the Reserve banks. Each Reserve bank has nine directors, six of whom are elected by member banks and three of whom are appointed by the Board of Governors.

Federal Reserve Board A board of seven members appointed by the president of the United States and confirmed by the Senate. The Board formulates monetary policy, regulates member banks and bank holding companies, and oversees the activities of the 12 Reserve banks.

Federal Reserve district A geographic area served by a specific Federal Reserve bank.

Federal Reserve float Extra reserves that exist in the banking system because the Federal Reserve credits banks for checks presented for collection in accordance with a pre-determined time schedule, but receives payment for those checks only after the checks have been presented to the banks on which they are drawn. Federal Reserve float is generated in the time interval between crediting and payment.

Federal Reserve membership All nationally chartered banks must be members of the Federal Reserve system; state-chartered banks can choose to be members as well.

Federal Reserve notes Nearly all the nation's circulating paper currency consists of Federal Reserve notes printed by the Treasury and issued to the Federal Reserve, which puts them into circulation through the commercial banking system.

Federal Reserve Wire Network (Fedwire) A payment service operated by the Federal Reserve for the electronic transfer of funds between depository institutions.

fiat money (1) Fiat money is a medium of exchange mandated by a government and backed by the law and power of the state. (2) Money whose value is not related to the inherent value of the metal or other material from which it is made.

finance companies Companies that specialize in making small loans to consumers or small businesses.

financial holding company A corporation that owns or controls one or more banks as well as companies that underwrite securities, issue and underwrite insurance, and provide specialized financial services.

financial intermediaries Financial institutions that take in funds from savers and then transfer the funds to investors by issuing their own liabilities to savers and using the funds thus acquired to make loans and investments for their own accounts.

fiscal agent (1) An agent for a corporation that handles its taxes in connection with an issue of bonds (2) An agent for a government that handles payment of its bonds and other financial matters.

fiscal policy The government's use of federal spending and taxation to change the pace and direction of the economy.

foreign agency *See* agency

foreign exchange (1) The currencies of other countries, primarily U.S. dollars to foreigners, and euros and Japanese yen to Americans. (2) Trading in or exchange of foreign currencies for U.S. funds or other foreign currencies.

foreign exchange market The institutional setting in which buyers and sellers of foreign exchange, mainly major banks and foreign exchange dealer firms, transact business.

foreign exchange rate The price at which one country's currency is valued in relation to another country's currency.

forward exchange option A contract, which need not be exercised, to buy or sell foreign exchange at a future date for a price set at the time of the contract.

forward purchase contract A contract to purchase a specific quantity of foreign currency at an exchange rate set today for delivery on a specific date in the future. The bank assumes the foreign exchange risk and charges an appropriate forward exchange rate.

fractional reserves A banking principle under which banks maintain reserves equal to a fraction of their outstanding deposits, which enables them to create a multiple of new deposit balances.

frictional unemployment Unemployment generated by workers who voluntarily quit jobs to seek higher wages, better working conditions, or broader advancement opportunities.

full employment Full use of the labor force; a condition where there is little or no involuntary unemployment.

full employment budgeting A budgetary approach whereby (1) an estimate is made of the total amount of tax revenue the government would receive if the economy were operating at full employment and (2) government spending is increased or decreased to match this estimated amount.

G

gap The difference between maturing assets and maturing liabilities in a given time period.

gap management The control of the repricing of assets and liabilities to maintain the desired relationship between expected interest income and interest expense.

general monetary policy controls Policy tools that seek to control the total quantity, availability or cost of money throughout the economy without regard to the purpose of the funds.

gold standard A way of valuing money in terms of a fixed weight of gold. During the nineteenth century, an international monetary system in which individual nations agreed to buy and sell unlimited amounts of gold at specified prices in terms of each nation's currency.

gold tranche The automatic borrowing privileges or credit lines at the International Monetary Fund (IMF) that can be used for international reserve assets by member nations.

government spending Spending by the federal government on goods, services, and entitlement programs.

grandfathered A provision of law that allows a business to continue to provide a service or engage in an activity after the service or activity has been restricted or prohibited.

Gresham's Law The principle that "cheap money" tends to drive "dear money" from circulation when different values exist for the same commodity money, such as gold or silver.

gross domestic product (GDP) A measure of the value of a country's total production of goods and services from all forms of economic activity for a given period, typically a calendar year.

H

hedging Controlling the risk of one transaction by engaging in an offsetting transaction. For example, a bank that wants to protect a segment of its securities portfolio from a rise in interest rates can hedge by selling the same amount of securities for future delivery at a current price.

hidden unemployment Job seekers who take jobs well below their skill levels or take part-time jobs because jobs at their skill levels or full-time work is unavailable.

hold order A request or order issued to a bank to freeze or hold back some or all funds in an account. Such orders, often issued by the courts in divorce or tax litigations, are routinely instituted when a bank learns of the death of an account holder.

income effect The redistribution of real income that occurs in an inflation as people whose incomes rise rapidly gain relative to those whose incomes rise slowly or not at all.

income-expenditure theory The theory of John Maynard Keynes on the workings of the economy based on the interrelationship between total income and total spending.

income statement A financial statement that shows a summary of a firm's or individual's income and expenses for a specific period.

independent floating An exchange rate policy adopted by the U.S. and the major industrial nations whereby the market determines each nation's exchange rate. Governments intervene only to moderate erratic or excessive exchange rate fluctuations.

indexation The process whereby all income and payments, such as wages, rents, interest, taxes, and government entitlements, are adjusted to changes in the cost of living so as to reduce the real income transfers associated with inflation.

individual retirement account (IRA) A tax-deferred account that allows a customer to deposit a stipulated amount and to earn interest. Tax on the account may be deferred until retirement, when it presumably will be taxable at a lower rate.

inelastic currency A currency whose supply is not responsive to the changing demands of businesses and consumers.

inflation A continuing increase in the general level of prices in an economy, which results from increases in total spending relative to the supply of goods on the market.

inflation hedging The consumer and business large-scale purchase of non-productive assets such as gold and art objects in order to avoid inflation risks, which distorts the economy's investment and savings flows.

insolvency (bank) A condition in which the accounting value of a bank's assets are less than the value of its liabilities.

insufficient funds Checks returned to a presenting bank because the account on which the checks have been drawn does not have a sufficiently large collected funds balance for the checks to be collected (paid).

interdistrict settlement account An account that each Reserve bank maintains on the books of the Interdistrict Settlement Fund, established in Washington, D.C., to handle check settlements among Reserve banks. A check presented to one Reserve bank drawn on a bank in another Federal Reserve district results in a transfer of interdistrict settlement account balances from one Reserve bank to another.

international competitiveness effect The effect inflation has on imports and exports, driving up imports and slowing down exports, leading to an expanding trade deficit.

international reserves Financial assets that governments throughout the world have agreed to accept from each other in payment or settlement of debt, such as gold, special drawing rights (SDRs), gold tranche, and foreign exchange.

investment (1) The purchase of capital assets by a business. (2) Assets acquired in order to earn income in the form of interest, dividends, or capital gains.

K

Keynesian theory The body of economic theory associated with the British economist

John Maynard Keynes. Key features of that theory are the interrelationship between income and spending and that fiscal policies are important determinants of short-run economic activity.

L

legal tender In the United States, currency and coin designated by the U.S. government as acceptable payment for goods and services and settlement of debt.

letter of credit A financial instrument in the form of a letter that declares a bank will make payments on behalf of a given party, such as a company, substituting the bank's credit for the company's credit. It typically is used in foreign trade in import-export contracts, under pre-arranged conditions.

liability sensitive A bank that has more liabilities than assets subject to repricing in a given time period.

liquid assets Assets that can be converted to cash with minimal cost or risk of loss. Examples of liquid assets are vault cash or near-money assets.

liquidity (1) The ability of a bank or business to meet its current obligations (2) The quality that makes an asset quickly and readily convertible into cash without significant loss.

liquidity preference theory Keynes' theory of interest, which states that people prefer to hold money rather than less liquid assets. Interest is the price that must be paid to get people to give up their preference for liquidity.

loan assets A major asset holding of banks, consisting of contracts in which borrowers agree to pay interest for the use of the bank's funds.

loan commitment fee A fee a borrower pays to a lender for a binding pledge that the lender will make a loan to the borrower usually at a stated interest rate, at a future date.

loan loss reserve account A balance sheet account that covers expected losses on loans. As losses occur, they are charged against this account.

loan participation An agreement between or among lenders to share part of an existing loan, with each advancing funds and accepting risk on nonpayment.

local clearing house A central site where banks in one locality present checks drawn on one another for collection and exchange. Each participating bank's balance at the clearing house is adjusted on a net basis to reflect the difference between the value of checks presented to, and the value of checks received from, other banks in the collection arrangement.

M

magnetic ink character recognition (MICR) Magnetic codes on the bottom of a check that allow a machine to read the check. MICR encoding can include the amount of the check, the account number, the bank's number, and the serial number of the check.

maintenance period The period for which banks must maintain reserves if they are required to do so. For large banks, this is a two-week period, and the amount of reserves is based on daily average deposits held in a two-week computation period that lags the maintenance period by two days.

managed liabilities Those sources of funds that bank management can control through purchase or borrowing actions, such as corporate CDs, Eurodollar borrowings, and federal funds purchases.

margin The difference, or spread, between the market value of securities used as collateral for a loan for the purpose of purchasing stock and the amount of the loan granted.

margin requirements Federal Reserve regulations T, U, and X that establish the maximum margin in percentage terms.

marginal efficiency of investment (MEI) A representation of the relationship between the costs of making investments and their expected returns, which determines the level of investment spending. The MEI is graphically depicted as a downward-sloping curve.

maturity The date on which a security, loan, or other financial instrument becomes due and payable.

medium of exchange An item that is generally accepted in exchange for goods, services, and settlement of debt. Providing an effective medium of exchange is the primary function of money.

monetarism The body of economic theory that holds that the quantity of, and changes in, the money supply are the single most important influence on a nation's economy.

monetary policy The management by a central bank of a nation's money supply to ensure the availability of credit in quantities and at interest rates consistent with specific economic objectives.

monetization of gold The Treasury's issuance of gold certificates to the Federal Reserve in return for an equal dollar credit to the Treasury's account at the Federal Reserve.

money (1) Legal tender; the coin and currency declared by a government as the accepted medium of exchange. (2) Anything that serves the functions of money; that is, providing a medium of exchange, a standard of value, or a store of value.

money creation The process by which banks create money by granting loans.

money market deposit account (MMDA) A type of savings account created in 1982 that pays a market interest rate and allows account holders limited check-writing privileges (three checks per month).

money market funds Mutual funds that buy high-quality short-term money market instruments issued by corporations and governments.

money supply The sum of all the funds that individuals and businesses have immediately available for spending in the domestic economy. The U.S. money supply has three basic measures: M1—sum of currency, demand deposits, traveler's checks, and other checkable deposits; M2—M1 plus overnight repurchase agreements (RPs) and Eurodollars, money-market mutual fund (MMMF) balances (general purpose and broker-dealer), money market deposit accounts, and savings and small time deposits; M3—M2 plus large time deposits, term RPs, term eurodollars, and institution-only MMMF balances.

multiple deposit creation The process by which the banking system can create amounts of money several times larger than the amount of reserves the system starts with.

municipal obligations Debt instruments issued by states and localities.

mutual fund A company that pools investors' funds for placement in a diversified portfolio of securities (stocks or bonds) from which investors can buy shares.

N

national charter A bank charter (license to operate) granted by the Office of the Comptroller of the Currency (OCC). All banks with a national charter must use the word *national* in their name or carry the initials N.A. (national association) after their name.

national economic objectives The broad objectives of monetary and fiscal policy to promote an economic environment of full employment, price stability, and economic growth.

national income The sum of all wages, rents, interest, and profits generated in an economy. An economy's total income.

near monies Noncash items that are good standards of value and good stores of value but are not accepted as mediums of exchange. These items can, however, be readily converted into cash. Near monies include U.S. government and corporate bonds, life insurance policies, pension funds, money market shares, and various types of interest-earning time deposits in financial institutions.

negotiable order of withdrawal (NOW) account An interest-earning transaction account on which check-like instruments may be used. Withdrawals from NOW accounts are made by using savings account withdrawal tickets as negotiable instruments that closely resemble checks. Although NOW accounts are transaction accounts, they are not demand deposit accounts, and banks must reserve the right to require seven days' notice before a withdrawal can be made. NOW accounts may be offered by commercial banks, mutual savings banks, and savings and loan associations, among others, and may be owned only by individuals, certain nonprofit organizations, and certain governmental units. For-profit businesses may not own a NOW account.

net domestic product A country's total output of goods and services minus the amount of capital consumed in producing the goods and services.

net interest income A bank's gross interest revenue minus its interest expense.

netting The process of valuing the payment obligations of participants in a clearing house or swap transaction and having the counter party's that pay more transfer only the differential.

nominal GDP A country's total output of goods and services without any adjustment for inflation.

nominal interest rate An interest rate actually paid without any adjustment for inflation.

nonbank bank A bank owned by a non-banking company that avoids being defined as a bank for regulatory purposes by divesting itself of either its demand deposits or its business loans.

nondiscretionary government spending Federal government spending that is not immediately subject to the discretionary control of the president or congress. This spending is largely for entitlements, such as Social Security, and interest on the federal debt that the government is obligated to pay.

nonaccelerating-inflation rate of unemployment (NAIRU) The lowest rate of unemployment that can be achieved without triggering cost-push inflation.

nonfinancial intermediary A non-depository business whose primary activity is not providing financial products and services.

O

Office of the Comptroller of the Currency (OCC) The federal regulatory agency responsible for chartering, examining, and supervising national banks.

Office of Thrift Supervision The federal regulatory agency responsible for chartering and supervising savings and loan associations.

on-us collection Checks collected through internal adjustments to one bank's books.

on-us items Checks deposited at the bank on which they are drawn.

open-account arrangement Trade credit for an exporter who ships goods with the good faith expectation that the importer will pay.

open market The primary dealer firms in government securities that directly buy securities from, and sell securities to, the Federal Reserve Bank of New York.

open market dealer firms *See* dealer firms.

open market operations The purchase and sale of government securities by the Federal Reserve. These operations influence the growth of the nation's money supply and are the principal means by which monetary policy is implemented.

opportunity cost The benefits that were foregone by choosing one alternative over another; often measured by the price or rate of return that the best alternative course of action would provide.

outsource A cost reduction strategy whereby back-office activities traditionally done in-house, such as payroll processing and check collection, are purchased from outside service providers.

overdraft A condition at the end of the banking day when a bank finds that it has paid out more funds from an account than it has on its books for that account (*see* daylight overdraft).

P

pass-through account An account held at a member bank by a nonmember bank or other depository institution that is required by the Federal Reserve to hold reserve accounts. Those requirements may be met by holding deposits in a bank that holds an equivalent amount on deposit at a Federal Reserve bank.

payments system The system of instruments used, and the procedures and practices followed, to transfer money, make payments, and settle debts.

Phillips curve A downward-sloping curve, named after New Zealand economist Alban Phillips, that shows the correlation between inflation and unemployment over particular time periods. The Phillips curve purports to demonstrate that higher unemployment will typically accompany lower inflation and that lower unemployment will typically accompany higher inflation.

point-of-sale (POS) terminal An in-store computer terminal that transfers information on the books of participating banks or funds between purchasers and merchants.

precautionary demand A preference for holding more money than needed for transactions purposes to cover unforeseen contingencies.

price index number A number that reflects the percentage change in prices between a selected year and the current year.

price stability (1) An economic environment without inflation. (2) An economic environment in which consumers and businesses do not base financial decisions on expectations of inflation.

primary reserves Bank reserves that provide immediate liquidity but do not generate income. Primary reserves consist chiefly of cash assets, cash in vault, reserves at the Federal Reserve bank, deposit balances at correspondent banks, and cash items in the process of collection.

prime rate A benchmark interest rate charge that some banks use in lending funds to their best, most credit worthy, corporate customers. *Also see* base rate.

productivity Output per hour worked.

profit illusion effect The illusion of profit gains in an inflation if the rising value of inventories is not taken into account as an increase in replacement costs.

proprietary fund A mutual fund managed by a bank, although the bank itself does not own the fund's assets or issue shares to customers. A separate company not affiliated with the bank owns the assets and issues shares.

purchase and assumption A procedure used by the FDIC to keep a failed bank open by having another bank buy only the good assets of the failed bank and assume all of its liabilities. The FDIC makes up the difference between the good and bad assets with a cash payment to the buying bank.

purchasing power The value of money as determined by what it can buy in the marketplace.

Q

quantity theory of money A theory based on the truism that $MV = PT$ (the quantity of money multiplied by its velocity equals the price level multiplied by the number of transactions). The key assumption is that changes in the quantity of money primarily influence prices because velocity is assumed to be constant and the number of transactions is determined by other factors.

quasi-governmental An organization that has characteristics of both a private corporation and a government agency. The Federal Reserve is quasi-governmental.

quota A physical quantity or dollar value limitation imposed by a government on specific imports or exports.

R

real GDP The nation's output of goods and services adjusted to allow for inflation.

real interest rate The rate of interest adjusted to allow for inflation. The nominal interest rate less the expected inflation rate is the real rate of interest.

recession A period in which most economic activity slows. As a specific phase of the business cycle, a recession begins when economic activity begins to decline and ends when economic activity begins to increase.

reciprocity An agreement between countries as to the validity of licenses or privileges granted by the other to its citizens. In banking, the laws and regulations governing a bank located in a foreign country would be similar in treatment to the laws and regulations in the bank's own country.

redlining An illegal practice in which certain geographic areas are eliminated from eligibility for mortgages or other loans, allegedly because the area is considered a poor investment risk but without regard for the creditworthiness of each mortgage applicant and property. In effect, a red line is drawn around the eliminated area on a map.

representative money A money item, usually in the form of paper currency, that represents a claim on one or more items of value held in a central depository. A silver certificate that could be exchanged for silver bullion would be an example.

representative office An administrative or sales office of a foreign bank that cannot accept deposits or make loans and investments.

repurchase agreement The purchase of a security, usually a three-month Treasury bill, under an agreement that the seller will buy back the security within a specified time (usually a day or two) at an agreed-upon price. Often called a repo.

required reserves The amount of funds that banks must keep by law as a kind of backing against their customers' deposits. To create more money a bank must have more reserves (excess reserves) than required by law.

reservable liabilities Depository institution liabilities that are subject to reserve requirements.

reserve deficiency A situation that occurs when a bank's daily average reserve balance is less than the daily average required reserve balance during a given reserve maintenance period (the period during which required reserves must be maintained). Banks are permitted to carry over a deficiency of up to 4 percent into the next maintenance period without penalty.

reserve requirements The ratio of reserves required by law that banks must hold against their customers' deposits.

reserves (1) Cash on hand in a bank's vault or deposited with the Federal Reserve or in pass-through accounts with correspondent banks, used by depository institutions to meet legal reserve requirements. A bank contemplating a loan must have reserves at least equal to the amount of money to be created. (2) Funds in cash or quickly convertible into cash, if necessary, to meet current needs.

Resolution Trust Corporation (RTC) A government-sponsored corporation created by Congress in 1989 to take over insolvent savings and loan associations and find buyers for them or liquidate their assets and pay off insured depositors. The RTC was disbanded in 1996.

respondent bank A bank that regularly buys the services of a correspondent bank for stipulated activities, such as check collection.

return on assets (ROA) A profitability ratio. Return on assets is net income divided by average total assets. ROA indicates how efficiently assets are employed.

return on equity (ROE) A profitability ratio. Return on equity is net income divided by average total equity. ROE indicates how efficiently equity capital is invested.

risk The degree of uncertainty that a loss will be sustained in a loan, investment, or payment transaction.

S

safekeeping A service provided by a bank in which customers' valuables are protected in the bank's vaults for a fee. The custody of securities is an important form of safekeeping.

Savings Association Insurance Fund (SAIF) The deposit insurance fund for savings and loan associations administered by the FDIC.

savings institutions Depository institutions that primarily accept savings and checkable deposits from the public and use these funds for mortgage loans. Savings banks, savings and loan associations, and credit unions are the nation's savings institutions. *Also see* thrifts.

scarcity-induced inflation An increase in prices caused by either a natural or governmentally-induced shortage of key commodities or goods.

seasonal unemployment Unemployment caused by temporary layoffs in response to seasonal changes in production and demand.

secondary market A market, such as the government securities market, where ownership of financial assets is transferred from one party to another.

secondary reserves A bank's securities portfolio. Because a bank's securities assets can be sold easily for liquid assets to meet demand claims, these assets are considered the second source of a bank's reserves. A bank's primary source of reserves is its liquid assets.

securitization The process of converting loans into securities. It is accomplished by originating loans, combining them into pools, and selling securities that are secured by the principal and interest payments from the original loans.

selective monetary policy controls Monetary policy tools that focus on controlling a specific financial market or component of total credit, such as stock market lending, consumer credit, or real estate.

sensitivity to market risk A criterion used by bank examiners in evaluating a bank's safety and soundness; how well positioned a bank is to handle changes in interest rates.

share draft An interest-bearing checking account that credit unions offer.

short-term adjustment credit Federal reserve loans to depositories through the discount window for short-term liquidity needs, usually for a day or two in the case of large banks and a week or longer for smaller banks.

special drawing rights (SDRs) International money balances created by the International Monetary Fund and allocated to its member nations. SDRs can be used only by governments to settle international debts.

specie Coins made from precious metal, usually gold or silver, as contrasted with paper money.

speculative demand A preference for holding more money than is needed for transactions and precautionary purposes in order to speculate about future interest rates.

Spot rate The price or rate in the spot (cash or immediate delivery) market.

spread The difference between a bank's return on assets and its cost of liabilities.

state charter A banking license issued by a state banking authority. A state-chartered bank may or may not be a Federal Reserve member and may or may not belong to the Federal Deposit Insurance Corporation (FDIC).

stop-payment order Order issued by a check writer to his or her bank, by phone or in writing, telling the bank not to pay a specific check that was previously written and presented as payment.

store of value A means to hold and accumulate purchasing power for future use. Serving as a store of value is one of the primary functions of money.

stored value card A prepaid wallet-size card containing a microchip that stores a predetermined amount of dollars to be used for purchases or other transactions.

structural unemployment Unemployment caused by the mismatch of employees' job skills and employers' job requirements.

supply-chain management A computer-based process that enables a seller to track and control every aspect of the production process from ordering and invoicing to loading and shipping.

swap drawings A mutual credit facility in which two central banks exchange, or swap, a predetermined amount of each other's currencies for several months. The exchanged currency is used in the foreign markets to stabilize exchange rates.

sweep accounts Accounts that receive the prearranged, automatic transfer of funds from a checking account into an interest-bearing account or into a general ledger account from which short-term investments are made.

system open market account The portfolio of government securities owned by the Federal Reserve banks.

T

T-account An abstract of a depository institution's balance sheet that shows changes in selected assets and liabilities.

tariff A tax imposed by a government on specific imports or exports.

tax-based income policy A government policy that would automatically increase or decrease corporate taxes for companies whose annual wage or price increases exceeded or were below the year's inflation rate.

tax effect The effect inflation has on people's tax burden; as prices and wages increase during an inflationary period, wage earners are pushed into higher tax brackets, requiring that a larger proportion of the wage gain be paid in taxes.

term federal funds Loans of immediately available funds from one bank to another for more than one day.

thrifts Institutions that primarily accept savings account deposits and make mortgage loans. Savings banks, savings and loan associations, and credit unions are examples of thrifts. *Also see* savings institutions.

time and savings accounts Interest-earning deposits in a bank account that cannot be withdrawn before a specified date or technically without advance notice.

too-big-to-fail policy A policy adopted by the FDIC in the 1980s to protect all of the deposits at a bank if, because of its size, its failure would destabilize financial markets or the economy of a region.

total reserves The sum of all bank assets eligible for meeting reserve requirements (cash on hand and reserve account balances with the Federal Reserve or in correspondent bank pass-through accounts).

total spending For economic modeling purposes, the sum of consumption plus investment plus government spending. *See* aggregate demand.

transaction accounts Accounts with financial institutions that allow for transfers of funds to third parties. The account holder is permitted to make an unlimited number of withdrawals using transferable instruments such as checks.

transaction demand The basic motive or demand for holding money as a convenience to meet day-to-day and week-to-week spending needs.

Treasury bill (T-bill) A marketable U.S. Treasury security with a life of one year or less, which is sold to the public at weekly auctions on a discount basis in minimum denominations of $10,000 and in book-entry-only form. Also called T-bill.

Treasury securities Federal government obligations issued by the U.S. Treasury as a means of borrowing money to meet government expenditures not covered by tax revenues.

Treasury tax and loan accounts (TT&Ls) Accounts in which tax deposits may be made through any authorized depository institution, where the deposits remain until the Treasury draws them out according to a predetermined schedule.

U

unanticipated inflation A period or degree of inflation that consumers and businesses failed to anticipate. In response to the surprise inflation, consumers and businesses tend to retrench and cut back on spending.

uncollected funds Check deposits the bank has not yet collected.

underwriting The purchase of new offerings of corporate stock or the debt securities of a corporation or government entity for resale in the secondary market.

unemployment rate The percent of the labor force currently not working but seeking employment.

unit of account A standard of measurement for the relative value, or worth, of goods and services. Serving as a unit of account is one of the primary functions of money.

unit banking A banking system made up largely of small, single-office (unit) banks. Until the 1980s, many states required banks to operate without branches, which led to the proliferation of single-office institutions called *unit* banks. Because of the changes in banking law that began in the 1980s, unit banking is no longer a requirement in any U.S. locality.

usury laws State laws that stipulate the maximum rates of interest to be charged on different types of loans.

V

vehicle money A currency used by the world's traders and investors in international dealings. The U.S. dollar is the world's predominant vehicle money.

velocity of money The rate at which money circulates within an economy, either in terms of spending or income.

W

wage-price controls Government-imposed regulations that attempt to limit wage and price increases.

wage-price spiral The inflationary process that drives workers to press for higher wages to offset losses in the purchasing power value of their incomes, which in turn, drives producers to mark up prices to protect profit margins, leading to another round of inflation.

wealth effect (1) Refers to the impact on spending and savings behavior of perceived changes in the public's financial wealth. (2) Refers to the redistribution of wealth that occurs during periods of unanticipated inflation from creditors, who are repaid in cheaper dollars than those originally loaned, to debtors, who repay loans with funds worth less than the money originally borrowed.

winners and losers effect The ultimate socio-economic effect of a prolonged period of inflation, including the creation of specific groups that are better off than before the period of inflation, such as debtors, and specific groups that are worse off, such as retirees.

Y

yield The rate of return on an investment.

INDEX

forward exchange options and, 257
foreign exchange rate, 252-255
    determination of, 254
    influences on, 254-255
    risk management and, 258
foreign investors
    and federal debt, 235, 236, 237
foreign-owned open market dealers,
    218, 219
forward purchase contract, 256
fractional reserves, 38
FRBNY. *See* Federal Reserve Bank of
    New York
free banking era, 167
frictional unemployment, 194-195
Friedman, Milton, 184-185. *See also*
    monetarism
FSLIC. *See* Federal Savings and Loan
    Insurance Corporation
full-employment budgeting, 234
functions of money, 2-3
futures market, 97

G

gap management, 95
Garn-St Germain Act (1982), 152, 153, 165
Glass-Steagall Act (1933), 84, 157
gold, 243
gold standard, 5
gold tranche, 243
goodwill, 75
government. *See also* regulation; *entries at*
    Federal Reserve; *entries at*
    U.S.
    as debtor, 27
    fiscal agent for, 133
    secondary mortgage market and, 68
    spending by, 20, 174, 180
Gramm-Leach-Bliley Act (1999), 66-67,
    157, 165
gross domestic product (GDP), 20
    change from GNP to, 26
    as measure of spending, 24-25
    money supply and, 185, 186
    real GDP and, 22-23
gross national product (GNP), 26

H

hedging, 97, 246
hidden unemployment, 194
holdover float, 114

I

imports, limitations on, 244
income effect, 199
income statement, 86-90
    key performance measures and, 89-90
    net income and, 89
    net interest and, 87-88
    noninterest income and, 88-89
    for U.S. banks (2001), 88
indexation, 245-247
individual retirement accounts (IRAs),
    71-72
inflation, 22, 197-203
    anticipation of, 198-201
    commercial loan theory and, 229-230
    effects of, 199-201
    federal debt management and, 239
    indexation and, 245-247
    measurement of, 196-197
    profile of, 199
    sources of, 197-198
    trade-off dilemma and, 201-203
    wealth effect and, 199-200
inflation hedging, 246
insurance companies, 65
Interdistrict Settlement Fund, 112
interest assets of Federal Reserve, 143
interest payments on federal debt, 235-236
interest rates. *See also* discount rate
    bank loan charges and, 31
    credit markets and, 30-31
    in Keynesian theory, 183-184
interest rate swaps, 96
international banking, 252-269
    countries permitting foreign control of
      banks, 266
    foreign banks in the U.S. and, 263-267
    foreign exchange and, 252-258
    largest companies and, 263
    payments devices in, 258-263
International Banking Act (1978), 263-264
international banks, U.S., 162, 163
international competitiveness effect, 200
international payments, 258-261

IMPROVE YOUR PERFORMANCE WITH THESE ABA PRODUCTS AND SERVICES

ABA Web Sites. The ABA has been the connecting link for bankers for more than 125 years. Now, technology allows us to put the world of banking right on your desktop through the Internet. Explore *www.aba.com* for more information about these and other products and services.

American Institute of Banking. ABA's American Institute of Banking (AIB) is a continuing education curriculum for the financial services industry. AIB courses are instructor guided, include learning measurements, and are designed to increase job skills and knowledge. Completion of prescribed courses can lead to industry-recognized AIB diplomas and certificates, or assist in professional licensing requirements. AIB courses are offered in flexible formats. In addition to traditional classroom instruction, today's AIB offers Internet delivery for many of its courses.

Performance Training Series. The ABA Performance Training Series addresses vital skills that every banker needs today. All training materials clearly outline objectives and all use interactive techniques, promoting group discussions and activities for reinforcement. The seminars are grouped in topic clusters: Business Fundamentals, Compliance, Managing People, Retail Banking (Product Knowledge and Sales), and Small Business (Product Knowledge and Sales).

ABA eLearning. Now there's a training solution that moves faster than your world does. Combining ABA's knowledge of the financial services industry with the technical expertise of the e-learning leaders, Digital Think, ABA eLearning delivers training faster, more effectively, and more efficiently than ever before. More than 50 individual courses support the curriculum in these areas: Basic Banking Knowledge, Fundamental Business Skills, Management and Leadership, Regulatory Compliance, Retail Banking Fundamentals, Retail Banking Sales Skills, Small Business Banking Fundamentals, Small Business Banking Sales Skills, Trust and Investments, as well as eBusiness fundamentals and Microsoft Application courses.

ABA Telephone Briefings. Get real-time expert information on your business challenges without leaving the office. No need to invest travel time and expense to participate. Educate 1 or 100 employees for the same low price. Each seminar provides a participant's guide. You may ask questions directly to leading experts on the issues. New topics are added all the time. Check *www.aba.com* for the latest schedule.

Payment Systems Today. This 15-hour short course provides you with a high level overview of the systems that power our nation's economy. The course shares with you basic information about the most common payment systems available today, their use in the economy, and regulatory and security concerns in the process. Topics include cash, checks, electronic checks, debit cards, credit cards, smart cards, stored value cards, prearranged and preauthorized ACH and funds transfers, inter-bank settlement, global payment systems, security and the laws and regulations governing payments.

For more information, call **1-800 BANKERS** or visit our web site, *www.aba.com.*

IMPROVE YOUR PERFORMANCE WITH THESE
ABA PRODUCTS AND SERVICES

ABA Retail Banking Survey Report. Information issues shaping today's retail banking landscape form the core of ABA's Retail Banking Survey Report. The survey presents detailed data about retail banking operations, performance management, deposit and other banking services, stratified by two asset categories: less than $500 million and $500 million or more. Divided into three main sections—an analysis of Internet banking, a management summary and detailed data tables—the report contains information on both traditional and special services that banks offer to individuals and small businesses, including: branch automation, automated teller machines, employee training and compensation, POS debit cards, package plans, and online banking.

Banking and Finance Terminology. The most reliable source for banking and finance terminology, the 4th edition of this industry resource will help you read with greater comprehension and write with greater authority in the such areas as accounting, asset and liability management, commercial and consumer lending, credit cards, economics and global banking, human resources management, insurance, investments and securities, law and regulatory compliance, marketing and sales, operations and payment systems, electronic funds transfers, real estate finance, trust and private banking, and more. The book presents a total of more than 7,000 definitions, with more than 1,000 new entries! Much more than a dictionary, this compact reference contains information that reflects today's expanding financial services industry, including appendices on industry acronyms and abbreviations, key performance ratios, economic indicators, Federal Reserve regulations, important banking legislation, and federal and state regulatory agency addresses.

Law and Banking Principles. Your legal aid for the fundamentals of banking law, this highly informative, revised and up-to-date, text outlines and illustrates in plain English how laws affect the business of banking. You will learn the fundamentals of banking law from the point of view of employees in direct contact with customers. This is a powerful information tool that will give you the confidence to grasp the legal and regulatory requirements of banking. You will be able to explain the regulatory system governing banks; identify the major laws that affect the business of banking today; describe differences between crimes and torts, and list those that affect banking today; and list property ownership types and how banks obtain an interest in customer property. Also in this edition are detailed chapters about the Uniform Commercial Code as it relates to banking and information on internet banking.

Reference Guide to Regulatory Compliance. Keep one copy of this easy-to-carry publication in your briefcase and keep another on your desk top. Updated annually, this comprehensive desktop reference book offers detailed information on more than 34 regulatory areas affecting banks, arranged by bank function—deposits, lending, information reporting, bank operations, safety and soundness, and social responsibility. Developed as an extended outline, the guide covers federal regulations, consumer legislation, and all the rules you need to know to meet all the demands of today's compliance requirements. The *Guide* also includes pertinent regulatory citations and self-study/review questions and answers.

For more information, call **1-800 BANKERS** or visit our web site *www.aba.com*.

STUDENT SURVEY

Thank you for participating in this American Bankers Association/American Institute of Banking course/seminar. Your responses on the following evaluation will help shape the structure and content of future courses. After completing the evaluation, please fold, staple, and mail this postage-paid response form.

TELL US ABOUT YOURSELF:

Name _____   Phone # _____

Title_____ E-mail_____ Fax no. _____

Department_____ Bank/Company _____

Address _____

City _____ State _____ Zip _____

Your education   ❑ high school   ❑ some college   ❑ BA/BS degree   ❑ advanced degree _____

TELL US ABOUT YOUR EMPLOYER

Your employer's business is in   ❑ banking   ❑ other
(specify)_____

Number of years you've worked for financial services industry:
❑ 0-2   ❑ 3-5   ❑ 6-10   ❑ more than 10

Your employer's asset size: ❑ up to $250mm
❑ $251mm - $500mm   ❑ $501mm - $5 B ❑ $5 B plus

TELL US ABOUT YOUR AIB EXPERIENCE

Number of courses/seminars taken in last 3 years:
❑ 0   ❑ 1-2   ❑ 3-5   ❑ 6 or more

AIB course taken through (please check all that apply)?
❑ Local ABA Training Provider
❑ AIB online program
❑ AIB correspondence study
❑ other (specify _____)

Are you working on another degree? ❑ yes ❑ no
(specify)_____
_____

Number of employees:
❑ up to 100   ❑ 101 to 300   ❑ 301 to 1,000   ❑ 1,001 plus

Does your employer have an in-house training department?
❑ yes   ❑ no

If the answer is *yes*, who manages that department?
Name: _____
Title: _____

Are you working on an AIB certificate/diploma program?
❑ yes (please specify)   ❑ no
❑ Bank Operations   ❑ Banking & Finance
❑ General Banking   ❑ Bank Marketing
❑ Performance Training Series Certificate
❑ Lending Diploma [❑ Commercial ❑ Consumer ❑ Mortgage]

Please list any other training providers you have used and the courses/seminars you have taken.

_____
_____
_____

TELL US YOUR OPINION OF THE COURSE MATERIALS

Please indicate your degree of agreement with the following:

	Strongly Disagree			Strongly Agree
Materials covered all important topics.	1	2	3	4
Learning objectives were clear.	1	2	3	4
Graphics well illustrated course content.	1	2	3	4
Theory and practical applications were well balanced.	1	2	3	4
Examples/case studies helped achieve learning objectives.	1	2	3	4
Exercises gave ample opportunity to apply learning.	1	2	3	4

Overall, how would you rate the following?

	Poor			Excellent
Course/seminar materials	1	2	3	4
Your experience with the course/seminar	1	2	3	4

Did your instructor use any supplemental materials to teach this course/seminar? ❑ Yes (What? _____)❑ No

TELL US WHAT OTHER SUBJECTS IN THE FINANCIAL SERVICES INDUSTRY YOU WOULD LIKE TO STUDY

Are there other banking areas you want to learn about? Please specify: _____
_____
_____

What course(s) would help you improve your performance in your current job? Please specify: _____
_____
_____

What type of courses best suit your needs?
❑   Instructor led classroom training
❑   Courses presented over the Internet
❑   Courses presented on CD-ROM multimedia
❑   Printed correspondence courses
❑   Other (please specify):_____

Please provide additional comments about the course/seminar, the materials, other training topics, ABA/AIB, and/or your training needs so that we may better serve you in the future:

_____
_____
_____
_____
_____
_____
_____

TELL US WHAT INFORMATION WE SHOULD SEND TO YOU   (check all that apply)
❑ AIB diploma programs   ❑ ABA conferences   ❑ AIB online programs
❑ ABA schools   ❑ ICB certification program   ❑ other products and services   (describe: _____)
May we contact you about courses/seminars under development for your input?   ❑ yes ❑ no

Thank you for completing this survey.
For more information about the ABA/AIB, please visit our Internet Web site at **www.aba.com** or call our Member Service Center at **1-800-BANKERS**.